Object-Oriented Design in C++

Using the Standard Template Library

Nicholas J. DeLillo
Manhattan College

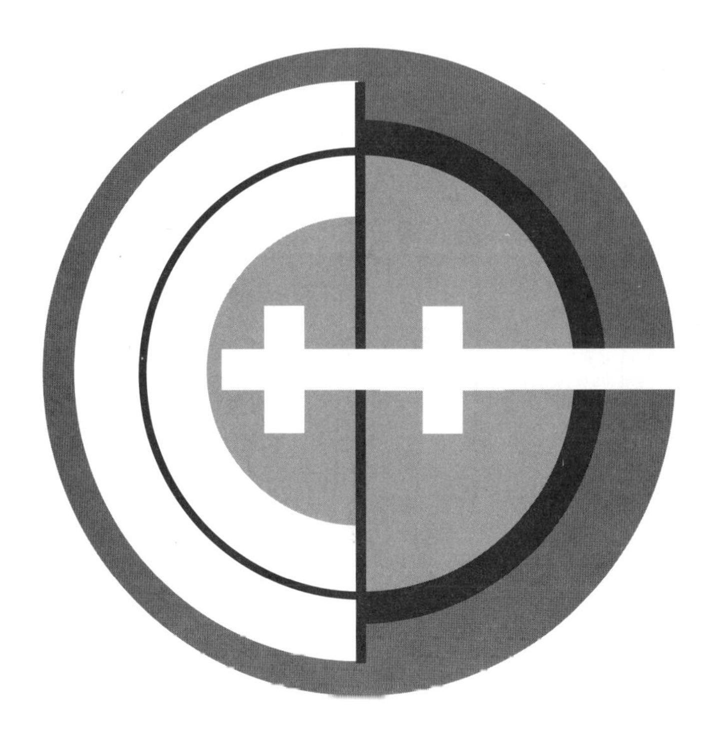

BROOKS/COLE
THOMSON LEARNING

Australia • Canada • Mexico • Singapore • Spain • United Kingdom • United States

BROOKS/COLE

THOMSON LEARNING™

Sponsoring Editor: *Kallie Swanson*
Marketing Team: *Chris Kelly, Samantha Cabaluna*
Editorial Assistant: *Carla Vera*
Production Editor: *Kelsey McGee*
Production Service: *Matrix Productions Inc.*
Manuscript Editor: *Frank Hubert*
Interior Design: *Lisa Devenish*
Cover Design: *Roy R. Neuhaus*
Cover Photo: *Phototake/David Bishop*
Print Buyer: *Vena M. Dyer*
Typesetting: *ATLIS Graphics & Design*
Cover Printing, Printing and Binding: *Webcom, Limited*

For more information about this or any other Brooks/Cole products, contact:
BROOKS/COLE
511 Forest Lodge Road
Pacific Grove, CA 93950 USA
www.brookscole.com
1-800-423-0563 (Thomson Learning Academic Resource Center)

Printed in Canada

10 9 8 7 6 5 4 3 2

Library of Congress Cataloging-in-Publication Data

DeLillo, Nicholas J.
Object-oriented design in C++ using the Standard Template Library/Nicholas J. DeLillo.
p. cm.
Includes bibliographical references and index.
ISBN 0-534-37782-3
1. Object-oriented programming (Computer science) 2. C++ (Computer program language) 3. Standard template library. I. Title.
QA76.64. D455 2002
005.13′3--dc21

2001037794

THIS BOOK IS PRINTED ON ACID-FREE RECYCLED PAPER

To my mother, Anna DeLillo . . . in beloved memory
and to my grandchildren, Nicholas and Michela

CONTENTS

CHAPTER 1 **Classes • 1**

CHAPTER 2 **Inheritance and Polymorphism • 54**

PREFACE

This book is designed for a course in computer science or computer engineering satisfying a number of distinct requirements. The first requirement is to provide a source for the study of object-oriented design (OOD) as implemented in the C++ programming language. This involves the presentation of three main concepts: encapsulation, inheritance, and polymorphism. These concepts are presented in the first two chapters, where each is defined and illustrated using easily understood and fundamental mathematical concepts. The second requirement is to introduce the major components of the Standard Template Library (also called the Standard Library, or STL). This is accomplished by first presenting "traditional" concepts such as search and sort, and hashing (the content of Chapters Three and Four). These chapters set the stage for the introduction of predefined container classes and generic algorithms comprising components of STL treated in the remaining chapters of the text.

The first four chapters may serve as the basis for a conventional course in data structures and algorithms, often referred to as the CS7 course by the Association for Computing Machinery. The text is also designed for use in other venues:

- an advanced undergraduate or early graduate course in special topics in computer science and computer engineering emphasizing the exposition of the components of the Standard Library and their functionality;
- an advanced undergraduate or early graduate course in computer science or computer engineering in object-oriented design involving the use of the Standard Library.

This text is not designed for a first course in data structures (the designated CS2 course in the ACM Curriculum). There are a number of texts satisfying this need; instead, the primary emphasis of this text is on object-oriented design using the Standard Library. In many instances, the text treats topics first introduced in the data structures course, such as linked lists, stacks, queues, and priority queues. However, in the CS2 course, the implementation of each of these structures in C++ usually does not involve the Standard Library. In addition, the CS2 course also gives a formal treatment of trees; the current text does not include this topic, since the design of STL does not include trees as a container class template. In fact, the only exposure to trees in STL is accomplished with the implementation of sorted associative container classes using red-black trees.

A prevailing opinion about STL is that its use does not encourage or emphasize the key ideas of object-oriented design, particularly with regard to inheritance and polymorphism. In Section 9.6 and in the Appendix, these ideas, along with those of virtual functions and class hierarchies merge with the use of components defined from several different STL class templates in two separate application domains. One of these involves the implementation of several graph abstract data types, and the second implements an object-oriented design of a local area network.

Several new approaches to teaching the data structures and algorithms (ACM's CS7) course using C++ as the implementation language use the Standard Library in a pivotal way. This is because the components of STL apply another important objective of commercial software design: to present solutions of a variety of software problems emphasizing correctness, efficiency, reusability, and portability. These are important concepts normally treated in courses in software engineering. These concepts are central in the design of code throughout this text.

This text is unusual in that, at present, not all of the topics presented are found in a single competing work. While there are several texts covering some of these topics, there is no single unified source, except for the present text, covering all of these. In most cases, each key topic is introduced first without any link to a predefined STL facility. Then this topic is revisited in the environment of the STL, with the assurance of correctness, efficiency, and portability. Several valuable goals are attained in establishing this association with STL:

- Programmers no longer have to be concerned with the correctness and efficiency of the codes they design—this is no longer a consideration, since the STL facility accessed is guaranteed to be correct and efficient.
- Because STL has been designed to be independent of any specific hardware configuration, the code is applicable across all platforms.
- Students preparing for careers as software development professionals using C++ as the implementation language attain two major milestones. The first is that of becoming acquainted with the theoretical description of the underlying data structure, and the second is the implementation details of that structure (using the Standard Library).

Each chapter begins with a listing of a number of objectives to be fulfilled by studying the concepts presented in that chapter. In addition, the last section of each chapter summarizes the more critical issues treated in the chapter, thus enabling students to return to the appropriate section(s) in the event that they missed an important idea. The exercises at the end of each chapter attempt to convert students from passive observers to active participants by having them demonstrate their problem-solving abilities using several concepts described in the chapter, in providing a solution to each exercise. Further, each chapter ends with the presentation of at least one programming project that goes beyond the usual level of problem-solving capability demanded in the solution of problems in the exercises section. These projects generally take the form of extending the general theory in some direction accessible to interested students or provide an alternate form of implementation from that described in the text of the chapter. In each case, the problems and projects have been thoroughly tested for correctness and, in most cases, the formal solutions appear in the accompanying disk.

We assume throughout that students are familiar with the content of a first course in data structures—consequently, the approach to topics covered in this text is more advanced. The description of the properties of certain data structures is provided only as these are needed for enhancing the readability of the text.

The book serves in part as a useful tutorial emphasizing the concept of object-oriented programming (OOP) and its implementation using the facilities of STL. Most of the concepts introduced in the text are motivated by examples of everyday problems encountered in software design. Their solutions are given in the form of programs, many of which include tools available in the Standard Template Library. The exercises at the end of each chapter involve variations and generalizations of the concepts presented in that chapter. These exercises range from the most elementary to very challenging extensions of these ideas. In fact, the most challenging exercises are placed in a separate programming projects section. As already stated, the exercises are designed to draw students into the environment of OOD as active participants rather than casual spectators.

The following is a list of the topics presented in each chapter:

Chapter One: Classes. In this chapter, a review of the preliminary topics involved in the definition, design, and coding of classes appears. The ideas of constructors, destructors, data members, and member functions are described with ample illustration of each concept. Design aspects will be stressed: which properties of the objects constructed will be designated as `private`, and which will be `public`. The idea of data abstraction will be stressed, and the implementation of abstract data type (ADT) as a C++ class. Included in this discussion are the concepts of function and class templates, use of `friend` functions, generic `void*` pointers, exceptions and exception handlers, and `static` members of a class. The presentation will be augmented by a generous number of illustrative examples, providing students with a number of familiar concepts seen, in part, in previous courses.

Chapter Two: Inheritance and Polymorphism. This chapter introduces and illustrates the importance of class hierarchies, base classes, derived classes, abstract classes, `virtual` functions, `protected` members of a class, and static and dynamic polymorphism. Specifically, the value of class inheritance and polymorphism and their role in contemporary commercial software, design are stressed.

Chapter Three: Search and Sort. The first exposure to the idea of an algorithm, along with some of the more frequently used algorithms used in sorting and searching are presented here. The implementation of each of these algorithms will be described without using the tools provided in the Standard Template Library, since this chapter may be regarded as a preview of these concepts as presented in Chapter Eight. In particular, we define the ideas of efficiency and its quantification, using big-O, and the idea of mathematical proofs, using Finite Induction. The idea of recursive programming and the principle of divide and conquer are presented. The use of these concepts in the traditional problems of linear and binary search, selection sort, insertion sort, quicksort, and mergesort is illustrated, along with other sorting techniques.

Chapter Four: Hashing: Prelude to the Standard Template Library. This chapter discusses introductory topics on data storage and retrieval in some depth. This includes the introduction of such concepts as hashing, hash functions, hash tables, open addressing, resolving hash collisions using various forms of probing, and linked lists. In addition, the chapter ends with a discussion of namespaces, which leads in a natural way into the environment of the Standard Template Library.

Chapter Five: Overview of the Components of the STL. This chapter is intended to bridge the gap between the more traditional aspects of OOD as discussed in the first four chapters and those devoted to the use of the STL components treated in Chapters Six through Nine. The coverage includes an outline of the ideas of containers, generic algorithms, iterators, adaptors, and allocators. All of these represent concepts to be discussed and illustrated in great detail, beginning with Chapter Six.

Chapter Six: Sequence Containers. This chapter presents the basics of the `vector`, `deque`, and `list` sequence container class templates, providing students with a detailed introduction to their value in commercial OOD, with particular stress on their efficiency of use. This chapter will provide numerous examples of the use of each form of these container class templates, with particular emphasis on how the choice of the appropriate form of container contributes to the efficiency of the solution of the problem under consideration.

Chapter Seven: Container Adaptors. After exposing students to the fundamental sequence containers illustrated in Chapter Six, a natural follow-up is to present the container adaptors `stack`, `queue`, and `priority queue`. Each of these will be accompanied by a number of examples taken from the students' experience with problems seen before in computer science. These examples are drawn primarily from the study of the design of compilers and operating systems. Examples of these applications include the checking for balanced parentheses, brackets, and braces, converting an arithmetic expression from infix form to its equivalent postfix form, the evaluation of postfix arithmetic expressions, and the simulation of a ready queue for processes in a mulitprogrammed timesharing operating system.

Chapter Eight: Generic Algorithms. This chapter exposes students to the STL `<algorithm>` and stresses the importance of a number of members of that library. These include `lower_bound`, `binary_search`, `find`, `sort`, and others. The idea here is not to provide an intensive and comprehensive treatment of these topics; instead, the emphasis will be on the efficiency of the functions presented in a number of frequently used areas of data processing, such as copying, searching, and sorting. Many of these ideas were first discussed in Chapter Three; these are now revisited using the strength and efficiency of the functions provided in `<algorithm>`.

Chapter Nine: Sorted Associative Containers. This chapter is devoted to introducing the `set`, `multiset`, `map`, and `multimap` class templates, distinguishing these from one another, and illustrating their use in a number of important application areas. These areas include sorting, searching, and the definition and implementation of various forms of graph data types. In this chapter, we also introduce the important idea of associative arrays and observe how it is used in data retrieval and hashing.

Appendix: A Local Area Network Simulator. This appendix supplies an additional and longer application of the ideas presented in STL to an important application area: simulating the activity of a local area token ring network.

All of the code presented in this text has been tested in different platforms, including Visual C++ version 6.0, Borland's C++ compiler version 5.02, and a number of UNIX-based platforms.

Acknowledgements

This book would not have been possible without the contribution of several groups of very talented people. The first group is the staff at Brooks/Cole, whose help and support were invaluable throughout every stage of production: Bill Stenquist, Kallie Swanson, Libby Blaker, Kelsey McGee,

Samantha Cabaluna, Sue Ewing, Grace Fujimoto, Carla Vera, and Chris Kelly. The help of production editor Merrill Peterson and copy editor Frank Hubert also was important.

I also wish to thank the group of individuals who reviewed the manuscript at various levels of development, and provided many constructive comments, corrections, and suggestions: Robert Judd, Ohio University; Stephen Kresbach, South Dakota State University; Barry Levine, San Francisco State University; Anne-Louise Radimsky, California State University, Sacramento; Peter Smith, California State University, Northridge; Yonglei Tao, Grand Valley State University; and Aaron Tenenbaum, Brooklyn College, CUNY.

Thanks also to my colleagues in the Department of Mathematics and Computer Science at Manhattan College, who by now I hope have become accustomed to, but still tolerate, my personality changes over the years in the development of this text and earlier works. Further, special warm thanks go out to my students, both undergraduate and graduate, who were often subjected to the indignity of serving as test subjects for the contents of this text.

Special thanks go to a small but select group of colleagues: Dan McCracken, Rod Angotti, John Mallozzi, Henry Ruston, and Jack Beidler, for many helpful suggestions, both direct and indirect, about the current direction of pedagogy and research as they apply to OOP and OOD. I wish particularly to thank Jack Beidler for his support and encouragement, and for letting me sample his rendition of a "good cappuccino," although, in my opinion, mine is of far better quality.

Finally, and in a very special way, I wish to thank my wife Rosalie and my children and grandchildren for their moral support, comfort, and encouragement during the various stages of the writing of this book. Now that it is just about finished, I look forward to spending more quality time with Rosalie, my children, and my grandchildren Nicholas and Michela, on the beach at Isla Verde in Puerto Rico.

CHAPTER 1

Classes

CHAPTER OBJECTIVES

- To introduce and explain the key aspects of object-oriented design, such as abstraction, encapsulation, and modularity.
- To present and illustrate the definition of classes and objects and their role in the design of contemporary software.
- To define and explain the idea of function and class templates and how they aid in software reuse.
- To describe and apply the concept of `friend` functions.

1.1 Introduction

Contemporary design of commercial software usually involves the *object-oriented paradigm.* This entails the design of a solution to a software problem in which two fundamental goals are kept in mind:

- correctness
- efficiency

A software design is *correct* if it produces the expected solution to the problem for all possible inputs that define the application domain, namely, the collection of input values for which the application (or problem) is defined. In other words, a design is correct if it works properly for all values in its domain of definition. For example, the design of an algorithm for searching for a value in a finite list of values of that type is correct if the value sought is retrieved whenever that value actually appears in the list, and an error message such as

```
VALUE SOUGHT DOES NOT EXIST
```

is issued whenever that value does not appear.

In addition, software solutions must be designed as *efficiently* as possible.

This simply means that executing the solution should be relatively fast and use only the computer resources that are absolutely necessary for its completion. In many instances, the speed of computation of a solution may be the determining factor between success and failure of the product. For example, the telemetry and guidance systems used in commercial aircraft should react as quickly as possible to changing weather conditions and to the sudden presence of unexpected obstacles during flight, landing, and takeoff. In summary, the design of correct and efficient solutions to relatively complicated software problems must be a key goal of our efforts. We will see that the proper implementation of the object-oriented paradigm usually satisfies these goals.

The attainment of these goals is not automatic; a great degree of preparation and testing of the design and implementation code must be done. The C++ programming language has the advantage of possessing a very rich and extensive collection of predefined libraries containing the correct and efficient encoding of many of the algorithms encountered in contemporary data processing. For example, the Standard Template Library (STL) contains the necessary operations for solving a large number of basic problems, such as copying a given finite list of values, sorting a finite list of values in some specific order, or searching through a list for some specific value.

A main objective of this book is to demonstrate how to produce solutions to software problems that are both correct and efficient. This will be achieved by studying a large and varied number of problems whose solution will keep these goals in mind either by using components of the STL or other techniques and concepts lying at the "high end" of C++.

1.2 Principles of Object-Oriented Design

Over the last thirty years, research and development of contemporary high-level general-purpose programming languages have concentrated on two key factors: *simplicity* and *power*. That is, much effort has been given to the development of programming languages whose code is relatively simple for programmers to write, is easily understood by others, and is sufficiently powerful to maintain the goals of correctness and efficiency mentioned earlier.

There have been a number of languages proposed over this period that have attempted to satisfy these goals but have failed in one or more respects. It is interesting to note that the problem-solving methodologies that have been successful in meeting these goals have been those implementing the object-oriented paradigm. The C++ programming language treated in this text is an example of such a language. Another is Java™, which differs from C++ in implementing the object-oriented paradigm in a number of ways. One difference is that Java makes direct use of the Internet in accomplishing its objectives.

What are the principal aspects of object-oriented design (OOD)? These are

- abstraction
- encapsulation
- modularity

Abstraction

The concept of *abstraction* is an important aspect of OOD. Abstraction is the ability of a language to implement a theoretical concept in simple and precise terms. Generally, the concept may involve a number of separate but cooperating parts. In applying this concept in this situation, abstraction enables us to define the distinct parts and formally express their functionality. As an example, let us define a *stack* (of values of some type T) theoretically as either the empty set or an ordered sequence of values into which additional values may be inserted (pushed) and from which values may be removed (popped) whenever possible. We understand that pushing and popping values of a stack is possible from one end only, known as the *top* of the stack. We may characterize the abstraction of a stack by Figure 1.1.

FIGURE 1.1

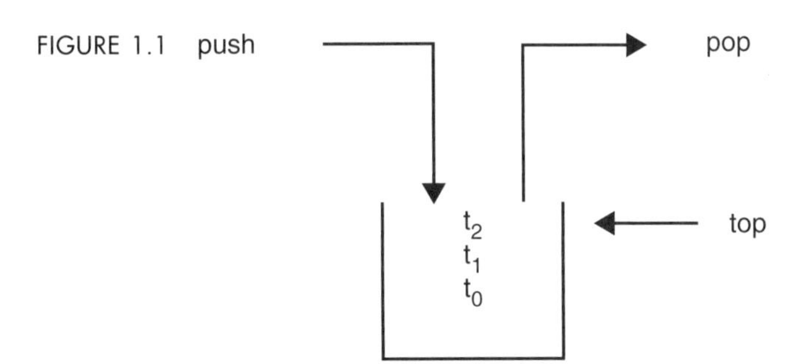

It would also be convenient to test whether the current stack is empty and to retrieve the value at the top of the current stack whenever it is not empty. This represents the complete description of the abstraction of a stack of values of type T. Once we are satisfied with this definition, the next step is to frame it in the form of an *abstract data type* (ADT). We may define an abstract data type as a mathematical model of a data structure specifying the type of data stored in that structure, the admissible operations applied to these data, and the necessary parameters required for the correct and efficient implementation of these operations. It is important to note that an

ADT describes what operations are admissible but does not necessarily supply any information as to how these operations execute.

As an example, an ADT for stacks of values of type `T` involves two components:

1. an *application domain* consisting of all possible stacks of values of type `T`
2. a finite collection of *admissible operations* applicable to any member of the application domain

In the case of stacks, we may list these admissible operations as

a. a *push* operation, which inserts an additional value into the current stack
b. a *pop* operation, which removes a value from the current stack whenever it is not empty
c. an *is-empty* operation, which tests whether the current stack is empty
d. a *top* operation, which retrieves the value at the top of the current stack whenever it is not empty

This represents the complete characterization of a stack of values of type `T` as an ADT. In C++, this ADT is generally implemented as a *class.* Classes enable us to define the type of data to be stored in the structure and the admissible operations applicable to instances of that class. These instances are called the *objects* of that class.

In C++, classes are generally designed using two major components:

- a *user interface*
- an *implementation file*

This subdivision is particularly useful when describing the other aspects of object-oriented design.

Encapsulation

Another key principle of OOD is *encapsulation,* or *information hiding.* This principle was first proposed by David Parnas in 1971.[1] Let us view the implementation of an ADT as a class in the sense just described. Then the idea of encapsulation enforces two major aspects of OOD:

1. The class must provide the intended client (user) with all of the information required to implement the abstraction and nothing more.
2. The class definition must provide the implementation with all of the information required to complete the definition of the class and nothing more.

[1]See Parnas in the References at the end of this chapter.

Thus, the user of a class does not know how the class is implemented and cannot write programs that are dependent on that specific implementation. This makes the class easier to maintain because class designers (implementers) know exactly what code may be changed without affecting any of the users' applications. From another perspective, once the class has been designed and made available to clients, the implementers have no way of knowing all of the specific applications of their work performed by clients, except that the necessary functionality has been provided in the user interface. This simplifies maintenance of user programs because programmers have a precise knowledge of what code may or may not be changed safely.

In the example of the stack ADT involving C++ class definitions, the user interface may be described with a listing of the operations available to the user (in the `public` part of the interface) and hide a number of the implementation details (in the `private` part). Thus, the user interface will contain a listing of the names of the stack operations available to the user, such as `push`, `pop`, `is_empty`, and `top`, and express some of the implementation details in the `private` part. The operations described in the `public` part of the user interface need only be described as *prototypes* because all the user has to know is their specific names and the number, order of appearance of any input values and their respective types, and the return data type, if applicable. There is no reason for the user to know how these operations are implemented; this is the concern of the contents of the implementation file.

For example, in the stack ADT, there are two popular implementations that we will discuss later in some detail. These are

- the *sequential implementation*
- the *linked implementation*

Each represents a separate implementation of the four admissible operations `push`, `pop`, `is_empty`, and `top`. The user has no direct interface with either implementation; these implementation details are of no concern to the user. In fact, a later decision in the design of a class definition of the stack ADT may be to change the implementation from one that is sequential to a linked implementation. In the true spirit of information hiding, this change will have no effect on the user's application.

In this context, we say that the class definition of stacks *encapsulates* the definition of the stack ADT. Hence, encapsulation yields adaptability because it allows the implementation details of sections of a program to change without affecting other sections of the program's code. The `public` and `private` parts of a class definition represent instances of how information hiding is applied in the object-oriented paradigm.

Modularity

Contemporary commercial software systems are typically comprised of a number of well-organized and well-planned autonomous units, to which we give the general name *modules.* These modules must be designed in such a way that they interact correctly to produce the solution of the problem for which they were designed. In the context of an object-oriented system, the design and proper organization of these modules are called *modularity* and may involve the design of a number of classes whose objects must coordinate properly to produce the desired solution. In a number of cases, these classes may be designed in a *hierarchical* framework, in which certain classes may depend on the existence of other more general classes. This is implemented in an OOD using the idea of *inheritance,* in which a *base class* is defined with one or more dependent *derived classes,* whose objects inherit some of the properties inherent in the base class.

In a hierarchical organization of classes, any object constructed in a derived class is said to satisfy an "is-a" relationship with the corresponding base class. Let us illustrate this idea with the following example.

EXAMPLE 1.1 Suppose we look at a group of classes representing a simple hierarchy of two-dimensional geometric figures, organized as in Figure 1.2. The organi-

FIGURE 1.2

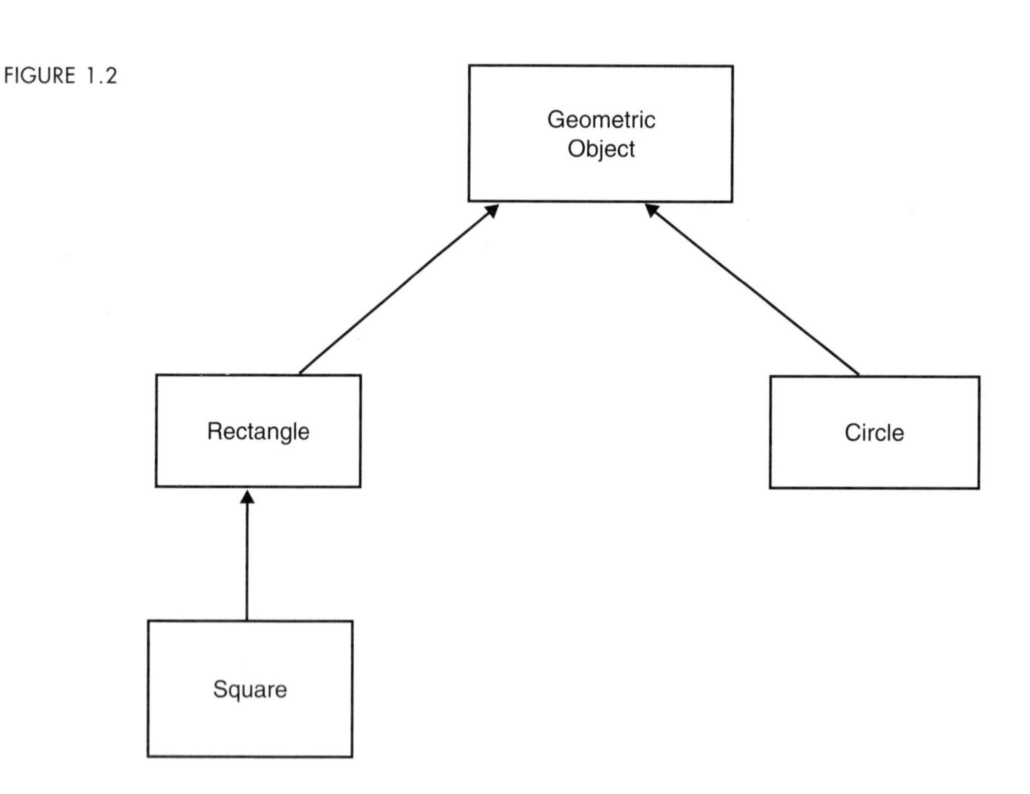

zational structure is such that each box defines a separate class, with the dependencies as illustrated. Thus, any object constructed from the class `Rectangle` is also a `Geometric Object`; this dependence is also true of any object constructed from the `Circle` class. The hierarchy descends one further level: It is possible to construct an object of the `Square` class, which is a kind of `Rectangle` and is in turn a kind of `Geometric Object`.

Class hierarchies are often very useful in designing solutions of large software problems. This is because the implementation of a hierarchical modular design respects the common functionality of a number of objects from a distinct derived class with the common and more general base classes. In addition, the specialized behavior of objects constructed in any of the derived classes is respected.

The use of modular design also promotes *reusability* of software. This means that a module designed to solve a specific software problem may also be applicable to the solution of a number of seemingly unrelated software problems. In this case, there is no need to completely recode a second version. Instead, all that need be done is to "plug in," or link, that module to the modules of the new system. This is certainly possible in C++, where classes designed for the solution of one problem may possess a functionality that may be reused to solve others because that functionality (in part) applies as well.

1.3 Classes and Objects

Classes undoubtedly represent the central construct of OOD as implemented in C++. With classes, we may group associated items of data together with a number of operations acting on those data. The aggregate consisting of a well-defined set of data and a finite collection of admissible operations acting on those data has already been defined as the necessary ingredients of an ADT. It then follows that classes represent an ideal implementation of an ADT.

The user interface of a class is defined in C++ by first writing the keyword `class`, followed by an identifier naming that class. The *text* (or *body*) of the interface follows, enclosed in braces, and describes (perhaps in the form of prototypes) the member functions of the class (in the `public` part) and the data members (in the `private` part). The description of the interface terminates with a semicolon (`;`).

The formal syntax for the user interface of a class definition may then be expressed as

```
class class_name {
      class_body
};
```

where `class` is a C++ keyword, *class_name* is an identifier naming the class, and *class_body* contains the definitions of the class members: the *data members* and *member functions.* The data members comprise whatever data are required to define the class, and the member functions formally describe the admissible operations of that class.

It is possible to manage the user's access to the members of the class by using the keywords `public` and `private` (and `protected` in certain instances using inheritance) preceding a group of definitions in *class_body*. The default access mode is `private`. Class members designated as `private` are accessible only to members of the same class. If a class operation is `public`, this operation is available to any user. Consequently, if class members are to be made available to any user, these must appear in a section of *class_body* headed by the keyword `public`.

A variable declared with *class_name* as its data type is an *object* of that class; that is, it is an instance of the underlying ADT named by *class_name*. The declaration of an object of that class invokes a *constructor,* which is a function allocating storage that possibly (depending on the form of the constructor) may install initial values for the data members of the new object or construct a duplicate object of an already existing object of the same class. A constructor is easy to identify because it always has the same name as *class_name*. In fact, a class may have more than one constructor or provide no explicit constructor in its definition. We will treat these in more detail in the next section.

class_body may contain variable and/or constant definitions used for clarifying the behavior of any object of that class. There is one difference between variables and constants defined within the text (scope) of *class_body* and ordinary variables and named constants. Those defined within the scope of *class_body* are not allocated storage until an object of that class is actually constructed. In fact, if several variables and/or constants are defined within *class_body*, each of these is allocated storage at once, and only when an actual object of that class is constructed.

How does the presence of classes aid in the general practice of contemporary software design? The design of a software solution to a problem generally progresses through three fundamental stages. First, the idea is to gain, in as precise a manner as possible, a clear understanding of the problem. This is often called the *analysis phase* of software development. The next stage is to identify the key components involved in the solution (the *design phase*). Finally, the solution is expressed in correct and efficient code (the *programming phase*). The details of the problem and the attempt to design and encode the proposed solution are often attained through a trial-and-error process consisting of efforts to implement these components in code, producing a solution that is correct and as efficient as possible.

In most contemporary designs, the solutions require more than the data types predefined with the language. In C++, these predefined types are the so-called *simple types:* `int`, `long`, `short`, `unsigned`, `char`, `bool`, `float`, and `double`. In an object oriented environment, the solution usually requires the definition of a sequence of cooperating classes.

A C++ class defines a *type*, which specifies the behavior of its objects. This behavior includes how these objects are constructed, how they may be manipulated, and how they may be destroyed when no longer needed. The main objective in writing effective object-oriented programs is to design classes that capture a simple, fundamental concept. With this in mind, the questions of how such objects are constructed, manipulated, and destroyed must figure heavily in the design.

1.4 Constructors and Destructors: An Example

A *constructor* is a member function whose name is *class_name;* that is, its name is the same as that of its underlying class and never specifies a return data type. A constructor is used to create objects of the class. When a constructor is invoked by the user, it allocates storage for each of the object's data members and also provides access for each of the member functions defined in the class.

Constructors may be defined so that initial values are provided for some or all of their data members. The process of constructing an object and initializing its data members is called *instantiation.* In addition, it is possible to define a constructor whose resulting object is an exact copy of an already existing object of the same class. Such a form of a constructor is called a *copy constructor.* In fact, we may define several different forms of constructors for the same class.

EXAMPLE 1.2 The user interface for a stack class storing integer values may be given as follows:

```
const int MAX_SIZE = <some fixed positive integer>;
class int_stack {
  public:
    // Constructor.  Constructs empty stack object.
       int_stack();
    // Push operator.  Pushes an int value onto the top of
    // the current stack.
       void push(int);
    // Pop operator.  Removes value at the top of the current
    // stack.
```

```
    // Precondition: Current stack is not empty.
       void pop();
    // Function testing whether the current stack is empty.
    // Returns true if so, false if not.
       bool is_empty() const;
    // Function returning value at the top of the current stack.
    // Precondition:  Current stack is not empty.
       int top() const;
  private:  // Data members.
       int info[MAX_SIZE];
       int top_value;
}; // Concludes user interface.
```

This class defines five `public` member functions, one of which is the constructor, whose prototype is given as

```
int_stack();
```

In addition, two data members are defined. One is a reference to an array of `int` values with `MAX_SIZE` components, indexed from `0` through `MAX_SIZE - 1`. The second, named `top_value`, stores an `int` value that locates the position in the array associated with the top of the current stack.

When this constructor is invoked in a user program, say in the form

```
int_stack i_stack;
```

we may view the allocation of storage for `i_stack` as in Figure 1.3. Here

FIGURE 1.3 i_stack

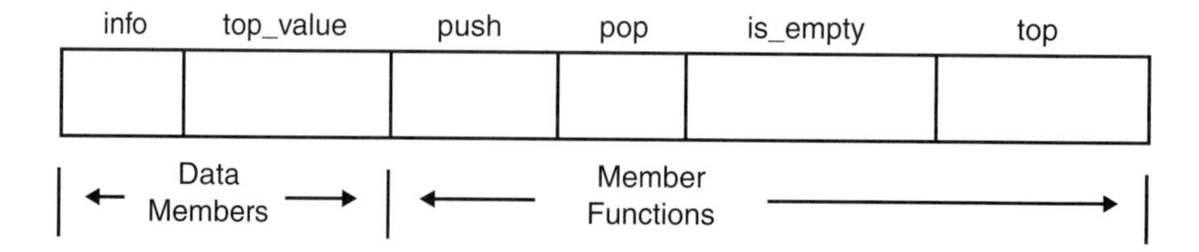

`info` is a reference to an array of `int` values of the form given in Figure 1.4. The constructor given by the prototype

```
int_stack();
```

is responsible for all of this storage. Later, when we discuss the implementation details of this class, we will see how the constructor initializes any `int_stack` object as empty.

The implementation file contains the code

```
int_stack::int_stack(){
   top_value = -1;
}
```

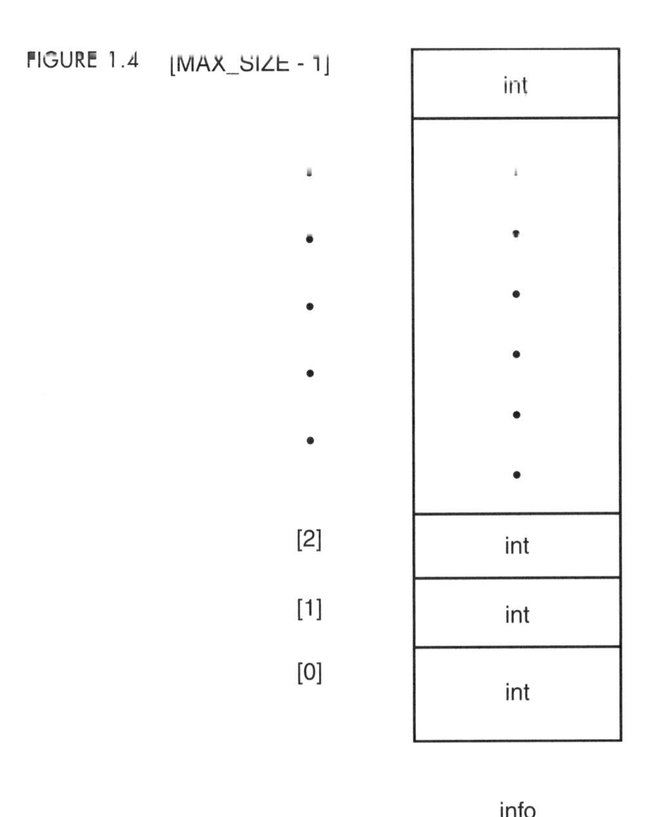

FIGURE 1.4

This ensures that any `int_stack` object (such as `i_stack`) is initialized as in Figure 1.5. The initial value of `-1` for `top_value` will ensure that no current value stored in the `info` array is associated with the current stack. Thus, effectively, `i_stack` in its current form describes an *empty stack.* This form of a constructor for `int_stack` is known as a *default constructor* because its implementation requires no arguments. If no explicit form of a constructor is supplied in the definition of a class, the default constructor is assigned to that class, with no initial values given to any of the object's data members.

A *destructor* is a member function whose name is *class_name* preceded by the character ~ . A destructor performs the inverse operation provided by any constructor—a constructor allocates storage to associate with the object, and the destructor frees *(deallocates)* that storage. Destructors are invoked implicitly when an object of its corresponding class must be destroyed, usually occurring upon exiting the text of a function or a block.

In the `int_stack` example, no explicit destructor is given; this implies an implicit use of the destructor. The action provided in this case would probably result in destroying the association of the components of the `info` array and the storage assigned to `top_value` with the object. This does not

FIGURE 1.5

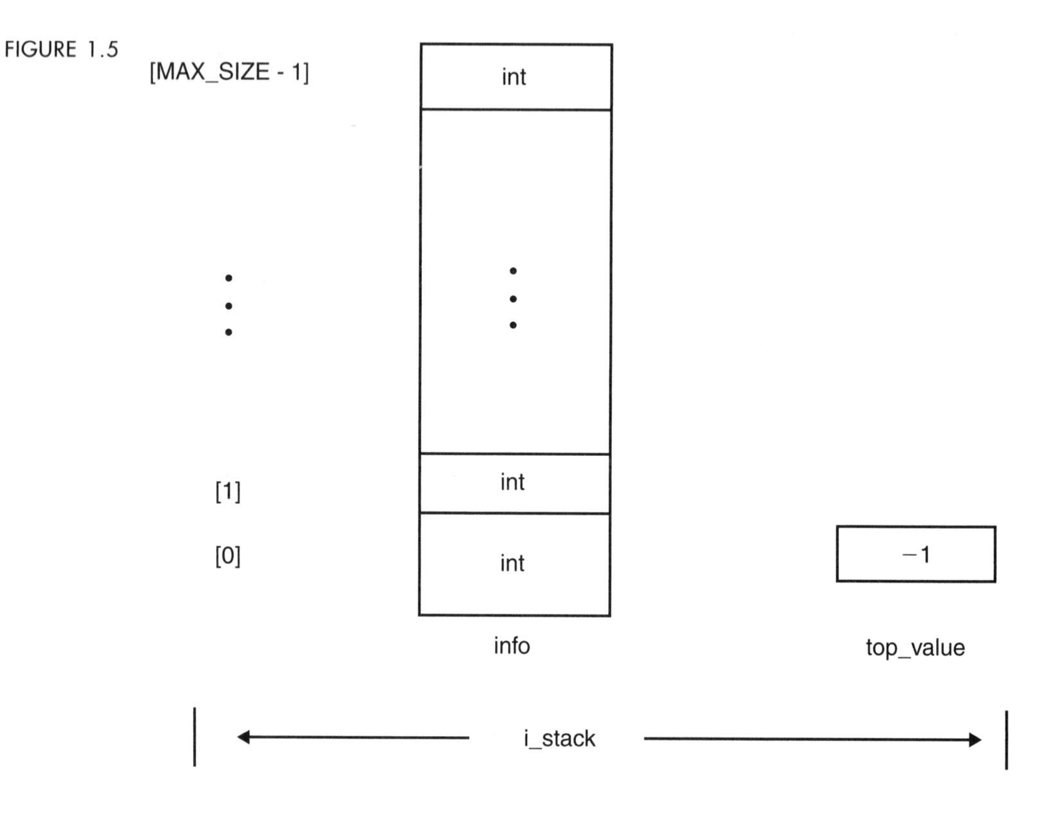

necessarily free the contiguous storage of the individual components of `info` for reuse. To ensure this (which would be regarded as a more efficient use of storage), we would have to give an explicit definition in the user interface as

```
~int_stack();
```

with an implementation

```
int_stack::~int_stack(){
 delete[] info;
}
```

Observation

The `const` declaration for the size of the `info` array given by

```
const int MAX_SIZE = <some fixed positive integer>;
```

appears before the code of the user interface for `int_stack`. A possible criticism to this might be that the interface does not completely encapsulate the class because the size of the array appears outside the code of the interface.

This is answered by replacing this declaration by an *anonymous* enum *declaration* of the form

```
enum {MAX_SIZE =  <some fixed positive integer>;}
```

in the private part of the interface. This enum declaration plays the role of a constant declaration within the scope of the interface, with one major difference. If we replace this by `const int MAX_SIZE = <some fixed positive integer>;` within the scope of the user interface, a compile-time error occurs. This is because a `const` definition, wherever it occurs, always allocates storage (`int-` valued storage in this case). But a class definition never allocates storage of and by itself—allocation of storage is possible only outside of the text of the class, when a constructor is used to generate objects of that class.

1.5 Implementation Details

If the file containing the user interface for `int_stack` is kept separate from the details of the implementation, we name it `int_stack.h`, and the corresponding implementation file is named `int_stack.cpp`. The contents of this implementation file use a number of properties (such as the use of named constants instead of constant literals), which are very useful in the general environment of correct and efficient design.

Because we assume that `int_stack.cpp` is a separate file from `int_stack.h`, `int_stack.cpp` must contain the preprocessor directive

```
#include "int_stack.h"
```

to establish a link with its associated user interface. We assume the code for the constructor (and destructor) as described in Section 1.4 is included.

Another very useful preprocessor directive uses the idea of *assertions*. An assertion is a Boolean-valued statement which, when true, allows a computation to proceed normally and aborts with a diagnostic when false. The C++ standard library contains the file `assert.h` containing the macro `assert`, whose syntax may be expressed as

```
void assert(<expression>);
```

where `<expression>` is Boolean-valued. When invoked, `<expression>` is tested first. If true, execution proceeds normally; if false, normal execution is aborted with the display accompanying diagnostic describing the cause of interruption of normal execution.

We may use this for the coding of `push`, as

```
void int_stack :: push(int value) {
// Pushes contents of value onto current stack.
// Postcondition: contents of value on top of stack
```

```
//    with previous contents below.
assert(top_value < MAX_SIZE - 1);
info[++top_value] = value;
}
```

The assertion checks to see whether there is still room in the info array for another value to be pushed onto the stack. That is, it checks to see whether the so-called *overflow condition* prevails. If info is completely filled with stack values, then the value of top_value is MAX_SIZE - 1, signaling the overflow condition. Consequently, there is no further room on info for another stack value, and the push operation is aborted. The overflow condition is inherent in any sequential implementation of stacks. This is because an array has only a finite number of components into which stack values may be stored, whereas, in theory, a stack has no upper bound on the number of values it may store. In later chapters, we will study other implementations of stacks in which the overflow condition may be avoided.

When deemed appropriate, the commentary accompanying the formal code should contain a description of the status of data upon entry into the text of the function *(preconditions)* and at the point of exit from the function *(postconditions)*, as well as *assertions* about the status of the data at some pivotal stage of processing.

If, on the other hand, there is room in info for another stack value, the index top_value is incremented, and the value of the parameter is copied into the array at position ++top_value.

The pop operator uses another form of an assertion. Its code is given by

```
void int_stack :: pop(){
// Removes value at top of current stack.
// Precondition: Current stack is not empty.
assert(top_value != -1);
top_value--;
}
```

Here the assertion tests whether the current stack is empty (sometimes called the *underflow condition*). If so, the current value stored in top_value is -1, signaling the presence of the underflow condition. If so, the expression top_value != -1 is false, aborting the pop operation. But if the current stack is not empty, this expression is true, and the pop operation proceeds without interruption. In the process, the value of top_index is decremented, indicating that the info array holds the resulting stack in positions 0 through the newly decremented value of top_value.

The function top() was included in the user interface. Its purpose is to return the value at the top of the current stack whenever it is not empty. We code this as

```
int int_stack :: top() const
// Returns value at the top of the current stack.
// Precondition: Current stack is not empty
{
 assert(top_value != -1);
 return info[top_value];
}
```

The same assertion as that used for `pop()` applies here for the same reasons. In addition, note the presence of the `const` modifier. This indicates that this function does not change the *state* of the object to which it is being applied. More specifically, the stack represented by the object has the same values and does not change its size as a result of applying this function. Applying `const` in this way may be regarded as issuing a directive to the compiler to report an error if the accompanying code attempts to change the object's state.

The code for `is_empty()` is

```
bool int_stack :: is_empty() const
// Tests whether the current stack is empty.
// Returns true if so, and false if not.
{
  return top_value == -1;
};
```

We should note that the assertions given for `pop()` and `top()` could also have been expressed as

```
assert(!is_empty());
```

1.6 Templates

Class Templates

In the last two sections, we began the design and produced a C++ implementation for the ADT for integer valued stacks using classes. But what about stacks whose values are not integer-valued, such as character-valued stacks or stacks whose values are real valued? Our previous design, although quite correct and efficient, does not apply. In fact, although the design of the underlying code turns out to be nearly identical with that which we have given for integer-valued stacks, it will have to be rewritten for each separate data type of the values for which the stack is defined. This is repetitive and tedious because we are faced with the alternative to supply an implementation for which the only change is to replace each occurrence of `int` by an occurrence of the specific new data type.

There is another alternative supported by C++: Rather than specify a specific data type, such as `int`, we may design a "generic" form of the implementation, with the data type of the values involved defined using a *type parameter* `T`. The class definition using this generic form is called a *class template.* The same subdivision into a user interface and an implementation file applies in this context, but each occurrence of the specific data type (such as `int`) is replaced by an occurrence of the parameter `T`. Besides this, there are some other relatively simple modifications in syntax, which we explain in the course of describing the syntax of the "templated" form for the stack ADT.

We illustrate these ideas by first describing the templated form of the user interface for stacks, where we use the *class_name* `stack` rather than `int_stack`:

```
const int MAX_SIZE = <some fixed positive integer>;
// User interface.
template<class T> class stack {
   public:
     // Constructor.  Constructs empty stack object.
        stack();
     // Push operator.  Pushes a value of type T onto the top of
     // the current stack.
        void push(T);
     // Pop operator.  Removes value on the top of the current
     // stack.
     // Precondition: Current stack is not empty.
        void pop();
     // Function testing whether the current stack is empty.
     // Returns true if so, false if not.
        bool is_empty() const;
     // Function returning value at the top of the current stack.
     // Precondition: Current stack is not empty.
        T top() const;
   private: // Data members.
        T info[MAX_SIZE];
        int top_value;
}; // Concludes user inteface.
```

Note that `template` is a new C++ keyword, and each of the member functions is again expressed as a prototype, but now in templated form, replacing `int` by `T` whenever referring to the data type of values on the current stack. C++ uses the phrase

```
template<class T> class stack
```

to indicate that the code that follows represents the user interface for the stack class using the parameter T. This is often referred to as the class template stack<T>. As a further illustration, note that the function push() described here is

```
void push(T);
```

This implies that whenever this class is defined for a specific data type (such as int), the push operator is simply the push operator for the int type whose behavior was described in earlier sections of this chapter. When we use the stack class template with T substituted by int, we say that the type parameter T has been *instantiated* by T.

The key advantage in using class templates is that we no longer have to write a separate class definition for stacks storing values of type char or stacks storing real values (such as float or double) or stacks of values defined by the user. All that need be done is to instantiate the data type of the stack(s) desired in the user function. For example, if a user function requires the use of two int-valued stacks called i_stack1 and i_stack2 and one char-valued stack called c_stack, all that need be done in the text of the user function is to first establish a linkage with the user interface of the stack class template and then invoke the constructor for two instances of int and one instance of char, as

```
stack(<int>) i_stack1, i_stack2;
stack(<char>) c_stack;
```

If we assume that the user interface is in stack.h, then the preprocessor directive appearing in the text of the user function is

```
#include "stack.h"
```

It also follows that the implementation details of the templated member functions appear in stack.cpp. Since we again assume that these represent two separate files, stack.cpp must also contain

```
#include "stack.h"
```

We will use assertions in stack.cpp just as they were used in int_stack.cpp, only now for member function templates. Consequently, the text of stack.cpp must also contain

```
#include <assert.h>
```

The templated version of the constructor is coded as

```
template<class T> stack<T> :: stack(){
 // Constructor.  Constructs empty stack with no values.
 top_value = -1;
}
```

The idea here is that the constructor will be invoked for specific instances of T, as was done earlier, twice for T substituted by int and once for T substituted by char, as

```
stack(<int>) i_stack1, i_stack2;
stack(<char>) c_stack;
```

The push operator again checks for overflow using the same assertion as that already described for the int_stack class:

```
template<class T> void stack<T> :: push(T value)
{
 // Pushes value onto stack.
 // Postcondition: value is at top of stack,
 //    with previous contents below.
 assert(top_value < MAX_SIZE - 1);
 info[++top_value] = value;
}
```

Similarly, the template version of pop checks whether the underflow condition exists. Its code is given as

```
template<class T> void stack<T> :: pop()
{
 // Removes value at the top of the current stack.
 // Precondition: Current stack is not empty.
 assert(top_value != -1);
 top_value--;
}
```

The template version of is_empty is

```
template<class T> bool stack<T> :: is_empty() const
{
 // Tests whether the current stack is empty.
 // Returns true if so, false if not.
 return top_value == -1;
}
```

Testing whether the current stack object is empty clearly does not depend on the type of values stored on the current stack. Thus, the same code executes regardless of the data type of the stack values. The only code that depends on the type of values on the stack is the push operator, described earlier, and the top operator, which again returns the value currently stored at the top of the current stack and whose template is

```
template<class T> T stack<T> :: top() const
{
 // Returns value at the top of the current stack.
 // Precondition: Current stack is not empty.
 assert(top_value != -1);
```

```
 return info[top value];
}
```

In summary, we conclude that class templates provide a higher level of abstraction and reuse because they may be defined when the same class structure is applicable on different types in exactly the same way. All that is necessary is that the user specify the type needed by instantiating the type parameter(s).

Function Templates

The C++ language allows for a second form of templates to be used when the same algorithm can be applied for different types of parameters. This form of abstraction and reuse is commonly known as *function templates.* To illustrate, we may observe that one of the most frequently used algorithms is that for interchanging (or swapping) the values stored in two variables. The swap is accomplished by executing the code sequence

```
temp_holder = value1;
value1 = value2;
value2 = temp_holder;
```

where `value1` and `value2` are variables holding the values to be swapped, and `temp_holder` is an auxiliary variable of the same type as that of `value1` and `value2`. Note that we have not specified any type because this sequence will work regardless of the type specified. For example, if we wish to swap the values of two `int` variables, the operable form of the swapping function would be coded as

```
void swap_values(int& value1,int& value2)
{
 int temp_holder = value1;
 value1 = value2;
 value2 = temp_holder;
}
```

The function for swapping two `char` values is

```
void swap_values(char& value1,char& value2)
{
 char temp_holder = value1;
 value1 = value2;
 value2 = temp_holder;
}
```

This same implementation would also work for any floating-point type or other well-defined data type in C++. Without templates, the problem is that a separate function is required for each different type. Since C++ allows overloading of function names, the same name (`swap_values` in this case) may be used for different versions of the swapping function as long as these different versions are distinguished by different type names in their respective formal parameter lists.

As an alternative, C++ permits the coding of a generic form for `swap_values` using a function template with a single type parameter `T` in the form

```
template<class T> void swap_values(T& value1,T& value2)
{
 T temp_holder = value1;
 value1 = value2;
 value2 = temp_holder;
}
```

This indicates that whenever we have to swap any two values of some specific type, all that we need do is instantiate the type parameter by that type. For example, assuming the coding of the function template for `swap_values` just presented, a user program may apply the sequence

```
int number1 = 3, number2 = 5;
swap_values(number1,number2);
float f_val1 = 7.3, f_val2 = -9.08;
swap_values(f_val1,f_val2);
```

The compiler will then produce two versions of `swap_values`: one for interchanging two `int` values and the second for interchanging two `float` values.

In other words, a function template allows for the creation of an entire category of specific functions, one for each distinct instance of the data type that substitutes the type parameter. In effect, we already did this for member functions for the class template `stack`. Indeed, if we look at the implementation of the `push` operator

```
template<class T> void stack<T> :: push(T value)
{
  // Pushes value onto current stack.
  // Postcondition: value is at the top of the stack,
  //   with previous contents below.
  assert(top_value < MAX_SIZE - 1);
  info[++top_value] = value;
}
```

we conclude that this represents a template of the `push` member function of `stack<T>`. However, we generally associate the term *function templates* with those that are not described as member functions of some class template, as is the case for `swap_values`.

An Alternative to Templates: The `void*` Type

The C++ language supports a `void*` pointer type. This serves as a *generic pointer type* because any ordinary pointer such as a value of type `int*` or of type `char*` can be assigned to it. In fact, the following observations hold:

a. An ordinary pointer can always be converted to a `void*` pointer using assignment operators.
b. A pointer of type `void*` *cannot be dereferenced.* Recall that dereferencing is the operation denoted by `*` applied to a pointer to access the current value being referenced by that pointer.

For example, if we have the declarations

```
void* gptr;
int* iptr;
```

then

```
gptr = iptr;
```

is a legal assignment by observation (a). But the reverse assignment is possible only if we explicitly *cast* the generic pointer as `int*`, namely,

```
iptr = (int*)gptr;
```

The generic pointer type `void*` is a useful alternative to class templates. We illustrate this for the stack ADT, where we replace the type parameter `T` by `void*`. We begin by rewriting the user interface for `stack<T>` seen earlier in this section by

```
const int MAX_SIZE = <some fixed positive integer>;
typedef void* gptr;

class stack {
 public:
  // Constructor
  stack();
  // Push operator
  void push(gptr);
  // Pop operator
  void pop();
  // Function retrieving value at the top of the current stack
  gptr top() const;
  // Function testing whether current stack is empty.
  // Returns true if so, false if not.
  bool is_empty() const;

 private:
```

```
  gptr* info;
  int top_value;
};
```

The implementation code for the constructor is

```
// Constructor.  Constructs empty stack.
stack :: stack()
{
 info = new gptr[MAX_SIZE];
 top_value = -1;
}
```

The `push` operator is coded as

```
// Push operator.
void stack :: push(gptr value)
{
 info[++top_value] = value;
}
```

Similarly, the code for the `pop` operator is

```
// Pop operator.
void stack :: pop()
{
 top_value--;
}
```

and that for the `top` operator is

```
// Function retrieving value at the top
// of the current stack.
gptr stack :: top() const
{
 return info[top_value];
}
```

Finally, the coding for `is_empty()` is nearly identical with the template version:

```
// Function testing whether current stack is empty.
// Returns true if so, false if not.
bool stack :: is_empty() const
{
 return top_value == -1;
}
```

The key fact to bear in mind is that the preceding code allocates no real storage—that allocation is done in the template version when `T` is instantiated as a specific type, such as `int`, `char`, `double`, and any other well-defined specific type. The same is accomplished in this new version by *casting*. This may be illustrated by the driver for the preceding code, which prompts the user for five `int` values, pushing each onto the stack as they are input and then outputting these values as they are popped. The output is the five input values in reverse order.

```
int main(){
 stack st;
 int number;
 cout << "Input five values:" << endl;
 for(int index = 0; index < 5; ++index)
 {
  cout << "Enter a value:" << endl;
  cin >> number;
  st.push((int*)number);
 }
 while(!st.is_empty())
 {
  cout <<(int)st.top() << '\t';
  st.pop();
 }
 cout << endl;
 return 0;
}
```

This may be repeated for, say, `char` values by replacing each instance of `int` by `char`. We leave this as an exercise for the reader, as well as the inclusion of tests for underflow and overflow using `<assert.h>` and the `assert()` macro.

1.7 An Abstraction for Complex Numbers

This section is devoted to a specific abstraction of an important data type used in mathematics and engineering. It is called the *complex number system,* and a typical complex number has the form

```
<real part> + <imaginary part>i
```

where `<real part>` and `<imaginary part>` are real numbers, and where `i` is the symbol used to denote the square root of `-1`. Here the `+` symbol performs no arithmetic operation; it simply acts as a *separator* between the real and imaginary parts.

In defining the ADT for complex numbers, the admissible operations are

- *addition* of any two complex numbers, defined as $(a_1 + b_1i) + (a_2 + b_2i) = (a_1 + a_2) + (b_1 + b_2)i$;
- *subtraction* of any two complex numbers, defined as $(a_1 + b_1i) - (a_2 + b_2i) = (a_1 - a_2) + (b_1 - b_2)i$;
- *equality* of two complex numbers, defined as $(a_1 + b_1i) == (a_2 + b_2i)$ if and only if $(a_1 == a_2)$ and $(b_1 == b_2)$;
- an *assignment operator* `=`, which permits the copying of an already existing complex value into a declared complex variable
- an *output function,* which outputs the real and imaginary parts of any complex number[2]

Our design involves an implementation of this ADT using a class named `complex`, any of whose objects represents a single complex number with two data members: `real_part` and `imaginary_part`, each of type `double`. The `public` member functions will consist of a constructor and an implementation of each of the functions just described.

The constructor we use has *default parameter values.* The prototype for the constructor is

```
complex(double = 0.0,double = 0.0);
```

This informs the compiler that any `complex` object will be constructed with two data members in the order `real_part` and `imaginary_part`. If the user wishes to construct a `complex` object `z1` with `4.1` as the value of `real_part` and `-3.8` as the value of `imaginary_part`, the user program must contain

```
complex z1(4.1,-3.8);
```

This constructs the `complex` object `z1` as described in Figure 1.6.

FIGURE 1.6

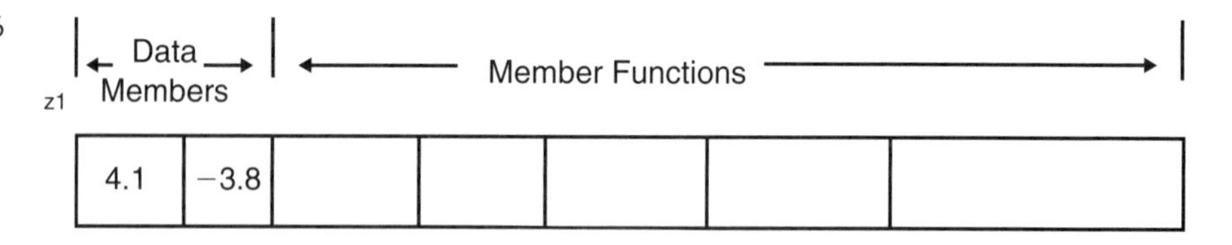

However, if the user fails to supply a pair of `double` parameter values for the constructor, as in

```
complex z2;
```

the default parameters will prevail, resulting in the construction of the `complex` object `z2`, as described in Figure 1.7.

[2]These operations may be extended to include a *multiplication operator* `*` and a *division operator* `/`, with the latter defined for any complex denominator having either a nonzero real part or a nonzero imaginary part. We leave this extension as an exercise.

FIGURE 1.7

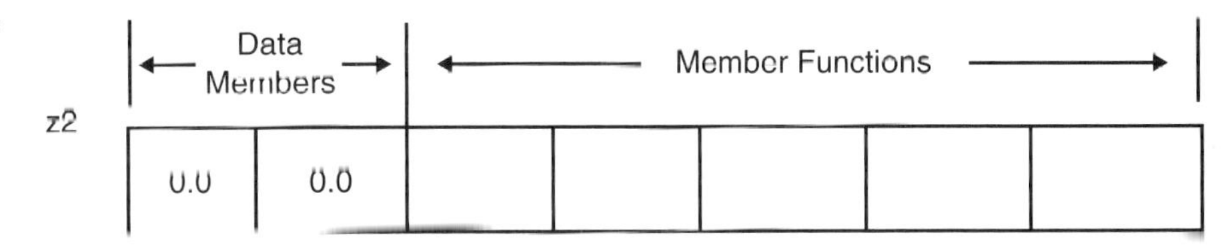

Another facility of C++ allows us to use the actual operator symbol `+` as the name of the member function for computing the sum of two complex numbers. This is accomplished by introducing `operator+`, where `operator` is a new C++ keyword, and `+` is the overloaded addition symbol for `complex` arguments as defined earlier for the complex ADT. A prototype for this is

```
complex operator+(const complex&) const;
```

But our definition of complex addition involves a *binary operation,* and yet the prototype displays only one parameter! The explanation is that `operator+` is defined as a *pure member function* of the `complex` class; it must be applied with a single `complex` parameter to an already existing `complex` object! Symbolically, this interpretation of the sum of the complex numbers $z = a_1 + b_1 i$ and $w = a_2 + b_2 i$ is given as `z.operator+(w)`. C++ permits the user to replace the formally correct version `z.operator+(w)` by the more familiar `z + w`. Since addition is a commutative operation, the same result would be obtained if the user applies `w.operator+(z)` or its replacement `w + z`. Similarly, C++ permits the use of `operator-` for the overloaded subtraction operator for complex numbers. The only distinction is that subtraction is not commutative; hence, `z - w` and `w - z` produce different results.

A prototype for the subtraction operator for complex numbers is

```
complex operator-(const complex&) const;
```

In each of the prototypes defined for complex addition and subtraction, we pass the single parameter *by reference,* preceded by a `const` modifier. The inclusion of `const` in the description of the parameter informs the compiler that the "state" of the parameter cannot be changed during the course of the computation of either addition or subtraction. This simply means that no changes in the values of the data members of the `complex` parameter are allowed during the function's computation.

The test of equality of two complex arguments is implemented by the prototype

```
bool operator==(const complex&) const;
```

Formally, if we use `w` as the name of the `complex` parameter and the operator is applied to the `complex` object `z`, as in `z.operator==(w)`, the value returned will be either `true` or `false` depending on whether the real parts and the imaginary parts agree. Again, C++ permits the user code to replace this formally correct version as `z == w`.

The overloaded assignment operator is defined by the prototype

```
complex& operator=(const complex&);
```

This permits an already existing `complex` value to be copied into the respective components of a previously constructed `complex` variable. This is not to be confused with the action of a *copy constructor* because the latter first constructs a `complex` object from scratch and then copies the values of the respective components of the `complex` parameter into the new `complex` object. In executing the assignment, the state of the object in which the copy is being sent changes, hence the omission of the `const` modifier outside of the parentheses.

The user interface for the `complex` class appearing in `"complex.h"` is

```
class complex {
  public:
  // Constructor
     complex(double = 0.0,double = 0.0);
  // Overloaded addition operator
     complex operator+(const complex&) const;
  // Overloaded subtraction operator
     complex operator-(const complex&) const;
  // Test for equality.  Returns true if equal,
  // and false if not.
     bool operator==(const complex&) const;
  // Overloaded assignment operator
     complex& operator=(const complex&);
  // Output function.  Outputs any complex
  // argument as a + bi
     void print() const;
  private:
     double real_part;
     double imaginary_part;
};
```

The corresponding implementation file `"complex.cpp"` contains the preprocessor directives

```
#include <iostream.h>
#include "complex.h"
```

and the implementation details of each member function.

The constructor is coded as

```
complex :: complex(double r,double i)
{
```

```
  real_part = r;
  imaginary_part = i;
}
```

Here the `real_part` component of the object being constructed is assigned the value contained in the first parameter, and the object's `imaginary_part` component is assigned the value currently contained in the second parameter. If no parameter values are supplied, the default value of `0.0` is assigned to each of the `real_part` and `imaginary_part` components.

The implementation file for the overloaded addition operator is

```
complex complex :: operator+(const complex&  operand2) const
{
  complex sum;
  sum.real_part = real_part + operand2.real_part;
  sum.imaginary_part = imaginary_part + operand2.imaginary_part;
  return sum;
}
```

In this form, the first identifier on the right side of each of

```
sum.real_part = real_part + operand2.real_part;
sum.imaginary_part = imaginary_part + operand2.imaginary_part;
```

refers to the `real_part` and `imaginary_part` components, respectively, of the `complex` object being acted on by `operator+`. For instance, if the user's code contains either `z.operator+(w)` (or `z + w`), `z` is the `complex` object being acted on by the member function `operator+(w)`. Thus, `real_part` and `imaginary_part` refer to the respective data components of `z`. The formal execution of this member first constructs a local `complex` object called `sum` and fills its respective `real_part` and `imaginary_part` components with the corresponding sum of the `real_part` and `imaginary_part` components of its two summands: the object being acted on by `operator+` and `operand2`. The resulting `complex` object `sum` is returned.

Similar observations exist for the implementation of subtraction, coded as

```
complex complex :: operator-(const complex& operand2) const
{
  complex diff;
  diff.real_part = real_part - operand2.real_part;
  diff.imaginary_part = imaginary_part - operand2.imaginary_part;
  return diff;
}
```

The `bool`-valued test for equality of two `complex` values tests whether the `complex` object being acted on by `operator==` has a `real_part` component matching that of `operand2` and an `imaginary_part` component matching that of operand2. If that is the case, true is returned; otherwise, false is returned:

```
bool complex :: operator==(const complex& operand2) const
{
 return (real_part == operand2.real_part)
      && (imaginary_part == operand2.imaginary_part);
}
```

The print() member function is coded as

```
void complex :: print() const
{
 cout << real_part << " + " << imaginary_part << "i" << endl;
}
```

The implementation of the overloaded assignment operator raises a number of interesting questions. It is coded as

```
complex& complex :: operator=(const complex& operand)
{
 real_part = operand.real_part;
 imaginary_part = operand.imaginary_part;
 return *this;
}
```

This coding makes use of the predefined this pointer, where this is a new C++ keyword. The result of applying this, which holds the address of the object whose member function (operator= in this case), is being invoked. The expression *this gives access to the object whose member function is invoked and whose return value is that object (of complex type in this case). Thus, for example, if z and w are complex objects and if we apply z.operator=(w); (or equivalently, z = w;), then *this references z, the complex object to which operator= is being applied.

The modifier & written as part of the description of a return type for a function denotes a *reference return,* as in

```
complex& operator=(const complex& operand);
```

In a *standard return,* as in

```
complex operator+(const complex operand2);
```

the return value is a *temporary object* created to store the (complex) value returned. The existence of the temporary object is bound to the invocation expression in the caller, as in

```
   .
   .
   .
```

```
complex z,w;
      .
      .
      .
(z + w).print();   // Invocation expression.
      .
      .
      .
```

In a reference return, no temporary object is created. Instead, the return value is an object whose scope includes the scope of the text of the function containing the invocation. Thus, the scope of `z` in

```
      .
      .
      .
complex z,w;
      .
      .
      .
   z = w;   //   Invocation expression.
      .
      .
      .
```

also contains the scope of the text of `operator=`. For a member function of a class with this form of a return data type, the object acted on by such a member function is the one invoked in the text of the user's code.

A driver for this implementation may be given by

```
#include "complex.h"
int main()
{
 complex x, y(4.3,8.2), z(3.3,1.1);
 cout << "x is " << x.print() << endl;
 x = y + z;
 cout << "x = y + z is " << x.print() << endl;
 x = y - z;
 cout << "x = y - z is " << x.print() << endl;
 if(x == y)cout << "x and y are equal" << endl;
 else cout << "x and y are not equal" << endl;
 return 0;
}
```

The output is

```
x is 0 + 0 i
x = y + z is 7.6 + 9.3 i
x = y - z is 1 + 7.1 i
x and y are not equal
```

1.8 Suggested Improvements of the Design of the `complex` Class

Our initial design of the `complex` class, although correct and efficient, raises a number of questions. First, we have already commented on the fact that the member functions defined for addition, subtraction, and testing equality show one parameter, yet each is viewed mathematically as a *binary function.* We explained that, to apply these as *pure member functions,* each had to be applied to a single `complex` argument as the object being acted on, with the second argument appearing as a parameter. For example, in the driver function just presented, the sum of the `complex` objects `y` and `z` could be expressed as `y.operator+(z)`, although C++ permits the alternative `y + z` as a replacement for the formally correct first version.

If we look at the text of the user interface, the prototype for addition is given as

```
complex operator+(const complex&) const;
```

There is thus no indication from this prototype that it implements the usual binary addition of two complex arguments. The same is true for `operator-` and `operator==`.

The question, then, is whether it is possible for a binary function to be expressed as a member function of a class and display both of its arguments as parameters. In the strict sense of pure member functions, the answer to this question is "no"; however, C++ has a facility that allows for a compromise. This is in the form of `friend` functions, where `friend` is a new C++ keyword.

A `friend` function of some class `A` is listed as a function in the user interface of `A`, but is coded in the implementation part without the necessary syntax for scope resolution as that for pure member functions. More precisely, the prototype of a `friend` function is defined within the scope of the user interface of `A` and has access to the `private` components of `A`, but is coded in the implementation part without using the scope resolution operator `::` required for pure member functions.

The syntax for the prototype of a `friend` function appearing in the user interface of a class is

friend *return_type function_name* (*formal_parameter_list*);

Observations

1. friend functions enhance readability and performance. Its prototype is defined within the scope of the user interface of the class but is coded in the implementation part without the usual scope resolution operator :: needed for the pure member functions of that class.
2. A friend function must be declared in the scope of the user interface of the class definition of which it is a friend. The function(s) involved must be prefaced by the keyword friend and may appear either in the public or private part without affecting its meaning or accessibility.
3. The most common occurrence of friend functions is in the public part of the user interface.
4. friend functions are often appropriate when a pure member function is not convenient for certain applications. This is the case in our coding of certain member functions of the complex class, as in the case of the somewhat "unnatural" forms implementing complex addition, subtraction, and equality.

We now introduce an alternative implementation of the complex class having the same functionality as its predecessor but now using friend functions. The user interface is given by

```
#include <iostream.h>
class complex {
public:
 // Constructor with default values.
 complex(double = 0.0,double = 0.0);
 // Overloaded addition operator.
 friend complex operator+(const complex&,const complex&);
 // Overloaded subtraction operator.
 friend complex operator-(const complex&,const complex&);
 // Test for equality.  Returns true if equal,
 // and false if not.
 friend bool operator==(const complex&,const complex&);
 // Overloaded assignment operator.
 complex& operator=(const complex&);
 // Overloaded output operator.
 // Outputs any complex value as a + bi.
 friend ostream& operator<<(ostream&,const complex&);
private:
 double real_part;
 double imaginary_part;
};
```

The prototype for the addition of two complex arguments now appears as

```
friend complex operator+(const complex&,const complex&);
```

Here two complex arguments are visible as operands, with a complex return type. This is more consistent with the formal mathematical view of complex addition. The coding of this version of operator+ in the implementation file is

```
// Overloaded addition operator.
complex operator+(const complex& operand1, const complex& operand2)
{
 complex sum;
 sum.real_part = operand1.real_part + operand2.real_part;
 sum.imaginary_part = operand1.imaginary_part +
                              operand2.imaginary_part;
 return sum;
}
```

The coding of the prototype and implementation for operator- and operator== follow similar lines.

One other change occurs in this version. The previous version defines a print() function used to output complex values in the form a + bi. It would seem more convenient to replace this by an overloaded version of cout, now designed for complex arguments. This is permitted in C++; in fact, the prototype in the form of an overloaded version of operator<< appears in the interface as

```
friend ostream& operator<<(ostream&,const complex&);
```

This is permitted by observing that the predefined <iostream> library defines two classes: istream and ostream. The first is designed for character stream input, and the second is for output. The ostream class is the mechanism for converting values stored internally (in the form of finite strings of bits) into legible char values. It is predefined for standard types, which simply means that the outputting of values of types such as int, char, float, double, and the like are done automatically using cout and an *output insertion operator* <<. This operator may be overloaded by defining a version of operator<< designed for a data type such as complex.

This may be accomplished for the complex class by defining a friend function that constructs an object of ostream (parameterized by os), then inserting values into os using operator<< predefined for double and char values, and then returning the current storage in os to the caller. The result is that operator<< is then defined for any complex argument. Let's assume that the implementation takes the form

```
ostream& operator<<(ostream& os,const complex& c)
// Overloaded output operator.
{
 // Deposit parts of complex argument in ostream object.
 os << c.real_part; // Deposit real_part component of c in os.
 os << "+"; // Deposit "+" in os
 os << c.imaginary_part; // Deposit imaginary_part
                          // component of c in os.
 os << "i"; // Deposit "i" in os.
 return os; // Return current contents of os to caller.
}
```

We may now write user functions in which the output of any `complex` value is performed using `operator<<`. As an example, consider the revision of the driver of Section 1.7 for the new version of `complex`:

```
int main()
{
 complex x, y(4.3,8.2), z(3.3,1.1);
 cout << "x is " << x << endl;
 x = y + z;
 cout << "x = y + z is " << x << endl;
 x = y - z;
 cout << "x = y - z is " << x << endl;
 if(x == y) cout << "x and y are equal" << endl;
 else cout << "x and y are not equal" << endl;
 return 0;
}
```

The output is identical with that of the previous version.

1.9 Exceptions and Exception Handling

In commercial or military systems, where software guides the flight of a satellite or monitors the environment of very delicate chemical processes, the occurrence of run-time errors such as hardware failures in peripheral sensing devices represents *exceptions* (that is, abnormal occurrences) that must be handled quickly and efficiently. In particular, the software should contain code that executes whenever an exception occurs. In response to this, the syntax of C++ contains a structure that deals with the detection of exceptions and branches to a code sequence that executes when such an exception occurs.

An exception is an event that interrupts normal program execution. There are two aspects involved in the processing of exceptions: *raising* (or *throwing*) the exception and *handling* the exception. An exception is thrown when a function detects a problem it cannot cope with in the course of normal execution. For example, for stacks using a sequential implementation, an exception is thrown when an attempt is made to push a value onto a stack when the associated `info` array is already full of stack values (the overflow condition alluded to earlier) or when an attempt is made to pop or retrieve the value at the top of a stack that is empty (underflow). The idea is, ideally, to transfer execution to a code sequence equipped to handle the exception. In C++, this code sequence to which execution transfers is said to *catch* the exception.

We have already discussed the use of `assert` statements and the predefined library `<assert.h>` in dealing with stack overflow and underflow. An objection to using `assert` is that it causes immediate termination of execution when an exception is detected. This may not necessarily be the most desirable situation in many commercial software applications. Thus, a better solution is sought for applications that cannot afford to crash, such as an onboard embedded guidance system for commercial aircraft that detects an obstacle to normal takeoff and landing operations.

In C++, three components of code are used for throwing and handling exceptions:

- a `throw` statement
- a `catch` statement
- a `try` block

A `throw` statement may assume one of two forms:

```
throw;
throw expression;
```

where `throw` is a new C++ keyword. The form described by the syntax `throw expression;` raises an exception whose description is given by *expression*. *expression* usually takes the form of an identifier naming a variable or a class, or a function (such as a class constructor). It operates in conjunction with a `try` block where the exception is raised and transfers control of execution to the corresponding `catch` statement used to process the exception. The first form (`throw;`) *rethrows* the current exception. It is used when a second exception handler called from the text of the original handler is required to complete the processing of the exception.

A `catch` statement contains the necessary code for handling the exception. Its syntax is

```
catch(formal-parameter-list)
  statement
```

where `catch` is a new C++ keyword. The appropriate `catch` statement is invoked by a matching `throw` statement. At that point, control transfers to the execution of the corresponding `catch` statement. The text of each catch statement immediately follows the try block in which such exceptions are raised. All objects constructed locally within the text of the try block are destroyed upon exiting.

A try block has the syntax

```
try {
  statement-sequence,
}
list of corresponding catch statements;
```

Note that try is another new C++ keyword.

The catch statements following the text of the try block contain all of the handlers of exceptions raised in that block

It is possible to nest try blocks. If no matching catch statement is appropriate from the try block currently executing, an appropriate catch statement is chosen from the enclosing try block and so on until an appropriate form is found. If no form matches the throw statement involved, a default statement executes.

The next example describes a new design of the int_stack class of Sections 1.4 and 1.5, replacing the assert statements by exceptions and exception handlers. Thus, an exception will be thrown if either an overflow or underflow condition occurs. The corresponding catch statement will be invoked when such an exception occurs. In each case, we define a class for processing each exception. We begin with

```
#include <iostream.h>


class underflow { // Class definition for underflow
  public:
    // Constructor
    underflow : message("Underflow error "){}
    // Output function
    void print() const { cout << message << endl; }
  private:
    const char* message;
};
```

This terminates the user interface code for the underflow class. Note that each of its member functions is coded *inline*—their implementation is included as part of the user interface. Therefore, there is no need for a separate implementation file. The member functions for underflow consist of a constructor, which creates an object whose only data member is the character string

```
Underflow error
```

The remaining member function print() displays this message when applied to any such object. Similarly, we define the overflow class as

```
class overflow { // Class definition for overflow
  public:
   // Constructor
   overflow : message("Overflow error "){}
    // Output function
    void print() const { cout << message << endl; }
  private:
    const char* message;
};
```

The user interface for `int_stack` is identical with that of Section 1.4, including preceding the user interface with the declaration

```
const int MAX_SIZE = <some fixed positive integer>;
```

However, there are a number of changes in the coding of the implementation details. For example, the implementation of the `push` member function throws an exception when overflow occurs:

```
// Push operator.  Watch for overflow.
void int_stack :: push(int value)
{
 if(top_value == MAX_SIZE - 1)
   throw overflow();
 info[++top_value] = value;
}
```

Thus, if the overflow condition exists, it is thrown as an exception by `push` and is caught by an exception handler treating the overflow condition. Otherwise, the normal execution of `push` proceeds as usual.

The implementation of `pop` and `top` each may throw an exception for underflow:

```
// Pop operator.  Watch for underflow.
void int_stack :: pop()
{
 if(is_empty())
   throw underflow();
 top_value--;
}

// Returns integer value at top of current stack.
// Precondition:  Current stack is not empty.
int int_stack :: top() const
{
 if(is_empty())
```

```
      throw underflow();
    return info[top_value];
  }
```

A possible driver function for this code may throw an overflow or underflow inside a `try` block. The version we provide may throw an overflow condition depending on how many integers are pushed onto the stack.

```
// Driver program.
int main()
{
  int_stack i_stack;
  try { // Contains code which may throw an exception
    int number_of_values, value;
    cout << "Input the number of values to be pushed onto the stack:"
         << endl;
    cin >> number_of_values;
    for(int i = 0; i < number_of_values; ++i)
    {
      cout << "Input an integer value:" << endl;
      cin >> value;
      i_stack.push(value);
    } // Ends for loop
    cout << "Popping from stack:" << endl;
    while(!i_stack.is_empty())
    {
      cout << i_stack.top() << '\t';
      i_stack.pop();
    } // Ends while loop
    cout << endl;
  } // Ends try-block

// Here come the exception handlers:
  catch(underflow error_message){ // Exception handler for underflow
    cout << "Error: ";
    error_message.print();
    cout << endl;
    return 1;
  } // Ends catch code for underflow

  catch(overflow error_message){ // Exception handler for overflow
    cout << "Error: ";
    error_message.print();
```

```
    cout << endl;
    return 2;
  } // Ends catch code for overflow

  return 0; // Terminate normal program execution
}
```

When we run this program, the message

```
Input the number of values to be pushed onto the stack:
```

appears. Assume the value of `MAX_INT` is `10`, and we respond to this message with `9`. The program responds with

```
Enter an integer value:
```

and we respond with an integer value. This process is repeated until nine integer values have been input. Suppose the sequence resulting from this is `8`, `4`, `-12`, `0`, `62`, `14`, `2`, `7`, and `12`. The output continues as

```
Popping from stack:
12      7       2       14      62      0       -12     4       8
```

On the other hand, if after being prompted with

```
Input the number of values to be pushed onto the stack:
```

we respond with `11`, after inputting the eleventh value, the program responds with

```
Error: Overflow error
```

and terminates execution. Overflow errors can be tested just as easily. We leave the programming details as an exercise.

1.10 `static` Members of a Class

Although `static` is a C keyword defining, for example, a particular type of storage behavior for variables,[3] its use is overloaded in C++ and is applicable to members of a class. A class may contain `static` data members and/or `static` member functions.

* `static` Data Members

Data members of a class may be declared using the `static` modifier. A `static` data member is a value that is shared by all objects constructed from that class and is generally stored in a memory location set apart from the

[3]Brian W. Kernighan and Dennis M. Ritchie, *The C Programming Language* (2nd ed.) (Upper Saddle River, NJ: Prentice Hall, 1988), p. 83.

storage allocated for any of the objects from that class. In contrast, the storage allocated for any ordinary (non-static) data member is part of the memory allocation for that object. In addition, if a class definition involves ordinary data members, each object constructed from that class contains storage for each such data member. In other words, there are as many distinct memory locations for ordinary data members as there are distinct objects constructed from that class.

Because a static data member is a value shared by all objects constructed from that class, it behaves like a global variable for that class. However, there are advantages in using static data members over global variables:

1. Information hiding may be enforced because a static data member can be defined as private (or later, protected), restricting access by user functions. A global variable does not have this property.
2. A static data member is not included among the list of global variables for any underlying user function using objects from a class having static data members. This removes the possibility of any conflict with name overloading. We will illustrate this in Example 1.3.

Because a static data member is independent of any particular instance (object) of that class, it is not accessed using the usual qualified reference. Instead, it is accessed using the syntax

```
data_type class_name :: expression;
```

for initialization, where expression includes the name of the static data member, as in

```
int static_class :: val1 = 3;
```

Such an initialization appears outside of the text of any user function invoking these static data members. We illustrate these ideas in Example 1.3.

EXAMPLE 1.3 This example illustrates the following ideas:

1. the distinction between a static data member and a global variable
2. the declaration and initialization of static data members

```
int val1 = 70;   // Ordinary global variable.


// User interface.
class static_class {

 public:
  // Output function.
```

```
  void print() const;

 private:
  static int val1;
  static int val2;
}; // Terminates coding of user interface for static_class.

// Initialization of each static data member
int static_class :: val1 = 3;
int static_class :: val2 = val1 + 1;

// Implementation file.
#include <iostream.h>

// Implementation of output function
void static_class :: print() const
{
  cout << "static_class :: val1 = " << val1 << endl;
  cout << "static_class :: val2 = " << val2 << endl;
}
```

The text of the user function is

```
int main()
{
 static_class cls;  // Default constructor invoked.
 cls.print();
 cout << "val1 = " << val1 << endl;
 return 0;
}
```

The output is

```
static_class val1 = 3
static_class val2 = 4
val1 = 70
```

Thus, the statement

```
cout << "val1 = " << val1 << endl;
```

interprets `val1` as an instance of the global variable. But what if we wish to access the `static` data member named `val1` in the user program? The user program may access the value of any `static` data member using the syntax

```
class_name :: static_data_member;
```

provided *`static_data_member`* is defined as part of the `public` components of the class named by *`class_name`*; otherwise, a compile-time error results.

For example, suppose we add the statement

```
cout << "val1 from static_class = " << static_class :: val1 << endl;
```

to our user program. The revised program will not compile because val1 was declared as private. If, instead, val1 was declared in the public section of the definition of static_class, the output would include

```
val1 from static_class = 3
```

* static Member Functions

An ordinary member function invoked from a user program in the form

object_name.function_name(actual_parameter_list);

has an *explicit* list of arguments (those appearing in *actual_parameter_list*) and an *implicit* list of arguments consisting of the data members of *object_name*. These implicit arguments represent a list that is accessible using the this pointer. A static member function of a class may be defined using the prototype

static *return_type function_name(formal_parameter_list);*

assumed to appear in the public part of the user interface and invoked in any user program by

class_name :: function_name(actual_parameter_list);

As was true of static data members, the reference to any static member function of a class appears outside of the allocated memory for any specific object constructed from that class.

EXAMPLE 1.4 This example illustrates the design, behavior, and the advantage of defining static member functions to solve a specific business-oriented problem. We wish to design a class employee based on the following design: Each object constructed from this class represents the salary data and behavior of any one employee. Each employee is issued a specific base salary, with the possible addition of a salary bonus that may differ from one employee to the next. The firm also has a policy that, when applicable, every employee will be awarded an additional common bonus. Our design of employee includes all of these considerations, and its user interface may be coded as

```
class employee {

 public:
  // Constructor. Computes base salary for each employee.
  employee(double);
  // Compute individual bonus based on a specific percentage
  // of base salary.
```

```
  void compute_bonus(double);
  // Static member function changing the amount of general
  // bonus awarded to each employee.
  static void adjust_general_bonus(double);
  // Member function computing each employee's salary,
  // including all bonuses.
  double compute_salary() const;

 private:
  double base_salary;
  double personal_bonus;
  static double general_bonus;
}; // Terminates code of user interface.

// Initialization of static data member.
double employee :: general_bonus = 225;
```

The implementation file contains the code

```
// Constructor.  Computes base salary for each employee.
employee :: employee(double base)
{
 base_salary = base;
}

// Computes individual bonus awarded to each employee.
void employee :: compute_bonus(double per_cent)
{
 personal_bonus = base_salary * per_cent;
}

// Member function adjusting the amount of general_bonus.
// Note that keyword static is omitted.
void employee :: adjust_general_bonus(double amount)
{
 general_bonus = amount;
}

// Computes salary for each employee, including all bonuses.
double employee :: compute_salary() const
{
 return base_salary + personal_bonus + general_bonus;
}
```

We illustrate the functionality of this class with the driver program

```
#include <iostream.h>

int main()
{
  // Construct two employee objects, establishing
  // base salary for each:
  employee emp1(4000), emp2(6000);
  // Compute personal bonus for each:
  emp1.compute_bonus(0.10);
  emp2.compute_bonus(0.25);
  // Output salary for each employee before general
  // bonus adjustment:
  cout << "Before general bonus adjustment" << endl;
  cout << "employee 1 earns $" << emp1.compute_salary() << endl;
  cout << "employee 2 earns $" << emp2.compute_salary() << endl;
  // Invoke static member function.
  employee :: adjust_general_bonus(500);
  // Now output salary for each employee after general
  // salary adjustment.
  cout << "After general bonus adjustment" << endl;
  cout << "employee 1 earns $" << emp1.compute_salary() << endl;
  cout << "employee 2 earns $" << emp2.compute_salary() << endl;
  return 0;
}
```

The ouput generated from this driver is

```
Before general bonus adjustment
employee 1 earns $4625
employee 2 earns $7725
After general bonus adjustment
employee 1 earns $4900
employee 2 earns $8000
```

We trace execution of this code using Figure 1.8:

When `emp1.compute_bonus(0.10)` executes, `emp1.personal_bonus` gets the value `400`.

When `emp2.compute_bonus(0.25)` executes, `emp2.personal_bonus` gets the value `1500`.

When `emp1.compute_salary()` executes the first time, the value `4625` is returned.

When `emp2.compute_salary()` executes the first time, the value `7725` is returned.

FIGURE 1.8

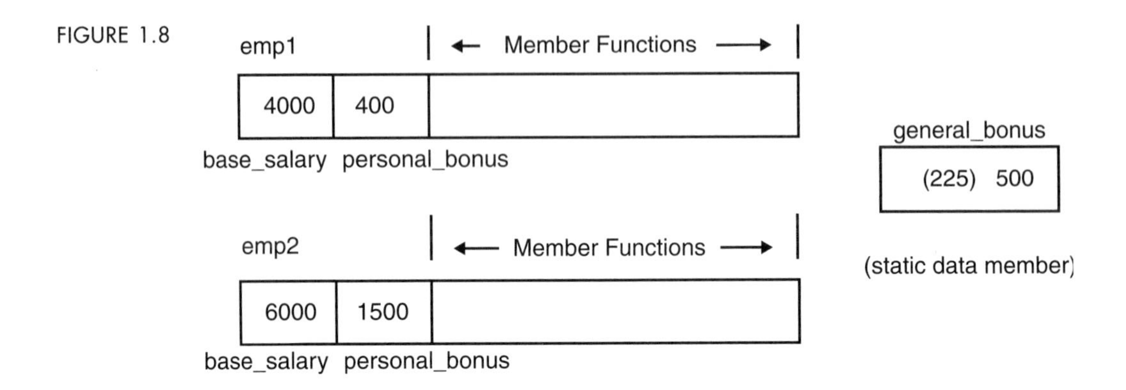

When `employee :: adjust_general_bonus(500)` executes, the initial value of `general_bonus of 225` is changed to `500`.

When `emp1.compute_salary()` executes the second time, the value `4900` is returned.

When `emp2.compute_salary()` executes the second time, the value `8000` is returned.

We may summarize the behavior of the various forms of member functions studied in this chapter. An ordinary member function (pure member function) has three distinct attributes:

1. It may access the `private` members of the class where it is defined.
2. It is in the scope of that class.
3. It must be invoked by an object of that class; that is, it uses the qualified reference applied to a specific object constructed from that class (thereby making an implicit use of the `this` pointer).

If we instead are dealing with a `static` member function, that function has only the first two attributes; if we are dealing with a function which is a `friend` of that class, such a function has only the first attribute.

1.11 Chapter Summary

Object-oriented software is designed for correctness and efficiency. The principal aspects of OOD involve three main factors:

1. *abstraction,* in which ADTs are created to aid in the formulation of the solution of the underlying software problem
2. *encapsulation* (or *information hiding*), in which the user is shielded from

the implementation details of the solution and is given access only to those components that he or she must apply and nothing more.

3. *modularity,* in which the problem is decomposed into smaller and autonomous units, each of which cooperates in contributing to that solution. Modular systems promote *software reuse,* in which a module designed to aid in the solution of one problem may also contribute to the solution of others.

The C++ language, especially with its support of the definition of classes and objects, is especially suited to promoting the solution to software problems by applying the design principles just listed.

Classes are generally designed with two major components: the *user interface* and the *implementation part.* Ideally, the user should have access only to the functions described in the `public` part of the user interface. Thus, the design of that component should be as user-friendly as possible. The typical user interface involves a `public` part consisting of one or several versions of a constructor, a destructor, and a finite collection of member functions designed for ease of use. The user interface includes a `private` part consisting of data members that are important in the description of the objects to be constructed from that class.

This chapter concentrated on the design of two examples: the implementation of the stack ADT and the system of complex numbers. The stack ADT was eventually implemented as a *class template,* allowing for the construction of stack objects, which store values of any type simply by instantiating the type parameter to the specific type of values to be stored on the stack. In the sequential implementation, an *overflow* condition may occur, in which the `info` array holding the stack values may be full, and another attempt is made to push a new value onto the stack. Besides this and independent of the implementation, an *underflow* condition is possible, in which we attempt to either pop or retrieve the value at the top of the current stack when that current stack is empty. This pair of situations was dealt with in two ways: by using the predefined `<assert.h>` library and by using exceptions and exception handlers.

The design of the class `complex` included some of the more elementary properties of the arithmetic of the system of complex numbers, which are useful in many application areas. We presented two alternative designs. The first involved defining a number of *pure member functions* for the addition, subtraction, and comparison for equality of two complex numbers, with each complex number viewed as a separate object of the `complex` class. Although this design embraced all of the desirable design principles we described earlier, we noted that it was somewhat unnatural because each of these functions is described mathematically as a *binary function,* requiring two arguments. The second design of `complex` provides an alternative that expresses each of these operations with two arguments and involves `friend` functions. These functions enhance the legibility of these operations because their implementation is closer to their formal mathematical description.

It is possible to define `static` data members and member functions of a class. There exist a number of special situations in the object-oriented design of solutions to problems in which such members are very useful and often quite indispensable. Such data members have the property that their values are shared by all objects constructed from that class in a specific application, with similar advantages attached to `static` member functions, whose reference is not part of the storage allocated to any object of the class. Instead, such `static` member functions are stored independently of any object.

The idea of object-oriented solutions to software problems may include the construction of a *class hierarchy,* consisting of a *base class* and a number of *derived classes.* In such situations, objects constructed in any one of the associated derived classes is said to exhibit an "is-a" relationship with any of its parent classes. This idea will be studied in greater detail in Chapter Two.

EXERCISES

1. Given the program

```
#include <iostream.h>

class counter {
 public:
  counter() { data = 0;}
  void print() const { cout << data << endl;}
  friend void reset_data(counter&,int);
 private:
  int data;
};

void reset_data(counter& c,int val)
{
 c.data = val;
}

int main(){
 counter count;
 cout << "count.data initial value:";
```

```
    count.print();
    cout << endl;
    reset_data(count,12);
    cout << "count.data after call to reset_data:";
    count.print();
    cout << endl;
    return 0;
}
```

a. Find the exact form of the output for the program.

b. Rewrite the `reset_data` function as a pure member function and test your result by running the version of the driver invoking the new version of `reset_data`.

2. Suppose we define an ADT for three-dimensional vectors with real-valued coordinates, whose list of admissible operations is defined as

a. *vector addition* defined as

$$<x_1, y_1, z_1> + <x_2, y_2, z_2> = <x_1 + x_2, y_1 + y_2, z_1 + z_2>$$

b. *vector subtraction,* defined as

$$<x_1, y_1, z_1> - <x_2, y_2, z_2> = <x_1 - x_2, y_1 - y_2, z_1 - z_2>$$

c. *vector cross-product,* defined as

$$<x_1, y_1, z_1> * <x_2, y_2, z_2> = <y_1z_2 - y_2z_1, z_2x_1 - z_1x_2, x_1y_2 - x_2y_1>$$

d. *vector assignment,* defined as `w = u`, where `w` is a three-dimensional vector variable and `u` is a three-dimensional vector whose components are copied into those of `w`

e. *vector dot product,* defined as

$$<x_1, y_1, z_1> * <x_2, y_2, z_2> = x_1x_2 + y_1y_2 + z_1z_2$$

f. an output function, which prints the values of the three components of any three-dimensional vector

Implement this as a class in C++, using pure member functions for vector sum, difference, cross-product, and dot product.

3. Redesign the user interface and implementation file for the class of three-dimensional vectors in Problem 2, but now use `friend` functions as the replacement for the pure member functions for vector addition, subtraction, cross-product, and dot product.

4. Design code for a templated `stack` class using a sequential implementation similar to the one designed in Section 1.6. The implementation should replace the form using assertions in that section by a version containing exceptions and exception handling. Test your implementation on the problem of checking a string for balanced parentheses, brackets, and braces.

5. Write a driver for the function template `swap_values` in which three swaps are attempted: one for `int` values, a second for `char` values, and a third for `double` values.

6. a. Describe the effect of applying the constructor for the `complex` object `z3` when the constructor is given as

```
complex z3(5.6);
```

b. Extend the definition of the `complex` class to include functions implementing multiplication and division. Multiplication is defined by

```
(a + bi)*(c + di) = (ac - bd) + (ad + bc)i
```

and division is defined by

$$(a + bi)/(c + di) = (a + bi)*(c + di)^{-1}$$

where $(c + di)^{-1}$ is defined as

$$\frac{c}{c^2 + d^2} - \frac{d}{c^2 + d^2} i$$

(Here we assume that at least one of `c` and `d` is nonzero.)

7. Given the class definition

```
class intpair {
 public:
  void initialize (int b) { second = b; first = b + 1;}
  intpair increase() { first++; second++; return *this; }
  void* location() { return this;}
  void print(){cout << first << ' ' << second << endl; }
 private:
   int first;
   int second;
};
```

with all member functions coded inline, and the driver

```
int main() {
 intpair value1, value2, value3;
 value1.initialize(3);
 value2.initialize(5);
 value3.initialize(9);
 value1.print();
 cout << " is found in " << value1.location() << endl;
 value2.print();
 cout << " is found in " << value2.location() << endl;
 value3.print();
 cout << " is found in " << value3.location() << endl;
 return 0;
}
```

Explain the output derived from executing this program. Is the output dependent on the choice of the compiler and the hardware?

8. Write a new driver for the generic stack implementation described in Section 1.6 using the generic pointer void*, which is similar to that written in the text for int, but now the stack constructed will store char values.

9. Given the definitions

```
void* gptr;
int* iptr;
char* cptr;
```

which of the following assignments are legal?

```
gptr = cptr;
cptr = (char*)gptr;
iptr = cptr;
*cptr = 'w';
*gptr = 0;
```

10. Include tests for overflow and underflow for the case of the implementation of the stack class using void*, using <assert.h>.

11. Given the generic function

```
void f(void* gptr1,void* gptr2)
{
 void* temp_holder = gptr1;
 gptr1 = gptr2;
 gptr2 = temp_holder;
}
```

which attempts to imitate the function template for swap_values described in Section 1.6, design a driver function to test whether the swapping of two int values is accomplished by invoking f. Then trace execution by hand between f and the caller to determine how the parameters are passed.

12. For any complex number $z = a + bi$, define its *conjugate* as $z = a - bi$. Further, define the *modulus* of z as $|z| = (a^2 + b^2)^{1/2}$.

    a. Extend the definition of the complex class to include public member functions that compute the conjugate and the modulus of any complex object. Represent these as pure member functions.

    b. Rewrite the code of part (a) of this problem, but now the functions computing the conjugate and the modulus are coded as friend functions involving a single argument.

Note: You must include the predefined <math.h> library to access sqrt().

13. Extend the definition of the complex class to include an overloaded version of the input operator operator> for complex values.

14. A *quaternion* is defined as an expression of the form $a = a_0 + a_1 i + a_2 j + a_3 k$, where a_0, a_1, a_2, a_3 are real numbers. The *sum* of any two quaternions $a = a_0 + a_1 i + a_2 j + a_3 k$ and $b = b_0 + b_1 i + b_2 j + b_3 k$ is defined as

$$a + b = (a_0 + b_0) + (a_1 + b_1)i + (a_2 + b_2)j + (a_3 + b_3)k$$

and the *difference* is defined as

$$a - b = (a_0 - b_0) + (a_1 - b_1)i + (a_2 - b_2)j + (a_3 - b_3)k$$

Further, their *product* obeys the conditions

$$i^2 = j^2 = k^2 = -1 \text{ and } ij = -ji = k,\ jk = -kj = i,\ ki = -ik = j;\ \text{thus,}$$

$$a*b = (a_0b_0 - a_1b_1 - a_2b_2 - a_3b_3) + (a_0b_1 + a_1b_0 + a_2b_3 - a_3b_2)i + (a_0b_2 + a_2b_0 + a_3b_1 - a_1b_3)j + (a_0b_3 + a_3b_0 + a_1b_2 - a_2b_1)k$$

and where we define the *equality* of two quaternions by

$$a == b \text{ if and only if } (a_0 == b_0)\ \&\&\ (a_1 == b_1)\ \&\&\ (a_2 == b_2)\ \&\&\ (a_3 == b_3)$$

Design a class for quaternions whose constructor uses four parameters with default values of `0` and with member functions for addition, subtraction, multiplication, equality, and an overloaded version for `operator<<` for output.

15. Suppose we define the class

```
#include <iostream.h>
class A{
 public:
  // Constructor coded inline.
  A(){x = 0;}
  void print() const { cout << x << endl;}
  friend void f(A&,int); // Prototype.
 private:
  // Data member.
  int x;
};
```

and the implementation of `f` as

```
void f(A& c,int val)
{
  c.x = val;
}
```

Describe the output obtained from the driver function

```
int main(){
 A value;
 cout << "value.x after instantiation = ";
 value.print();
 cout << endl;
 cout << "value.x after call to friend function = ";
 f(value,12);
 value.print();
 cout << endl;
```

```
return 0;
}
```

16. Write the complete text of a user function in which the class named `static_class` described in Example 1.3 now defines the `static int` data member `val1` as a `public` component of that class, allowing the user function to output its value.

17. Describe the behavior of the following program and give the exact form of the output:

```
// User interface.
class int_class {
 public:
  // Static data member.
  static int static_value;
  // Constructor.
  int_class(int);
  // Output function.
  void print() const;
 private:
  int int_value;
};

// Initialization of static data member:
int int_class :: static_value = 0;
// Implementation details

#include <iostream.h>
// Constructor.
int_class :: int_class(int val)
{
 int_value = val;
}

// Output function.
void int_class :: print() const
{
 cout << "value of class = " << int_value << endl;
}
```

The corresponding user function is coded as

```
int main()
{
 int_class obj1(5);
 int_class :: static_value++;
```

```
    int_class obj2(25);
    int_class :: static_value++;
    cout << "The current value of static_value is: ";
    cout << int_class :: static_value << endl;
    return 0;
}
```

PROGRAMMING PROJECTS

1. Design a class template `rational` implementing the ADT for *rational numbers.* That is, the ADT should define a *constructor* that defines a `rational` object that takes the form of a quotient *a/b* whose numerator is any integer and whose denominator is any integer > 0. Also define an *assignment operator* `=` that assigns the value of an already existing `rational` object to another. In addition, define the usual binary arithmetic operations for `rational` objects according to the definitions

   $a/b + c/d = (ad + bc)/bd;$
   $a/b - c/d = (ad - bc)/bd;$
   $(a/b) * (c/d) = (ac)/(bd);$
   $(a/b) / (c/d) = (ad)/(bc).$

   Your code should also define *relational operators* `==` and `<` for `rational` objects according to the definitions

   $a/b = c/d$ *if and only if* $ad = bc;$
   $a/b < c/d$ *if and only if* $ad < bc.$

   Your coding of this class should take the necessary precautions about zero denominators and should reduce any `rational` value to lowest terms. In the latter case, for example, the `rational` value *15/12* should be reduced to *5/4*. In addition, your code should take all of the necessary precautions regarding the encapsulation of code and information hiding. The class should include an output function using an extension of `operator<<`, which outputs any `rational` value in the form *a/b*, where *b* is not zero.

   Finally, your code should include a *driver program* that illustrates the use of all of these facilities.

2. (Note: This project is for those with some prior knowledge of linearly linked lists.) Implement the stack ADT as a class template with the same fundamental set of `public` member functions as those defined for the implementation of stacks as described earlier in this chapter. Thus, a `stack` object for some instantiation of the type parameter `T` is constructed as an initially empty linked list of nodes whose data components will contain specific values of the instantiated type. In addition, when the stack is not empty, the initial node will be viewed as the top of the stack. Therefore, the push operation will insert a new node at the front of the current linked

list, and a pop operation will be implemented (whenever possible) as the removal of that initial node. To test if the current stack is empty, determine whether the current list is NULL, and the operation that retrieves the top of the current stack, whenever it is nonempty, is implemented as the return of the initial data value of the corresponding node.

Test this version of a stack using the test for balanced parentheses, brackets, and braces for an input character string.

REFERENCES

Parnas, D. L., "Information Distribution Aspects of Design Methodology," *Proceedings of the IFIP Congress,* Ljubljana, Yugoslavia, 1971, pp. 339–344.

CHAPTER 2

Inheritance and Polymorphism

CHAPTER OBJECTIVES

- To introduce the concept of inheritance and class hierarchies and their value in object-oriented design.
- To study the relationship between base classes and derived classes and the objects constructed from each.
- To distinguish between simple and multiple inheritance and the value of each in problem solving.
- To define the concepts of virtual function and abstract classes, their importance in creating class hierarchies, and the run-time selection of member functions of objects constructed in such hierarchies (polymorphism).

2.1 Introduction

We have seen that object-oriented design (OOD) models real-world situations with software simulations using classes and objects. One important aspect of OOD alluded to in Chapter One is its ability to take advantage of relationships between classes, where objects of certain classes share the same set of characteristics. More specifically, an object-oriented design may be applied to display a *hierarchical organization* among classes, in which newly created classes may be derived from existing classes by inheriting characteristics of these existing classes and yet display certain unique characteristics of their own. Such a design paradigm is known as *inheritance,* and C++ supports two general classifications of this concept: *simple inheritance* and *multiple inheritance.*

The relationship among classes designed using inheritance is known as an "is-a" relationship. This relationship specifies that one abstraction (realized as a *derived class*) is a particular instance of another (a *parent class*). In Example 1.1, we illustrated this concept by noting that any `Square` object is a special kind of `Rectangle` object, which in turn is a special kind of `Geometric Object`; similarly, a `Circle` object is a kind of `Geometric Object`.

Another useful attribute connected with class hierarchies is *polymorphism,* which may be defined as the ability of an entity to assume a number of different forms. In an object-oriented design, we may view polymorphism as the property of a message to be interpreted in a number of different ways depending on the class in the hierarchy of which the current object is a member. For example, in the class hierarchy of Example 1.1, if we are currently referencing an object of the `Rectangle` class and wish to compute its perimeter, the value returned by that object would be computed using the formula `2*length + 2*width`, where the respective values of `length` and `width` would be given as data members of the class definition of `Rectangle`. On the other hand, if an object of the `Circle` class was currently being referenced and we wished to compute its perimeter, the value returned would be `π*diameter`, where the value of `diameter` would be stored as a data member of that object. Our design of the hierarchy of geometrical shapes of Example 1.1 presumes that a `public` member function called `perimeter` is defined in each of the classes. This clearly overloads the `perimeter` function because it assumes different forms depending on which class of the hierarchy was used to construct the object.

As we will see, by defining and using `virtual` functions in an inheritance hierarchy, C++ supports a *dynamic* form of polymorphism by permitting run-time selection of member functions associated with the currently referenced object. In the example of the geometric hierarchy just described, we will observe that the perimeter value returned depends on the current class of geometric object selected (pointed at) during execution of a program in which the hierarchy appears.

We begin this treatment by investigating ideas associated with class hierarchies and inheritance. We then turn to a study of how polymorphism is implemented in such hierarchies.

2.2 Inheritance, Base Classes, and Derived Classes

Inheritance is the mechanism of defining new classes using existing ones as a basis. The new classes are called *derived classes,* and the existing classes are generally referred to as *base classes.* Inheritance promotes code reuse because each derived class inherits the code existing from the base class. It is generally true that any derived class is developed from one (or possibly more than one) base class either by adding more code than that existing in the base class or by altering code (via overloading) in the base class.

We may illustrate this with the hierarchy of classes defined in Example 1.1. If we look at the *inheritance diagram* given by Figure 1.2, the base class is identified as `Geometric_Object`. The user interface for this class may be given by

```
class Geometric_Object {
  public:
   // Perimeter function coded inline.
   double perimeter() const { return 0;}
};
```

This class has no `private` section and defines a single member function `perimeter()`, which is coded *inline* (the code appears in the text of the user interface). Because of this, there is no need for a separate implementation file for this class. As a matter of fact, using this definition of `Geometric_Object`, it is possible for any user function to apply the default constructor for this class to construct an object `obj` and then compute `obj.perimeter()`, returning a value of `0`. This is not a good base class design for this hierarchy because the description of the base class is too general to admit the construction of objects—after all, what do we mean by a "geometric object"? Is it a circle, a rectangle, a square, or perhaps some other figure we have not yet considered, but which may be included in this hierarchy? Our intention here is to use `Geometric_Object` as a hub (or root) for the derived classes in this hierarchy, where each derived class constructs well-defined and useful geometric objects (such as circles, rectangles, and squares).

Our design shows that `Circle` and `Rectangle` are each direct descendants of `Geometric_Object`. How do we define this in syntax? In general, to declare that a class is a derived class of a base class requires the syntax

```
class derived_class_name : public base_class_name
{
  public:
  // Public components of derived_class
      .
      .
      .
  private:
  // Private components of derived_class
      .
      .
      .
};
```

The occurrence of the keyword `public` in

```
class derived_class_name : public base_class_name
```

describes the situation that the class named by *`derived_class_name`* is derived from the class named by *`base_class_name`* using *public inheritance.*

This form of inheritance is most likely to be applied in designing a class hierarchy, but it is not the only possibility: Derived classes could be derived from base class using *private inheritance* or *protected inheritance*.

In our example, we may define

```
const double PI = 3.14159;

class Circle : public Geometric_Object
{
  public:
   // Constructor
   Circle (double d): diameter(d) {}
   // Perimeter function coded inline
   double perimeter() const { return PI * diameter; }
  private:
   double diameter;
};
```

Similarly, we may code the class `Rectangle` as

```
class Rectangle : public Geometric_Object
{
  public:
   // Constructor
   Rectangle(double lt,double wd):length(lt),width(wd){}
   // Perimeter function coded inline
   double perimeter() const { return 2*length + 2*width; }
  private:
   double length, width;
};
```

How do we code `Square`? Observe that `Square` is not derived directly from `Geometric_Object`, but it is derived directly from `Rectangle`, implementing the idea that any square "is a" kind of rectangle; in fact, we view any square as a rectangle whose length and width have the same value. We may express this as

```
class Square : public Rectangle
{
  public:
   // Constructor
   Square(double x):Rectangle(x,x){}
   // Perimeter function coded inline
   double perimeter() const { return Rectangle::perimeter(); }
};
```

Note the form of the constructor for `Square`:

```
Square(double x):Rectangle(x,x){}
```

This makes direct use of the is-a relation between the Rectangle and Square classes. That is, to construct a Square object, we must view it as a special kind of Rectangle object whose length and width are identical.

Is it possible to override this form and instead consider the alternative design for Square given by

```
class Square : public Rectangle {
 public:
  // Constructor
  Square(double x){ side = x; }
  // Overloaded perimeter function

 private:
  double side;
};
```

The answer is *no* because the semantics of C++ expects a design for Square that inherits properties handed down from Rectangle. In the case of the constructor for Square, its coding must directly reflect the is-a relationship. Hence, any attempt of a user program to construct a Square object using

```
Square(double x){ side = x; }
```

will generate a compile-time error. Likewise the attempt to compute the perimeter of a Square object using

```
double perimeter() const { return 4 * side; }
```

will fail for similar reasons.

2.3 `public` Inheritance

We have already stated that the use of the keyword public following the colon in

```
class derived_class_name : public base_class_name
```

allows for public access of information between the base and derived classes. This means that the public (and later, protected) members of the base class are inherited as public (and later, protected) members of the derived class, respectively. As a consequence, the statement of each of these inherited properties need not appear in the definition of the derived class unless they are redefined there. On the other hand, any private members of the base class are inaccessible to the derived class.

As an example, suppose we modify the definition of the Rectangle class to include the additional public member function diagonal(). The revised version of Rectangle then takes the form

```
class Rectangle : public Geometric_Object {
 public:
  // Constructor
  Rectangle(double lt, double wd):length(lt),width(wd){}
  // Perimeter member function, coded inline
  double perimeter() const { return 2*length + 2*width; }
  // Member function computing length of the diagonal
  double diagonal() const {
          return sqrt(length*length + width*width); }
 private:
  double length, width;
};
```

Note that here we must include the additional preprocessor directive

```
#include <math.h>
```

to access the square root function `sqrt`.

There is no need to rewrite the definition of `diagonal()` for the `Square` class because any `Square` object will simply inherit the same `diagonal()` function from its parent class (superclass) `Rectangle`. This is illustrated in Figure 2.1.

FIGURE 2.1

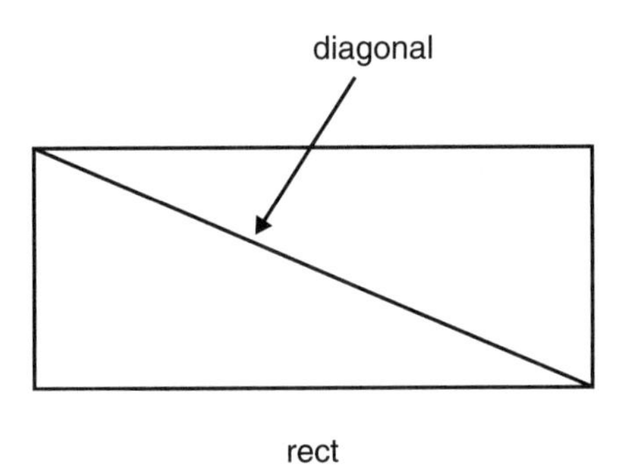

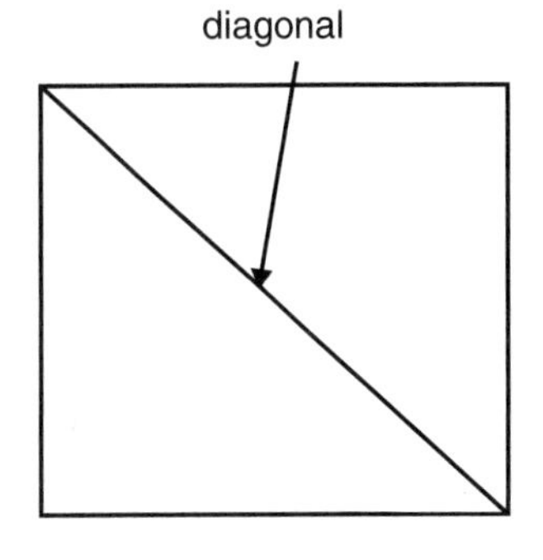

If we execute the driver function for this revised hierarchy given by

```
int main()
{
 Geometric_Object obj;
 Rectangle rect(3,5);
 Circle circ(4);
 Square sq(6);
 cout << "Perimeter of obj = " << obj.perimeter() << endl;
 cout << "Perimeter of rectangle = " << rect.perimeter() << endl;
```

```
 cout << "Perimeter of circle = " << circ.perimeter() << endl;
 cout << "Perimeter of square = " << sq.perimeter() << endl;
 cout << "Diagonal of rectangle = " << rect.diagonal() << endl;
 cout << "Diagonal of square = " << sq.diagonal() << endl;
 return 0;
}
```

the output is

```
Perimeter of obj = 0
Perimeter of rectangle = 16
Perimeter of circle = 12.5664
Perimeter of square = 24
Diagonal of rectangle = 5.83095
Diagonal of square = 8.48528
```

2.4 `protected` Members of a Base Class

In an inheritance hierarchy, `public` members of a base class are accessible to any function invoking the hierarchy. On the other hand, `private` members of a base class are accessible only to member and `friend` functions of the base class. Besides these forms of access, C++ provides a form of access between `public` and `private`, known as `protected` access, where `protected` is a new C++ keyword.

If a member of a base class is `protected` (that is, appears as a component of the `protected` part of the user interface), it may be accessed only by member and `friend` functions of the base class and member and `friend` functions of any derived class in the hierarchy, assuming `public` inheritance. Thus, it is possible to extend the syntax of user interfaces to include a possible `protected` part, as in

```
class base_class_name {

  public:
  // Public members
       .
       .
       .
  protected:
  // Protected members
       .
       .
       .
  private:
```

```
  // Private members
        .
        .
        .
}; // Terminates definition of user interface
```

This represents the syntax for the user interface of the base class. A similar syntax form exists for derived classes in which

```
class base_class
```

is replaced by

```
class derived_class_name : public base_class_name
```

Semantically, any member of a derived class may access any `public` or `protected` member of the base class simply by invoking its name. However, any revision of the design of `protected` members of the base class may produce a ripple effect, causing corresponding changes in all of its derived classes. Because of this, using a design involving `protected` members requires a considerable amount of additional testing of software in the case of revisions of `protected` members. Example 2.1 shows how `protected` members of a base class are applicable in a simple design.

EXAMPLE 2.1 We design a class hierarchy with a base class called `Vertex`, whose objects are two-dimensional vertices—that is, two-dimensional points in the plane. The constructor for this class requires two `double` parameters, representing the respective x- and y-coordinates of the point. The class also contains a single overloaded output function that returns these coordinates in order. The syntax is given by

```
#include <iostream.h>

class Vertex {  // Base class
  public:
   // Constructor
   Vertex(double = 0, double = 0);
   friend ostream& operator<<(ostream&,const Vertex&);
  protected:
   double x_coord, y_coord;
}; // Terminates user interface for Vertex
```

The implementation code for the member functions of `Vertex` is

```
// Constructor
Vertex :: Vertex(double x,double y)
{
  x_coord = x;
  y_coord = y;
```

```
}

// Overloaded output function
ostream& operator<<(ostream& os, const Vertex& v)
{
 // Deposit components of Vertex argument in
 // ostream object os.
 // Deposit "(" in os:
 os << "(";
 // Deposit x_coord component of v in os:
 os << v.x_coord;
 // Dcposit "," in os:
 os << ",";
 // Deposit y_coord component of v in os:
 os << v.y_coord;
 // Deposit ")" in os:
 os << ")";
 // rcturn current contents of os:
 return os;
}
```

The hierarchy continues with the definition of the class `Ellipse`, viewed as a derived class of `Vertex`. We use the fact that any ellipse is completely characterized by its vertex (the *center*) and by the length of its horizontal and vertical axes. These lengths represent the respective horizontal and vertical distances from the center to the periphery of the ellipse.[1] The `Ellipse` class also contains an overloaded output function that yields the coordinates of the center, whether the major (longer) axis is vertical or horizontal, and similarly for the minor (shorter) axis. The class also contains an area function, which computes the area of the ellipse using the formula `π * (length of horizontal axis) * (length of vertical axis)`. The user interface for this derived class may then be given as

```
// Derived_class user interface
class Ellipse : public Vertex
{
 public:
  // Constructor.  First two parameters are the coordinates
  // of the vertex, the next two are the respective lengths
  // of the axes in the x-direction and y-direction,
  // respectively.
```

[1]We assume the ellipse is not tilted: Its axes are horizontal and vertical, as opposed to those ellipses that are tilted, namely, with nonhorizontal and nonvertical axes.

```
  Ellipse(double,double,double,double);
  // Overloaded output function.  Determines whether the
  // major (minor) axis is horizontal (vertical)
  friend ostream& operator<<(ostream&,const Ellipse&);
  // Member function computing area of ellipse
  double area() const;
 protected:
  double horiz_axis, vert_axis;
}; // Terminates user interface for Ellipse class
```

The implementation code for Ellipse is given by

```
// Implementation details for Ellipse class.
const double PI = 3.14159;
// Constructor
Ellipse :: Ellipse(double x,double y,double h,double v)
  : Vertex(x,y),horiz_axis(h),vert_axis(v){}

// Overloaded output function.
ostream& operator<<(ostream& os,const Ellipse& ell)
{
 os << "Ellipse has vertex = (" << ell.x_coord << ",";
 os << ell.y_coord << ")" << endl;
 if(ell.horiz_axis >= ell.vert_axis)
 {
  os << "Major axis is horizontal of length = "
        << ell.horiz_axis << endl;
  os << "Minor axis is vertical of length = "
        << ell.vert_axis << endl;
 }
 else
 {
  os << "Major axis is vertical of length = "
        << ell.vert_axis << endl;
  os << "Minor axis is horizontal of length = "
        << ell.horiz_axis << endl;
 }
 return os;
}

double Ellipse :: area() const
{
  return PI * horiz_axis * vert_axis;
}
```

The hierarchy continues with the definition of the `Circle` class, designed as a derived class with `Ellipse` as the parent class. The is-a relation exists between `Circle` and `Ellipse`, using the intuitive idea that every circle is a special kind of ellipse—one whose major and minor axes are equal and whose joint value is the radius. It follows that the reason for the `protected` definition of `horiz_axis` and `vert_axis` in `Ellipse` is to apply this to the implementation code for member functions of `Circle`. The same is true in `Vertex`: Its data members `x_coord` and `y_coord` were declared as `protected` so that they may be applied to both `Ellipse` and `Circle` objects.

```
// User interface for Circle class as a derived class of Ellipse.
class Circle : public Ellipse
{
 public:
 // Constructor.
 Circle(double,double,double);
 // Overloaded output function.  Returns the
 // center and radius of Circle object.
  friend ostream& operator<<(ostream&,const Circle&);
  // Member function computing area of circle
  double area() const;
 private:
  double radius;
}; // Terminates user interface for Circle class.

// Implementation details for Circle

// Constructor.
Circle :: Circle(double x1,double y1,double r):Ellipse(x1,y1,r,r)
{
  radius = horiz_axis;
}

ostream& operator<<(ostream& os,const Circle& c)
{
 os << "Center = (" << c.x_coord << "," << c.y_coord << ")"
        << endl;
 os << "Radius of circle = " << c.radius << endl;
 return os;
}

double Circle :: area() const
```

```
{
  return PI * radius * radius;
}
```

The hierarchy diagram for these classes is given in Figure 2.2.

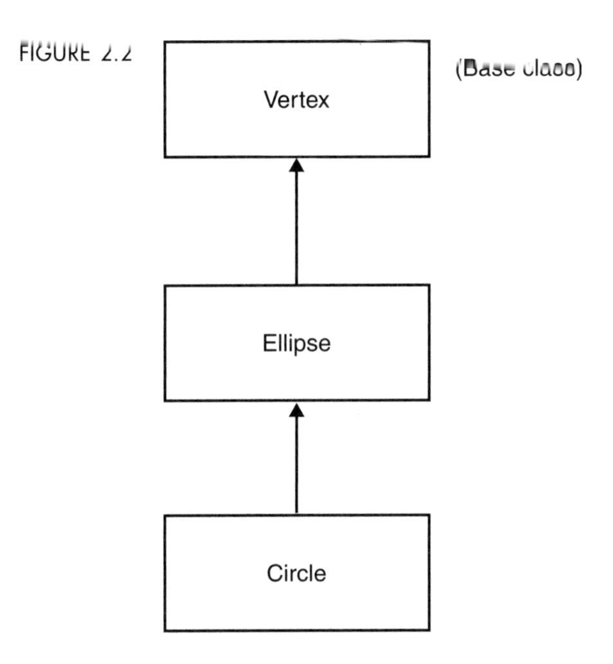

FIGURE 2.2

This design of `Circle` represents a variant of the design of `Circle` seen earlier. In the current design, we characterize any circle by defining its center (or vertex) and its radius. A driver function for this hierarchy is

```
int main()
{
 Vertex vert(0,-3);
 cout << vert << endl;
 Ellipse e_object1(4,2,6,4);
 cout << e_object1 << endl;
 cout << "Area of first ellipse = " << e_object1.area() << endl;
 Ellipse e_object2(2,1,5,9);
 cout << e_object2 << endl;
 cout << "Area of second ellipse = " << e_object2.area() << endl;
 Circle circ(2,-1,6);
 cout << circ << endl;
 cout << "Area of circle = " << circ.area() << endl;
 return 0;
}
```

The output obtained by executing this code is

```
(0,-3)
Ellipse has vertex = (4,2)
Major axis is horizontal of length = 6
Minor axis is vertical of length = 4
Area of first ellipse = 75.3982
Ellipse has vertex = (2,1)
Major axis is vertical of length = 9
Minor axis is horizontal of length = 5

Area of second ellipse = 141.372
Center = (2,-1)
Radius of circle = 6
Area of circle = 113.097
```

2.5 private and protected Inheritance

We discussed public inheritance in Section 2.3 and have been using it exclusively. Recall that the compiler recognizes public inheritance if the derived class is defined using the header

```
class derived_class_name : public base_class_name
```

This use of the public keyword is as an *access specifier:* It declares the level of access between the designated base class and derived class. The C++ language also supports two other forms of access: private and protected inheritance.

private inheritance is declared when the header assumes the form

```
class derived_class_name : private base_class_name
```

Here private is the designated access specifier. When deriving from a base class under private inheritance, public and protected members of the base class become private members of the derived class. As an illustration, let us consider the following variant of Example 2.1. In this case, x_coord and y_coord are not accessible because the class Ellipse uses private to inherit from Vertex. That is, the header for Ellipse is now given by

```
class Ellipse : private Vertex
```

The error is detected in the code of the overloaded output function operator<< in the user interface for the Circle class. The text of this function is

```
ostream& operator<<(ostream& os,const Circle& c)
{
 os << "Center = (" << c.x_coord << "," << c.y_coord << ")"
```

```
        << endl,
  os << "Radius of circle = " << c.radius << endl;
  return os;
}
```

When the access specifier between the base and derived classes is protected, protected inheritance is declared:

`class derived_class_name : protected base_class_name`

When deriving from a base class using protected inheritance, public and protected members of the base class become protected members of the derived class, and private members of the base class are, as usual, inaccessible in the derived class.

If we change the access specifier between Vertex and Ellipse and between Ellipse and Circle to protected, the resulting code executes in exactly the same way as described in Section 2.4. This is because every public member function in the base class is redefined as protected in the corresponding derived class, and all data members are inaccessible to any user function in any case.

In practice, public inheritance is the form used in the overwhelming majority of applications because it affords the greatest amount of flexibility in many detailed inheritance hierarchies, as well as a reasonable amount of protection. In this text, unless we state otherwise, we will use public inheritance throughout.

2.6 Multiple Inheritance

Each of the situations discussed so far in this chapter uses a form of inheritance in which each derived class comes from a single parent (base) class. This form of inheritance is commonly known as *simple inheritance.* Besides this, C++ supports another form of inheritance in which hierarchies involve a derived class that is inherited from two or more base classes. This form is known as *multiple inheritance.* In such a situation, any object constructed from such a derived class inherits the behavior and attributes of each of its parents. As a simple illustration of these ideas, consider the hierarchy described in Figure 2.3. The idea of this design is as follows: Any object constructed from base_class_1 has a single int-valued data member called int_value, and any object constructed from base_class_2 has a single char-valued data member called char_value. Further, any object constructed from derived_class contains three data members:

- an int-valued data member inherited from base_class_1
- a char-valued data member inherited from base_class_2
- a double-valued data member defined in the private part of derived_class

FIGURE 2.3

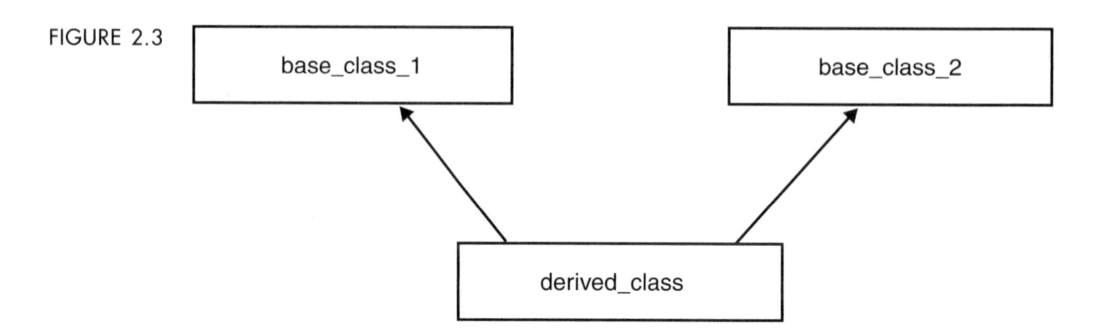

To make the `int`-valued data member and the `char`-valued data member available to the object constructed in `derived_class`, the respective data members of `base_class_1` and `base_class_2` are defined as `protected`.

Another issue to settle is the syntax for declaring a derived class using multiple inheritance. In the case of multiple inheritance involving two base classes, the syntax for the user interface for the derived class is

```
class derived_class : public base_class_1, public base_class_2
{

 public:
  // Public members of derived_class
         .
         .
         .

 protected:
  // Protected members of derived_class
         .
         .
         .

 private:
  // Private members of derived_class
         .
         .
         .

};
```

This syntax generalizes in a natural way when multiple inheritance involves three or more base classes.

Returning to the design we described earlier in this section, let us consider Example 2.2.

EXAMPLE 2.2

```
// Coding of user interface for base_class_1:
class base class_1
{
 public:
  // Constructor
  base_class_1(int);
  // Overloaded output operator
  friend ostream& operator<<(ostream&,const base_class_1&);
 protected:
  int int_value;
}; // Terminates user interface for base_class_1

// Implementation details for base_class_1

// Constructor
base_class_1 :: base_class_1(int val):int_value(val){}

// Overloaded output operator
ostream& operator<<(ostream& os,const base_class_1& b1)
{
 os << "Output from base_class_1: " << b1.int_value << endl;
 return os;
}
// Coding of user interface for second base class
class base_class_2
{
 public:
  // Constructor
  base_class_2(char);
  // Overloaded output operator
  friend ostream& operator<<(ostream& ,const base_class_2&);
 protected:
  char char_value;
}; // Terminates user interface for base_class_2

// Implementation details for base_class_2

// Constructor
base_class_2 :: base_class_2(char cval): char_value(cval){}

// Overloaded output operator
ostream& operator<<(ostream& os,const base_class_2& b2)
```

```
{
 os << "Output from base_class_2: " << b2.char_value << endl;
 return os;
}
// User interface for derived class

class derived_class : public base_class_1, public base_class_2
{
 public:
  // Constructor
  derived_class(int,char,double);

  // Overloaded output operator
  friend ostream& operator<<(ostream&,const derived_class&);
 private:
  double dbl_value;
}; // Terminates user interface for derived_class

// Implementation details for derived_class

// Constructor
derived_class :: derived_class(int i_val,char c_val,double d_val)
 : base_class_1(i_val),base_class_2(c_val),dbl_value(d_val){}

// Overloaded output operator
ostream& operator<<(ostream& os, const derived_class& d)
{
 os << "output from derived class: " << endl;
 os << "Value derived from base_class_1: " << d.int_value << endl;
 os << "Value derived from base_class_2: " << d.char_value << endl;
 os << "Value derived from derived_class: " << d.dbl_value << endl;
 return os;
}

// Driver function

int main(){
 base_class_1 base_1_object(4);
 base_class_2 base_2_object('W');
 derived_class derived_object(8,'T',7.19);
 cout << base_1_object << endl;
 cout << base_2_object << endl;
```

```
  cout << derived_object << endl;
  return 0;
}
```

The output obtained by executing this driver is

```
Output from base_class_1: 4

Output from base_class_2: W

output from derived_class:
Value derived from base_class_1: 8
Value derived from base_class_2: T
Value derived from derived_class: 7.19
```

2.7 Polymorphism and `virtual` Functions

In Section 2.1, we defined polymorphism as the ability of an entity to assume a number of different forms. In other words, polymorphism is a means of providing different meanings to a message by localizing the response to the type of data being processed. For example, consider the instruction in a program to divide one value by another. A different response occurs if the values involved are of some integer type (`int`, `unsigned`, `long`, `short`) from those of a floating-point type (`float`, `double`, `long double`). For another example, we have overloaded the output function `operator<<` so that we may apply such statements as

```
cout << object_value ;
```

to objects of different classes (such as `complex`, `Ellipse`, `Circle`, `base_class_1`, `derived_class`, and others), as well as to predefined values of some integer or floating-point type.

Function and class templates provide another form of polymorphism depending on the value(s) assigned to the type parameters involved. The decision as to the specific form assumed by the operation is decided at *compile time*—that is, as the underlying code is compiled. This form of polymorphism is commonly called *parametric polymorphism* or *compile-time polymorphism.*

Besides these, C++ offers another form of polymorphism known as *run-time polymorphism,* sometimes called *pure polymorphism.* This form allows for choosing the appropriate form of a member function from among those appearing in a base class of some hierarchy and those with the same name in a derived class during program execution. To accomplish this, every such function appearing in the base class is specified with the `virtual` keyword. Thus, by supplying `virtual` as a modifier for each such function appearing in the base class, C++ "knows" that its functionality is subject to change during the course of execution to that of a corresponding function in some derived class. Example 2.3 gives a simple illustration of this idea.

EXAMPLE 2.3

```
 #include <iostream.h>
class base_class
{
 public:
  // Constructor
  base_class(char);
  // virtual output function
  virtual void print()const;
 protected:
  char ch_value;
}; // Terminates user interface for base_class.

// Implementation details for base_class

// Constructor
base_class :: base_class(char b):ch_value(b){}
// Print function
void base_class :: print()const
{
 cout << "Outputting value " << ch_value
      << " inside base_class" << endl;
}

// User interface for derived_class

class derived_class : public base_class{
 public:
  // Constructor
  derived_class(char);
  // Output function
  void print()const;

  // No private or protected parts
}; // Terminates user interface for derived class.

// Implementation details for derived_class

// Constructor
derived_class :: derived_class(char b) : base_class(b){};
```

```
// Output function
void derived_class :: print() const
{
 cout << "Outputting value " << ch_value
       << " from derived_class" << endl;
}

// Driver function
int main()
{
 base_class base_object('b');
 base_class *ptr = &base_object;
 derived_class derived_object('d');
 ptr -> print();
 ptr = &derived_object;
 ptr -> print();
 return 0;
}
```

The output is

```
Outputting value b inside base class
Outputting value d from derived class
```

Let us trace execution of this program. First, a base_class object called base_object is constructed with data member 'b'. Next a pointer ptr is defined, and initially refers to base_object, as in Figure 2.4a. Then an object named derived_object is constructed from derived_class with data member 'd', as in Figure. 2.4b.

FIGURE 2.4a

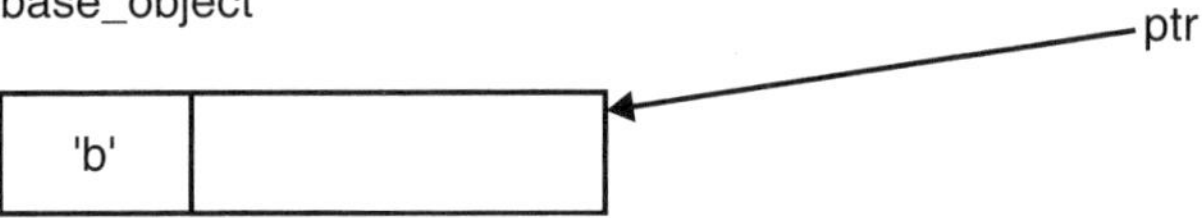

FIGURE 2.4b

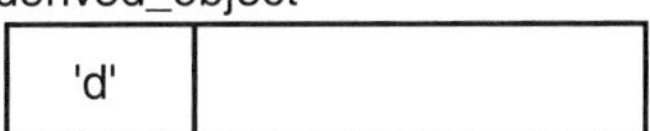

When

```
ptr -> print();
```

executes for the first time, ptr is still pointing to base_object, causing the print() member function of base_class to be invoked, producing the output

```
Outputting value b inside base class
```

Then `ptr` is redirected to `derived_object` by executing

```
ptr = &derived_object;
```

The result is pictured in Figure 2.4c.

FIGURE 2.4c
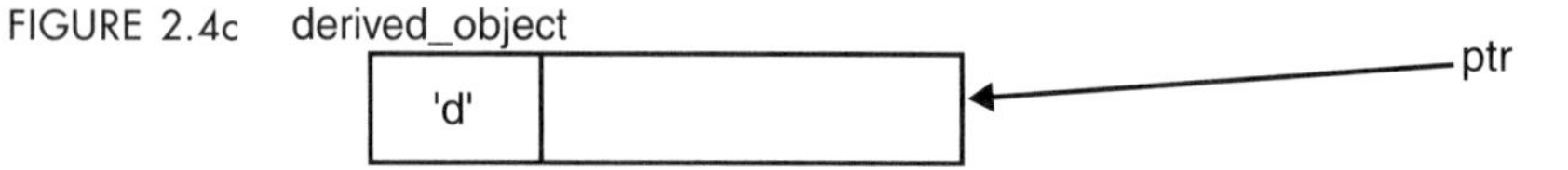

When

```
ptr -> print();
```

executes again, `ptr` is now pointing at an object constructed from `derived_class`, producing the output

```
Outputting value d from derived class
```

The key idea is that this selection of objects by `ptr` is occurring during the course of execution of the program. This illustrates run-time polymorphism.

Suppose we contrast this to the execution of the driver

```
int main()
{
 base_class base_object('b');
 base_object.print();
 derived_class derived_object('d');
 derived_object.print();
 return 0;
}
```

The output obtained from this version is identical with that of the previous version, but the progress of execution is quite different. In the latter case, the decision as to which version of `print()` is made at compile time. This is because no pointer is defined; hence, no trace of its movements during program execution occurs. Thus, the version of polymorphism being applied is compile-time polymorphism.

The type of `virtual` function we have described is commonly called an *ordinary `virtual` function.* Such functions take the form of executable code. When an ordinary `virtual` function is invoked, its semantics are exactly the same as those for non-`virtual` functions. Any such function may be overridden in the derived class, as was the case for `print()`, and the prototype for the derived function must have the same *`function_name`* and the same formal parameter list (sometimes called the *signature*) as that of the corresponding `virtual` function appearing in the base class.

The selection of which version of the virtual function is made at run time. The typical case occurs when the base class has an ordinary virtual function, and the derived classes have their own versions of this function. A pointer declared in the base class may point to an object constructed in the base class or to an object constructed in a derived class. The member function selected depends on the class of the object selected by the pointer, not on the pointer type.

Once declared virtual, this property is carried along to all redefinitions of the function in each of the derived classes. It is not necessary to use the virtual modifier when redefining the function in the derived class or in its coding in the implementation file. Moreover, the inclusion of virtual functions promotes *code reuse* because the inclusion of any newly created derived classes in the hierarchy containing a member function with the same *function_name* as that of a virtual function in the base class simply involves referring to an object constructed in the newly derived class by a pointer and then invoking the new form of the member function.

2.8 Pure virtual Functions and Abstract Classes

C++ also supports the definition and implementation of a second category of virtual functions known as *pure virtual functions.* Any such function is declared as virtual in the base class and plays the role of a *dummy:* The body of the function is empty in the base class, but has a specific meaning in each of the derived classes in which it is a member function. The general syntax of the definition of a pure virtual function in the base class is given by

```
virtual return_data_type function_name()const = 0;
```

A base class containing at least one pure virtual function is called an *abstract class.* Up until now, our view of a class has been as an implementation of a specific ADT from which instances (objects) may be considered. For example, we described a hierarchy for geometric objects in Example 1.1 and Section 2.2, whose base class Geometric_Object has the interface

```
class Geometric_Object {
 public:
 // Perimeter function coded inline.
  double perimeter() const { return 0; }
};
```

We commented in Section 2.2 that it is possible to construct specific objects of this class and assign to each a perimeter value of 0. However, we also commented that this represents a poor design because we never intend to use this base class as a *concrete class,* namely, one in which objects may be constructed. Instead, our view of this class is to serve as a *hub* (or *interface*) for any number of derived classes using `Geometric_Object` as a hub. This was certainly true for the derived classes `Rectangle`, `Circle`, and `Square`. In fact, we may also add other derived classes to this hierarchy. For example, we may add

```
class Triangle : public Geometric_Object
{
  public:
   // Constructor.
   Triangle(double s1, double s2, double s3)
    : side1(s1), side(s2), side3(s3) {}
   // Perimeter function coded inline.
   double perimeter() const { return side1 + side2 + side3; }
  private:
   double side1, side2, side3;
};
```

The resulting hierarchy is described by Figure 2.5. This underscores the fact that our design never intended to construct specific objects from the

FIGURE 2.5

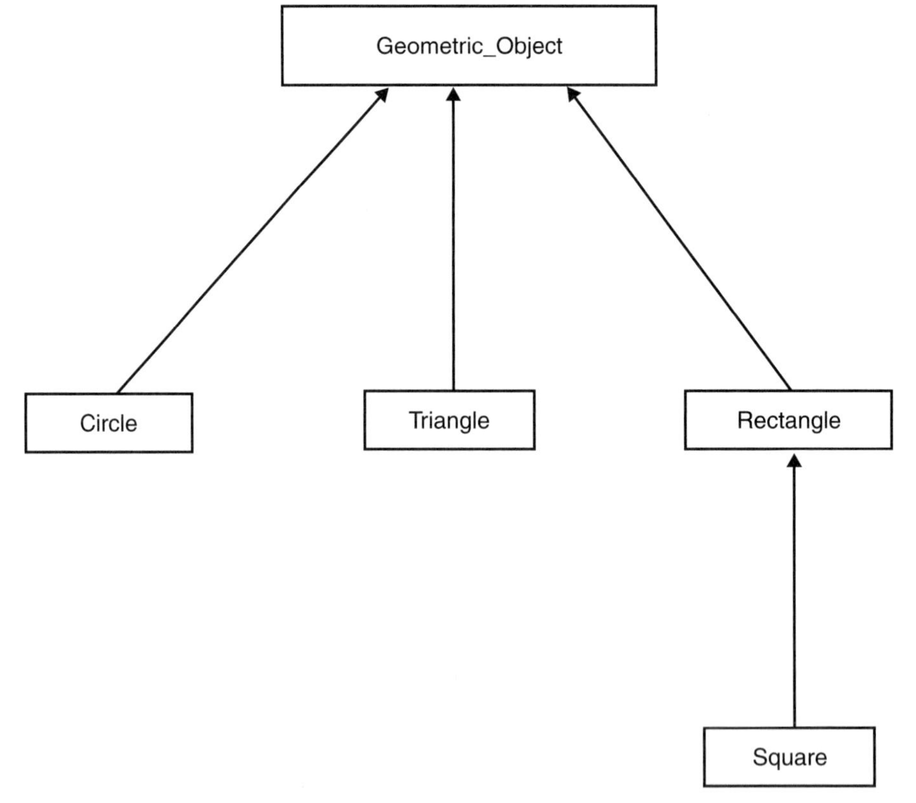

base class. This is enforced in C++ by replacing the current interface for `Geometric_Object` by an abstract class version, whose code is given by

```
class Geometric_Object
{   // Abstract class.
 public:
  // Perimeter function defined as a pure virtual function.
  virtual double perimeter() const = 0;
};
```

By defining `Geometric_Object` in this way, it is no longer possible to construct objects directly from `Geometric_Object`. This is exactly what we intended all along when we designed this hierarchy.

```
int main(){
 Geometric_Object *ptr;
 Rectangle rect(3,5);
 Circle circ(4);
 Square sq(6);
 Triangle tri(3,4,5);

 ptr = &rect;
 cout << "Perimeter of rectangle = " << ptr -> perimeter() << endl;
 ptr = &circ;
 cout << "Perimeter of circle = " << ptr -> perimeter() << endl;
 ptr = &sq;
 cout << "Perimeter of square = " << ptr -> perimeter() << endl;
 ptr = &tri;
 cout << "Perimeter of triangle = " << ptr -> perimeter() << endl;
 return 0;
}
```

The output obtained from executing this is

```
Perimeter of rectangle = 16
Perimeter of circle = 12.5664
Perimeter of square = 24
Perimeter of triangle = 12
```

Suppose we trace execution of this user program. After the first sequence of constructions and initializations, we have the situation described in Figure 2.6a. After executing `ptr = ▭` we have the situation described in Figure 2.6b. After executing `ptr = ˆ` we obtain the situation described in Figure 2.6c. After executing `ptr = &sq;` the situation is as described in Figure 2.6d. Finally, after executing `ptr = &tri;` we have Figure 2.6e.

In our earlier design of the class hierarchy of Example 2.1, `Vertex` was a concrete base class containing a constructor and an overloaded version of

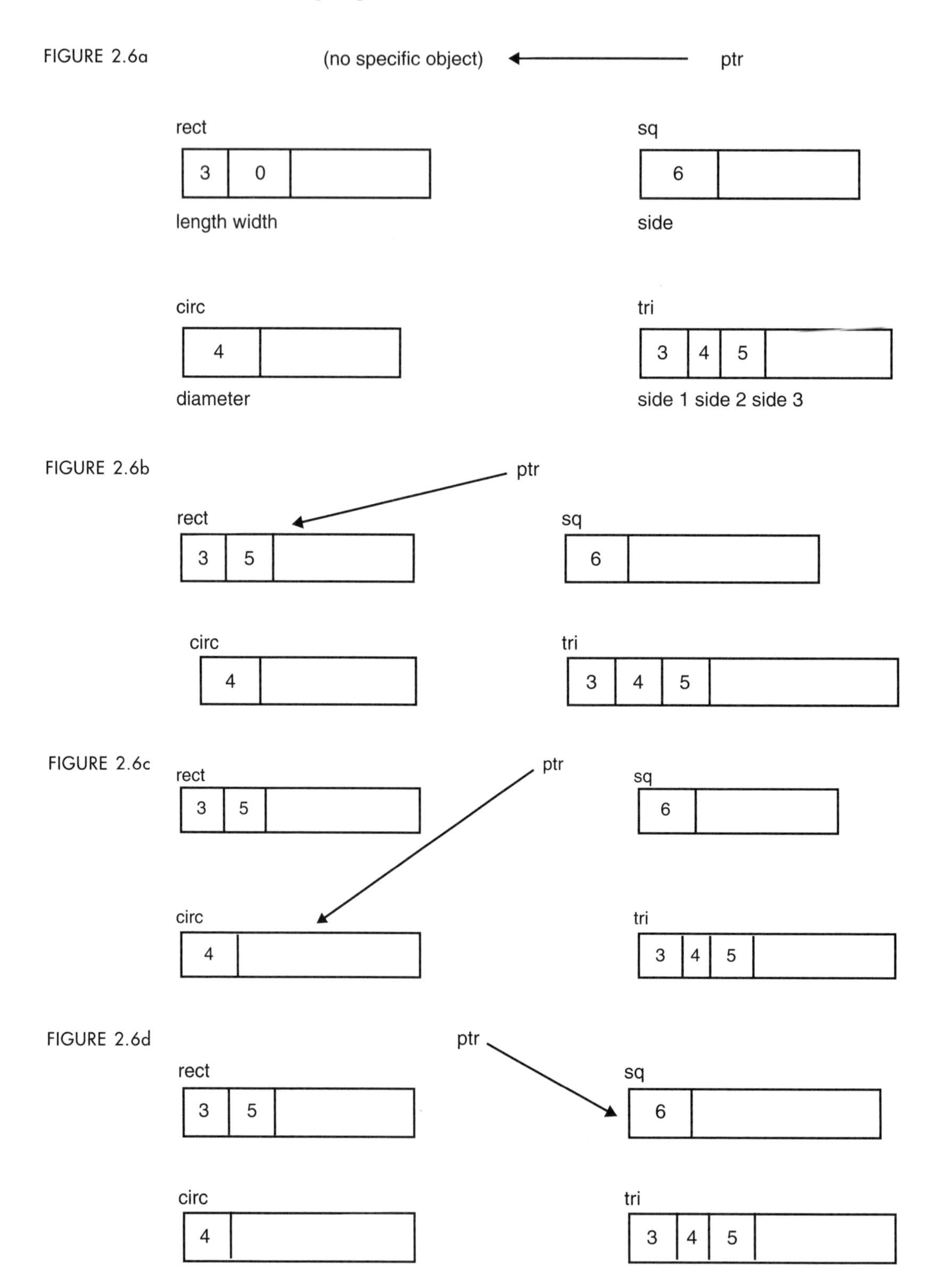
FIGURE 2.6a
(no specific object)
ptr
rect
3
0
length width
sq
6
side
circ
4
diameter
tri
3
4
5
side 1 side 2 side 3
FIGURE 2.6b
ptr
rect
3
5
sq
6
circ
4
tri
3
4
5
FIGURE 2.6c
ptr
rect
3
5
sq
6
circ
4
tri
3
4
5
FIGURE 2.6d
ptr
rect
3
5
sq
6
circ
4
tri
3
4
5

FIGURE 2.6e

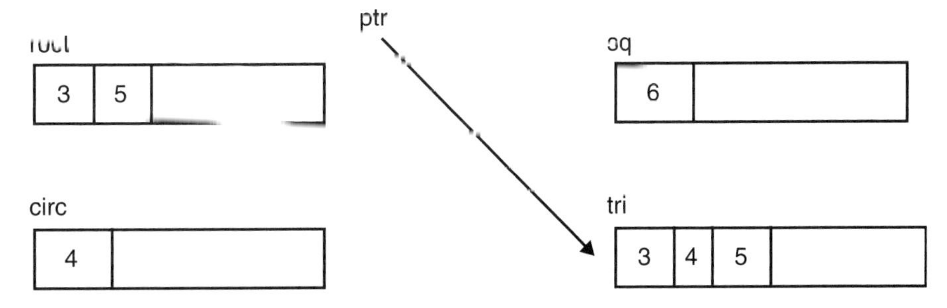

`operator<<`, in which the coordinates of any `Vertex` object are output. In fact, this base class did nothing more than produce a pair of coordinates for the center of any `Ellipse` or `Circle` object. Thus, constructing specific objects of the `Vertex` class contributes nothing of any value to the hierarchy: The sole purpose of this class is to establish a hub for the hierarchy. Consequently, in the presence of `virtual` functions and polymorphism, it would be more sensible to redefine `Vertex` as an abstract class, using it as a hub for the current sequence of classes in the hierarchy, and as well for other classes that can be adjoined as derived classes, such as a version of `Rectangle` in which the vertices are input, as in Figure 2.7.

FIGURE 2.7

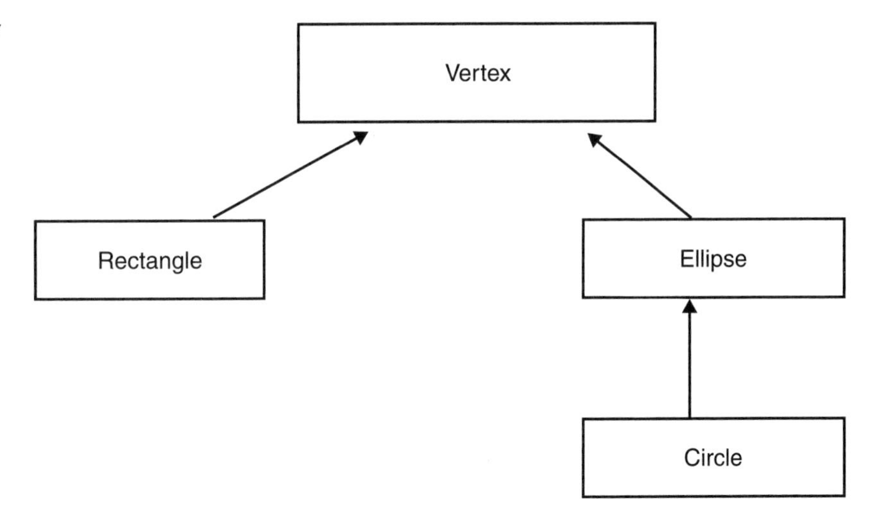

The formal details of the coding of `Vertex` as an abstract base class are given by

```
class Vertex {   // Abstract base class
  public:
   virtual double area() const = 0;
 }; // Terminates user interface for Vertex
```

Note that this version of `Vertex` does not include a `protected` section defining the coordinates of any object. This is accomplished in the derived classes `Ellipse` and `Rectangle`, whose user interfaces and implementation files are given as

```
class Ellipse : public Vertex
{
 public:
  // Constructor.  First two parameters are the coordinates
  // of the vertex, the next two are the respective lengths
  // of the axes in the x-direction and y-direction,
  // respectively.
  Ellipse(double,double,double,double);
  // Overloaded output function.  Determines whether the
  // major (minor) axis is horizontal (vertical).
  friend ostream& operator<<(ostream&,const Ellipse&);
  // Member function computing area of ellipse
  double area() const;
 protected:
  double x_coord, y_coord;
  double horiz_axis, vert_axis;
}; // Terminates user interface for Ellipse class.

// Implementation details for Ellipse class.
const double PI = 3.14159;
// Constructor
Ellipse :: Ellipse(double x,double y,double h,double v)
  : x_coord(x), y_coord(y),horiz_axis(h),vert_axis(v){}

// Overloaded output function.
ostream& operator<<(ostream& os,const Ellipse& ell)
{
 os << "Ellipse has vertex = (" << ell.x_coord << ",";
 os << ell.y_coord << ")" << endl;
 if(ell.horiz_axis >= ell.vert_axis)
 {
  os << "Major axis is horizontal of length = "
         << ell.horiz_axis << endl;
  os << "Minor axis is vertical of length = "
         << ell.vert_axis << endl;
 }
 else
 {
  os << "Major axis is vertical of length = "
```

```
        << ell.vert_axis << endl;
    os << "Minor axis is horizontal of length = "
        << ell.horiz_axis << endl;
  }
  return os;
}

double Ellipse :: area() const
{
  return PI * horiz_axis * vert_axis;
}
```

The definition of `Circle` as a derived class of `Ellipse` is essentially the same as before, but the constructor uses the fact that the coordinates of the center of any `Circle` object are all derived directly from `Ellipse` because `Vertex` is now an abstract class.

The user interface for `Rectangle` has a `protected` part defining the respective x- and y-coordinates of the vertices of any object. We have omitted the possibility of checking whether the user has properly input the vertices of a rectangle, leaving the details as an exercise. Further, this implementation depends on the order of initialization of the parameters representing these vertices and assumes that these have been input, in order, in a clockwise fashion beginning with the upper left vertex. It also assumes that the objects constructed from this class are rectangles with two vertical and two horizontal edges. Finally, the implementation details require the preprocessor directive

```
#include <math.h>
```

to take advantage of the predefined absolute value function `abs`.

```
// User interface for derived class Rectangle.
class Rectangle : public Vertex
{
 public:
  // Constructor
  Rectangle(double,double,double,double,double,double,double,double);
  // Overloaded output operator
  friend ostream& operator<<(ostream&,const Rectangle&);
  // Area member function.
  double area() const;
 protected:
  double x_coord1, y_coord1, x_coord2, y_coord2, x_coord3, y_coord3,
   x_coord4, y_coord4;
}; // Terminates user interface for Rectangle.
```

```
// Implementation details for Rectangle class

// Constructor.  Constructs Rectangle object, given four sets
// of coordinates for its vertices.
Rectangle :: Rectangle(double x1,double y1, double x2, double y2,
                       double x3,double y3, double x4, double y4)
{ x_coord1 = x1; y_coord1 = y1; x_coord2 = x2; y_coord2 = y2;
 x_coord3 = x3; y_coord3 = y3; x_coord4 = x4; y_coord4 = y4;
}
// Overloaded output operator
ostream& operator<<(ostream& os,const Rectangle& re)
{
 os << "Coordinates of rectangle are:" << endl;
 os << "First vertex: (" << re.x_coord1 << "," << re.y_coord1 << ")" <<endl;
 os << "Second vertex: (" << re.x_coord2 << "," << re.y_coord2 <<")" << endl;
 os << "Third vertex: (" << re.x_coord3 << "," << re.y_coord3 <<")" << endl;
 os << "Fourth vertex: (" << re.x_coord4 << "," << re.y_coord4 <<")" << endl;
 return os;
}
#include <math.h> // For absolute value function abs.
// Overloaded area function
double Rectangle :: area() const
// This function presumes the vertices are presented in
// a clockwise order beginning with the upper left vertex.
{
 return abs(x_coord2 - x_coord1)* abs(y_coord3 - y_coord2);
}
```

You should write a driver for this new version of the hierarchy and also explore the possibility of adjoining a derived class of `Rectangle` called `Square`, whose objects are rectangles with all sides equal.

2.9 Implications of Inheritance and Polymorphism for Software Engineering

Inheritance is a design paradigm promoting code reuse, which is very desirable from the standpoint of efficiency. In addition, most software problems are solvable by observing that the problem domain consists of a number of subproblems whose solution involves designing hierarchies beginning with a base class and having a number of derived classes, each of which contributes to the solution of the original problem and for which an is-a relationship exists with the base class. This was certainly the case with the geometric hierarchies studied in this chapter. In each case, the respective base classes Geometric_Object and Vertex were designed optimally as abstract classes with a number of concrete derived classes.

A sensible decomposition of a simple inheritance hierarchy also promotes the inclusion of new derived classes into the original hierarchy without causing a major revision of the existing code. This was demonstrated when the Triangle class was added as a new derived class into the hierarchy having Geometric_Object as the base class.

In the case of multiple inheritance as a problem-solving tool, the relationship between a derived class and several distinct base classes causes a number of conceptual complications. First, the is-a relationship is unclear because no single parental attribute exists between parent (base) class and derived class. Second, in principle, when an object is constructed from a derived class that is multiply inherited from several parents, the object is the summation (or absorption) of objects that are constructible from each of the parents. Such an object may be viewed as a form of each of its parent classes. The behavior of this object has to be carefully controlled; otherwise, the original plan of design becomes cloudy at best. All of this notwithstanding, a carefully controlled environment involving multiple inheritance becomes an important design paradigm promoting code reuse and often represents an extremely powerful and useful alternative to simple inheritance.

The idea of run-time polymorphism represents another extremely useful and efficient design paradigm. When programs involving hierarchies also use virtual functions and polymorphism, the text of the user program assumes an appearance that is relatively easy to follow. This simplification also creates simpler venues for testing, debugging, and maintaining code. When designing and writing code using virtual functions and polymorphism, the design of the underlying classes may remain general and close to the theoretical concepts being implemented. It also permits the user's code invoking this design to become more specific, using instances of the application domain. This again results in software design that is easier to maintain and with relatively few bugs.

2.10 Chapter Summary

This chapter concentrates on two major tools of OOD: inheritance and polymorphism. Inheritance is the facility enabling a new class to be derived from old ones, in which we designate the existing class as the *base class* (or *parent class*) and the newly defined class as the *derived class*. In defining the derived class, the data members of the base class are present as data members of any object constructed from the derived class, with the possibility of defining new and extra data members in the derived class. Any member function derived in the base class becomes a member function of any object constructed in the derived class, unless overridden by a new definition of that function in the derived class. Thus, we say that an is-a relation exists for any object constructed in the derived class with the corresponding base class.

A derived class may be designed from a single existing base class using the syntax

```
class derived_class_name : public | private | protected base_class_name
{
                         .
                         .
                         .
     // Member declarations of derived_class
                         .
                         .
                         .
};
```

where the *access specifiers* `public`, `private`, or `protected` designate specific forms of access between objects constructed in a class defined in the hierarchy. The default access specifier is `private`. This establishes a state of *simple inheritance* between the derived class named by *`derived_class_name`* and the base class named by *`base_class_name`*.

A `public` member of a class is accessible throughout its scope, including any user functions. A `private` member is accessible only to member functions defined in its own class and to `friend` functions of that class. A `protected` member is a compromise between `public` and `private` members: It is accessible to other functions within its class and any class immediately derived from it, as well as to `friend` functions of that class.

Multiple inheritance allows for the possibility of a class to be derived from two or more base (parent) classes. Unlike the situation for simple inheritance, the is-a relationship is no longer definable.

The derived class may have its own specific constructors, which must invoke the constructor defined in its base class. The syntax needed to pass parameters from the derived class to the base class is given by

```
derived_class_name(formal_parameter_list) : base_class_name(arguments)
```

as in

```
Square(double x) : Rectangle(x,x)
```

We may view a publicly derived class as an implementation of a subtype of a data type implemented by its base class. In view of this, it is possible to assign the value of any object defined in a derived class to an object of the base class, but not vice versa. In addition, a pointer reference defined initially to an object of the base class may refer to an object defined in any of its derived classes, but not vice versa.

C++ uses the keyword `virtual` to provide a mechanism for the dynamic selection of an appropriate member function from among objects defined either in the base or derived classes. This implies that the `virtual` function must be defined as such in the base class, with possible redefinition in any derived class. In fact, in many instances, the base class may be an *abstract class*, in which the `virtual` function defined there is known as a *pure `virtual` function*, which prohibits the construction of any specific object in that class. The capability of the dynamic selection of member functions of objects coming from either a base or a derived class is known as *polymorphism*.

Public inheritance is an important tool for software engineering, as it promotes code reuse. Further, it allows for an organized way of separating more general forms of modules into simpler and more specific forms, using the idea that the base class is a *hub* for a number of more specific derived classes solving a number of subproblems generated by this decomposition. Facilities permitting the implementation of encapsulation, inheritance, and polymorphism are critical for OOD.

EXERCISES

1. Extend the hierarchy for `Geometric_Object` discussed in Section 2.2 and then enlarge to contain the derived class `Triangle` as follows:

   a. Construct a new class `Isosceles_Triangle` as a derived class of `Triangle`, where the constructor passes only two parameter values: the common length of the two equal sides and the length of the third side. The `perimeter` function should return the result of computing twice the length of the common sides plus the length of the third side.

   b. Then construct a new class `Equilateral_Triangle` as a derived class of `Isosceles_Triangle`, where the constructor passes only one parameter: the common length of all three sides. The `perimeter` function for this class should return the result of computing three times the length of each side.

   Then write a driver tracing polymorphism for objects constructed from each of the classes in the hierarchy.

2. Extend the hierarchy with abstract base class `Vertex` to contain a derived class `Square` of `Rectangle`, whose constructor contains the same number of parameters as that for `Rectangle`, but whose `area()` member function exploits the fact that all sides of a `Square` object have the same length.

   Write a driver tracing polymorphism between objects constructed from this extended hierarchy.

3. Look at the following variation of Example 2.3:

```
#include <iostream.h>

class base_class
{
 public:
  // Virtual output function.
  virtual void print() const;
  // Public data member
  char ch_value;
}; // Terminates user interface for base_class

// Implementation details for base_class
// Print function.
void base_class :: print() const
{
 cout << "Outputting value " << ch_value
      << " inside base_class" << endl;
}

// Now for the derived_class:

class derived_class : public base_class
{
  public:
   // Public data member
   base_class :: ch_value;
   // Output function
   void print() const;
}; // Terminates user interface for derived_class

// Implementation details for derived_class

// Output function
void derived_class :: print() const
{
      cout << "Outputting value " << base_class :: ch_value
      << " from derived class" << endl;
}

// Driver function

int main()
```

```
{
  base_class base_object;
  base_class *ptr = &base_object;
  derived_class derived_object;
  base_object.ch_value = 'b';
  ptr -> print();
  derived_object.ch_value = 'd';
  ptr = &derived_object;
  ptr -> print();
  return 0;
}
```

a. Describe the output (if any) obtained from executing this program.

b. Is there any change if `derived_class` is inherited from `base_class` using `private` inheritance?

4. Use `<assert.h>` to safeguard against any forms of illegal input in the `Vertex` hierarchy as it applies to the input of vertices for `Rectangle` and `Square` objects.

5. Trace execution and find the exact form of the output for

```
#include <iostream.h>

// User interface for base_class
class base_class
{
  public:
   // Constructor
   base_class(char= 'c');
   // Virtual output function, with no parameters
   virtual void print() const;
   // Output function with character string parameter
   void print(char*) const;
  private:
   char ch_value;
}; // User interface for base_class
// Implementation details for base_class

// Constructor
base_class :: base_class(char c_val) : ch_value(c_val){}
// Virtual parameterless output function
void base_class :: print() const
{
 cout << "value = " << ch_value << endl;
}

// Output function with string parameter.
```

```
void base_class :: print(char* str) const
{
 cout << str << ch_value << endl;
}

// User interface for derived_class
class derived_class : public base_class
{
 public:
  // Constructor
  derived_class(char c_val = 'd') : base_class('a'),
             char_value(c_val) {}
  // Overloaded parameterless output function
  void print() const;
  // Output function with string parameter
  void print(char*) const;
 private:
  char char_value;
}; // Terminates user interface for derived_class

// Implementation details for derived_class
// Constructor
//derived_class :: derived_class(char c_val = 'b') : base_class('b');

// Overloaded parameterless output function
void derived_class :: print() const
{
  cout << "value = " << char_value << endl;
}

// Overloaded output function with string parameter
void derived_class :: print(char* str) const
{
 cout << str << char_value << endl;
}

// Driver
int main()
{
 base_class b1, b2('A'), *ptr1;
 derived_class d1, d2('C'), *ptr2 = &d2;
 b1.print();
 b2.print();
```

```
  d1.print();
  d2.print();
  ptr1 = ptr2;
  ptr1 -> print();
  ptr1 -> print("derived_class value = ");
  ptr2 -> print();
  ptr2 -> print("derived_class value = ");
  return 0;
}
```

6. a. Does the following program compile? It represents an attempt to use a forward declaration by defining the base class `Geometric_Object` using a prototype, delaying its formal definition until later:

```
#include <iostream.h>
class Geometric_Object;  // Base class forward declaration.
class Rectangle : public Geometric_Object
{
 public:
  Rectangle(double lt, double wd) : length(lt),width(wd){}
  double perimeter() const { return 2*length + 2*width; }
 private:
  double length, width;
};

class Geometric_Object
{
 public:
  virtual double perimeter() const = 0;
};

int main()
{
 Rectangle rect(3,4);
 cout << rect.perimeter() << endl;
 return 0;
}
```

b. Examine the following version for compilation:

```
#include <iostream.h>

class Geometric_Object; // Base class forward declaration.
class Rectangle; // Derived class forward declaration.

class Geometric_Object
```

```
{
 public:
  virtual double perimeter() const = 0;
};

class Rectangle : public Geometric_Object
{
 public:
  Rectangle(double lt, double wd) : length(lt),width(wd){}
  double perimeter() const { return 2*length + 2*width; }
 private:
  double length, width;
};

int main()
{
 Rectangle rect(3,4);
 cout << rect.perimeter() << endl;
 return 0;
}
```

c. Test the following version for compilation:

```
#include <iostream.h>

class Geometric_Object;  // Base class forward declaration.
class Rectangle : public Geometric_Object;
// Derived class forward declaration.

class Geometric_Object
{
 public:
  virtual double perimeter() const = 0;
};

class Rectangle
{
 public:
  Rectangle(double lt, double wd) : length(lt),width(wd){}
  double perimeter() const { return 2*length + 2*width; }
 private:
  double length, width;
};

int main()
```

```
{
 Rectangle rect(3,4);
 cout << rect.perimeter() << endl;
 return 0;
}
```

7. Is there a default access specifier between a base class and a derived class? To answer this question better, compile the following code, which represents a variation of Example 2.3:

```
#include <iostream.h>

class base_class  // Base class user interface
{
 public:
  base_class(char);
  virtual void print() const;
 protected:
  char ch_value;
};

// Implementation details for base_class
base_class :: base_class(char b) : ch_value(b){}
void base_class :: print() const
{
 cout << "Outputting value " << ch_value
   << " inside base_class" << endl;
}

// User interface for derived_class.  Shows attempted default
// for access specifier.
class derived_class : base_class
{
 public:
  derived_class(char);
  void print() const;
};

// Implementation details for derived_class
derived_class :: derived_class(char b) : base_class(b){}
void derived_class :: print() const
{
 cout << "Outputting value " << ch_value
  << " from derived_class" << endl;
}
```

```
// Driver
int main()
{
 base_class b_object('b');
 base_class *ptr = &b_object;
 derived_class d_object('d');
 ptr -> print();
 ptr = &d_object;
 ptr -> print();
 return 0;
}
```

a. Insert `private` and then `protected` as the specific form of the access specifier and compile each of these versions.

b. Compare the result of (a) to the result of compiling the default version. What may be concluded on the basis of these observations?

8. Is it possible for a class to be a derived class of itself?

a. Test this by defining the class `Geometric_Object` as in Section 2.2 and attempt to compile the derived class definition

```
class Geometric_Object : public Geometric_Object
{
  public:
   double perimeter() const { return 0; }
};
```

b. Then attempt to compile and execute the program given by

```
#include <iostream.h>
// Base class declaration.
class Geometric_Object
{
 public:
  double perimeter() const { return 0;}
};

class Geometric_Thing : public Geometric_Object
{
 public:
  double perimeter() const { return 0;}
};

// Driver
int main()
{
```

```
    Geometric_Object obj;
    cout << obj.perimeter() << endl;
    Geometric_Thing thing;
    cout << thing.perimeter() << endl;
    return 0;
  }
```

What conclusions may we make based on these observations?

9. Suppose we consider the class user interfaces for `base_class_1`, `base_class_2`, and `derived_class` of Example 2.2 with the driver given by

```
int main(){
 derived_class *ptr = new derived_class(3,'a',5.1);
 base_class_1 *ptr1 = ptr;
 base_class_2 *ptr2 = ptr;
 cout << *ptr << endl;
 cout << *ptr1 << endl;
 cout << *ptr2 << endl;
 return 0;
}
```

a. Trace execution of this program and give the exact form of the output.

b. What happens if the multiple inheritance of `derived_class` is `private` for each of `base_class_1` and `base_class_2`? That is, we have

```
class derived_class : private base_class_1, private base_class_2
```

Explain your answer.

10. Use `<assert.h>` to check for `Circle` objects with nonnegative diameters in each of the geometric hierarchies of Sections 2.1 and 2.4. Do the same to test for nonnegative values for the parameter values for `Rectangle` and `Square` objects.

11. Change the access specifier from `public` to `private` and again from `public` to `protected` in the geometric hierarchy described in Example 2.1. Comment on the results produced by your compiler.

12. Trace execution, explain the behavior, and give the exact form of the output for

```
#include <iostream.h>


class base_class
{
 public:
  // Default constructor.
  //base_class();
```

```
  // Two virtual member functions, coded inline:
  virtual void virt(char v){ cout << v << " inside base_class" << endl;}
  virtual void virt(int i){ cout << i << " inside base_class" << endl;}
 }; // Terminates coding of base_class.

class derived_class : public base_class
{
 public:
 // Default constructor.
 //derived_class();
 // Derived version of virtual member function, coded inline:
 void virt(int i){ cout << i << " inside derived_class" << endl;}
}; // Terminates coding of derived_class

int main()
{
 derived_class d_object, *ptr = &d_object;
 base_class b_object;
 b_object.virt('a');
 b_object.virt(25);
 d_object.virt('a');
 d_object.virt(25);
 ptr -> virt('a');
 ptr -> virt(25);
 return 0;
}
```

13. a. Given the class definitions

```
#include <iostream.h>

const double PI = 3.14159;

class Axes
{
 protected:
  double x_axis, y_axis;
};

class Vertex
{
 protected:
  double x_coord, y_coord;
```

```
};

class Ellipse : public Axes, public Vertex
{
 public:
 // Constructor prototype
 Ellipse(double,double,double,double);
 // Area function, coded inline.
 virtual double area() const { return PI * x_axis * y_axis; }
 // Overloaded output function
 friend ostream& operator<<(ostream&,const Ellipse&);
};

// Implementation details for Ellipse class.

// Constructor
Ellipse :: Ellipse(double x,double y,double maj, double min)
{ x_coord = x; y_coord = y; x_axis = maj; y_axis = min;}

// Overloaded output function.
ostream& operator<<(ostream& os,const Ellipse& e)
{
 os << "Vertex of ellipse has coordinates:" << endl;
 os << "(" << e.x_coord << "," << e.y_coord << ")" << endl;
 if(e.x_axis >= e.y_axis)
 {
  os << "Major axis has length " << e.x_axis << endl;
  os << "Minor axis has length " << e.y_axis << endl;
 }
 else
 {
  os << "Major axis has length " << e.y_axis << endl;
  os << "Minor axis has length " << e.x_axis << endl;
 }
 return os;
}

class Circle : public Ellipse
{
 public:
 // Constructor prototype.
 Circle(double,double,double);
```

```
 // Overloaded output function
 friend ostream& operator<<(ostream&, const Circle&);
 // Area function for Circle objects coded inline
 double area() const { return PI * x_axis * x_axis; }
};

// Implementation details for Circle class
// Constructor
Circle :: Circle(double x, double y, double r)
: Ellipse(x,y,r,r){}

// Overloaded output function.
ostream& operator<<(ostream& os, const Circle& c)
{
 os << "Circle has center with coordinates:" << endl;
 os << "(" << c.x_coord << "," << c.y_coord << ")" << endl;
 os << "and has radius = " << c.x_axis << endl;
 return os;
}
```

and the driver

```
int main()
{
 Ellipse ell(3,-2,6,8);
 Circle circ(-9,-2,5);
 cout << ell << endl;
 cout << ell.area() << endl;
 cout << circ << endl;
 cout << circ.area() << endl;
 return 0;
}
```

Find the exact form of the output.

b. Suppose we now consider the driver

```
int main()
{
 Ellipse ell(3,-2,6,8), *ptr = &ell;
 Circle circ(-9,-2,5);
 cout << *ptr << endl;
 cout << "Area of current ellipse = " << ptr -> area() << endl;
 ptr = &circ;
 cout << *ptr << endl;
 return 0;
}
```

Explain the behavior of this program and why `ptr -> area()` does not compile after redirecting `ptr` to point at `circ`.

14. Consider the following variant of Example 2.3:

```
#include <iostream.h>
class base_class
{
 public:
  // Constructor
  base_class(char);
  // virtual output function
  virtual void print() const;
 protected:
  char ch_value;
}; // Terminates user interface for base_class.

// Implementation details for base_class

// Constructor
base_class :: base_class(char b):ch_value(b){}
// Print function
void base_class :: print() const
{
 cout << "Outputting value " << ch_value
      << " inside base_class" << endl;
}

// User interface for derived_class

class derived_class : public base_class{
 public:
  // Constructor
  derived_class(char);
  // Output function
  void print() const;

  // No private or protected parts
}; // Terminates user interface for derived_class.

// Implementation details for derived_class

// Constructor
derived_class :: derived_class(char b) : base_class(b){};
```

```
// Output function.
void derived_class :: print() const
{
 cout << "Outputting value " << ch_value
       << " from derived_class" << endl;
}

// Driver function
int main()
{
 base_class base_object('b');
 base_class *ptr = &base_object;
 derived_class derived_object('d');
 ptr -> print();
 derived_class *ptr1 = &derived_object;
 ptr1 -> print();
 base_object = derived_object;
 ptr -> print();
 *ptr = *ptr1;
 ptr1 -> print();
 return 0;
}
```

Trace execution of this program and justify the output generated.

PROGRAMMING PROJECT

Define the following hierarchy of employees for a large firm:

1. `Employee` names a base class containing the following data common to all employees:
   a. social security number (as an 11-character string)
   b. date of initial employment (using the format `mm/dd/yy`)
   c. status—choose between the `char` values
      `'a'` for administrator (chief executive, other executives, department heads)
      `'b'` for assembly line worker
      `'c'` for clerical staff
2. `Full_Time_Employee` names a derived class of `Employee`, every object of which contains these additional fields:
   a. weekly gross pay (based on a standard 40-hour workweek)
   b. overtime wages (based on the number of weekly hours greater than 40)
   c. deductions (for employee credit union, health insurance)
      Each of these should be in a `double` format.

3. `Part_Time_Employee` names a second derived class of `Employee`, every object of which contains these additional fields:
   a. numbers of hours worked this week (`int` value, total must be less than 40)
   b. hourly rate of pay (as a `double` value)

   Design and code a driver program that first creates a list of employees interactively and then outputs the records just created in that list.

CHAPTER 3

Search and Sort

CHAPTER OBJECTIVES

- To study methods of searching for and sorting a finite sequence of values stored in an array using a variety of algorithms designed for this purpose.
- To define and develop efficient algorithms for search and sort using the techniques of object-oriented design.
- To quantify the concept of efficiency of algorithms using formal mathematics.
- To introduce the Principle of Finite Induction and to demonstrate its importance in testing the efficiency and correctness of algorithms.

3.1 Introduction

Two of the most important problems encountered in commercial data processing are, undoubtedly, the problems of sorting a sequence of values and searching for a value from a given finite collection of values stored in some fixed data structure. One objective of this chapter is to define and develop efficient algorithms for search and sort using object-oriented design (OOD). The ideas presented here begin a sequence leading to Chapter Eight, where we discuss predefined facilities for searching and sorting offered by the Standard Template Library (STL).

We begin by defining the concept of an algorithm and then examine the design and refinement of algorithms. The design process begins with a somewhat naive first description and, through a process of refinements, culminates in a "final" version that can be translated into formal code in a seamless manner. A very important consideration we will always keep in mind is the efficiency of the algorithm and formal mathematical techniques providing a quantification of efficiency.

3.2 The Concept of an Algorithm

We may define an algorithm as a carefully constructed finite sequence of instructions which, when executed in order of their appearance, constitutes a solution of a specific programming problem. Once we have formulated an algorithm, the path to a solution of the problem involves testing whether the sequence of instructions succeeds in arriving at that solution. Our emphasis in this text involves describing an algorithm as a finite sequence of well-formulated instructions for the purpose just described. But what constitutes a "well-formulated" instruction? This chapter emphasizes what constitutes well-formulated instructions as they apply to solving sorting and searching problems.

Several key factors are involved in the design of well-formulated algorithms:

- *There must be a clear and unambiguous description of the input data required for the solution.* This implies that the problem presented for solution must be stated in a clear and unambiguous form so that the input data, when presented in this environment, permit the algorithm to complete its execution in a finite number of steps. Moreover, this execution must yield an anticipated output, at which point the computation terminates.
- *Each instruction must be clearly and unambiguously stated, without any chance of misinterpretation.* A well-formulated instruction eliminates the possibility that there exists more than one possible consequence of its execution. That is to say, a well-formulated instruction must be deterministic. As an example, attempting to formulate instructions in some spoken language, such as English or French, generally leads to ambiguities. This is because such languages are by their very nature filled with terms having several alternative interpretations.
- *The algorithm must be correct.* As described in Chapter One, the algorithm must yield the anticipated output as the value(s) solving the stated problem for the given input value(s). In certain cases, the proof of correctness may be quite formal and rigorous. Such proofs may use such formal mathematical tools as the Principle of Finite Induction, seen later in this chapter.
- *The algorithm must produce a computation that terminates in a finite number of steps.* We must safeguard against a design which, for example, may result in an infinite loop or in an infinite chain of function calls. However, it is not necessary that we predict the exact number of computational steps involved. Instead, the only requirement is that we determine an upper bound beyond which no further computational steps occur. This determination will rely on concepts studied later in this chapter, when we study methods of quantifying the efficiency of algorithms.

- *The output and purpose of the algorithm must be clearly specified in advance.* There should be no doubt as to the intended purpose of the algorithm. It often happens that certain unanticipated side effects arise, even from very carefully formulated code. These side effects may be very subtle in nature and arise in very subtle ways. They often appear as run-time bugs, often requiring a very carefully planned strategy of code examination and testing to track down their origin. We will not go into any great detail describing such strategies in this text; this is properly the concern of the study of software engineering. It is a commonly accepted fact that even the most carefully defined and well-formulated algorithms contain a number of occurrences of run-time bugs. Our objective, then, is to minimize the number of such occurrences and to purge the resulting code of as many of these as possible.

3.3 Design with Classes and Objects

There are a number of powerful tools for designing algorithms involving classes and objects. If the problem to be solved can be cast in an environment whose application domain may be modeled using classes and objects, several questions arise:

- Which classes and objects are required in the design of the solution?
- Does the most suitable solution require predefined classes, such as those in the Standard Template Library?
- Does the solution require the facilities of classes of our own design?
- Which facilities of classes of our own design should be made `public`?
- If several classes are involved in the solution, do they form a hierarchy involving a well-defined base class and several well-defined derived classes?

In the traditional design process, the algorithm first appears in a comparatively crude form and then evolves gradually by a sequence of refinements into a form that very closely resembles the final coded version. In our earlier work, we have emphasized solving problems using classes and objects. In the sequel, we will show that many of these problems are solvable using certain predefined classes of the STL. One advantage derived from using these predefined tools is that a large burden of the design of these solutions is lifted from our shoulders because we may now rely on the fact that they represent reusable functions that have already been thoroughly tested for efficiency. The only question is how well suited these facilities are to the solution of the specific problem at hand.

Our approach in this chapter is that of studying techniques for searching and sorting values stored in an array using a variety of traditional algorithms designed for this purpose. In later chapters, beginning with Chapter Five, we will study a number of facilities available in the predefined container objects of classes defined in the STL for storing finite sequences of values. In so doing, we hope to acquire a deeper appreciation for the STL as a valuable tool for the software designer using C++ as the implementation language for solving such problems.

Before we begin this study, we introduce some of the more important and fundamental mathematical concepts needed to place this analysis on a more formal and rigorous foundation. Consequently, the next several sections will introduce the idea of complexity measures and their application to algorithms for searching and sorting, as well as the Principle of Finite Induction as an important tool in the analysis of algorithms that follow throughout the remainder of this text.

3.4 Efficiency Issues: Preliminary Discussion

We have emphasized the importance of efficient software solutions to problems from the beginning of this text. However, up to this point, our idea of efficiency has been intuitive and little more. To add more precision to this, we may pose the question:

> *Is it possible to quantify efficiency in some way, in the form of some common metric, to compare the efficiency of a number of algorithms that serve as alternative solutions to some specific software problem?*

One way to measure efficiency is the amount of processing time, in the form of the number of processing steps, required to complete the algorithm's execution. As we will see later, when the Standard Template Library is involved, efficiency is directly related to the time required to process the data stored in some container. In this context, we use the current size `n` of the container as an argument and define a (time) complexity function `t(n)` for an algorithm as the (maximum) number of processing steps required for the algorithm to complete execution.

More precisely, suppose `f(n)` is a function with nonnegative values and defined for all positive integers `n`. We say that an algorithm has order of complexity `f(n)` if

```
t(n) <= C*f(n) for n >= K
```

for suitable choices of the positive constants `C` and `K`, and we use the terminology that the algorithm is `O(f(n))`.

We now list some of the more important orders of complexity attached to algorithms we will encounter in this text.

- A very important and fundamental search algorithm is known as *sequential* (or *linear*) *search*. We will show that the amount of processing

time required to complete execution of this search algorithm is proportional to the number n of values in the sequence. Since this form of search involves at most n comparisons and each comparison is regarded as a separate processing step, we may conclude that sequential search is of order O(n). We say that this algorithm processes its data in linear time.
- Another important search algorithm is called *binary search*. In the sequel, we will show that this algorithm is of order $O(\log_2 n)$.[1] We may characterize this as an algorithm that processes its data in logarithmic time.
- Several of the popular sorting algorithms, such as selection sort and insertion sort, have complexity n^2; that is, they are of order $O(n^2)$. We say that such algorithms process their data in quadratic time.
- Some versions of sorting algorithms, such as quicksort and (internal) mergesort, have complexity that on the average is of order O(n log n).
- Certain algorithms do not depend on the number of elements appearing in the sequence. That is, there are constants C and K such that t(n) <= C for n >= K. We say such algorithms execute in constant time and denote this as O(1).

In analyzing the time complexity of algorithms, much stress is placed on what is called worst-case complexity and average-case complexity. This entails finding upper bounds for the number of computations involved in executing the algorithm for the worst possible and average situation, respectively. For instance, in executing quicksort, the worst possible case occurs when the sequence of values to be sorted appears in exactly the wrong order; for example, it appears in descending order when we wish to sort the values of the sequence in ascending order. Similarly, in the average case, quicksort involves placing a "pivot" value in its proper position in the sequence by splitting the sequence into two parts, each of which has roughly the same number of elements. In the average case, quicksort is O(n log n) and is $O(n^2)$ in its worst case (when one of the parts contains a single element).

3.5 The Principle of Finite Induction

We state the following mathematical result, known as *the Principle of Finite Induction:*

Principle of Finite Induction: Let P(n) *be a Boolean-valued statement whose value depends on the choice of the value of the nonnegative integer argument*

[1]We will drop the subscript with the understanding that, unless we specify otherwise, any reference to log will be a reference to $\log_2$.

> *n. If P(0) is true (that is, if P is true for the case n = 0), and if, for each value of k, k >= 0, P(k + 1) is true whenever P(k) is true, then P(n) is true for every choice of a nonnegative integer n.*

An important step described in the statement of the principle is

```
for each k, P(k + 1) is true whenever P(k) is true
```

This is called the inductive step and provides the means of moving to the next highest level of `P`, knowing that `P` is true at the current level. The way to use finite induction in mathematical proofs is first to prove separately and independently that `P(0)` is true for the proposed `P(n)`. Once this is established, the inductive step will verify `P(1)`; applying the inductive step once again, we obtain the truth of `P(2)` and so on.

EXAMPLE 3.1 Finite induction is useful in verifying certain inequalities for integers. Some of these inequalities also prove to be invaluable for comparing the efficiency of certain key algorithms. One such inequality states that $n < 2^n$ for all choices of a nonnegative integer `n`. Suppose we denote this statement by `P(n)`. We first show that `P(0)` is true. This is done by replacing each occurrence of `n` in `P(n)` with `0`, yielding $0 < 2^0$, which is certainly true. We next assume `P(k)` is true for some choice of a nonnegative integer `k`; thus, we assume $k < 2^k$ for this `k`. If we add `1` to both sides of this inequality, we get $k + 1 < 2^k + 1$. But we can show (by a separate argument using finite induction) that $2^k + 1 <= 2 * 2^k = 2^{k+1}$ for every nonnegative integer `k`. This yields $k + 1 < 2^{k+1}$, which establishes the truth of `P(k + 1)`. By finite induction, it follows that $n < 2^n$ is true for all nonnegative integers `n`.

3.6 Comparing Algorithms: Big-O Notation

We have already observed that a number of questions arise in a natural way in analyzing the efficiency of algorithms:

- How can we measure efficiency?
- What factors enter into the decision as to which of a number of candidates represents the most efficient and desired version of an algorithm for solving a given software problem?

The choice of the most efficient algorithm from a list of possible candidates is a very important factor in solving a software problem. The detailed study of the comparison of algorithms for efficiency is at the heart of the discipline in computer science known as algorithm analysis.

There are two commonly used measures for efficiency of algorithms: space efficiency and time efficiency. Space efficiency is concerned primarily with the amount of storage required to implement the underlying algorithm in hardware. It is generally understood that algorithm A is more space efficient than algorithm B if A requires less storage than B to solve the underlying problem. On the other hand, time efficiency involves counting the number of processing steps required to solve the problem. We say that algorithm A is more time efficient than algorithm B if A requires fewer computational steps than B to solve the problem.

Before proceeding further, it is important to observe that correctness should never be sacrificed either for time or space efficiency. If a proposed algorithm is being considered over other candidates because it is either more time or space efficient, but does not perform satisfactorily in all cases, then there should be no doubt as to the decision: Choose the candidate that exhibits correctness in all cases.

EXAMPLE 3.2 *The Factorial Function.*

Define the factorial function for all nonnegative integers n by

$$\text{factorial}(n) = \begin{cases} 1, \text{ if } n = 0 \text{ or } n = 1, \\ n * (n - 1) * (n - 2) * \ldots * 3 * 2 * 1, \text{ if } n > 1 \end{cases}$$

Thus, factorial(0) = factorial(1) = 1, factorial(2) = 2*1 = 2, factorial(3) = 3*2*1 = 6, factorial(4) = 4*3*2*1 = 24, and so on. We may observe that the rate of growth of the values returned by factorial is very rapid. In fact, we may use big-O to find an upper bound on its growth. We will show that factorial(n) is $O(n^n)$. To see this, note that for $n > 0$,

$$\begin{aligned} \text{factorial}(n) &= n * (n - 1) * (n - 2) * \ldots * 3 * 2 * 1 \\ &<= \underbrace{n * n * n * \ldots * n * n}_{n} = n^n \end{aligned}$$

factorial(n) is more commonly denoted by n!.

3.7 Search Algorithms for Arrays: Linear (Sequential) Search

Our objective in this section and the next is to analyze search strategies for values stored in an array. In doing so, we should seek search strategies that are relatively easy to implement and are as efficient as possible. The analysis of the efficiency of the search algorithm under consideration will be somewhat rigorous and will involve some basic mathematical concepts.

An array is a form of linear container, and we may view the values currently stored in an array as arranged in some linear path. However, we should be aware that there are other forms of linear containers: the properties of vectors, deques, and linked lists will be studied later in the text.

We begin with an analysis of linear (sequential) search as it applies to an array. Assume T is some given data type and assume there exists a finite sequence of values of type T in which the search is to be conducted. Our version of linear search will retrieve the first occurrence of the value we seek in the array, returning true if such a value occurs in the array; otherwise, false is returned. Informally, we may state the linear search algorithm as

> *Begin by probing the initial value of the sequence. If the value we seek appears there, stop the search and report success; otherwise, continue the search by examining the next value in the sequence. This process eventually terminates either by finding the value sought at some component in the array (in which case* true *is returned), or by exhausting all of the array's components without finding that value (in which case* false *is returned), indicating an unsuccessful search.*

Our final version of the algorithm expresses linear search as a function template, returning a bool value and a for loop ranging over the pointer indices referring to the array containing the sequence. The coding is given by

```
template<class T> bool linsrch(T* a,int the_size,const T& value,
                               int& steps)
{
 // Function implementing linear search algorithm
 // Precondition: array components have been assigned values
 // with no specific ordering.
 // Postcondition: "true" is returned whenever the first occurrence
 // of the value sought (if it exists) is found, and "false" if the
 // value sought does not appear in the array.

 bool UNSUCCESSFUL_SEARCH = false;

 for(int index = 0; index < the_size; ++index)
 // Invariant: the values in a up to and including position
 // index - 1 have already been inspected.
 {
  ++steps;
  if(*(a + index) == value) // Search is successful
   return true;
 }
  return UNSUCCESSFUL_SEARCH;
}
```

Note that the function uses a for loop with the comment

```
// Invariant: the values in a up to and including position
// index - 1 have already been inspected.
```

This is an example of a loop invariant, which is an assertion that

1. in some sense captures the essence of the computation performed in the loop
2. is true when control of execution enters the loop for the first time
3. is true each time that control of execution reenters the loop

In the case of the invariant as stated, we may observe that initially the invariant is satisfied vacuously because no component of the array has been tested upon initial entry into the loop. If the need exists to reenter the loop at some later time, it is because the value sought has not as yet been found.

This version also includes an `int`-valued formal reference parameter `steps`. The value of the corresponding actual parameter at the point of the call to `linsrch` must be zero. When control of execution is passed back to the caller after `linsrch` completes execution, the new value of that actual parameter will represent the number of comparisons required for `linsrch` to arrive at a conclusion. For example, if `linsrch` searches the values of the `int`-valued array storing the sequence `2,-3,4,0,2,7,3,2` and the value `7` is sought, the return to the caller will yield a value of the actual parameter corresponding to `steps` is `6`, indicating that `6` comparisons were required to find the (first) occurrence of the value `7` in the array.

In later chapters, we will study other implementations of linear search as it applies to other forms of linear containers.

3.8 Analysis of Linear Search

Suppose we have a sequence of `n` values of some fixed type `T`. We wish to determine the *average* number of comparisons (that is, processing steps) necessary to decide whether a specific value is a member of the sequence. For linear search, the value sought may be the initial member of the sequence (in which case only one comparison is necessary) or the next (in which case two comparisons are required) and so on. If we assume that examining each position of the array occurs with the same probability, the average number of comparisons involved is

$$\frac{1 + 2 + 3 + \ldots + n}{n}$$

A well-known mathematical result is

$$1 + 2 + 3 + \ldots + n = \frac{n*(n + 1)}{2}$$

for any positive integer n. This last result may be shown using finite induction and is left as an exercise. Since

$$\frac{1 + 2 + 3 + \ldots + n}{n} = \frac{n + 1}{2}$$

the average number of comparisons required to perform a linear search is (n + 1)/2.

The *worst possible case* for linear search occurs when either the value sought is the last value in the array or the value sought does not appear at all. In either case, exactly n comparisons are required. In fact, even if we apply linear search only to sequences that are already sorted in order of increasing size, then on the average n/2 comparisons are required to arrive at a conclusion. The advantage in searching an ordered sequence is that the search may terminate earlier in the case of an unsuccessful search; once the values in the sequence become larger than the value sought, we can terminate at that point and announce that the search was unsuccessful. Nevertheless, linear search is O(n) on the average.

3.9 Review of Recursive Programming

This section is devoted to a review of *recursion*, an important problem-solving tool with many key ramifications. The concepts discussed in this section will be used extensively in the remainder of the text. It also represents a self-contained exposition of recursive methods in software design and programming. As a consequence, the reader who is already familiar with the subject may effectively skip this section without loss of continuity.

There are problem-solving methods using functions that invoke themselves from their own scope. This method is called *recursive design* and *recursive programming*, and the resulting functions are called *recursive functions*. In a very natural way, stacks are employed in implementing recursion. We may illustrate this with Example 3.3.

EXAMPLE 3.3 *The Factorial Function, Recursive Form.*

In Section 3.6, we defined the *factorial function* as

$$\text{factorial(n)} = \begin{cases} 1, \text{ if } n = 0 \text{ or } n = 1 \\ n * (n - 1) * (n - 2) * \ldots * 3 * 2 * 1, \text{ if } n > 1 \end{cases}$$

for all nonnegative integers n.

A simple way to compute values of factorial is to use loops—that is, to give an *iterative* implementation of factorial as

```
int factorial(int n)
// Iterative form computing the values of the factorial
// function.
// Precondition: n >= 0.
{
 if(n == 0) return 1;
 else
 {
  int prod = 1;
  for(int index = 1; index <= n; ++index)
    // Invariant: prod = 1 * 2 * ... * (index - 1) for
    // 1 <= index <= n.
    prod *= index;
  return prod;
 } // terminates else
} // terminates factorial.
```

We may also design a recursive version of `factorial` using the observation that for all nonnegative integers `n`, we have

```
                 ┌ 1, if n = 0;
factorial(n) =   │
                 └ n * factorial(n-1), if n > 0.
```

Here we note that `factorial(0) = 1`, `factorial(1) = 1 * factorial(0) = 1`, `factorial(2) = 2 * factorial(1) = 2`, `factorial(3) = 3 * factorial(2) = 6`, and so on. C++ allows us to capture this recursive version in formal code as

```
int factorial(int n)
// Recursive form computing the values of the factorial
// function.
// Precondition: n >= 0.
{
 if(n == 0) return 1;
 else return n * factorial(n-1);
} // terminates factorial.
```

Suppose we invoke `factorial(4)`. Tracing execution of the recursive version, the initial call to `factorial` involves assigning the value `4` to the formal parameter `n`. If we now trace execution of the text of `factorial` for `n = 4`, we note that

```
4 * factorial(3)
```

must be computed. Since the value of `factorial(3)` is not yet known, control of execution pushes `4` onto an initially empty run-time stack, and then the attempt to compute the value of `factorial(3)` follows. This is accomplished by reentering the text of `factorial` with the new formal parameter value `3`. As this text executes, the value of

```
3 * factorial(2)
```

must be found. Again, since the value of `factorial(2)` is not yet known, `3` is pushed onto the run-time stack, and the text of `factorial` is reentered with `2` as the new value of the formal parameter. In a similar manner, the value of

```
2 * factorial(1)
```

must be determined. Since the value of `factorial(1)` is not yet known, `2` is pushed onto the stack, and the text of `factorial` is reentered with parameter value `1`. The same outcome occurs, leading to the execution of

```
1 * factorial(0)
```

pushing `1` onto the stack and then invoking `factorial(0)`. At this point, the run-time stack is as in Figure 3.1.

FIGURE 3.1

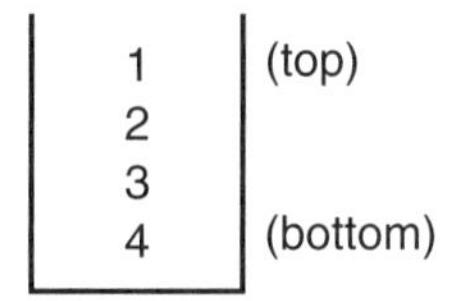

When `factorial(0)` executes, the `if` clause returns a value of 1 to the caller, which is

```
1 * factorial(0)
```

inside the text of `factorial(1)`. The value `1 * factorial(0) = 1` is returned to the text of `factorial(2)` and `1` is popped from the stack. In turn, the value `2 * factorial(1) = 2` is returned to the text of `factorial(3)` and `2` is popped from the stack. Similarly, `3` is popped from the stack, and `3 * factorial(2) = 6` is returned to the text of `factorial(4)`, the original call. This prompts the popping of `4` from the stack, rendering the stack empty, and returns the value `4 * factorial(3) = 24` to the caller.

The successive calls to `factorial` generated by executing the `else` clause when executing `factorial(4)`, `factorial(3)`, `factorial(2)`, and `factorial(1)` continue until the call to `factorial(0)` occurs. This last call provides the necessary "escape" that prevents the occurrence of an infinite sequence of calls to `factorial` and also prompts a popping of the run-time stack until it becomes empty, signaling the end of the computation.

Summarizing, it is possible to design *recursive algorithms* to solve specific programming problems if we can establish each of the following criteria:

- The original problem is decomposable into several "smaller" versions of the same problem.

- Each subsequent call to the algorithm diminishes the value(s) for which the problem is originally defined.
- There must exist an instance of the problem whose solution does not involve another call to the algorithm (the "escape").
- The escape is realized after a finite sequence of calls to the algorithm.

There are a number of problems at the end of this chapter whose solutions are obtained by recursive methods. In addition, we will study a number of problems in the sequel whose solution requires the application of recursive design and programming.

3.10 Binary Search

In this section, we consider a new search strategy called *binary search*, whose algorithm may be designed either iteratively or recursively. Binary search executes very differently from linear search and assumes a precondition that is not required in linear search: The values in the sequence are assumed to be sorted in order of increasing size, counting any possible repetitions. This strategy mimics the kind of search we would perform when we seek a student's record in some file, where these records are assumed to be sorted in lexicographic order according to surname. We first look at the "middle record." If that is the record we seek, we stop the search successfully; if not, we compare the record we have located to the one we seek. If the record we seek appears before this middle record, we resume the search for the record in the "upper half" consisting of the records of students whose surnames occur before that contained in the current middle record. However, if the record we seek appears after this middle record, we resume the search in the "lower half" consisting of the records of students whose surnames appear after that of the current middle record. Eventually, we either locate the record we seek, or there is no region left to search, indicating that the record is not in the current file.

Binary search is an example of a design strategy known as *divide and conquer* because we break down the problem of searching for a specific student record into the problem of searching for that record (if not located initially) in a file whose size is half that of the original file, and so on, until we arrive at a conclusion either by locating the record sought or by discovering that the record sought does not appear in the file.

Intuitively, this strategy is more efficient than that for linear search because we are discarding entire sections of the file each time we determine a new middle record when we do not find the record we seek. Although we use the example of seeking a student record in an alphabetized file, there is no reason this cannot be generalized to the problem of searching for a value of type T in a sorted finite sequence of values of that type.

Here is a pseudocode version of the algorithm, first using iterative methods:

// Initialize the array
int low = 0, high = ARRAY_SIZE - 1;
while(there are more components to search and the value sought has not as yet been found)
{
// Compute the current middle index.
int mid = (low + high)/2;
if(a[mid] == value) // If we find the value we seek in the mid position of the array.
return "true" to signal a successful search;
else // Value sought has not as yet been found
if(value < a[mid]) // Value we seek is smaller than that found in mid position of the // array
high = mid - 1; // Resume search in "upper half"
else // Value we seek is larger than that found in mid position of the array
low = mid + 1;
} // Terminates while-loop
// Processing resumes here only in the case of an unsuccessful search
return "false" to signal an unsuccessful search;

The formal coding of this algorithm, given as a function template, is almost a literal copy of this pseudocode. This version also counts the number of iterations needed to arrive at a conclusion as to whether the binary search was successful or not.

```
 template <class T> bool binsrch(T* a, int the_size, const T& value,
      int& steps)
// Binary search function, iterative form.
// Precondition:  the components of a are sorted
//  in order of increasing size.
// Postcondition: "true" is returned if the value sought is found
//  among the components of a; otherwise "false" is returned.
{
  int low = 0, high = the_size - 1;
  int mid;
  while(low <= high)
  {
    // Invariant: value sought has not as yet been found
         // and low <= high.
    ++steps;
```

```
      mid = (low + high)/2;
      if(a[mid] == value) // Value sought has been found:
                          // prepare to exit.
      return true;
   else if (value < a[mid])
      // Value sought is too small.  Resume search in "upper half"
      high = mid - 1;
     else
      // Value sought is too large.  Resume search in "lower half"
      low = mid + 1;
   } // Terminates while-loop.
   // At this point, search for value is unsuccessful.
   return false;
} // Terminates iterative form of binsrch.
```

The syntax for the initial call to this iterative version of `binsrch` takes the form

`binsrch(`*`array_name,array_size,value_sought,loop_iterations`*`);`

The recursive version of the algorithm makes very few changes. For example, the `while` loop in the iterative version is replaced by successive calls to `binsrch` from within its text for updated values of some of the parameters. The values of these parameters change based on the continuation of the search either in the upper half or lower half of the remaining array segment, whichever is appropriate. Its formal code is given by

```
template <class T> bool binsrch(T* a,const int first,
                        const int last, const T& value, int& steps)
// Binary search function, recursive form.
// Precondition:  the components of a are sorted
//  in order of increasing size.
// Postcondition: "true" is returned if the value sought is found
// among the components of a; otherwise "false" is returned.
{
  ++steps;
  int low = first, high = last, mid = (low + high)/2;
  if(low > high) return false; // Return unsuccessful search.
  else if(a[mid] == value) // Value sought has been found:
                          // prepare to exit.
   return true;
  else if (value < a[mid])
       // Value sought is too small.  Resume search in "upper half"
   return binsrch(a,low,mid-1,value,steps);
  else
```

```
    // Value sought is too large.  Resume search in "lower half"
  return binsrch(a,mid+1,high,value,steps);
} // Terminates binsrch, recursive version
```

Here, the syntax for the initial call to `binsrch` assumes the form

`binsrch(`*`array_name`*`,`*`array_size`*`,first,last,`*`value_sought`*`,`*`recursive_calls`*`),`

3.11 Analysis of Binary Search

Regardless of whether we choose the iterative or recursive form of binary search, the analysis of the underlying algorithm is essentially the same. Assume that the sequence involved in the search has already been sorted in order of increasing size. The algorithm begins execution by inspecting the middle value of the array where the sequence is stored and then "halving" the sequence (if necessary) until we find the value sought, if it occurs in the array.

The worst possible case occurs if we arrive at a subset of the original sequence containing exactly one value. The search thus ends successfully if the value sought matches that value and otherwise ends unsuccessfully. Thus, the worst possible case involves m "halving" operations, where

$$\frac{n}{2^{m-1}} = 1$$

and where n is the size of the original sequence.

This yields $2^{m-1} = n$ and $m - 1 = \log n$. This in turn implies that in the worst possible case, binary search is of order $O(\log n)$.

For sequences with a relatively small number of values, there is hardly any difference in the processing speed of linear and binary search. However, as the size of the sequence gets increasingly larger, it becomes apparent that binary search is more efficient than linear search.

3.12 Sorting Algorithms: Selection Sort and Insertion Sort

The specific problem we wish to solve here may be stated as

> *Given a fixed finite list of values, we wish to rearrange these values (if necessary) in order of increasing size.*

A combinatorial and straightforward way to solve this problem would be to store the list in some data structure, usually a one-dimensional array, and then apply some sort algorithm on that structure. One possibility uses *selection sort*: This begins by scanning the entire list (of size n) to find the smallest value. Once that value is found, it is swapped with the value currently occupying the initial position in the list. The processing continues by finding the smallest value in the remaining list beginning with the value immediately following the initial value, then swapping this value with that currently occupying the second position, and so on until only one unsorted value remains. This last value remains exactly where it is, and the entire list is sorted.

The following version of selection sort is in the form of a function template and uses `swap_values` from Section 1.6. This version also contains a counter that keeps track of the number of swaps required when two values in the array are not already in proper size order.

```
template<class T> void selsort(T* a,int the_size,int& swaps)
// Performs selection sort on array a.
// Postcondition: The array a will have components
// sorted in order of increasing size.
{
 int smallest; // Holds index of smallest remaining array value.
 for(int index1 = 0;index1 < the_size - 1; ++index1){
  // Invariant: components of a in positions index1 to
  // the_size - 1 remain unsorted.
  // Initialize the value of smallest as the first remaining
  // array index.
  smallest = index1;
  // Then find index of the smallest remaining array value.
  for(int index2 = index1 + 1;index2 <= the_size - 1;++index2)
   if(a[index2] < a[smallest]) smallest = index2;
  // Swap array values, if necessary.
  if(a[index1] > a[smallest])
   ++swaps;
  swap_values(a[index1],a[smallest]);
 } // Closes outer for-loop
} // Terminates selsort.
```

This function may be invoked using the syntax

`selsort(`*`array_name`*`,`*`array_size`*`,swap_counter);`

where *array_name* is an identifier naming the array whose values are to be sorted, *array_size* is the size of that array, and `swap_counter` is an `int`-valued variable with initial value zero, which counts the number of swaps required to complete the sort.

Insertion sort obtains the same result by a markedly different computation. Unlike selection sort, the complete list of n values in the array is not immediately visible to the algorithm. In fact, the values are revealed one at a time during the execution of each new cycle of an outer loop, with an inner loop performing the sorting of the values that are already visible. Thus, insertion sort proceeds as follows: (trivially) sort the first value, then the first two, then the first three, and so on, until the entire sequence is visible, at which time the resulting sort produces the desired sorting of the entire array.

Accordingly, we may describe the underlying algorithm as follows: Assume the initial segment of values in positions `0,1,2,...,q-1` are already sorted among themselves, `where 1 <= q < n`. We use position `temp` as a temporary storage location to hold the next value in the sequence until it is compared to the values contained in the current initial segment. The inner loop in the implementation code that follows is used to make room for the new value by shifting all of the values of the current initial segment larger than the new value down one position. This enables the new value to be placed in its proper location in the revised initial segment.

Similar to selection sort, the following version of insertion sort is coded as a function template and also contains a counter for the number of interchanges required to complete the sort.

```
template<class T> void insort(T* a,int the_size,int& interchanges)
// Performs insertion sort on array a.
// Postcondition: The array a will have components
// sorted in order of increasing size.
{
 for(int index1 = 1;index1 <= the_size - 1;++index1){
  // Invariant: Values in initial segment from position 0
  //  up to index1 - 1 are sorted among themselves.
  T temp = a[index1]; // Create temp to hold reference to the next
                      // value to be sorted in the new initial
                      // segment.
  int index2 = index1;
  while(index2 != 0 && a[index2 - 1] > temp){
   // Move larger values in current initial segment down one
   // position in order to make room for new value.
   ++interchanges;
   a[index2] = a[index2 - 1];
   --index2;
  } // Terminates inner while-loop.
  // Now place new value in its proper position.
  a[index2] = temp;
     } // Terminates for-loop
} // Terminates insertion sort.
```

3.13 Analysis of Selection Sort and Insertion Sort

Recall from the last section that the selection sort algorithm presupposes that the entire sequence is visible initially. Also recall that the sorting operation begins by singling out the smallest value in the entire sequence and placing it in the initial position in the array. The operation continues by determining the next smallest value and placing it in the next available position in the array, and so on, until the entire sequence is exhausted. The resulting array is the sorted version of the original sequence in order of increasing size.

We now show that selection sort is an $O(n^2)$ algorithm. To see this, we note that the implementation uses a pair of nested `for` loops. The first cycle of the outer loop finds the smallest value in the array and places that value in the initial position. This involves comparing `n-1` members of the sequence and is accomplished by executing the inner loop. The next cycle of the outer loop looks for the next smallest value to place in the second position, requiring `n-2` comparisons by the inner loop, and so on. This continues until the inner loop makes a single comparison of the remaining two (unsorted) values. Thus, the total number of comparisons required to sort the entire sequence is

$$(n-1) + (n-2) + \ldots + 3 + 2 + 1 = \frac{n*(n-1)}{2}$$

This implies that selection sort is an $O(n^2)$ algorithm.

In analyzing insertion sort, we note that at the completion of the initial cycle of the outer `for` loop, the first two values of the sequence are sorted among themselves; after completion of the next cycle, the first three values of the sequence are sorted among themselves, and so on, until the completion of the last cycle. At that point, the entire sequence is sorted. The inner `while` loop executes as many times as is necessary to adjust positions in the new initial segment to place the next new value in its proper location. Thus, in the worst case, one shift is required for the first loop cycle, two for the next, three for the next, until the last, which requires a shift of `n-1` positions to make room for the new (and last) value. Thus, in the worst possible case, the total number of shifts amounts to

$$(n-1) + (n-2) + \ldots + 3 + 2 + 1 = \frac{n*(n-1)}{2}$$

Thus, in the worst possible case, insertion sort is an $O(n^2)$ algorithm. The best possible case for insertion sort occurs when the input sequence is already sorted in order of increasing size, thus requiring no shifts at all in the resulting insertion sort. This may be illustrated by executing `insort` for the case of `n` values in reverse order for the worst possible case and for the case of `n` values that are already sorted for the best possible case.

If we were to consider all possible representations of an input sequence of n values, we would conclude that, on the average, the number of shifts required in the inner while loop would cause insertion sort to be proportional to n^2. Consequently, on the average, insertion sort is $O(n^2)$.

3.14 Quicksort and Recursive Algorithms

Selection sort and insertion sort have been shown to be $O(n^2)$ algorithms. However, there are a number of sort algorithms defined for one-dimensional arrays as well as for other data structures that are more efficient. In this section, we describe an O(n log n) sort algorithm called *quicksort,* which uses such design strategies as recursive programming and divide and conquer. Quicksort was first designed by C. A. R. Hoare (see Hoare in the References section at the end of this chapter). In fact, quicksort is O(n log n) in almost all cases. To get some idea as to the relative processing speed of selection sort and insertion sort to quicksort, we consult Table 3.1.

TABLE 3.1 **Growth Rates for Certain Selected Functions**

n	log n	n log n	n^2	n!	n^n
1	0	0	1	1	1
2	1	2	4	2	4
4	2	8	16	24	256
8	3	24	64	256	1677216
16	4	64	256	40320	*
32	5	160	1024	*	*
64	6	384	4096	*	*

The asterisks at certain positions in the table indicate that the number is too large to be listed. Using Table 3.1 for the case n = 32, we note that n^2 = 1024 and n log n = 160. From these observations, we may conclude that in sorting 32 values, selection sort and insertion sort require approximately 1024 processing steps, whereas quicksort, or for that matter, any other O(n log n) sort algorithm, requires only around 160. Thus, the efficiency of an O(n log n) sort algorithm over one that is generally $O(n^2)$ is evident. In fact, this difference becomes even more striking as the number of values to be sorted gets progressively larger.

We may illustrate how quicksort works with the analogy used earlier for selection sort and insertion sort. We begin quicksort by choosing any one of the values of the sequence at random and refer to that value as the *pivot.* We then compare the pivot to each of the other values in the sequence: Any value less than or equal to the pivot is placed to the left of the pivot in no particular order, and every value greater than the pivot is placed to its right. Once this is done, we choose a pivot from each of these smaller sequences and continue as before on each sequence. This process continues until we arrive at sequences whose size is no greater than one. When we reach this stage, the sorting of the original sequence is completed.

How do we design the quicksort algorithm? After choosing the pivot from the original sequence, we partition the sequence as we have described and then apply the same strategy to the *initial segment* (the sequence whose members are no greater than the pivot) and to the *final segment* (those greater than the pivot). We may then give a preliminary pseudocode description of quicksort as

Choose a pivot from among the sequence members;
Partition the sequence by placing individual members into either
    an initial or a final segment relative to the value of the current pivot;
Apply quicksort to the initial segment;
Apply quicksort to the final segment;

The pivot is placed in its proper position each time the segments are partitioned.

This is an example of a recursive algorithm because quicksort calls itself (twice) from its own text. As already described in Section 3.9, the key to using recursion is that each subsequent invocation of the algorithm is for a smaller collection of values, with an eventual escape from the recursion. For quicksort, the escape is realized when there is no more than one value on each side of the pivot. In this case, divide and conquer is implemented through a sequence of calls to quicksort, ending with the escape condition just described. Applying these ideas, a final refinement of the quicksort algorithm may be given as

```
void quicksort(array_type a,int first,int last)
{
int pos;
if(first < last)
{
  Partition a using the pivot by placing the pivot in position pos;
  quicksort(a,first,pos-1);
  quicksort(a,pos+1,last);
 }
}
```

The key problem that must be solved is the implementation of the partition algorithm. To accomplish this, we must be able to interchange values of the sequence. The proper position for the pivot is determined by ensuring that any value in the sequence larger than the current pivot is moved to the right of the pivot, and any value less than or equal to the pivot is moved to its left. A systematic way of doing this is to begin with the initial member of the segment and move forward until we locate a member whose value is larger than the pivot. The forward movement eventually stops at some position referenced by the current value of the index `i` (see the final coding of the `place_pivot` function that follows). The next step is to begin a backward movement in the current segment starting with the last value in that segment, until a value smaller than the current pivot is found, say at position `j`. We then interchange the values of the components referenced by `i` and `j`. Next we resume the forward movement from position `i+1`, looking for the next value greater than the pivot. Then we move backward again from position `j`, looking for the next value less than the pivot. This sequence of forward and backward movements eventually stops when we arrive at a "crossover": when the current value of `i` is greater than or equal to that of `j`. Finally, the sequence position holding the pivot interchanges with the current value in position `j`. The result of this processing is that the pivot is now in its proper position. The function `place_pivot`, described next, summarizes this processing, returning the proper position of the pivot.

```
template<class T> int place_pivot(T* a,int first,int last)
// Places pivot in its proper position, and returns that
// position. Chooses value with largest subscript as pivot.
{
 // Begin partition.
 int i,j;
 // Choose pivot as last value of array segment.
 T pivot = a[last];
 // Set i equal to the first subscript of array segment.
 i = first;
 // Set j equal to last subscript of array segment.
 j = last;
 for(;;){
  // Move forward, looking for first array component
  // not less than pivot value.
  while(a[i] < pivot)
   // Invariant: a[first],...,a[i] < pivot.
   ++i;
  // Move backward, looking for first array component
  // less than pivot value.
  while(a[j] >= pivot)
```

```
      // Invariant: a[last],...,a[j] >= pivot.
      --j;
     // Now test for "crossover":
     if(i >= j) break;
     // Swap values of a[i],a[j].
     swap_values(a[i],a[j]);
    } // Terminates for-loop.
    // Place pivot in its proper position.
    // The proper position is current value of i.
    swap_values(a[last],a[i]);
    // Return position of pivot.
    return i;
   } // Terminates code for place_pivot.
```

The next function template is the implementation of `quicksort`, using `place_pivot` as the partition algorithm. The last parameter, passed by reference, keeps track of the count on the number of recursive calls to `quicksort`.

```
template<class T> void quicksort(T* a,int first,int last,int& calls)
// Implements quicksort algorithm on array a from position first
// through position last.  The parameter calls counts the number
// of recursive calls to quicksort.
{
 ++calls;
 if(first<last){
  // Find proper positioning of pivot.
  int pivot_location = place_pivot(a,first,last);
 // Apply quicksort to initial segment.
  quicksort(a,first,pivot_location-1,calls);
  // Apply quicksort to final segment.
  quicksort(a,pivot_location+1,last,calls);
 } // Terminates if-statement.
} // Terminates quicksort.
```

Note that the *signature* of `quicksort` (the list of formal parameters defined in the function) is not identical with those of `selsort` or `insort`. In a sense, the version of the coding of `quicksort` we have described allows for more generality: By choosing the initial values of `first` and `last`, we may apply `quicksort` to a smaller segment of the entire array. If we wish to supply a version of `quicksort` with the same signature as those given for `selsort` and `insort`, all that we need to do is apply the following version, which we will call `q_sort`:

```
template<class T> void q_sort(T* a,int the_size,int& calls)
// Implements quicksort with the same signature as selsort
```

```
// and insort.
{
  // Invoke the quicksort function
  quicksort(a,0,the_size-1,calls);
}
```

Thus, the user function should define the size of the array to be sorted and also define and initialize an `int`-valued variable counting the number of recursive calls to `q_sort`, such as

```
int call_counter = 0;
```

Consequently, the call to `q_sort` will take the form

q_sort(*array_name*,*array_size*,call_counter);

EXAMPLE 3.4 *Tracing* `place_pivot`.

We illustrate the action of the `place_pivot` function on an `int`-valued array with nine components. Suppose this array is called `a`, initially appearing as in Figure 3.2a. The processing begins at component `0`, incrementing

FIGURE 3.2a

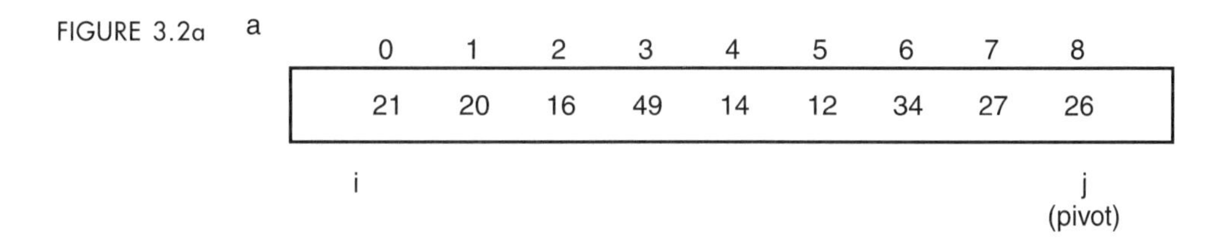

the value of `i` until the value of `a[i]` is larger than the current pivot value of `26`. This value is found at component `3`, as illustrated in Figure 3.2b. Next `j` decrements until the value of `a[j]` becomes less than that of the current pivot. This occurs at position `5`, as indicated in Figure 3.2c.

FIGURE 3.2b

FIGURE 3.2c

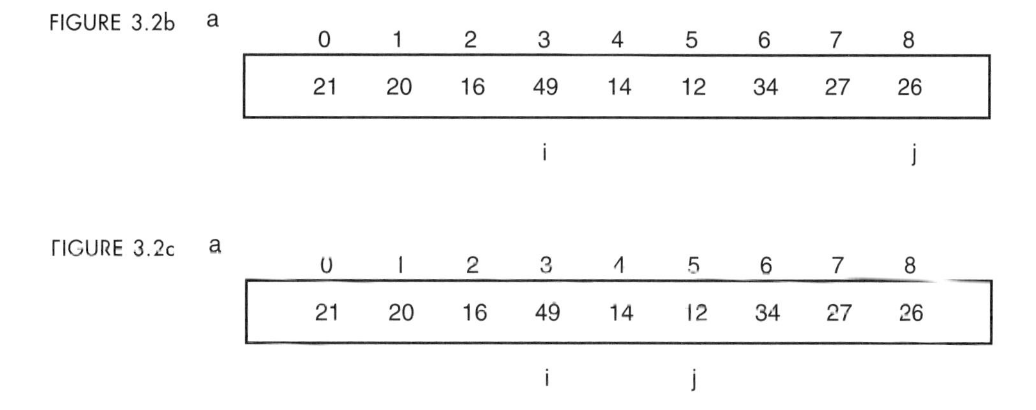

This completes a single sweep of a pair of forward and backward movements. We now test whether the values of `i` and `j` have crossed over—that is, whether `j < i`. Since this has not yet occurred, the resulting values of `a[i]` and `a[j]` are interchanged, with the result described in Figure 3.2d.

FIGURE 3.2d

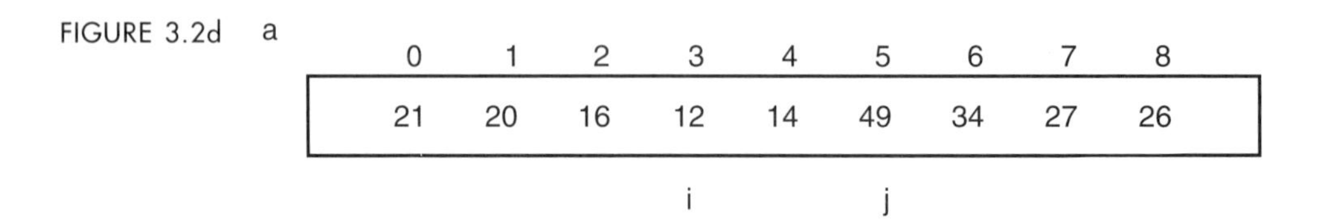

We resume with a second cycle of forward and backward movements. The forward movement resumes at position `4`, looking for the next array component with a value at least as large as the current pivot. This occurs at position `5`, as shown in Figure 3.2e. We resume the backward movement from

FIGURE 3.2e

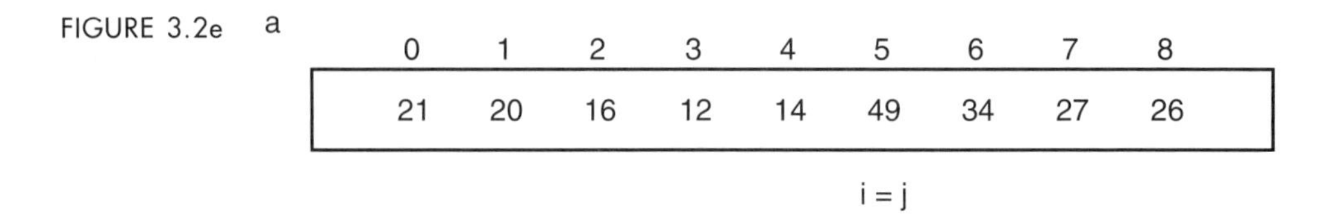

position `5` until we find the next array component with a value less than the current pivot. This occurs at position `4`, with the result described in Figure 3.2f. At this point, another cycle of a pair of forward and backward movements has completed. We again test for crossover: This has occurred, so we swap the values of `a[i]`and `pivot` to obtain the result in Figure 3.2g.

FIGURE 3.2f

FIGURE 3.2g

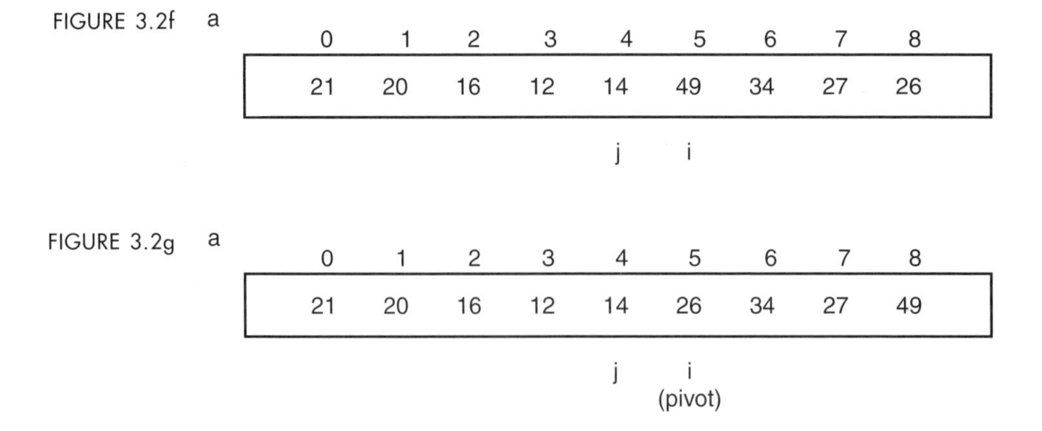

Quicksort is not stable; that is to say, there is no guarantee that equal values in the original (unsorted) sequence will retain their relative ordering in the final sorted result. On the other hand, from the very nature of their description, selection sort and insertion sort are stable.

3.15 Analysis of Quicksort

Let $C(n)$ be the number of comparisons performed by quicksort when applied to a sequence of n values. Then

$$C(0) = C(1) = 0 \qquad \textbf{3.15.1}$$

because no comparisons are necessary either for an empty sequence or for a sequence with exactly one value. In any other case, quicksort compares the pivot with every other value in the sequence once. Thus, quicksort involves exactly $n - 1$ comparisons for sequences of length $n >= 2$. Suppose the two segments created by the partition have the respective lengths k and $n - 1 - k$. Then the number of recursive calls that count the number of comparisons required to properly place the pivots involved are given by $C(k)$ and $C(n-1-k)$, and

$$C(n) = n - 1 + C(k) + C(n-1-k) \qquad \textbf{3.15.2}$$

Equation 3.15.2 is an example of a *recurrence relation* because it equates a value of C to values of C for smaller arguments. In fact, this equation shows that the value of $C(n)$ depends on the choice of k.

We first consider the worst case, occurring when the partition fails to split the sequence. This happens when the members of the sequence are close to, or actually are, in order of increasing or decreasing size. In the most extreme case, one of the segments contains all of the values, and the other segment is empty. Setting $k = 0$ in Equation 3.15.2 and using 3.15.1 produces

$$
\begin{aligned}
C(n) &= n - 1 + C(n-1) \\
C(n-1) &= n - 2 + C(n-2) \\
C(n-2) &= n - 3 + C(n-3) \\
&\;\;\vdots \\
C(3) &= 2 + C(2) \\
C(2) &= 1 + C(1) = 1
\end{aligned}
$$

Thus

$$C(n) = (n-1) + (n-2) + (n-3) + \ldots + 3 + 2 + 1 = \frac{n*(n-1)}{2}$$

which affirms that in the worst case, quicksort is $O(n^2)$.

In the average case, we observe that any value in the sequence may be chosen as the pivot. Let p denote the index of the proper position for the pivot. Setting k = p-1 in Equation 3.15.2, we get

$$C(n) = n - 1 + C(p-1) + C(n-p) \qquad \textbf{3.15.3}$$

for p = 1,2,...,n. If we add these n instances of Equation 3.15.3 and solve for C(n), we obtain

$$C(n) = n - 1 + \frac{2}{n}[C(0) + C(1) + \ldots + C(n-1)]$$

If we replace n by n-1 in the last equation, we get

$$C(n-1) = n - 2 + \frac{2}{n-1}[C(0) + C(1) + \ldots + C(n-2)]$$

Then

$$nC(n) - (n-1)C(n-1) = 2(n-1) + 2C(n-1)$$

which in turn yields

$$\frac{C(n)}{n+1} = \frac{C(n-1)}{n} + \frac{4}{n+1} - \frac{2}{n}$$

This reduces to

$$\frac{C(n)}{n+1} = \frac{4}{n+1} + 2\left[1 + \frac{1}{2} + \ldots + \frac{1}{n}\right]$$

Finally, multiplying this last equation by n+1, we get

$$C(n) = 4 + 2(n+1)\left[1 + \frac{1}{2} + \ldots + \frac{1}{n}\right]$$

where the sum 1 + 1/2 + ... + 1/n estimates the area under the graph of f(x) = 1/x from 1 to n, which is log n. This shows that, in the average case, quicksort is of order O(n log n).

3.16 Mergesort

Mergesort is another recursive sorting algorithm employing divide and conquer. The divide and conquer strategy applied in mergesort differs from that described for quicksort. In quicksort, the sequence is rearranged so that when the initial and final segments are sorted around the pivot, the entire sequence is sorted. In contrast, mergesort breaks down the original sequence into two parts, each of which is sorted and then combined into a single sorted sequence. Thus, quicksort first calls for a decomposition of the original sequence and then sorts each part. Instead, mergesort first sorts each segment and then merges the results into a single sorted entity. In addition, mergesort is more "even-tempered" than quicksort and will be shown to be of order `O(n log n)` for all situations, although it is slightly less efficient in the same average cases than quicksort.

Here is a preliminary version of the mergesort algorithm:

if(first < last)
{
Find index of the midpoint mid of the segment;
Apply mergesort to the segment referenced from first to mid;
Apply mergesort to the segment referenced from mid+1 to last;
Merge the sorted segments;
}

EXAMPLE 3.5 *Tracing Mergesort.*
We illustrate mergesort with the same `int`-valued array used in Example 3.4. Thus, we begin with

`a`

0	1	2	3	4	5	6	7	8
21	20	16	49	14	12	34	27	26

This is broken up into the two halves described in Figures 3.3a1 and 3.3a2.

FIGURE 3.3a1

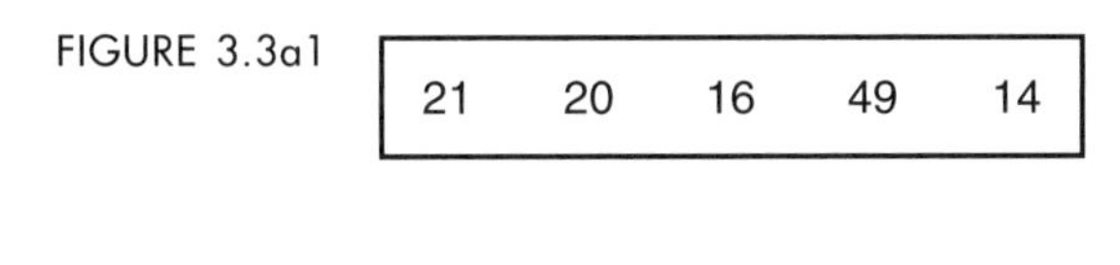

FIGURE 3.3a2

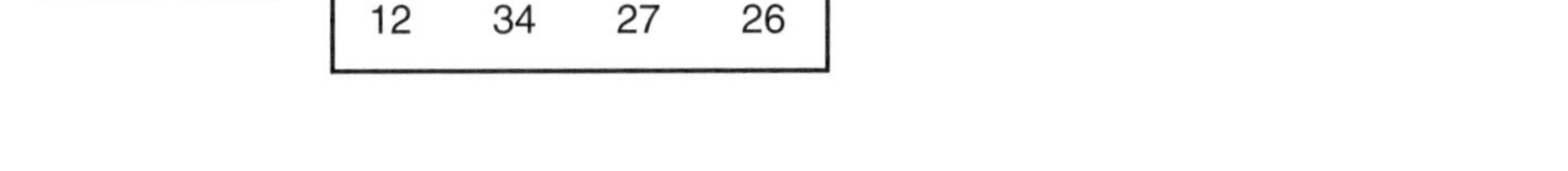

The first half illustrated in Figure 3.3a1 is further decomposed as in Figure 3.3b. In turn, each of these last two segments described in Figure 3.3b

FIGURE 3.3b

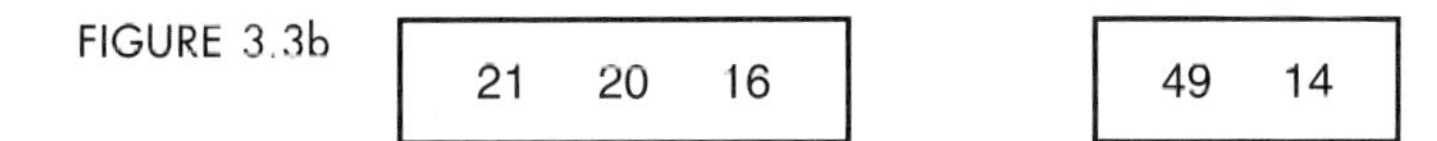

decomposes further as

A further decomposition of these two-member array segments produces

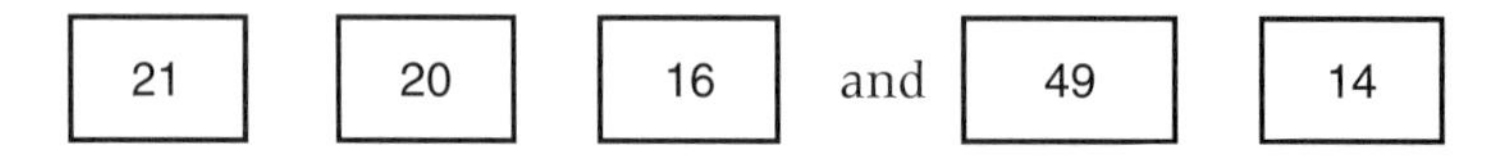

The following sequence of sorts and merges are performed in the order as given:

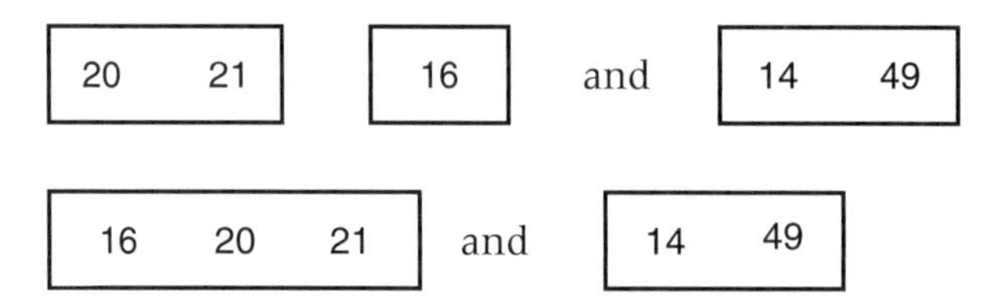

and then

FIGURE 3.3c1

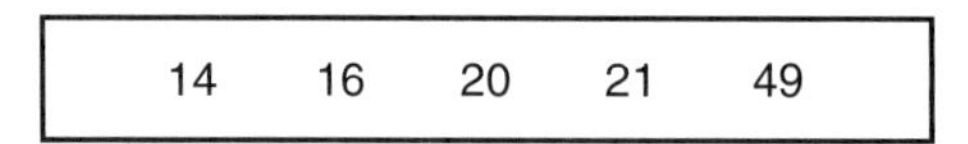

Similarly, Figure 3.3a2 is decomposed and merged into Figure 3.3c2. Finally, the sorted halves described in Figures 3.3c1 and 3.3c2 are sorted and merged into Figure 3.3d.

FIGURE 3.3c2

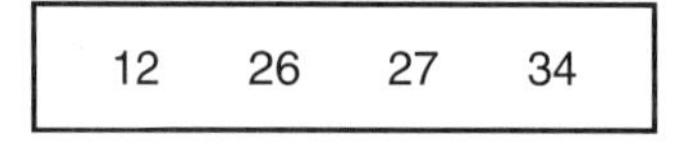

FIGURE 3.3d

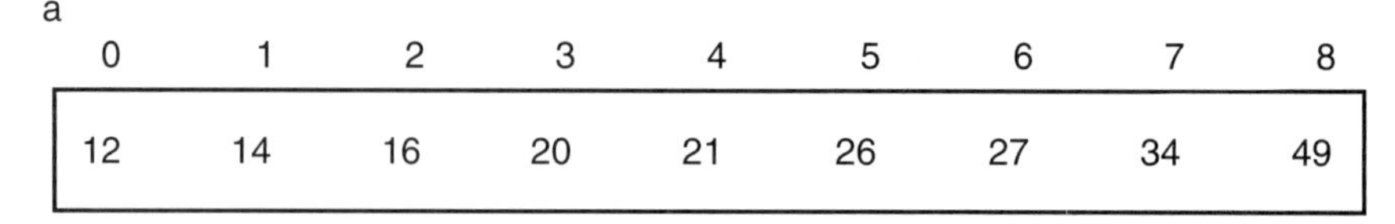

How do we implement the merge operation? We define a second array called `temp` to hold the merged halves at each stage of the decomposition. According to the mode of application of recursion in this case, sorting does not begin until after the halving process produces single-member sequences. Merging and sorting begin with these sequences until the process is applied to all of the members of `temp`, completing the sorting phase of the algorithm. After this completes, the members of `temp` are copied back into the original array, terminating execution.

The merging operation is implemented as a `void` function template called `merge` and will require five parameters: a reference to the original array `a`, a reference to `temp`, `first` = index of the initial value of the current array segment, `last` = index of the final value of the current array segment, and `mid` = index of the midpoint value of the current array segment. Accordingly, `merge` is coded as

```
template<class T> void merge(T* a,T* temp,int first,int mid,int last)
// Function which merges two sorted array segments
// into a single sorted array segment.
{
  // Precondition: a[first],...,a[mid] and
   // a[mid+1],...,a[last] are already sorted.
  int first1 = first; // Beginning index of first array segment.
  int last1 = mid; // Last index of the first array segment.
  int first2 = mid+1; // Beginning index of the second array segment.
  int last2 = last; // Last index of the second array segment.
  int index = first1; // Next usable component of temp array.

  // While both segments are not empty, copy the smaller
  // value into temp.
  while(first1 <= last1 && first2 <= last2)
  // Invariant: temp[first1],...,temp[index-1] is sorted,
   // and temp[first2],...,temp[index-1] is sorted.
  {
   if(a[first1] < a[first2])
    temp[index] = a[first1++];
   else
    temp[index] = a[first2++];
   ++index;
  }  // Terminates while-loop.

  // At this point, at least one of the array segments
  // has been copied completely into temp.
  // Fill in the empty components of the leftover segment.

  // Fill in the remaining components of the first segment
  // if necessary.
  while(first1 <= last1)
  // Invariant: temp[first1],...,temp[index-1] is already sorted.
  {
```

```
    temp[index] = a[first1++];
    ++index;
  }
  // Fill in the remaining components of the second segment
  // if necessary.
  while(first2 <= last2)
  // Invariant:  temp[first2],...,temp[index-1] is already sorted.
  {
    temp[index] = a[first2++];
    ++index;
  }

  // Copy the current contents of temp back into a.
  for(index = first;index <= last;++index)
    a[index] = temp[index];

} // Terminates merge function.
```

The recursive code for mergesort follows. It contains an additional `int`-valued reference parameter `count`, which keeps track of the number of calls to the `mergesort` function.

```
template<class T> void mergesort(T* a,T* temp,int first,int last,
                                          int& count)
// Sorts an array a of values of type T using mergesort.
// Last parameter, passed by reference, counts the number
// of recursive calls to mergesort.
// Postcondition: a[first],...,a[last] is sorted in order
//   of increasing size.
{
  int mid; // Middle index.
  if(first < last)
  {
    ++count;
    // Determine the middle index of the current array segment.
    mid = (first + last)/2;
    // Sort first segment.
    mergesort(a,temp,first,mid,count);
    // Sort second segment.
    mergesort(a,temp,mid+1,last,count);
    // Merge the two sorted segments.
    merge(a,temp,first,mid,last);
  } // Terminates if-clause.
} // Terminates mergesort.
```

We may also design a version of mergesort called `m_sort`, containing only four parameters: a reference to the original array and to the temporary array, along with an `int`-valued parameter holding the common size of the original and temporary arrays, and an `int`-valued reference parameter described earlier. Its implementation is

```
template<class T> void m_sort(T* a,T* temp,int the_size,int& count)
// Code for mergesort with a signature similar to those given for
// q_sort,selsort, and insort.  The only difference is that m_sort
// contains an additional array parameter for the temporary array.
{
  mergesort(a,temp,0,the_size-1,count);
}
```

The syntax of the original call to `m_sort` may then be given by

`m_sort(`*`array_name`*`,`*`temporary_array_name`*`,`*`array_size`*`,call_counter);`

where *`array_size`* is the common size of the original array and temporary array named as *`array_name`* and *`temporary_array_name`*, respectively.

3.17 Analysis of Mergesort

Each call to `merge` for the segments `a[first],...,a[mid]` and `a[mid+1],...,a[last]` involves a total of `k = last - first + 1` members and requires a maximum of `k-1` comparisons.

For example, suppose we trace the merging of the segments

16	20	21

from Example 3.5, with `k = 5`. The following comparisons were made:

1. Since `16 > 14`, copy `14` from `a[mid+1],...,a[last]` into `temp[0]`.
2. Since `16 < 49`, copy `16` from `a[first],...,a[mid]` into `temp[1]`.
3. Since `20 < 49`, copy `20` from `a[first],...,a[mid]` into `temp[2]`.
4. Since `21 < 49`, copy `21` from `a[first],...,a[mid]` into `temp[3]`.
   At this point, `a[first],...,a[mid]` is exhausted. Copy the remaining value `a[last] = 49` into `temp[4]`.

This results in

`temp`

0	1	2	3	4
14	16	20	21	49

and required `4` comparisons.

Each call to `mergesort` involves two further calls to itself and halves the current segment. The next set of recursive calls halve each of these segments to form four segments of the original sequence, and so on, until there remain nothing but segments consisting of single values. If `n` is the size of the original segment, there are `(int)(1 + log n)` calls to `mergesort`.

The first call to `mergesort` calls `merge` once, and `merge` merges all of the members of the sequence, using a maximum of `n - 1` comparisons. This call results in two subsequent calls to `mergesort` and, hence, two more calls to `merge`, each of which involves `(n/2) - 1` comparisons. If we generalize, then at any level `j` of the recursion, there are 2^j calls to `merge`, each of which requires $(n/2^j) - 1$ comparisons. Consequently, there are a total of $n - 2^j$ comparisons. Since there are `(int)(1 + log n)` calls to `mergesort`, we conclude that mergesort is of order `O(n log n)` in any case.

Mergesort is judged to be slightly slower than quicksort because it involves the additional overhead of copying the sorted values into `temp`, and then finally copying the completed `temp` back into `a`. This could involve substantial extra processing time for large sequences.

3.18 Chapter Summary

An *algorithm* is a formal description of the steps involved in the solution of a specific programming problem. The initial version of the algorithm is usually stated in informal terms, containing a general yet accurate description of the steps involved in solving the problem in pseudocode. After a sequence of successive refinements, the final result is very close to the implementation in formal code.

In any object-oriented design of a solution, we must give serious attention to each of the following factors:

1. the classes and objects needed to contribute to the solution
2. the specific behavior of the classes and objects chosen in (1) used for the solution
3. in case several classes are used, the contribution of each and the relationship between these in arriving at the final solution
4. the interface between these classes and users

Important considerations in the ultimate choice of the solution are the algorithm's efficiency and correctness. In earlier chapters, we discussed the correctness of a proposed solution either in formal or informal terms. Informal methods for testing correctness involve a clearly stated set of pre- and postconditions that accompany member functions of some class or the formal coding of some algorithm. An example of formal tests for correctness involve loop invariants, applying such mathematical results as the Principle of Finite Induction.

A key criterion used in choosing the most appropriate version of an algorithm is its efficiency. A metric used for measuring the relative efficiency of algorithms is big-O. More precisely, we use `O(f(n))`, where `f(n)` gives a quantitative estimate of the number of computations involved in completing execution of the algorithm. When `O(f(n))` produces the smallest values, the underlying algorithm is then judged to be in its most efficient form. However, correctness should never be sacrificed for the sake of some streamlined and more efficient alternative. We must assume that each candidate has been thoroughly tested for correctness and efficiency before it is incorporated as part of the solution of the original problem.

This chapter is primarily devoted to solving problems in searching and sorting as these apply to arrays. In later chapters, we will revisit these as they apply to other containers for data, such as those predefined in the class templates available in the Standard Template Library. In each case, we may consider these solutions as *reusable software tools,* which are stored permanently and invoked when necessary. The quality of reusability is enhanced by the flexibility of application to sequences of values from any well-defined data type `T` because such solutions are presented in the form of function and class templates.

We also studied the use of *recursive algorithms* and their implementation. These were used in binary search, as well as in quicksort and mergesort, and are important and concise applications of the problem-solving paradigm known as *divide and conquer*. However, using recursive methods usually involves the additional overhead of extra internal bookkeeping because the processor must keep track of the current value assigned to each parameter in the current call to the recursive function. This is particularly critical when the original call to the function requires a considerable number of subsequent recursive calls. In defense of this methodology, the coding of a recursive algorithm is usually easily legible and in many cases represents the only viable alternative. In summary, the use of recursive functions generally enhances the efficiency of the entire design of the solution. This became particularly evident when we analyzed quicksort and mergesort and compared them to selection sort and insertion sort.

EXERCISES

1. Write a driver for `linsrch`.

2. Using the Principle of Finite Induction, show: For any positive integer `n`,

$$1 + 2 + 3 + \ldots + n = \frac{n*(n+1)}{2}$$

3. Design a version of linear search that counts all of the occurrences of the value sought in an array and returns the number of such occurrences.
4. Write a version of binary search that returns an `int` value: the array index where an instance of the value sought is found. Otherwise, return the value `-1` (for `UNSUCCESSFUL_SEARCH`), as in the case of `linsrch`.
5. Design a version of binary search in which we also pass a lower and upper index of the array segment in which the search is to be conducted.
6. Design a version of selection sort in which, instead of passing the array size, we pass two `int`-valued parameters, indexing the beginning and the end, respectively, of the array segment to be sorted.
7. Redo Problem 6 using insertion sort.
8. Apply `insort` to the sequence of integers

   ```
   10 9 8 7 6 5 4 3 2 1
   ```

   and conclude that exactly `45 = 10*9/2` interchanges are necessary to complete the sort. Similarly, apply `insort` to the sequence

   ```
   1 2 3 4 5 6 7 8 9 10
   ```

   and conclude that `0` interchanges are necessary.
9. Test the code of each of `selsort, insort, q_sort,` and `m_sort` on the same 10-component `int`-valued, then `char`-valued, then `double`-valued array. Compare the number of swaps for `selsort` to complete the sort with the number of interchanges needed for `insort`, with the number of recursive calls to each of `q_sort` and `m_sort`.
10. Rewrite `place_pivot` where the pivot value chosen is the *initial value* of each array segment.
11. Is mergesort an example of a stable sort algorithm? Give reasons to support your answer.
12. Design an algorithm that searches a finite sequence of values of type `T` for the maximum value contained in that sequence. Then design an algorithm that searches the same sequence and retrieves both the maximum and minimum value of that sequence.
13. Design and implement an algorithm that conducts a linear search on a finite sequence of values of type `T` whose values are already sorted in order of increasing size. Discuss the benefits of searching a sequence with this property over a random sequence of values.
14. Rewrite the algorithms of selection sort and insertion sort to conduct the sort on the "high end" of the sequence; that is, the new version of each should contain a loop invariant

   ```
   // Invariant:  the values in the array from position p
   //  to position last - 1 are sorted among themselves.
   ```

15. Write code for a recursive version of the *power function* defined for two `int`-valued parameters `u,v`, with `u` $\neq$ `0` and `v >= 0`, as `power(u,v)`, as

```
               ┌ 1, if v = 0
power(u,v) =   │
               └ u * power(u,v-1), if v > 0
```

Thus, for any such u, v, power(u,v) = u^v.

16. The *Ackermann function* is defined as ACK(m,n) for any two nonnegative integers m,n according to the equations

```
(i)   ACK(0,n) = n + 1
(ii)  ACK(m,0) = ACK(m-1,1), if m > 0
(iii) ACK(m,n) = ACK(m-1,ACK(m,n-1)), if m > 0 and n > 0.
```

a. Compute ACK(0,4), ACK(2,0), ACK(1,2), and ACK(2,2) by hand.

b. Write code for a recursive version computing the values of ACK. Include a counter that keeps track of the number of recursive calls to ACK.

17. The *Fibonacci function* FIB is defined for all positive integers n by

```
         ┌ 1, if n = 1,2
FIB(n) = │
         └ FIB(n-1) + FIB(n-2), if n > 2.
```

a. Compute the values of FIB(1), FIB(2), FIB(3), FIB(4), and FIB(5) by hand.

b. Design an algorithm and write code for a recursive function computing the values of FIB. Also include a counter int-valued parameter that keeps track of the number of recursive calls to FIB.

18. Show that the following alternative also computes the values of the Fibonacci function:

```
int fast_fib(int a, int b, int n)
{
   if(n == 0) return b;
   else if(n == 1) return a;
   else return fast_fib(a+b,a,n-1);
}
```

What should be the values of a and b in the caller? Use a counter and compare the number of recursive calls to fast_fib to those for the version from (b) of the previous problem.

19. Use the Principle of Finite Induction to prove each of the following, valid for any positive integer n:

a. $1^2 + 2^2 + 3^2 + \ldots + n^2 = n*(n+1)*(2n+1)/6$

b. $1 + 3 + 5 + \ldots + (2n - 1) = n^2$

c. $1 + 1/2 + 1/2^2 + \ldots + 1/2^n = 2 * [1 - 1/2^{n+1}]$

d. $1/1*2 + 1/2*3 + \ldots + 1/n*(n+1) = n/(n+1)$

20. Use the Principle of Finite Induction to show that

$2^n <= n^n$ for all $n > 1$

21. Design and implement a recursive function called `write_backwards` defined for character strings `str` of any finite length `str_length` by `write_backwards(str,str_length)` = characters of `str` written backwards. For example, if `str = "Hello, there!"` then

`write_backwards(str,str_length) = "!ereht ,olleH".`

22. Use the code for `write_backwards` from Problem 21 to design and implement a `bool`-valued function called `palin_test`, having any character string as its only argument. The role of `palin_test` is to determine whether the current argument is a *palindrome,* namely, a string that is the same whether read from left to right or from right to left.

23. a. Show that `place_pivot` may be rewritten as

```
template <class T> int place_pivot(T* arr,int first,int last)
// Precondition: Pivot is chosen as arr[first].
// Postcondition: Returns the subscript of the proper location
// of the pivot in arr, with initial segment arr[first],..., arr[i-1],
// and final segment arr[i+1],...,arr[last].
{
 T pivot = arr[first];
 int i = first;
 for(int index1 = first + 1;index1 <= last;++index1)
 // Invariant: arr[first+1],...,arr[i] < pivot and
 // arr[i+1],...,arr[index1+1] >= pivot.
 {
  if(arr[index1] < pivot)
  {
   ++i;
   swap_values(arr[index1],arr[i]);
  } // terminates if-clause
 } // terminates for-loop
 // place pivot in its proper location.
 // Its proper location is the current value of i.
 swap_values(arr[first],arr[i]);
 // Return pivot location.
 return i;
} // terminates text of place_pivot
```

b. Trace the execution of this version on the input sequence `21 20 16 49 14 12 34 27 26.`

PROGRAMMING PROJECTS

1. Let `a,b` be positive integers, with `a > b`. Define `gcd(a,b)` = *greatest common divisor* of `a,b` = largest positive integer dividing both `a,b`. Show each of the following:

a. if b is not a divisor of a, then gcd(a,b) = gcd(b,a%b)
b. using (a), show

```
           ┌ b, if a%b = 0
gcd(a,b) = │
           └ gcd(b,a%b), if otherwise
```

Then use this recursive version of gcd(a,b) to design code computing gcd.

c. There is an algorithm for finding gcd(a,b) for any positive a,b called the *Euclidean algorithm*: Assuming a >= b, divide a by b, obtaining

```
a = b*q + r
```

If r = 0, then b = gcd(a,b); otherwise, continue. It then follows that gcd(a,b) = gcd(b,r). Now divide b by r to obtain

$b = r*q_1 + r_1$

Note also that $r_1 < r$. Now divide r by r_1, and so on, repeating this process until $r_{n+1} = 0$ for some n. This must certainly occur because the remainders are decreasing. Then r_n = gcd(a,b). Using a loop and the Euclidean algorithm, write code for an iterative version of an implementation for gcd.

d. Maintain counters in each of the iterative and recursive versions of gcd(a,b), and design drivers for each, comparing the count of loop cycles in the iterative version to the number of function calls for the recursive version.

2. The following represents an "improvement" on insertion sort, called *Shell sort* (see the References). The algorithm sorts separate components of the original array using components that are spaced k units apart from one another for a finite sequence of diminishing values of k. The value of k is called an *increment*. After k array segments are sorted (using insertion sort), a new and smaller value of k is chosen, and the array is partitioned once again into a new set of segments. Each of the larger segments is sorted, and the process continues with a yet smaller value of k, culminating in the last phase where k = 1, at which point the resulting array is completely sorted. Initially, a finite sequence of diminishing increments is input, with the last value 1.

For example, if the original int-valued array arr contains the values, in sequence, given by

```
8  15  24  6  -3  12  0  5
```

and the sequence of increments is

```
5  3  1
```

then the first iteration (k = 5) produces the sorted segments

```
arr[0], arr[5]
arr[1], arr[6]
```

```
arr[2], arr[7]
arr[3]
arr[4]
```

The second iteration `(k = 3)` produces the sorting of

```
arr[0], arr[3], arr[6]
arr[1], arr[4], arr[7]
arr[2], arr[5]
```

The final iteration `(k = 1)` produces the sorting of the entire array.

a. Show that Shell sort may be implemented by

```
template<class T> void shellsort(T* arr,int the_size,int* increments,
  int increments_size)
// Performs Shell sort on arr.
// "increments" is an int_valued array containing the diminishing
// increments of the sort.
{
 for(int index = 0, index <= increments_size-1;++index){
 // Invariant: increments[index] is the size of the increment.
  int inc_size = increments[index];
  for(int i = inc_size; i <= the_size-1;i++){
  // Insert arr[i] in its proper position.
  int value = arr[i];
  for(int i2 = i - inc_size;i2 >= 0 && value <arr[i2];
         i2 -= inc_size)
    arr[i2 + inc_size] = arr[i2];
   arr[i2+inc_size] = value;
   }
  }
}
```

by tracing this code by hand on the array component of `arr` given earlier and then by writing a driver for this function.

b. Compare the number of processing steps involved between Shell sort and insertion sort, using loop counters for each.

REFERENCES

Hoare, C. A. R., "Quicksort," *Computer Journal,* 5, 1962, pp. 10–12.

Knuth, Donald E., *The Art of Computer Programming, Volume 3: Sorting and Searching* (Reading, MA: Addison-Wesley, 1973).

Shell, D. L., "A High Speed Sorting Procedure," *Communications of the ACM,* 2(7), July 1959, pp. 30–32.

CHAPTER 4

Hashing: Prelude to the Standard Template Library

CHAPTER OBJECTIVES

- To define the concept of hashing.
- To justify hashing as an important tool in contemporary data processing.
- To examine various forms of hashing and some of the drawbacks inherent in each form.
- To present a specific design of a hashing method using objects and classes.
- To introduce the idea of namespaces and how they are used to establish a bridge to the facilities of the Standard Template Library.

4.1 Introduction

In Chapter Three, we studied search algorithms for data stored in one-dimensional arrays. In each case, the search was conducted using a *key,* which either was the value sought or was part of an aggregate containing other related values, such as the data usually given in student or employee records. This chapter is devoted to the study of efficient methods of data storage and retrieval using the idea of hashing and its implementation in various forms.

In addition, we will begin a discussion of some of the facilities available in the Standard Template Library (STL) and how these may be used to implement some of the hash strategies. In so doing, we may view this chapter, in part, as an introduction to the predefined structures and algorithms available to users of the Standard Library. Finally, we introduce the concept of *namespaces* and study their particular importance in the context of linking the facilities of the Standard Library to user programs.

4.2 Hashing as an Efficient Method of Data Storage and Retrieval

Let us consider the problem of storing and retrieving employee records maintained in a one-dimensional array. Suppose the employee's social security number is used both as a search key and as an array subscript. Since the values of a social security number may be viewed as integers ranging from a lowest possible value of `0` (formally represented by `000000000`) and a highest value of `999999999`, the array would have to contain as many components as there are distinct possible social security numbers—10^9 in all!

More precisely, suppose we design employee records in C++ using

```
struct employee_record
{
 char[30] surname;
 char[20] name;
 char mi;  // Middle initial.
 char[6] dob; // Date of birth, using ddmmyy format
      .
      .
      .
 // Other pertinent employee information.
      .
      .
      .
}; // Terminates definition of employee-record.
```
[1]

We may then define the array of employee records (assuming a suitable integer type large enough to handle the range `0. . . 999999999`)[2] as

```
employee_record employees[1000000000];
```

See Figure 4.1.

Although there is no difficulty in finding any specific employee record, there is clearly a serious problem in maintaining an array of this size. Allocating storage for this array is certainly inefficient because only a very small number of components will contain pertinent employee information. For example, suppose the firm employs 300 workers. Then all but 300 components of the array will be void, yet this excessive storage will still be allocated. Arrays of this kind are generally characterized as *sparse.*

[1] In similar later discussions when the STL is available, these character strings will be defined using the predefined `string` type.

[2] If necessary, we may define a "big integer" type such as that discussed in De Lillo. See the References at the end of this chapter.

FIGURE 4.1

employees

	surname	name	mi	dob	
[000000000]		...	...	...	....
.	...	...	...	...	....
.	.	.	.	.	.
[086364036]	Procach	Rosalie	A	020140	....
.	.	.	.	.	.
[099364150]	Boccia	Horace	J	140739	....
.	.	.	.	.	.
[999999999]	...	...	...	...	....

To provide a more efficient means of storing and retrieving such data, we first define the idea of an *address calculator.* This is a function whose argument is a key and whose value is an address in a data structure containing the actual data. If the data structure is an array, the address calculator uses the array indices as access values. The process of converting the search key into an access value is called *hashing,* and the function performing the conversion is called a *hash function.* The data structure holding the actual data is generally called the *hash table.*

How does hashing influence the efficiency of data retrieval? In Chapter Three, we described two strategies for searching and retrieving data: linear (sequential) search and binary search. We also showed that for an array of size `n`, linear search is of order `O(n)` and binary search is of order `O(log n)`. For sufficiently large `n`, we observed that binary search is substantially more time-efficient than linear search (see Table 3.1). In each case, the efficiency of the search strategy depends on `n`, the size of the underlying hash table.

Is it possible to improve on this? Specifically, does hashing establish a level of efficiency better than `O(log n)`? If we reexamine the example of maintaining employee records, hashing on the key of employee social security number yields the exact location (using array indices) of the data we seek, provided the individual with that social security number is an employee of the firm. In effect, the search for employee data using his or her social security number as the search key is of order `O(1)`. That is, it is a search strategy that completes execution in *constant time,* no matter where the data we seek appear in the array. The only drawback so far is that the array serving as the hash table is too large and sparse if the hash function simply produces an array subscript of the actual social security number.

Can we effect a compromise? That is, can we diminish the size of the hash table to make it more manageable and at the same time maintain a level of efficiency of `O(1)`? As an example, we continue with the problem of maintaining employee records using social security number as the key. Suppose we define the following hash function `H`:

`H(`*`social security number`*`) = `*`sum of its digits`*

Then the hash table becomes an array of employee records with subscripts ranging from `0 = H(000000000)` to `81 = H(999999999)`. In particular, `H(086364036) = 36` and `H(099364150) = 37`, and referring to Figure 4.2, all of the pertinent information about `Rosalie A. Procach` appears in the hash table at position `36`, and that of `Horace J. Boccia` is in position `37`.

FIGURE 4.2

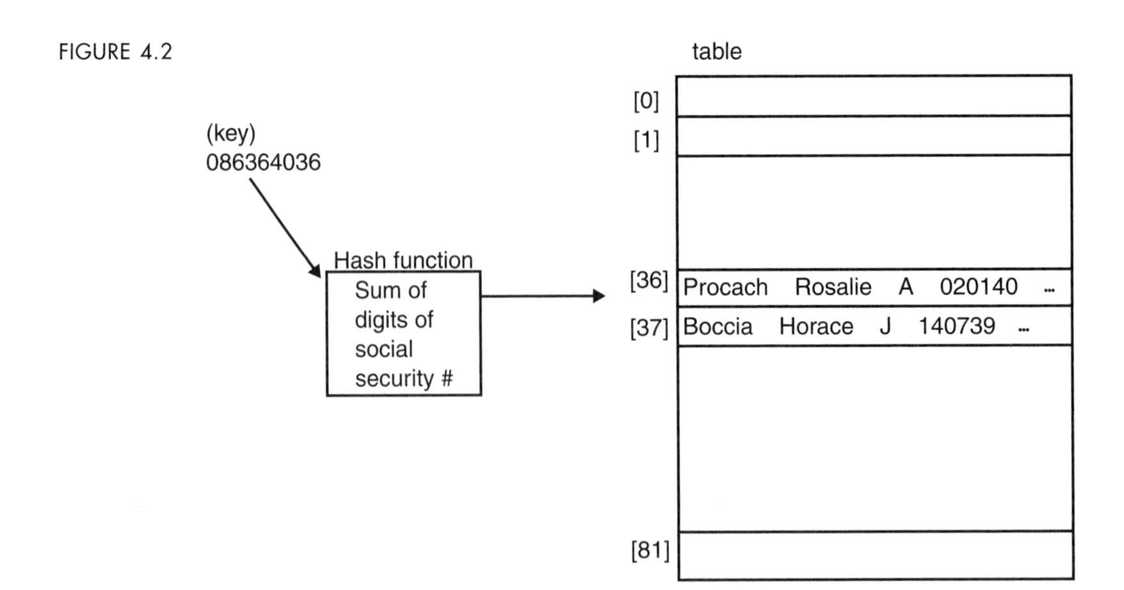

A number of potential problems arise with many hashing operations. To illustrate one using the hash function just described, suppose another employee has the social security number `066606661`. Then `H(066606661) = 37`, a position already occupied by `Horace J. Boccia`. This results in a *hash collision* because there are at least two candidates vying for the same location in the hash table. A hash function producing no collisions is called *perfect*. An example of a perfect hash function is

```
H(social security number) = social security number, omitting leading
                            zeros.
```

This uses the observation that no two individuals share the same social security number. In this case, the price of "perfection" is too costly for the reasons that have been given.

We must therefore face the reality of choosing hash functions that are practical, efficient, and appropriate for our needs. Several factors should influence our decision in choosing a suitable hash function:

1. It should produce values lying in the subscript range of the resulting hash table.
2. It should be easily and efficiently computable.
3. It should avoid as many hash collisions as possible.

Given the reality that any choice of a reasonable hash function is prone to producing a certain number of hash collisions, we must decide on a course to follow when a collision occurs.

4.3 Choosing an Appropriate Hash Function

The efficient storage and easy and timely retrieval of large volumes of data are very important considerations in the design of a large segment of commercial software. Inevitably, the design requires the use of hash functions. In this section, we explore some of the more commonly used hash functions and the course to follow in the event of a hash collision.

We have stated earlier that one of the criteria to consider in choosing a hash function is its *ease of computation*. We should anticipate applying the hash function very frequently because the associated software will generally involve a large number of searches in the hash table either for data currently stored there or for locations that are currently unoccupied so as to store newly acquired data. Consequently, computing values of the hash function should be done as simply and as efficiently as possible.

Another factor to consider is the ability of the hash function to produce values that are *widely distributed throughout its complete range*. Thus, the hash function should avoid a frequent repetition of a relatively small number of specific values and neglect the rest of the possible values. Choosing a hash function with this property will have the favorable side effect of avoiding the occurrence of a large number of possible hash collisions. For example, suppose we choose a hash function `H` for the employee example which maps a social security number into the nonnegative integer obtained by extracting its first three digits, omitting any leading zeros.[3] Then `H(099364150) = 99` and `H(237498710) = 237`, and if we assume that the hash table is in the form of an array, then it will have `1000` components ranging from `0` to `999`. However, this hash function has the undesirable side effect of producing an unequal distribution of hash values because relatively few individuals have social security numbers whose first three digits are close to `0` or `1000`. This results in a *clustering* of values in a small segment of the hash table.

Any one of a number of different approaches may be applied in choosing an appropriate hash function. Many of these choices are treated in greater detail in Knuth. (See the References at the end of this chapter.)

Method 1: The Middle Square Technique

This method takes the square of the key and then extracts a small number of consecutive digits (usually three) from the middle digits of the result. For example, using three consecutive digits on the social security numbers, the possible hash results range from `0 = 000` through `999`. As an illustration, $(099364150)^2 = 9873234305222500$, omitting any leading zeros. If we then extract the seventh through the ninth digits, the hash value is `430`. Experimental evidence shows that a fairly even distribution of values throughout the complete range of subscripts of the hash table occurs when this technique is applied. The downside is that the process of squaring a key as large as a social security number, even when omitting any leading zeros, and then dividing the result by an appropriate power of 10 to extract the desired digits requires integer values generally beyond the range supported by any of the usual predefined integer types. A "big integer" type would have to be designed to accommodate the values produced by this computation (see De Lillo in References, for example).

Method 2: Random Number Generators

This method defines the hash function as a *random number generator* whose values are restricted to the subscript range of the hash table. Such random number generators usually initiate by passing an `int`-valued parameter (the *seed*) and then computing a finite sequence of random integers lying in the subscript range of the hash table. In C++, we may define the seed as the initial value of some `static` integer-valued variable. The number of

[3] If the social security number begins with at least three zeros, this number hashes to zero.

random values to be generated is then set by the programmer. The rationale for generating more than one random number is to provide several alternative hash table subscripts in the event of a hash collision. In fact, using such a random number generator in the context of hashing generally involves presenting the value of the search key as the initial seed.

Method 3: Folding

This method uses the digits of the key in some arithmetical combination, with a result falling in the numerical range of the hash table subscripts. Method 1, the middle square technique, is a special case of folding. In fact, another form of folding using social security numbers was also discussed earlier: Take the sum of the digits.

Another version is called *shift folding,* in which the social security number is broken down into smaller groups and then added. For instance, `099364150` is first decomposed as `99`, `364`, `150` (omitting any leading zeros) and then added as `99 + 364 + 150 = 613`. If the keys are not big integers, such as character strings, a conversion of each `char` value in the string, in the order presented, into its equivalent ASCII code number would precede any folding operation. As an example of this, suppose the key is the character string `"money"`. The equivalent ASCII code for this string would be `109111110101121`, which is then folded as `109 + 111 + 110 + 101 + 121 = 552`.

Projection is another form of folding in which certain digits of the key are removed before the key is mapped to a subscript of the hash table. To illustrate this, suppose serial numbers of products handled by a firm are to be hashed, where these numbers may begin or end with a certain fixed group of digits (or characters). For example, suppose the serial numbers of all items stored in a warehouse are nine-digit integers beginning with `011`, with each of the remaining six digits ranging over the integers from `0` to `9` inclusive. An efficient projection map would ignore the first three digits and hash the remaining six digits by some specific method. One such possibility adds the remaining six digits, as in `H(011236809) = 28` and `H(011364150) = 19`. The hash values would then lie in the range from `0` to `54` inclusive. However, not all of these values are equally likely.

Method 4: Division with Remainder

In this case, the hash value is the remainder obtained when the key is divided by some suitably chosen positive integer `MAX_SIZE`, as in

`H(`*`key`*`) = `*`key`*` %MAX_SIZE`

The hash values lie in the range from `0` through `MAX_SIZE - 1`. It is not difficult to code this hash function, and if `MAX_SIZE` is chosen to be a suitable prime number, the number of possible hash collisions is minimized. For example, suppose `MAX_SIZE = 2011`, and we use the example of folding the last six digits of the serial numbers described earlier. Then `H(011236809) = 1522` because `236809 = 2011 * 17 + 1522`, and `H(011225909) = 677` because `225909 = 2011 * 112 + 677`. These values lie in the subscript range from `0` to `2010` inclusive.

4.4 Strategies for Resolving Hash Collisions

Despite the efficiency of some of these proposed hash functions, there remains the inevitable reality that hash collisions may still occur. In response to this, we consider several alternative strategies to pursue in the event of a hash collision. We classify these into two major categories: *open addressing and separate chaining.*

Strategies for Open Addressing

When a hash collision occurs in an open addressing scheme, we look for some unoccupied position in the hash table. This implies that the number of records capable of being stored in the hash table cannot exceed the size of the table. We now describe some of the more frequently used open addressing strategies.

Linear Probing

A simple open addressing strategy is *linear probing,* which may best be described by an example. Suppose *key* hashes to `k` for some specific value of *key*, and suppose that the component of the hash table at position `k` is already occupied. Thus, we have a hash collision. If we assume the hash table has subscripts in the range from `0` through `MAX_SIZE - 1`, we then probe the next component in the hash table, located at position `(k+1)%MAX_SIZE`. If this location is empty, the data will be inserted there; if not, we continue the linear search for the first available unoccupied slot. The hash function in this case takes the form `H(key) = key%MAX_SIZE`.

The effect of combining linear probing with searching the hash table using modular arithmetic is that, if all table positions from `k` through `MAX_SIZE - 1` are currently occupied, we "wrap around" to position `0` and test whether it is occupied, and so on, until an available slot is found. Figure 4.3 illustrates the use of linear probing in a hash table of `int` values with `MAX_SIZE = 11` for the sequence `23,36,89,12,134`.

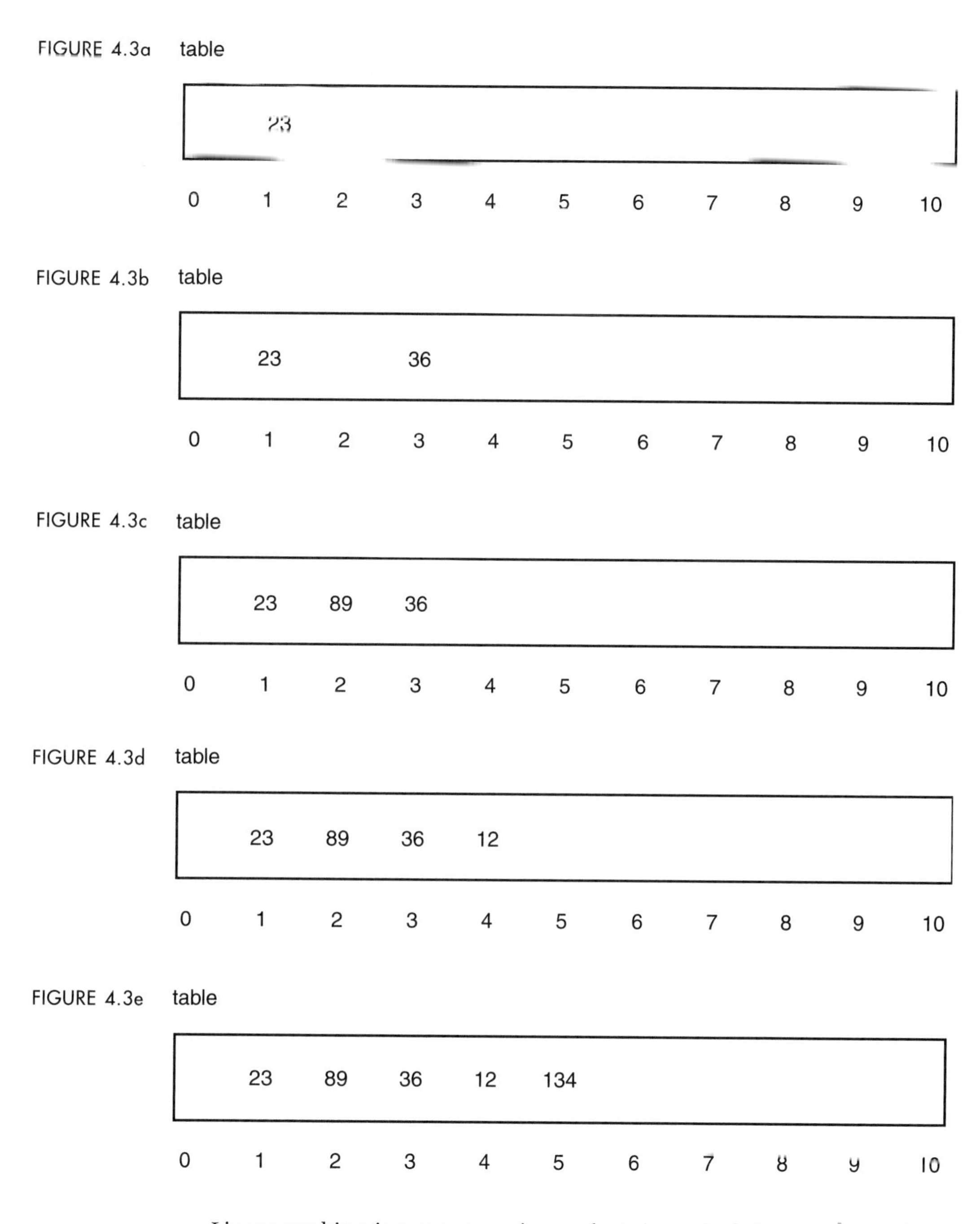

Linear probing is prone to *primary clustering,* which is a tendency for a large number of keys to hash to a relatively small group of locations close to one another. When this happens, searching for a location in which to insert a new value will be unsuccessful for a large number of probes if the search is currently going on in a large cluster. This diminishes the efficiency of linear probing; in fact, the efficiency diminishes dramatically as the set of values to be hashed increases because there is a tendency for smaller clusters spread through the hash table to collect into increasingly larger clusters.

Quadratic Probing

Quadratic probing is an alternative to linear probing that eliminates (to some extent) the type of clustering associated with linear probing. As an example of how quadratic probing works, suppose we once again apply the hash function `H(key) = key%MAX_SIZE`, and suppose `H(key) = k`. In this case, if the location with subscript `k` is occupied, we probe position $(k + 1^2)\%MAX\_SIZE = (k + 1)\%MAX\_SIZE$. If this position is occupied, we next probe position $(k + 2^2)\%MAX\_SIZE = (k + 4)\%MAX\_SIZE$, then position $(k + 3^2)\%MAX\_SIZE$, and so on, until an unoccupied location is found.

Quadratic probing has its own set of subtle setbacks. For example, if `MAX_SIZE = 16` and `H(key) = 5`, then any future probing in the event of an initial collision will inspect only positions `6,9,14`, and no others. This phenomenon is called *secondary clustering,* and it severely limits the effectiveness of quadratic probing, especially if these table positions are already occupied. Figure 4.4 illustrates quadratic probing for the same hash table and input sequence already used in linear probing.

FIGURE 4.4a

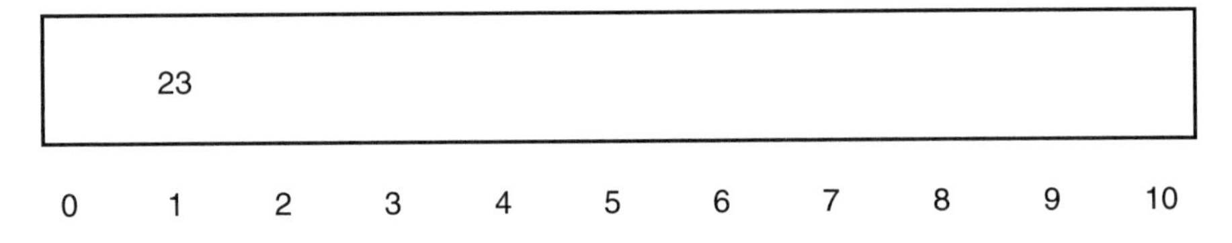

FIGURE 4.4b

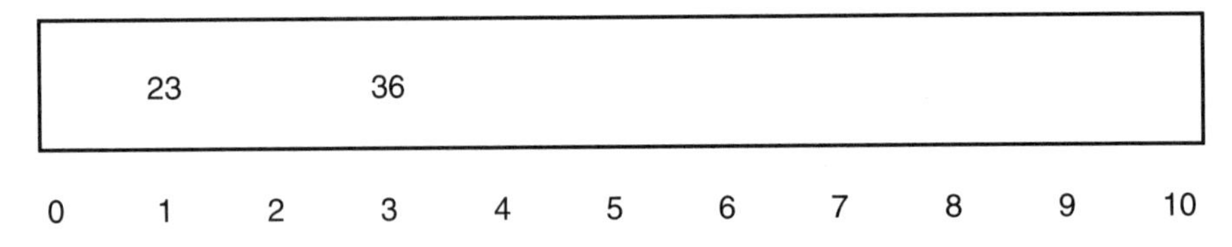

FIGURE 4.4c

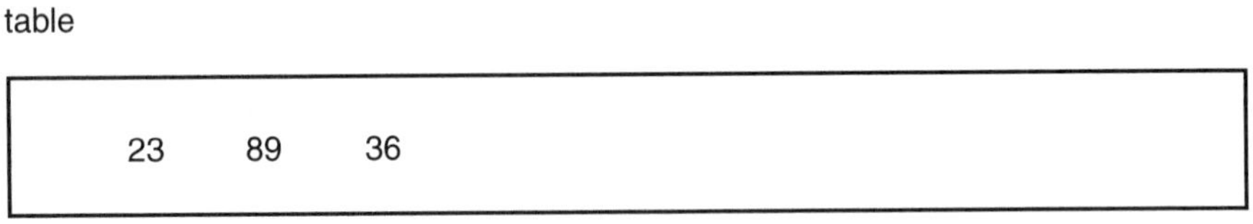

table

23 89 36

FIGURE 4.4d table

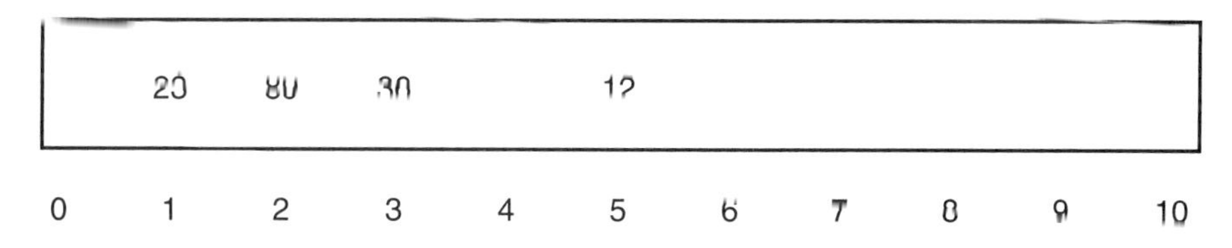

FIGURE 4.4e table

0	1	2	3	4	5	6	7	8	9	10
	23	89	36		12	134				

One way to avoid secondary clustering is to generate more than one table subscript at a time by applying several hash functions to the key when a collision occurs. This technique is called *rehashing,* and it proceeds as follows: If a collision occurs on a specific key with the first hash function, then apply the second hash function, and so on, until an unoccupied location is found in the table. If the sequence does not produce a suitable location, attempt linear or quadratic probing from the value produced from the first hash function until an unoccupied location is found. If this does not work for the first hash function, then proceed to the second and repeat the entire sequence, and so on. The worst possible case arising from this is that none of the hash functions using any of the probing strategies results in the successful placement of the data in the table. At that point, we may simply declare that the table is full and abort the operation. This strategy clearly depends on the sequence of hash functions chosen and the tendency of each of these to produce primary and secondary clustering. We will say no more about this here. Instead, we discuss one rehashing method (called *double hashing*) that has proven successful in a large number of specific situations.

Each of the strategies for resolving collisions so far are characterized as *circular hashing methods* because the course of probing leads to a wrapping around to the initial locations of the hash table if we come to the end of the table before locating an unoccupied position.

Double Hashing

In *double hashing,* we define a primary hash function H_1 and a secondary hash function H_2. These work in combination by using `H1(key)` to provide the initial probe into the hash table and then using H_2`(key)` to give an interval length in the probe sequence if necessary. H_2 is chosen so as to always give a value relatively prime to the value of `MAX_SIZE`. This causes maximum efficiency in the implementation of double hashing. The underlying reason behind this is that the size of a hash table is usually a prime number; hence, it will be relatively prime to all step sizes.

For example, suppose `MAX_SIZE = 17` so that `table` has components `0,1,...,16`. In addition, suppose we define H_1`(key) = key%MAX_SIZE = key%17`, and H_2`(key) = 11 - (key%11)`. If `key = 39`, then H_1`(key) = 5`, and if `table[5]` is unoccupied, then the data are placed there. On the other hand, if a collision results, H_2 is called to produce a probe sequence with increment given by H_2`(key) =` H_2`(39) = 11 - (39%11) = 5`. The probe sequence is then given by `5,10,15,3,8,13,1,6,11,16,4,9,14,2,7,12,0`. Note that each component of `table` is probed at some point owing to the fact that `MAX_SIZE = 17` and `11` are relatively prime. Since each location of `table` is probed at some point, clustering is reduced because two keys hashing to the same location generally follow different probe sequences.

Figure 4.5 illustrates the application of double hashing on the same input sequence used earlier for linear and quadratic probing, but now using H_1`(key) = key%11` and H_2`(key) = 7 - (key%7)`. Note that the probe sequence is `1,6,0,5,10,4,9,3,8,2,7,` if `key = 23`.

FIGURE 4.5a table

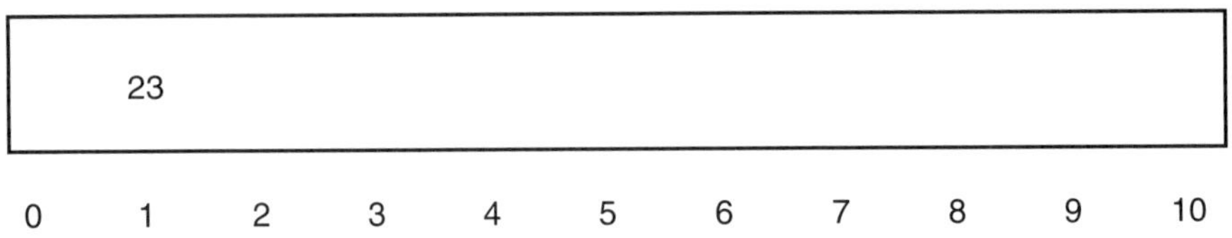

	23									
0	1	2	3	4	5	6	7	8	9	10

FIGURE 4.5b table

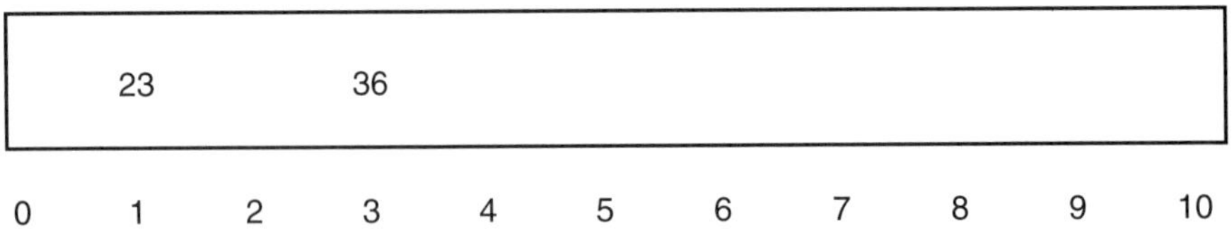

	23		36							
0	1	2	3	4	5	6	7	8	9	10

FIGURE 4.5c table

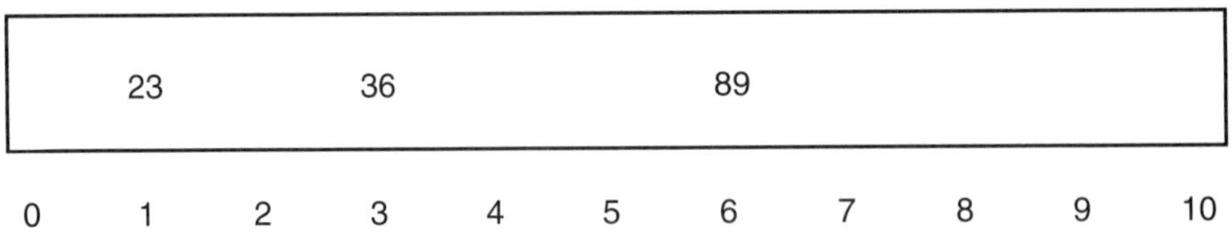

	23		36			89				
0	1	2	3	4	5	6	7	8	9	10

FIGURE 4.5d table

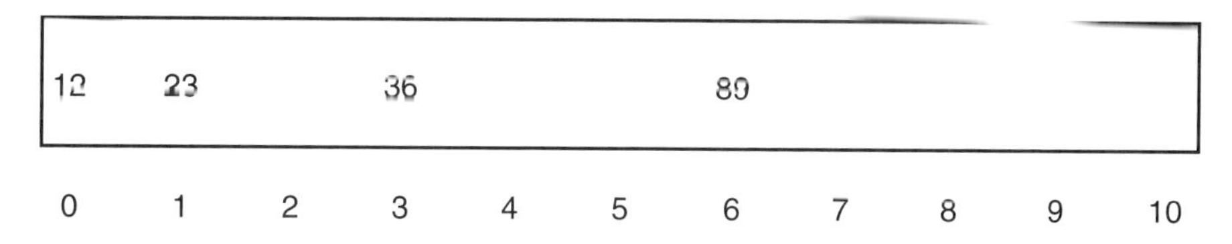

FIGURE 4.5e table

0	1	2	3	4	5	6	7	8	9	10
12	23	134	36			89				

4.5 Resolving Hash Collisions Using Buckets and Linked Lists

In the last section, we discussed the problem of hash collisions based on the principle of *open addressing:* Only one data record is permitted to occupy any position in the hash table. But what if hash collisions could be avoided by somehow permitting more than one data record to be stored at the same position in the hash table? There are two possible ways to implement this: *bucket hashing* and *separate chaining.*

Buckets

Here we visualize the hash table as capable of maintaining an array of records (called a *bucket*) at each location. The buckets will have a common size fixed in advance. Thus, the hashing operation may be captured in pseudocode as

Compute `H(key) = k;`
Let `table[k]` = *kth bucket. Search the components*
    `table[k][0],...,table[k][bucket_size-1]` *of* `table[k]`
for an unoccupied component;
if(no unoccupied component is available) abort the operation;
else place data in `table[k][j]`, *where* `j` = *subscript of the next available unoccupied component in* `table[k]`;

It is important in the implementation of this design to define buckets whose common size is not too small (to avoid collisions when a bucket becomes full) and not too large (to avoid wasting storage). The search for the next available unoccupied component in a bucket is done sequentially, beginning with component `table[k][0]`, if linear search is used, or the search may be conducted using binary search.

We illustrate bucket hashing using (Figure 4.6) with `bucket_size = 4` for the same hash function and input sequence treated earlier.

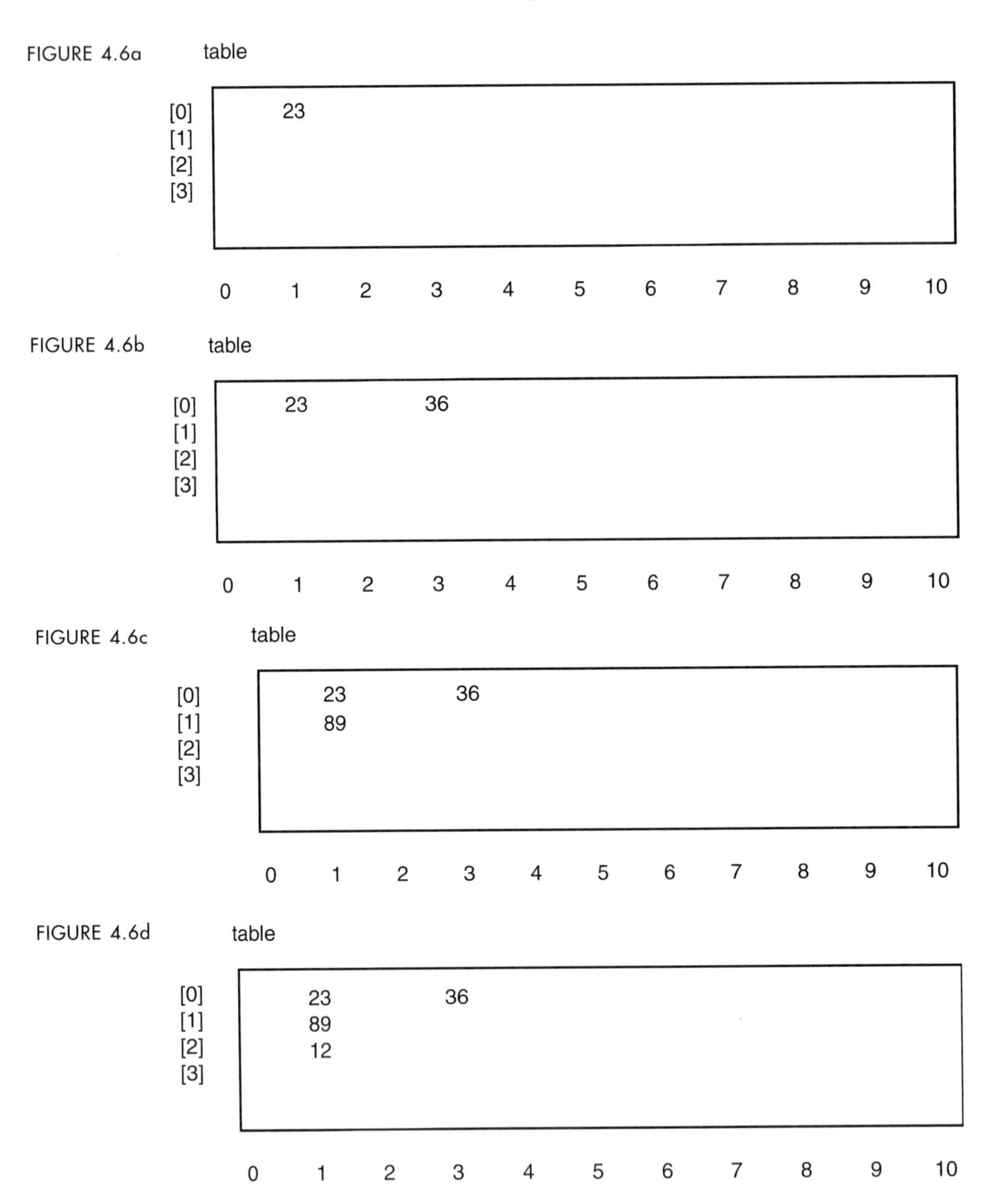

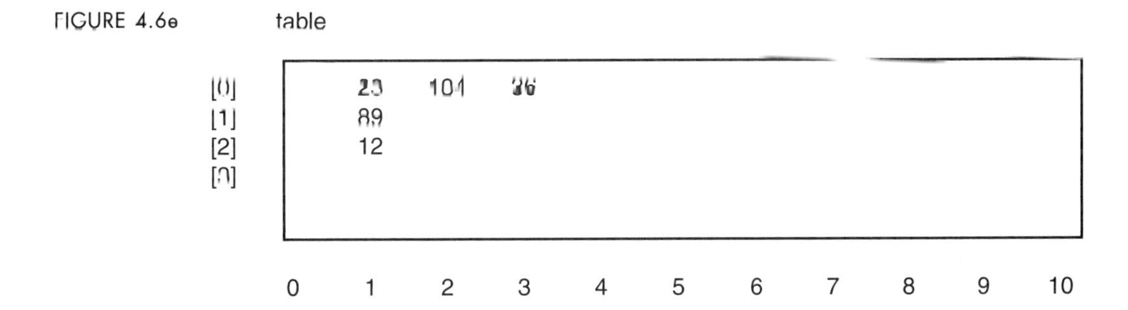

FIGURE 4.6e

Bucket hashing is a viable candidate for a paradigm that avoids as many hash collisions as possible, but it has limitations in efficiency and represents an alternative that is no better than separate chaining. To see how efficiency is compromised, note that `H(key) = k` implies that an unoccupied location in `table[k]` is sought. Since `table[k]` is itself an array, we must search that bucket (using linear or binary search) for an unoccupied location in case we wish to deposit a new data record in the hash table. Therefore, bucket hashing eventually becomes an operation that is either `O(n)` or `O(log n)`.

Linked Implementations: Separate Chaining

Separate chaining involves a design in which the hash table is an array of references to linearly linked lists. This approach avoids the threat of hash collisions entirely, unlike the situation with buckets. In this case, if a new data record hashes to a value in `table` that is already occupied, the new record is inserted in the same linked list given by that table location. For example, suppose we revisit the example of employee records discussed earlier in this chapter. After the records of `Rosalie A. Procach` and `Horace J. Boccia` have been inserted, `table` looks like Figure 4.7.

Suppose an employee named `Bart W. Jones` with social security number `066666610` joins the firm. Note that Jones's social security number also hashes to `37`. Instead of experiencing a hash collision, this record is inserted into `table` in location `37` as described in Figure 4.8.

Accordingly, each component of `table` is a reference to a *chain* (linearly linked list) of records hashing to the same value. In this way, the only limitations we face are those imposed by the hardware involving the amount of storage allocated for creating new nodes. Searching for a specific record involves first hashing to the proper location in `table` and then performing a sequential search through the list (if not empty) for the desired record. Adding, removing, and retrieving records then become familiar list operations.

FIGURE 4.7

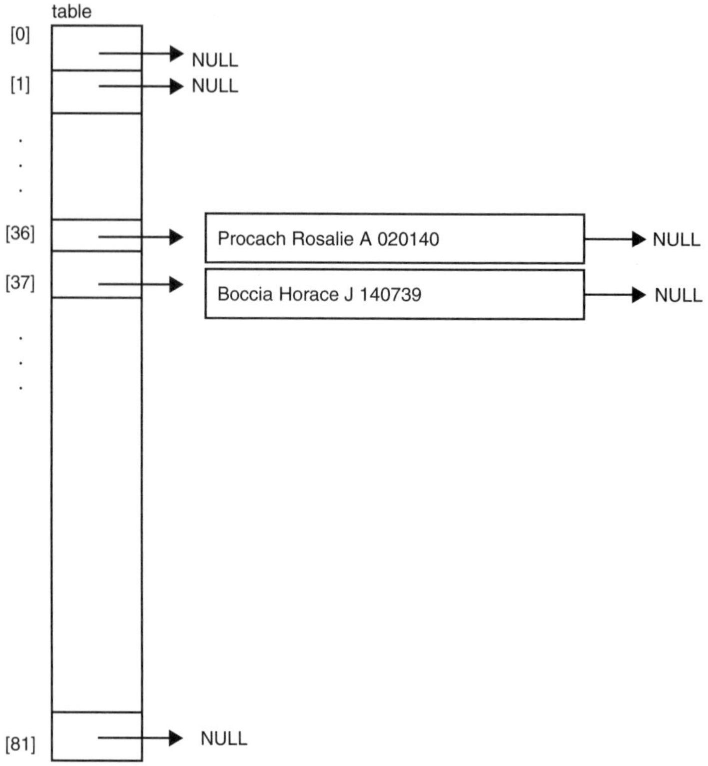

table

[0] → NULL

[1] → NULL

.
.
.

[36] → Procach Rosalie A 020140 → NULL

[37] → Boccia Horace J 140739 → NULL

.
.
.

[81] → NULL

FIGURE 4.8

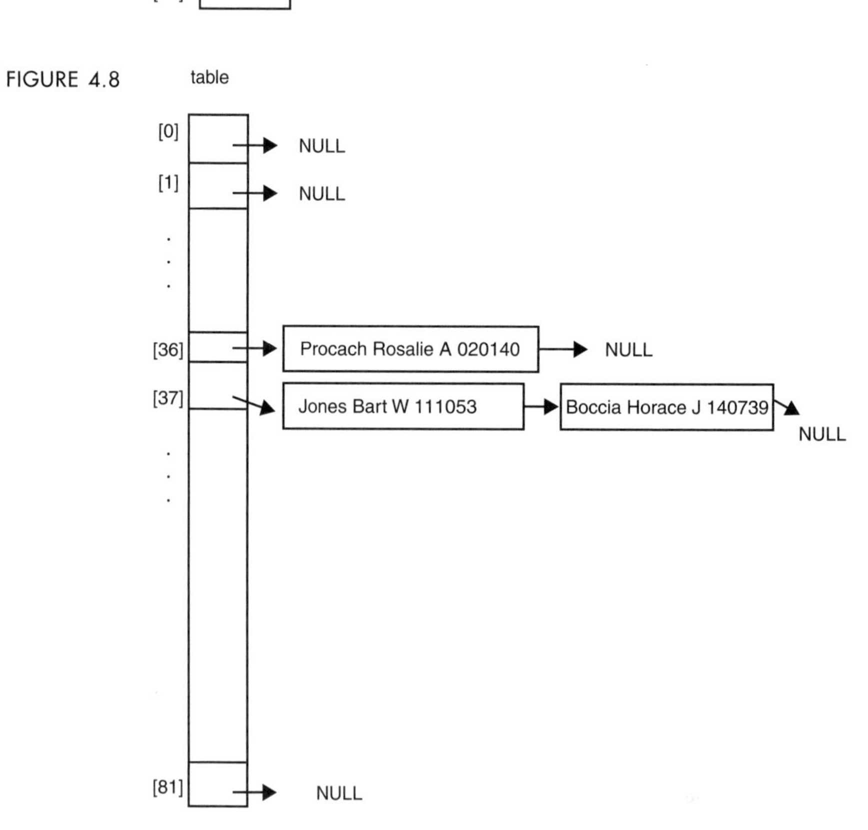

Suppose we apply separate chaining to the 11-component array `table`. The components of `table` now are references to linked lists whose nodes contain `info` components that hash according to `H(key) = key%MAX_SIZE = key%11`. If we again use the same input sequence as before, the result is as described in Figure 4.9.

FIGURE 4.9

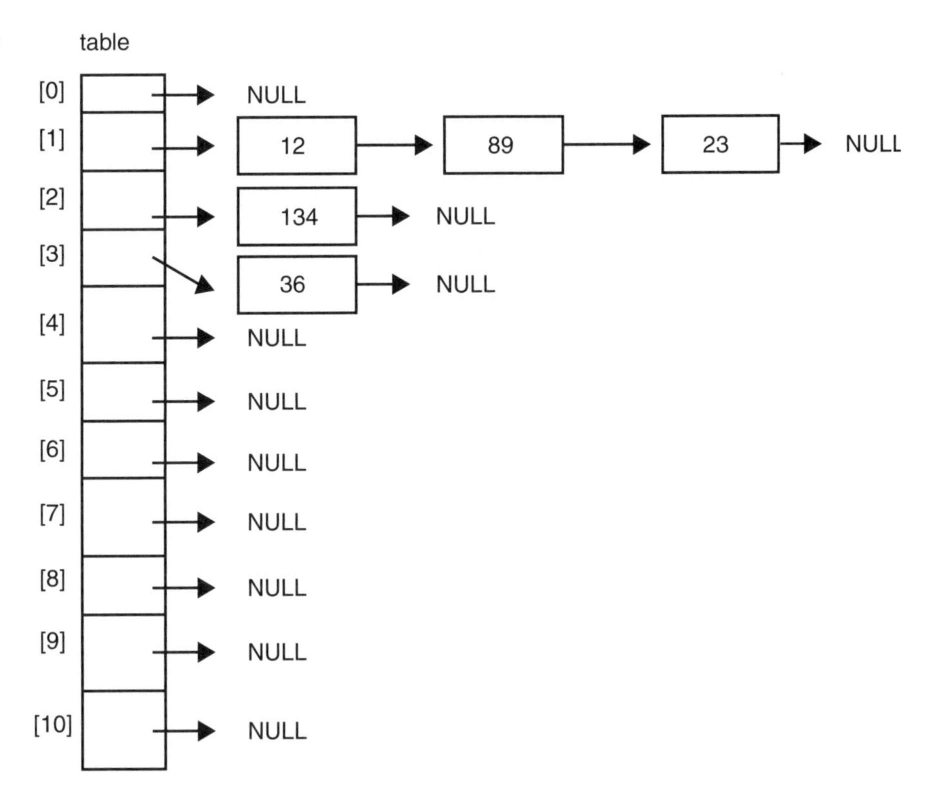

4.6 Implementation of Hashing Using Class Templates

Our primary objective is to place hashing in an application domain using classes and objects. This would imply that it is possible to define an ADT having its foundation in the hashing process. To accomplish this, we anticipate the design of a class template that we will call `hash_table`, whose objects will be specific hash tables with certain operations important to hashing and ultimately becoming the associated member functions defined for that class.

Several preliminary observations about hashing influence this design:

1. In describing the user interface, we observe that the user need not be aware of the specific choice of the hash function.

2. The user has no need to know which strategy for resolving hash collisions is adopted (whether linear or quadratic probing, double hashing, buckets, or separate chaining).
3. The only operations available to the user should be
   a. a *constructor,* which creates a new `hash_table` object, with a key value coming from a type parameterized by `K` and with any remaining data from a type parameterized by `D`
   b. a *destructor,* which systematically and efficiently destroys all storage allocated to the `hash_table` object
   c. an *insertion operator,* in which the user provides the specific data record to be inserted into the table
   d. an operator *retrieving* the data from that record, assuming the existence of a specific record in the table
   e. a *deletion operator,* which permits the removal of records that are no longer needed from the table

Our design includes the design of a parameterized `struct` type characterizing the structure of any record to be processed in the hash table. Our initial design views any such record as consisting of two major components:

1. a *key field* (of type `K`) specifying the data type of the keys used in the hashing operation
2. a *data field* (of type `D`) containing the remaining pertinent data found in each such record

Thus, any such record assumes the form pictured in Figure 4.10.

FIGURE 4.10

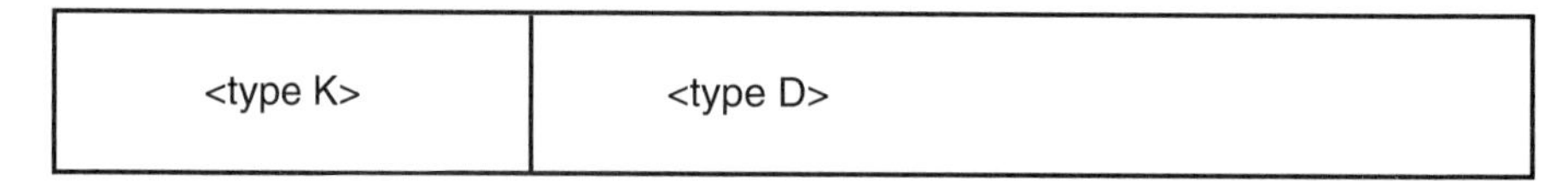

All of the examples we have described so far in this chapter may be viewed as `hash_table` objects for which `K` is instantiated as `int`. Consequently, the hash function defined explicitly in the `private` part of the proposed `hash_table` class will be an `int`-valued function of a single `int` variable. In general, returning an `int` value is not mandatory. A subsequent design uses arrays whose indices may come from any enumerated type and are known in C++ as *associative arrays.* These arrays are described in Chapter Nine. However, at this point, we will consider only hash functions returning an `int` value lying in the range `0. . . MAX_SIZE - 1`.

We begin by formally defining the structure `keyed_structure` of records to be hashed, with a single type parameter `D`, assuming we are enforcing the case that the type `K` is instantiated as `int`. We use `int` because it is relatively easy to work with; however, we can generalize this to any choice of a data type for which a "less than" relation is defined between any two of its values. Our design of keyed_structure will also include a third bool-valued field empty_val, whose initial value is true and remains true for that component in hash_table until an insertion is performed at that location. After the insertion, empty_val is assigned false. This also simplifies the removal operation because all that is required to decide whether a component in the hash table is empty is whether the current value of its empty_val field is true (regardless of the contents of that component's data_val value). In the case of removal, all that need be accomplished is to change the component's empty_val field value from false to true. A subsequent insertion at that location will perform two operations: copy over the previous value of the data_val value with the new value and change the value of that component's empty_val field from true to false. With these modifications, our code for keyed_structure is given in the form of a struct template as

```
template<class D> struct keyed_structure
{
  int key_val;
  D data_val;
  bool empty_val;
};
```
[4]

We also define the size of the hash table array using

```
const int MAX_SIZE = some convenient positive integer;
```

which is ordinarily a prime number.

We now turn to the design of hash_table. In doing so, we must make some preliminary decisions about whether to use an open addressing strategy or if we wish to implement buckets or separate chaining. In the case of open addressing, we must decide whether to resolve hash collisions, should they occur, by linear or quadratic probing or double hashing. We will choose an open addressing scheme using linear probing as a collision resolution strategy.

The user interface for hash_table uses the single parameter D, as already assumed for keyed_structure. The public portion lists prototypes for a parameterless constructor, a destructor, and member functions implementing insertion, retrieval, and removal. In addition, we provide an additional public parameterless member function called print_table that outputs the value of the data_val field of each nonempty component of the hash_table object and otherwise outputs the message

```
component is empty
```

[4]A struct template is handled in exactly the same way as a class template, as seen in Section 1.6.

If the type of the `data_val` field of a `keyed_structure` value is not predefined, it will be necessary to define `operator<<` in a manner similar to the examples seen in earlier chapters, so as to apply `cout` correctly in the implementation of `print_table`.

We begin the coding of the implementation details for the member functions of `hash_table` with the constructor. The object constructed will contain an array `h_table`, all of whose components will have `empty_val` fields initialized as `true` to simulate an initially empty array. The formal code is given by

```
// Constructor.  Constructs hash table of specified size
//  with all empty components.
// Postcondition: the empty_val field of each component
//  of the hash table is initialized as true, indicating
//  each such component is empty.
template<class D> hash_table<D> :: hash_table()
{
 for(int index = 0; index < MAX_SIZE; ++index)
  h_table[index].empty_val = true;
}
```

The destructor of `hash_table` releases all storage allocated to the `h_table` array and returns it to the free store.

```
// Destructor. Deallocates h_table array and returns
//  storage to free store.
template<class D> hash_table<D> :: ~hash_table()
{
  delete[] h_table;
}
```

The insertion operation implements open addressing with linear probing. It is coded as a `void` function with a single `keyed_structure` parameter, which is passed by reference:

```
// Insertion operation.  Implements open addressing with
//  linear probing.
// Postcondition: value is copied in h_table at position
//  given by H(key_value) or the next available location
//  determined by linear probing.
template<class D> void hash_table<D>
               :: insert(keyed_structure<D>& value)
{
 int position;
 position = H(value.key_val);
 while(!h_table[position].empty_val)  // Linear probing enforced.
  position = (position + 1)%MAX_SIZE;
```

```
  h_table[position].data_val = value.data_val;
  h_table[position].empty_val = false;
}
```

The retrieval operation uses a bool valued variable continue_search that is assigned true initially and remains true until the value sought (the value of the data_val field of the first parameter) is found (if ever). The second parameter is assigned true upon exiting the function just when the search is successful and false otherwise.

```
// Retrieval operation.
// Postcondition:  value of second parameter becomes true
//  if value sought appearing as first parameter is found
//  in hash table; otherwise false.
template<class D> void hash_table<D>
   :: retrieve(keyed_structure<D>& value, bool& found_it) const
{
  int position, initial_position;
  bool continue_search = true;

  initial_position = H(value.key_val);
  position = initial_position;
  do
  {
   // If the value sought is located at position, or position
   // is empty, terminate the search.
      if(h_table[position].data_val == value.data_val
            || h_table[position].empty_val)
       continue_search = false;
      else // Continue search
      position = (position + 1)%MAX_SIZE;
  } while(position != initial_position && continue_search);
  found_it = (h_table[position].data_val == value.data_val);
  // Return value is data_val field of value found.
  if(found_it) value.data_val = h_table[position].data_val;
}
```

The design of the removal function reflects the philosophy about determining when a component of the hash table is judged empty. The function returns true in the case of a successful removal and otherwise returns false.

```
// Removal function.  This version maintains the value of the
// data_val component until copied over.  Effectively,
// that data_val component has been removed because its empty_val
// is changed from false to true in the case of a successful
```

```
// removal.
// Postcondition: returns true in the case of a successful
// removal, otherwise returns false.
template<class D> bool hash_table<D>
  :: remove(keyed_structure<D>& value)
{
 int position, initial_position;
 initial_position = H(value.key_val);
 position = initial_position;
 do
 {
   // If value is found in hash table
   if(h_table[position].data_val == value.data_val)
   {
      // Empty hash table at that position and announce
      // successful removal.
      h_table[position].empty_val = true;
      return true;
   }
   else  // Otherwise, resume search.
      position = (position + 1)%MAX_SIZE;
 } while(position != initial_position);
 return false;   // Report unsuccessful search.
}
```

The remaining `public` member function prints the current contents of the hash table.

```
// Outputs current hash table.  In the case of an empty
// component, the output for that component is the string
// "is empty".
template<class D> void hash_table<D> :: print_table() const
{
 for(int index = 0; index < MAX_SIZE; ++index)
  if(!h_table[index].empty_val) // Component not empty
   cout << "index = " << index << ": " << h_table[index].data_val
        << '\t';
  else
   cout << "index = " << index << " is empty" << '\t';
  cout << endl;
}
```

Finally, the code for the hash function `H` is in the `private` part of the interface, conforming to our design plan. We also decided that this version will always involve keyed structures whose `key_val` field has values of type `int`. Thus, we have

```
// Coding of hash function. Uses division with remainder.
template<class D> int hash_table<D> :: H(int value) const
{
 return(value%MAX_SIZE);
}
```

The user interface is given as

```
template<class D> class hash_table
{
 public:
  // Constructor.  Constructs empty hash table
  //  with the specified size.
  hash_table();

  // Destructor.  Destroys hash_table object.
  ~hash_table();

  // Insertion operator. Inserts parameter value
  // in the hash table.
  // Precondition: Open addressing with linear probing
  // is applied.
  void insert(keyed_structure<D>&);

  // Retrieval of value of first parameter.  Second
  // parameter is true if value sought is found; otherwise
  // value of second parameter is false.
  void retrieve(keyed_structure<D>&, bool&) const;

  // Removal function.   Returns true if value of parameter
  // is found in hash table and is removed.  Otherwise,
  // there is no value to remove, and false is returned.
  bool remove(keyed_structure<D>&);

  // Output function.  Prints contents of the current
  // hash table.
  void print_table() const;

 private:
  // Hash function.
  int H(int) const;

  // Definition of hash table.
  keyed_structure<D> h_table[MAX_SIZE];
};
```

The fact that linear probing was applied appeared in the code of three member functions of hash_table: insert, retrieve, and remove. For example, insert contains the code segment

```
while(!h_table[position].empty_val)
   position = (position + 1)%MAX_SIZE;
```

If we decide to apply quadratic probing instead, this would be changed to

```
int increment = 1;
while(!h_table[position].empty_val)
{
 position = (H(value.key_val) + increment*increment)%MAX_SIZE;
 ++increment;
}
```

Similar changes must be made in retrieve and remove. We leave these coding details as an exercise. (See Problem 6 in the Exercises at the end of this chapter.)

Suppose we decide to implement separate chaining in our design of hash_table. As stated earlier, this would involve viewing each component of h_table as a reference to a (possibly empty) linked list of nodes, each of whose info components is capable of storing a value of type D, however D is instantiated. Thus, the user interface for hash_table will have a public segment identical to that already given for open addressing, but whose private segment is rewritten as

```
private:
 // Hash function.
 int H(int) const;
 // Definition of hash table.
 vector<list<keyed_structure<D>>> h_table[MAX_SIZE];
```

The interface uses the definition

```
vector<list<keyed_structure<D>>> h_table[MAX_SIZE];
```

This definition presumes the existence of several of the classes of "containers" (forms of data structures) that are predefined and available in the Standard Library. In brief, as we will see beginning with the next chapter, vector generalizes the idea of (one-dimensional) arrays, and list names a predefined class template of the STL containing all of the necessary operations for the general processing of linked lists, without the necessity of having to supply any of this code on our own.

The question before us now is whether we choose to design and code a class template for linearly linked lists "by hand" or instead invoke some predefined version, should this exist, from the Standard Library. We choose the latter. This is the bridge to the STL that we described in the introduction. For the moment, however, we introduce and discuss *namespaces,* a concept that is important in its own right and also serves as a necessary link to the facilities available in the STL.

4.7 Namespaces

A *namespace* is a mechanism used by C++ to group together a number of logically related programming entities under a single identifier. The identifier serves as a name for that grouping. The syntax for a namespace is given by

```
namespace identifier
{
        .
        .
        .
    // declarations and functions.
        .
        .
        .
}
```

where `identifier` names the namespace. Note also that `namespace` is a C++ keyword, and unlike the definition of a `struct` or the user interface for a class, the text of the namespace does not end with a semicolon. In addition, a namespace can be separated into an interface and an implementation part, each using the same identifier. These two parts are compiled separately and in fact may be stored in two separate files. In this context, the entities (classes, functions, objects, and others) defined in the namespace are limited by its scope (unless qualified by the scope resolution operator `::` or by some other device).

EXAMPLE 4.1 We recall the class definition for `int_stack` given in Example 1.2. In this example, we consider an alternative definition for `int_stack`, not as a class, but as a namespace construct. Just as we did for the class definition given in the earlier example, we may separate the namespace into an interface and a separate implementation file. The user interface is coded as

```
namespace int_stack {   // Interface.
 void push(int);
 int pop();
 bool is_empty();
 int top();
}  // No semicolon here.
```

The implementation details appear in a separate namespace with the same name as that for the interface and are given by

```
namespace int_stack { // Implementation details
 const int MAX_SIZE = 20;
 int info[MAX_SIZE];
 int top_value = -1;
 void push(int value)
 {
  if(top_value == MAX_SIZE - 1)
   cout << "Overflow -- push operation aborted." << endl;
  else
   info[++top_value] = value;
 }
 int pop()
 {
  if(top_value < 0){
   cout << "Underflow -- pop operation aborted." << endl;
   return 0;
  }
  else{
   int return_value = info[top_value];
   --top_value;
   return return_value;
 }
}

int top()
{
 if(top_value < 0){
  cout << "Underflow -- top operation aborted." << endl;
  return 0;
 }
 else
  return info[top_value];
}

bool is_empty()
{
 return top_value == -1;
}
} // closes namespace implementation details
```

The following main function drives the namespace:

```
int main()
{
 int_stack::push(3);
 int_stack::push(-7);
 cout << int_stack::pop() << endl;
 cout << int_stack::top() << endl;
 if(int_stack::is_empty())
  cout << "Current stack is empty" << endl;
 else
  cout << "Current stack is not empty" << endl;
 int_stack::pop();
 int_stack::pop();
 return 0;
}
```

The output is

```
-7
3
Current stack is not empty
Underflow--pop operation aborted.
```

General Observations About Namespaces

1. As a result of separating the implementation from the interface, each function now has exactly one definition (in terms of its formal code in the implementation part) and one declaration (its prototype in the interface).
2. In this last form, users may access only the interface containing the declarations (prototypes). In the case of `int_stack` given in namespace form, the implementation (in the form of function bodies) is placed in a separately compiled file to which users have no direct access.
3. It is impossible to declare a new member of a namespace outside of the text of a namespace interface using scope resolution, as in

   ```
   void int_stack :: new_operation();   // prototype
   ```

   This is not permitted. For this to have been acceptable, it must be defined within the scope of the `int_stack` namespace, as in

   ```
   namespace int_stack
   {  // Interface
      void push(int);
      int pop();
      bool is_empty();
   ```

```
    int top();
    void new_operation();
}
```

4. In namespaces, C++ does not permit the inclusion of the `const` modifier for functions defined in namespaces making no changes to the underlying structure being processed by that function. Thus, the definitions

   ```
   bool is_empty() const;
   ```

   and

   ```
   int top() const;
   ```

   defined in the `int_stack` interface, do not compile.

Why do we need namespaces? A namespace names a particular scope, nothing more. From the standpoint of good programming and design practice, the larger the text of the program, the more likely it is that there will be a need for blocking off segments of the code using namespaces. This device enables us to express logical separation of related program segments and remain within the accepted syntax of C++. We have already used "anonymous" versions of namespaces: Ordinary local scopes (in unnamed program blocks), global scopes, and class interfaces are examples.

Here are a few more observations about namespaces:

1. When an identifier is used outside of the namespace where it is defined, it must be qualified using the scope resolution operator `::`, as in

   ```
   int result = int_stack :: top();
   ```

   appearing in some user program. The `int_stack` qualifier is needed to state that the invocation of `top()` is for that declared in `int_stack` and not for some unrelated global function with the same name.
2. User-defined namespaces may be nested. Nested namespaces may be used to further improve the organization of the underlying code. The next example illustrates this.

EXAMPLE 4.2 We define an enclosing namespace `outer` and a properly nested namespace `inner` as

```
namespace outer {  // Beginning of scope of namespace outer.
 void f() { cout << "Calling f from outer namespace" << endl; }
 void g() { cout << "Calling g from outer namespace" << endl; }
 namespace inner { // Nested within namespace outer.
  void g() { cout << "Calling g from inner namespace" << endl; }
 } // Terminates text of inner namespace
} // Terminates text of outer namespace
```

Now execute the driver:

```
int main()
{
 outer :: f();
 outer :: g();
 outer :: inner :: g();
 return 0;
}
```

The output is

```
Calling f from outer namespace
Calling g from outer namespace
Calling g from inner namespace
```

If we insert the statement

```
inner :: g();
```

anywhere in the main text, a compile-time error results because the syntax rules regarding nested namespaces demand that the entire enclosing sequence of namespaces be given, from the outermost to the innermost, to properly specify the scope of the component invoked.

3. When an identifier defined in a namespace is used frequently out of its scope, it is very annoying to qualify it with its namespace every time it is used. For this reason, the syntax rules of C++ permit the application of a `using` directive as an alternative, where `using` is a keyword. The `using` directive may assume one of two possible forms:
   a. `using namespace` *`name;`*
   b. `using` *`name`* `::` *`member;`*

   where `name` identifies the namespace where the facility we wish to apply is defined, and *`member`* identifies the specific component of *`name`* where that facility appears. The `using` directive also respects nested scopes, as illustrated in Example 4.3.

EXAMPLE 4.3 The next user program refers to the same coding of nested namespaces as Example 4.2, but it applies the `using` directive at various locations. Suppose the user code is

```
int main()
{
 using namespace outer :: inner;
 g();
 using namespace outer;
 g();
 outer :: g();
 using namespace outer;
```

```
 f();
 return 0;
}
```

The attempt to compile this code produces an error at the segment

```
using namespace outer;
g();
```

This is because the compiler sees this as an *ambiguous call* to `g()`, since any such call to `g()` at this point is viewed as a call to `g()` from the "environment" of `inner`. In fact, if we instead execute

```
int main()
{
 using namespace outer :: inner;
 g();
 g();
 outer :: g();
 using namespace outer;
 f();
 return 0;
}
```

the code compiles and outputs

```
Calling g from inner namespace
Calling g from inner namespace
Calling g from outer namespace
Calling f from outer namespace
```

This is because the compiler sees no ambiguity in the second call to `g()`. It is viewed as a call to `g()` from the same namespace (`inner`) specified by the first `using` directive.

What happens when we omit the `using` directive on `f()`? That is, what is the effect of attempting to compile

```
using namespace outer :: inner;
g();
g();
outer :: g();
f();
return 0;
```

The result is a compile-time error because the call to `f()` is regarded as a call to an *undeclared global identifier* `f`. For `f()` to be properly understood by the compiler, and since `f()` is not defined globally (outside of the scope of any user-defined namespace), this occurrence of `f()` is viewed as *undeclared*.

How does the presence of a globally defined function with the same name affect the processing of functions redefined in user-defined namespaces? Let us consider the next example, whose complete list of namespaces is

```
// Global version -- not in any user defined namespace
void g() { cout << "Calling global g" << endl; }

<Definitions of outer and inner as above>

int main()
{
 g();

 outer :: g();
 outer :: inner :: g();
 g();
 return 0;
}
```

If we attempt to replace either of the qualified statements by the appropriate `using` directive, the compiler views the result as an ambiguous call to the overloaded function `g()`. The completely qualified version just described outputs

```
Calling global g
Calling g from outer namespace
Calling g from inner namespace
Calling global g
```

We may also qualify a global function using `::`. The result is written as `:: g();`

Example 4.4 illustrates how namespaces are used to encapsulate code segments using declared variables.

EXAMPLE 4.4 Suppose we define the namespaces `one`, `two`, and `three` by

```
namespace one {
  int x = 1;
  int y = x;
} // Terminates text of one.

namespace two {
  char x = 'c';
  namespace three {
   char x = two :: x;
   char y = ++x;
  } // Terminates text of three.
} // Terminates text of two.
```

Suppose we test the effect of these namespaces using qualified references, as in

```
int main() {

cout << "x = " << two :: x << endl;

cout << "x = " << one :: x << endl;
cout << "y = " << one :: y << endl;

cout << "x = " << two :: three :: x << endl;
cout << "y = " << two :: three :: y << endl;

return 0;
}
```

The output is given by

```
x = c
x = 1
y = 1
x = d
y = d
```

Key Observation

Our main motive for including a discussion of namespaces in this text is due to the observation that all of the components of the Standard Library are declared and defined within the scope of the predefined namespace called `std`. Therefore, the programmer who wishes to apply some of the facilities of the Standard Library, such as the class template `vector`, has the option of either using qualified references for each occasion of the use of such a facility or applying `using` directives, which is clearly much simpler and thus more desirable.

If we wish to apply operations and objects available, for example, in the `vector` class template, the simplest solution is to begin with a preprocessor directive

```
#include <vector>
```

and then add a `using` directive, either of the form

```
using namespace std;
```

or

```
using std :: vector;
```

If our application has a large number of such directives, a useful principle of good programming style would be to create a separate header file containing all of the `using` directives for members of the namespace `std` needed by that application. This is particularly important if the application requires disclosing all of the separate components needed. In this text, unless we specify otherwise, the `using` directive we will apply is

```
using namespace std;
```

4.8 Chapter Summary

The main goal of hashing is to provide a search paradigm that is reasonably efficient from the standpoint of the amount of memory required to store the data items to be accessed and whose time complexity for data retrieval is as close to `O(1)` as possible. To attain this goal, we studied a number of diverse hashing methods: middle squares, random number generators, folding, and division with remainder. Thus, the choice of a suitable form of a hash function is an important factor in our design.

Another important factor is whether to apply open addressing, buckets, or separate chaining. In each of these, there exists the possibility of several different data items yielding the same value when the hash function is applied. This is called a *hash collision.* Accordingly, our design must consider a suitable strategy to follow in the case of an occurrence of a hash collision. Popular among these are linear and quadratic probing and rehashing in the form of applying several cooperating hash functions when using either open addressing or buckets.

The technique of separate chaining resolved hash collisions by adding new nodes to a linearly linked list of nodes, in which the `info` component of each contains the pertinent data to be stored in the table. The hash table consists of a sequence of references to nodes in the linked lists, any one of which refers to the list of nodes whose `info` components have the same key value when acted on by the underlying hash function. This method resolves the problem of hash collisions, but the downside is that generally more processing time is required to maintain and update a hash table using linked lists.

We also presented the implementation of a hashing method using parameterized classes whose objects are hash tables, using a hash function employing division with remainder, with open addressing and linear probing. In addition, we suggested ways of implementing other forms of resolving hash collisions using our design as a prototype.

This chapter ended with a brief discussion of namespaces and how these may be used as a link between an object-oriented design of a hashing methodology employing hash tables and predefined facilities available in the STL. In so doing, we observed that this chapter provides a bridge between the earlier chapters and the content of the remainder of this text.

EXERCISES

1. Suppose we have a hash table in the form of the `int`-valued array `arr` given by

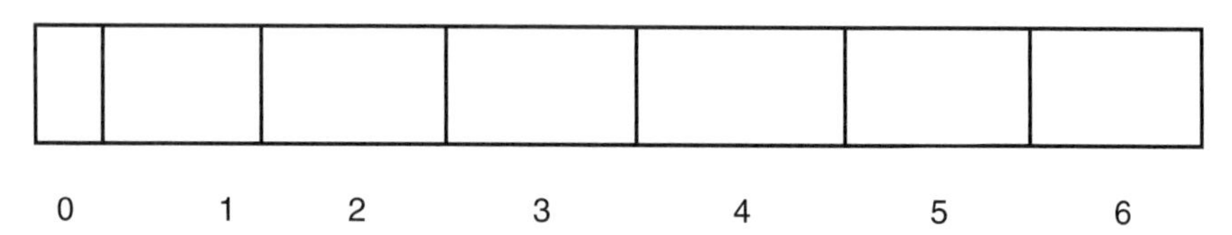

Apply the hash function

`H(search_key) = search_key % 7`

to the sequence `9,1,2,8,16`

a. using linear probing

b. using quadratic probing

c. using double hashing with the secondary hash function

H_2`(search_key) = 5 - (search_key % 5)`

2. Suppose we have a hash table in the form of an `int`-valued array `arr`, whose storage is represented as

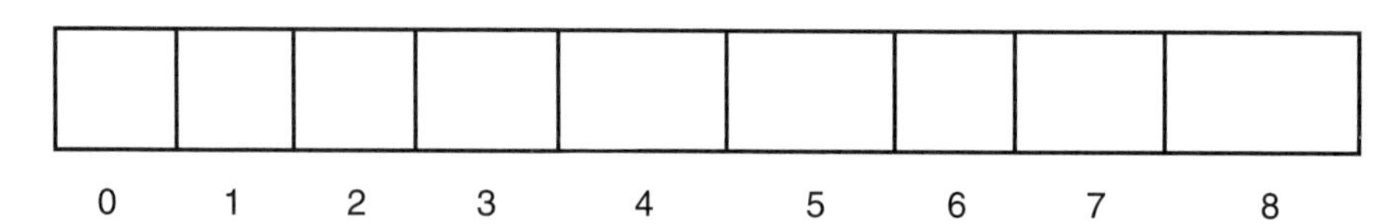

Apply the hash function `H(search_key) = search_key % 9` to the `int`-valued sequence `9,1,2,18,27`

a. using linear probing

b. using quadratic probing

c. using double hashing with the secondary hash function

H_2`(search_key) = 7 - (search_key % 7)`

3. a. Suppose the hash table `arr` of Problem 1 is now defined to store pointers to `int`-valued nodes of linked lists. Using the hash function `H` as defined earlier, and separate chaining, and the input sequence `9,1,2,8,16`, describe the result of applying the hash operation to that input sequence.

b. Do the same as (a), but now assume the array `arr` of Problem 2 is defined to store pointers to `int`-valued nodes of linked lists. Using the same input sequence `9,1,2,18,27`, describe the result of applying the hash operation `H` given in Problem 2 to this sequence.

4. Use the same input sequence and hash function as defined in Problem 1, but now assume each component of arr is defined as an int-valued bucket of size four.

5. Test the code for hash_table by instantiating the parameter D for keyed_structure and hash_table as int and by applying the insert member function to the sequence 23,36,89,12,134.

6. Complete the coding details for the implementation file for hash_table, now using quadratic probing as the strategy for resolving hash collisions.

7. Given the namespace sequence

```
namespace one {
  int x = 2;
  int y = x + 4;
}

namespace two {
  char x = 'w';
  char y = 't';
  namespace three {
   int x = one :: x--;
   char y = two :: x;
  }
}
```

a. Using a code trace, explain the output obtained when the following program executes:

```
int main() {

cout << "x = " << two :: x << endl;

cout << "x = " << one :: x << endl;
cout << "y = " << one :: y << endl;

cout << "x = " << two :: three :: x << endl;
cout << "y = " << two :: three :: y << endl;

return 0;
}
```

b. Explain any changes in the output if the nested namespaces change to

```
namespace one {
  int x = 2;
  int y = x + 4;
}

namespace two {
```

```
    char x = 'w';
    char y = 't';
    namespace three {
     int x = one :: x - 1;
     char y = two :: x;
    }
  }
```

8. Given the sequence of namespaces

```
namespace outer {  // Beginning of scope of namespace outer.
 void f() { cout << "Calling f from outer namespace" << endl; }
 void g() { cout << "Calling g from outer namespace" << endl; }
 namespace inner { // Nested within namespace outer.
  void g() { cout << "Calling g from inner namespace" << endl; }
 } // Terminates text of inner namespace
} // Terminates text of outer namespace

int main()
{
 outer :: f();
 outer :: g();
 outer :: inner :: g();
 return 0;
}
```

a. Explain the output obtained by executing the program.

b. Explain the result obtained when we attempt to run the program

```
int main()
{
 outer :: f();
 outer :: g();
 outer :: inner :: g();
 inner :: g();
 outer :: inner :: f();
 return 0;
}
```

9. Given the sequence of namespaces defined in Problem 7 and the user program

```
int main() {

using namespace two;
cout << "x = " << x << endl;

using namespace two :: three;
cout << "x = " << one :: x << endl;
```

```
cout << "y = " << one :: y << endl;
cout << "x = " << two :: three :: x << endl;
cout << "y = " << two :: three :: y << endl;

return 0;
}
```

a. Does the current program compile and execute? If so, give the exact form of the output.

b. What would occur if all of the qualified references that have been given were omitted? That is, would the following revision execute?

```
int main() {

using namespace two;
cout << "x = " << x << endl;

using namespace two :: three;
cout << "x = " << x << endl;
cout << "y = " << y << endl;
cout << "x = " << x << endl;
cout << "y = " << y << endl;

return 0;
}
```

c. What would be the result of omitting the `using` directive in the program described in (a)? Explain the reasoning behind your answer.

d. What would be the result of executing (c), except now for the revision as described in (b)? Again explain the reasoning behind your answer.

10. Rewrite the code for the `insert` operator for open addressing and linear probing of Section 4.6 so as to first check, using a linear search, whether the value to be inserted is already in the hash table. If so, the operation aborts, and the following message is issued:

```
Value already in hash table.  Insertion aborted.
```

PROGRAMMING PROJECT

1. Design and implement the `hash_table` class template using separate chaining. To do this, there is no need to design an accompanying `list` class template implementing linked lists. All that needs to be done is rewrite the member functions of `hash_table` using pointers and linked lists with the revision of `keyed_structure` given as

```
template<class D> struct keyed_structure
{
```

```
 int key_val;
 D data_val;
};
```

REFERENCES

DeLillo, Nicholas J., "An Implementation of Big Integers Using STL," *Proceedings of the Fourteenth Annual Eastern Small College Computing Conference,* October 23–24, 1998, Marist College, Poughkeepsie, NY, pp. 81–101.

Knuth, Donald E., *The Art of Computer Programming, Volume 3: Sorting and Searching* (Reading, MA: Addison-Wesley, 1973).

CHAPTER 5

Overview of the Components of the STL

CHAPTER OBJECTIVES

- To provide a general classification of the key components of the Standard Template Library.
- To define the various versions of STL container types.
- To introduce the concept of generic algorithms and their importance in contemporary and efficient software design and implementation.
- To present the various forms of iterators and their importance in connecting algorithms and suitable forms of containers.
- To present function objects and adaptors and to describe their importance in providing further flexibility and extending the functionality of other STL components.

5.1 Historical Introduction

The development and ultimate standardization of the C++ programming language began in 1989 and was completed in 1997, although some final decisions and resolutions delayed the publication of the standard until September 1998. The standard includes the STL, also referred to as the Standard Template Library, which may be characterized as a general-purpose library consisting of generic algorithms and data structures serving as containers for finite sequences of data from some type `T`.

The development of the STL is mainly the product of the efforts of Alexander Stepanov and Meng Lee, both from Hewlett-Packard Laboratories. Much of the original work on generic programming, which is part of the foundation of many of the constructs of the STL, was initiated by Alexander Stepanov and David Musser of Rensselaer Polytechnic Institute in the early 1980s. Originally, Stepanov and Musser implemented their work in Ada'83 and in Scheme. It was not until later, when the decision was made to include templates in C++ to support generic programming, that the STL evolved to its current state in C++. In fact, it is common to refer to the facilities provided in the STL as part of those supported in the *C++ Standard Library.*

5.2 Overview of the STL and Its Importance

The facilities of the STL support five distinct categories of language features, which may be classified as follows:

a. ***algorithms:*** One of the libraries in the STL is `<algorithm.h>` or, more simply, `<algorithm>`, which provides numerous implementations of the more commonly used algorithms in general data processing. These include implementations of linear and binary search, sort algorithms, and many others. These implementations are generally applicable to any well-defined data structure supported by the STL, such as ordinary one-dimensional arrays and various forms of data structures defined in the STL and to be studied shortly.
b. ***iterators:*** These represent generalizations of pointers (references) to any value stored in any of the data structures (containers) defined in the STL. Iterators allow the programmer to refer to any value stored in any container in a systematic manner and also allow for the progression of references to a succession of values stored in any well-defined STL data structure.
c. ***containers:*** These are the data structures defined and supported by the STL, which are classified either as fundamental (vectors, deques, and lists) or which modify a fundamental container in some specific and pragmatic way (sets, multisets, maps, and multimaps). These will be defined in detail in the remaining chapters of this text.
d. ***function objects:*** These represent a facility that permits passing a function as a parameter to an algorithm to adapt that function to the special kind of processing specified by that algorithm. Although this explanation at this point is somewhat vague, we will later describe situations where it is applicable.
e. ***adaptors:*** These take three forms: *Container adaptors* are STL classes that use objects defined as fundamental containers (vectors, deques, lists) as a "background" and provide a different interface, causing that container to be interpreted differently (as a stack, queue, or priority queue). *Iterator adaptors* are STL components that change the interface of an iterator defined on some fundamental container. *Function adaptors* adapt function objects definable in the STL for the purpose of extending their functionality.

Thus, we may say that the STL provides a number of "off-the-shelf" components available for commercial software design, allowing for the availability of efficient, easy-to-apply, and reusable tools.

What are some of the advantages in using STL components?

- Since the STL is now part of the ANSI/ISO standard for C++, its facilities are available across all compilers for the language and all platforms. Thus, the same version of the STL is available regardless of the underlying hardware configuration. Further, all forms of software developed using C++ as the implementation language will be independent of any significant hardware constraints.
- The STL provides a wealth of *reusable software components,* enhancing software development capability. This is because the components developed using the STL no longer require the programmer to design basic algorithms such as those for elementary searching and sorting or basic data structures such as linked lists, stacks, queues, and priority queues by hand. This work has already been done as part of the coding of STL components.
- Applications using the STL are guaranteed to produce efficient implementations from the standpoint of processing speed and utilization of storage because the design of the underlying STL components emphasize these efficiency factors.
- The general legibility of code using STL components is enhanced because much of the spadework present in the coding by hand of the implementation that the STL is replacing would have to be otherwise included. In addition, the unit testing of the code for various modules comprising a software application is easier to apply and maintain. These represent important ideas seen as integral parts of software engineering.

In summary, there is clearly much to recommend in the inclusion of the STL as a design paradigm, particularly for those who are training for a career in commercial software development where C++ is the primary implementation language.

5.3 Containers

A *container* is a data structure that stores a finite collection of values, all of which are of the same type `T`. These values may be objects themselves because their type `T` may be defined as a class. There are several classes of containers since no single container class has all of the necessary properties needed to solve every problem to which containers apply. Choosing the proper class of containers is very important because they are used to group together finite collections of objects of a single type and process these objects in a systematic way. The container storing these objects is identified by constructing it as an object of some underlying container class; this container class has a number of member functions that manipulate the objects inside the container in a specific way.

Containers may be divided into two general categories: sequence containers and associative containers. Sequence containers store a collection of values of a common type `T` in a linear arrangement in which each member of the sequence occupies a specific position. This position is in no way dependent on the value of the member; rather, it depends on the time of insertion of the member into the container and the position in the container where that member is inserted.

The STL sequence container types are described as

- *Ordinary array types:* Objects of this type are ordinary one-dimensional arrays. Containers of this type (the arrays) permit *random access* to any value stored in the sequence stored in the array. Informally, random access means that the processing time required to access the `i`th member of the sequence is *constant*—that is, it is of order `O(1)`. Access time does not depend on the position of the value in the sequence.
- *Vector types:* These are identified by the STL class template `vector<T>`. Objects of this type provide random access to a sequence whose length is allowed to vary *dynamically* (as the program executes). Processing vector objects permits constant-time insertions and deletions at one end (called the *back* of the vector). Insertions are identified by the member function `push_back`, and deletions are identified by the member function `pop_back`.
- *Deque types:* These are identified by the STL class template `deque<T>`. Objects of this type provide random access to a sequence of values of varying length, with constant-time insertions and deletions at each extremity of the container (the front and the back). Insertions are identified as `push_front` and `push_back`, and deletions are identified as `pop_front` and `pop_back`.
- List types: These are identified by the STL class template `list<T>`. Objects of this type are typically bidirectional linearly linked lists and thus permit *linear-time access*—that is, access of order `O(n)`, where `n` is the current length of the list—to any member of the sequence of varying length, but with *constant-time* insertions and deletions at any position in the sequence.

In contrast, associative containers associate a key value with each value stored in the container. The current C++ standard identifies these containers as *sorted associative containers.* Sorted associative containers provide for speedy retrieval of their values based on the value of the associated key.

In fact, the values stored in any sorted associative container are sorted automatically according to a specific ordering, which may be the default ordering given by `operator`. This default ordering may be overridden by an order relation explicitly supplied by the programmer. Again, the size of any sorted associative container varies dynamically. The STL defines four sorted associative container types:[1]

- *The `set` type:* This is identified by the class template `set<Key>`, which supports unique keys (that is, contains no more than one of each distinct key value) and permits speedy retrieval of the keys.
- *The `multiset` type:* This is identified by the class template `multiset<Key>`. Objects of this class support duplicate keys; that is, they support possible multiple objects with a common key value. Speedy retrieval of the key values themselves is supported.
- *The `map` type:* This is identified by the class template `map<Key,T>`. Objects of this type support unique keys (of type `Key`) and permit speedy retrieval of values of type `T` based on the underlying key values.
- *The `multimap` type:* This is identified by the class template `multimap<Key,T>`. Objects of this class support duplicate keys (of type `Key`) and permit speedy retrieval of values of type `T` based on the underlying key values.

5.4 Iterators

An important consideration at this point is how, in the course of processing the values of members of a sequence stored in some container, it is possible to move from one member to another. This is accomplished by the choice of an appropriate form of an *iterator* defined for that container. We may think of an iterator as an object capable of moving through and accessing some or all of the members of some STL container in some predefined order. Conceptually, iterators generalize the concept of a pointer, and each STL container class defines its own collections of iterators. In the case of ordinary one-dimensional arrays, vectors, deques, and lists, iterators are pointers of some kind.

Another important consideration is whether the value currently referenced by an iterator is permitted to change through the use of that iterator. Thus, we must distinguish between *(mutable) iterators* and *constant iterators* for each container class. This distinction is based on the definition of ordinary (mutable) pointers and how they differ from constant pointers. An ordinary (mutable) iterator refers to a member of a sequence stored in

[1]The sorted associative container types will be discussed in greater detail in Chapter Nine.

some container whose value may change during the course of a computation where the iterator is defined, whereas a constant iterator does not permit such a change to occur.

In C++, the identifier naming any ordinary one-dimensional array also serves as a constant pointer; in fact, the array name points to the location of the initial component. We may illustrate the distinction between mutable and constant iterators using arrays because, as we have already stated, iterators defined for ordinary arrays are just pointers to components of that array. To illustrate this, suppose we define an `int`-valued array `int_array` of size `MAX_SIZE` and then define

```
int *ptr = int_array;
```

This yields the situation described in Figure 5.1.

FIGURE 5.1

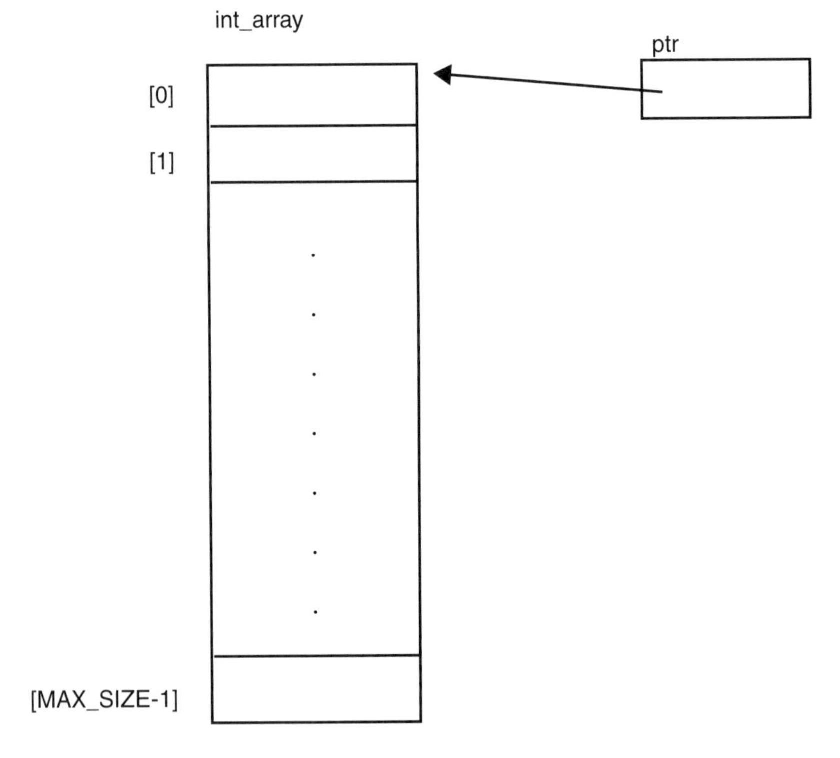

The value stored in `ptr` is the same as that stored in `int_array`, the (hexadecimal) address of the initial byte of `int_array[0]`. This defines `ptr` as a mutable iterator because it is possible to change the value of any component of `int_array` using

```
*ptr = some int-valued expression;
```

and to move the reference of `ptr` to any position of `int_array` using `++` or `--`.

How do we define ptr as a constant iterator? This is done by replacing the definition of ptr given earlier by

```
const int *ptr = int_array;
```

or equivalently by

```
const int *ptr = &int_array[0];
```

This permits movement of ptr through any of the components of int_array but prohibits any of the current values of the components of int_array to change using ptr. This describes ptr as a *pointer to a constant.* It also describes the behavior of a constant iterator applied to ordinary array containers.

It is important to distinguish this and a completely different concept using the const modifier and pointers. We may observe that C++ also permits the definition

```
int* const ptr = &int_array[0];
```

describing a completely different behavior from that described earlier for pointers to constants. In this case, the pointer is a constant: You cannot move the pointer from its initial position in the array to another. However, the value referenced by ptr is permitted to change using

```
*ptr = some int-valued expression;
```

This version of ptr is commonly referred to as a *constant pointer,* distinguishing it from the version associated with constant iterators described earlier. (See Exercises 1 and 2 at the end of this chapter.)

All of the STL container classes define the same basic member functions enabling the objects constructed from these classes to use iterators to access their members and (whenever possible) process them in some programmer-defined way. As an illustration, in vector, the identifiers iterator and const_iterator distinguish mutable and constant iterator types. More precisely, in vector,

```
vector<T> :: iterator
```

defines a mutable iterator type, and

```
vector<T> :: const_iterator
```

defines a constant iterator type.[2]

A basic pair of member functions using iterators are

- begin(), which returns an iterator (namely, const_iterator) value, referring to the initial member of a sequence stored in a container
- end(), which returns an iterator (namely, const_iterator) value, referring to the location just past the last member of a sequence stored in a container. (This is also called a *past-the-end iterator.*)

[2]We will have more to say about the distinction between mutable and constant iterators for containers in Chapter Six.

These are illustrated in Figure 5.2.

FIGURE 5.2

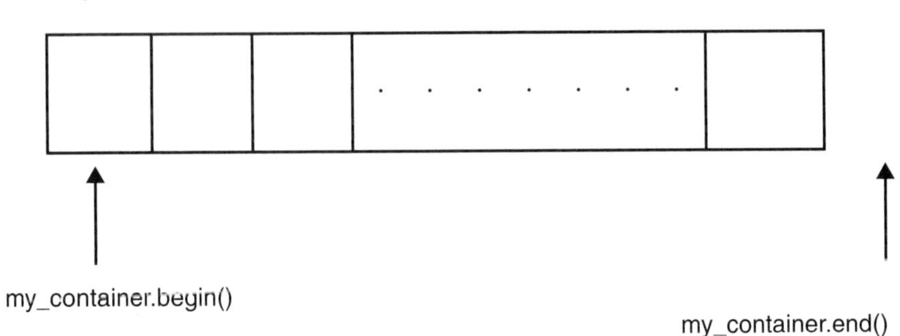

In effect, `begin()` and `end()` define a *half-open interval* of values

```
[my_container.begin(),my_container.end()]
```

including the left endpoint value and excluding the last. These form the basis for sequential loop processing over STL containers, which we illustrate for a `vector` container `my_vector` and constant iterators as

```
for(vector<T>::const_iterator ptr = my_vector.begin();
        ptr != my_vector.end(); ++ptr)
process each value in my_vector;
```

Thus, the processing begins with the initial value of the sequence in the container and continues sequentially through each member of the sequence, as long as the iterator does not refer to `my_vector.end()`. In the case of an empty container, `begin()` and `end()` refer to the same location. Thus, the same loop structure applies to this case as well. The result is that no actual processing is done.

5.5 Description and Classification of Iterators

Certain algorithms require iterators with a special functionality. In this section, we give a classification of iterators according to the functionality necessary for the implementation of the algorithm to complete execution.

Input Iterators

Consider the function template

```
template<class Iter,class T>
 Iter look_for(Iter first,Iter last,
      const T& value)
```

```
{
 for(; first != last; ++first)
  if(*first == value) return first;
 return NULL;
}
```

This implements a generic version of linear search.[3] Note that two type parameters are defined: `Iter` and `T`. The parameter `T` defines the type of data stored in the container, and `Iter` defines a parameter for a type of iterator necessary to process the members of the container. The iterator requires the following kind of functionality: It must respond to the comparison operator `operator!=`, to the prefixed version of `operator++`, and to the dereferencing operator `*`. Thus, all that is required for such operators is to move forward through successive members of the underlying container (using `operator++`), and they should have the ability to read any value (using `*`) they reference in the container and should finally respond to a condition halting their movement (using `operator!=`). Iterators having this functionality are called *input iterators.* In fact, the predefined pointer types defined for ordinary one-dimensional array types as well as iterators defined on vectors, deques, and lists have this functionality. In addition to these, pointers to `istream` objects also share this functionality. (See Section 1.8 for a discussion of `istream`.) Each of the predefined container classes supports iterators having this functionality and more; this suggests that there is a hierarchical relationship between the classes of iterators supported by each of the container classes and input iterators.

We may invoke `look_for` for an `int`-valued array `int_array` with six components using

```
look_for(int_array,int_array + 6,number);
```

where `number` is the name of an `int`-valued variable storing the value sought in `int_array`. The reaction to this by C++ is to instantiate `T` as `int` and `Iter` as the iterator type associated with ordinary arrays. These are random-access iterators, which are far more than what is required of input iterators. That is to say, random-access iterators are a special kind of input iterator possessing considerably more functionality than that required for `look_for` to execute. In effect, for ordinary arrays, C++ "sees" the type `Iter` as random access.

There is one further observation about the use of `operator++` for input iterators. Both the prefix and postfix forms of `++` are supported. For the prefix version, the dereferenced version of the prefix form returns the value in the sequence that the iterator advances to, whereas the postfix

[3]This generic implementation of linear search appears in `<algorithm.h>` using a while loop under the name `find`. We will discuss `find` later in the text.

form returns the previous value referenced. For example, suppose we have a sequence of `int` values `7,-3,6,0,5` stored in an array called `int_array` and suppose `ptr` is a (pointer) currently referring to `0`. Then `*ptr++` outputs `0`, and `*++ptr` outputs `5`.

None of the iterators defined on any specific STL container type are identified as input iterators. Each of these types associates with iterators that are much more than merely input iterators.

Output Iterators

Consider the functionality of the iterators described in the function template

```
template<class Iter1,class Iter2>
  Iter2 duplicate(Iter1 first,Iter1 last,Iter2 result)
{
 for(;first != last;++first)
 {
  *result = *first;
  result++;
 } // Terminates for-loop
 return result;
} // Terminates duplicate.
```

We pass two iterator parameters `Iter1` and `Iter2`. The reason is that the behavior of iterators of type `Iter1` is different from that of type `Iter2`. The former are input iterators, whereas the latter are defined as *output iterators.* If we examine the assignment

```
*result = *first;
```

we observe that `result` (as an iterator of type `Iter2`) has the capability of storing a value written to it. As a matter of fact, the functionality of output operators is the complete opposite of that for input iterators because an output operator permits values to be written to members of a sequence to which it refers, but does not necessarily permit these values to be read. That is to say, there is no guarantee that using `*result` in an expression guarantees that this value is read. Output iterators respond to dereferencing so that in the assignment

```
*result = *first;
```

it is possible to gain access to the current storage referenced by `*result`. Furthermore, this shows that output iterators respond to the assignment operator `operator=` in conjunction with deferencing. No such functionality is assumed for input iterators.

Unlike input iterators, there is no demand that output iterators respond to `operator==` or to `operator!=`; however, as is true for input iterators, output iterators respond to both prefix and postfix versions of `operator++`.

Again, as was observed for input iterators, there is no specific predefined container class in the STL defining its iterators as output iterators. All of the predefined containers define iterators (not constant iterators) with functionality much more than that for output iterators.

Forward Iterators

Input iterators have been defined as such because they are capable of reading values in a sequence and advancing forward, whereas output iterators have the capability of writing a value in a sequence and advancing forward to the next available position. But so far, we have defined no single iterator class capable of doing both. Having such a class of iterators is important because it may be used to solve a number of basic problems in data processing. One such problem is: Given a sequence stored in some container, we wish to substitute each occurrence of a specific value `u` of type `T` stored in the container by another such value `v`. The type of iterator involved must then be able to read any value in the sequence, and each time an occurrence of `u` is encountered, that occurrence must be written over with `v`. The iterator must also be able to advance forward from the initial member in the sequence to the last. We propose the following function template as a solution to this problem:

```
template<class Iter, class T> void substitute(Iter first,
  Iter last, const T& u, const T& v)
// Substitutes every occurrence of u in container by v.
{
 for(;first != last;++first)
  if(*first == u) *first = v;
} // Terminates code for substitute.
```

For example, if we execute the code sequence

```
int int_array[] = {4,3,2,7,4,2,7};
const int VALUE_REPLACED = 2;
const int REPLACEMENT = 0;
substitute(int_array,int_array + 7;VALUE_REPLACED,REPLACEMENT);
```

the contents of `int_array` in Figure 5.3a become those of Figure 5.3b.

Iterators possessing the functionality of both input iterators and output iterators are called *forward iterators*. The iterator class `Iter` defined in `substitute` requires the use of forward iterators. Again, the iterators (not constant iterators because such iterators must be mutable) have this functionality.

FIGURE 5.3

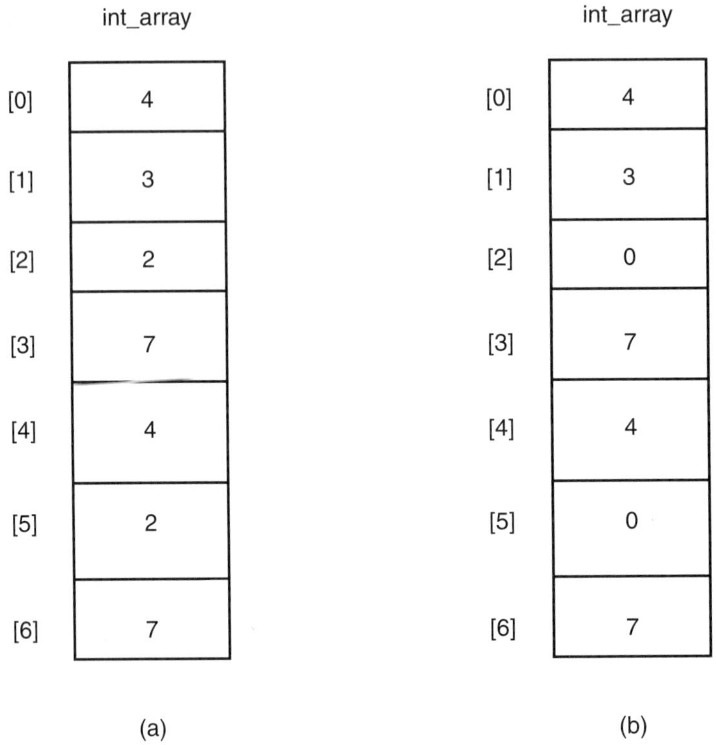

(a) int_array

Index	Value
[0]	4
[1]	3
[2]	2
[3]	7
[4]	4
[5]	2
[6]	7

(b) int_array

Index	Value
[0]	4
[1]	3
[2]	0
[3]	7
[4]	4
[5]	0
[6]	7

Bidirectional Iterators

Bidirectional iterators are similar to forward iterators, but a bidirectional iterator has the additional functionality of permitting the traversal of a sequence in either a forward or backward direction. Thus, bidirectional iterators support all of the operations defined earlier for forward iterators and also support the implementation of `operator--`, permitting the reversal of the direction of traversal in a sequence.

Both the prefix and postfix versions of `operator--` are defined, where the prefix version decrements the iterator and returns the new value, while the postfix version decrements the iterator and returns the old value. This is similar to the behavior of `operator++` for output iterators. Indeed, if we have the `int`-valued sequence `7, -3, 6, 0, 5` stored in `int_array` and if `ptr` currently points to the value `0` in that sequence, then `*ptr--` outputs `0`, and `*--ptr` outputs `6`.

Both forward iterators and bidirectional iterators may be either constant or mutable. In addition, we have already noted that output iterators have the capability of duplicating the values in a sequence, placing the copy of these values in a second container. The underlying algorithm presumes that the order of appearance of the sequence stored in the duplicate container is identical with that of the source sequence. The algorithm is implemented by the function template duplicate, which was discussed and coded earlier in this section. On the other hand, there are a number of important processing applications where it is critical that an iterator has the capability of traversing the values in a sequence in reverse order. A simple algorithm of this kind is to copy those values stored in one container in reverse order of appearance in a second container. For example, if int_array is the int-valued array described in Figure 5.4a, then reverse_array described in Figure 5.4b is the result of applying the algorithm just described on int_array.

FIGURE 5.4

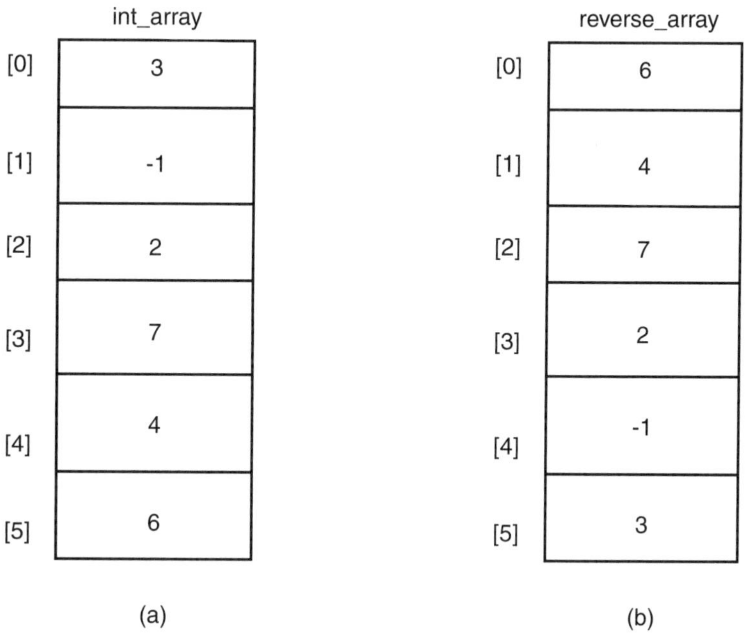

The implementation of the algorithm as a function template is described as copy_reverse and is coded as

```
template<class Iter1, class Iter2>
  Iter2 copy_reverse(Iter1 first,Iter1 last,Iter2 result)
// Makes a copy of the values stored in [first,last) in
// original container in reverse order in second container.
{
  for(;first != last;)
  {
   --last;
   *result = *last;
   ++result;
```

```
  }
  return result;
}
```

The execution of the algorithm is as follows: As the iterator `last` moves backward through the values in the source array, the dereferenced value of type `T` is copied into the next available location in the target array. The iterator `result` defined in the target array moves forward as the copying is done. The parameter `Iter1` must be at least bidirectional to allow `last` to decrement. Also, the parameter `Iter2` must be instantiated by at least an output iterator for the dereferenced value `*last` to be copied into `*result` and for `result` to advance forward, using `operator++`, in the target array. Certainly, if we apply `copy_reverse` to arrays, the itrerators are defined as random access; hence, these iterators have (more than) the necessary functionality for `copy_reverse`.

In Section 3.12, we discussed selection sort and insertion sort as they apply to ordinary one-dimensional arrays. Using iterators, we may generalize each of these sort algorithms to any container type supporting bidirectional iterators by replacing the first two parameters by two iterators: The first refers to the initial value of a finite sequence, and the second refers to the location immediately following the last member of that sequence. The advantage of this new version is that selection sort and insertion sort generalize to these new container classes—specifically, to vectors, deques, and bidirectional lists. In each case, the implementation is coded as a function template, passing two parameters: the iterator type and the data type of the sequence values.

The result for selection sort is given as

```
template<class Iter,class T>
  void selsort(Iter first,Iter last,T v,int& counter)
{
 // Selection sort implementation for containers.  The parameter
 // counter counts the number of possible swaps.
 // Postcondition: The container has values sorted in order of
 //  increasing size.
 Iter smallest;  // Reference to smallest remaining value
 for(Iter p = first; p != last; ++p){
  // Invariant:  values in container from position p up to
  // position immediately preceding last remain unsorted.

  // Initialize smallest as the first remaining value for p.
  smallest = p;
  // Then find position of the smallest remaining value.
```

```
    for(Iter q = p; q != last; ++q)
     if(*q < *smallest)
      smallest = q;
     // Swap container values.
     ++counter;
     T temp = *p;
     *p = *smallest;
     *smallest = temp;
  } // Terminates outer for-loop.
} // Terminates selsort.
```

The third parameter `v` of type `T` is a *dummy:* Its purpose is to inform the compiler that the values in the sequence are of type `T`. Without this information, the compiler has no way of determining the data type of the sequence members. The typical call to this version of `selsort` for any `int`-valued array `int_array` of size given by `MAX_SIZE` is

```
selsort(int_array,int_array + MAX_SIZE,0,swap_counter);
```

or

```
selsort(&int_array[0],&int_array[MAX_SIZE],0,swap_counter);
```

where the third parameter (`0`) is an integer informing the compiler that `selsort` is to be instantiated for `int`-valued arrays.

A similar set of observations apply to an iterator version of insertion sort. See the exercises at the end of this chapter (Problem 8) for more details.

Random Access Iterators

The four iterator categories discussed so far provide a functionality that is useful in implementing a large number of different algorithms. However, there still remains a significant number of algorithms requiring an even more powerful functionality. The iterators designed in the STL to handle this higher level of functionality are called *random-access iterators,* and they can be either constant or mutable.

Random-access iterators have all of the capabilities of bidirectional iterators and more. They have the ability to move in either direction at once in increments (or decrements) greater than one. In effect, such iterators have the functionality of moving from one position in the sequence to any other in constant time. Thus, these iterators implement algorithms for which movement from any position in the sequence to any other is efficiently accomplished with complexity `O(1)`.

In addition, random-access iterators support all of the operations defined for bidirectional iterators plus the following:

a. Addition of an integer offset, expressed as `iter + n`, where `n` is a nonnegative integer or the result of an expression whose value is a nonnegative integer. The result returned is the reference to the `nth` successor in the sequence of the current reference by `iter`. Thus, for example, if `iter` currently refers to the value `0` in the sequence given by Figure 5.5a, then `iter + 3` (or `3 + iter`) refers to the value `1` as

FIGURE 5.5a

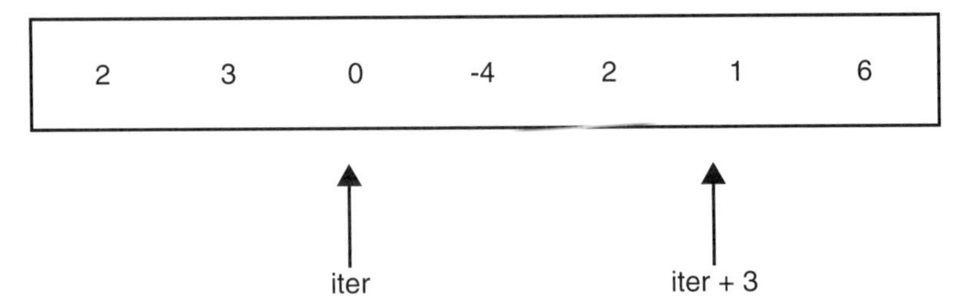

shown. It is important to observe that `iter` jumps to `iter + 3` in a single movement, not through a sequence of successive applications of `operator++`.

b. Subtraction of an integer offset, expressed as `iter - n`, where `n` is a nonnegative integer or the value of an expression evaluating to a nonnegative integer. If we refer to the current position of `iter` as given in Figure 5.5b, then `iter - 2` refers to the value `2`, as described in the same figure.

FIGURE 5.5b

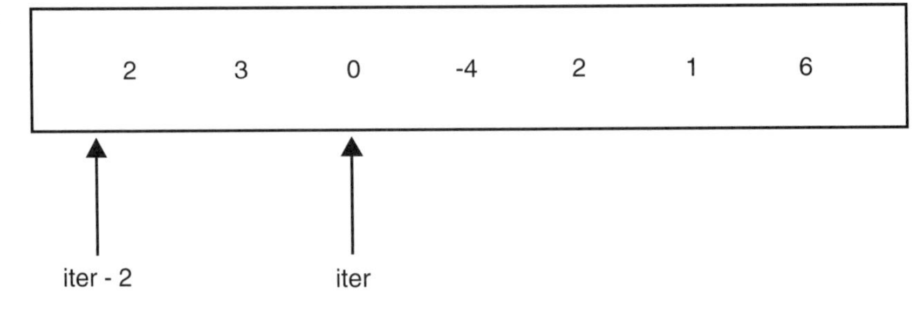

c. Bidirectional *jumps* from one position to any other in the container, expressed as `iter += n` or `iter -= n`, where `iter` is a random-access iterator and `n` is an `int`-valued expression. Thus, if we have the sequence in Figure 5.6a and if we execute `iter += 3;` the result is as described in Figure 5.6b. But if we instead execute `iter -= 2;` the result is as described in Figure 5.6c.

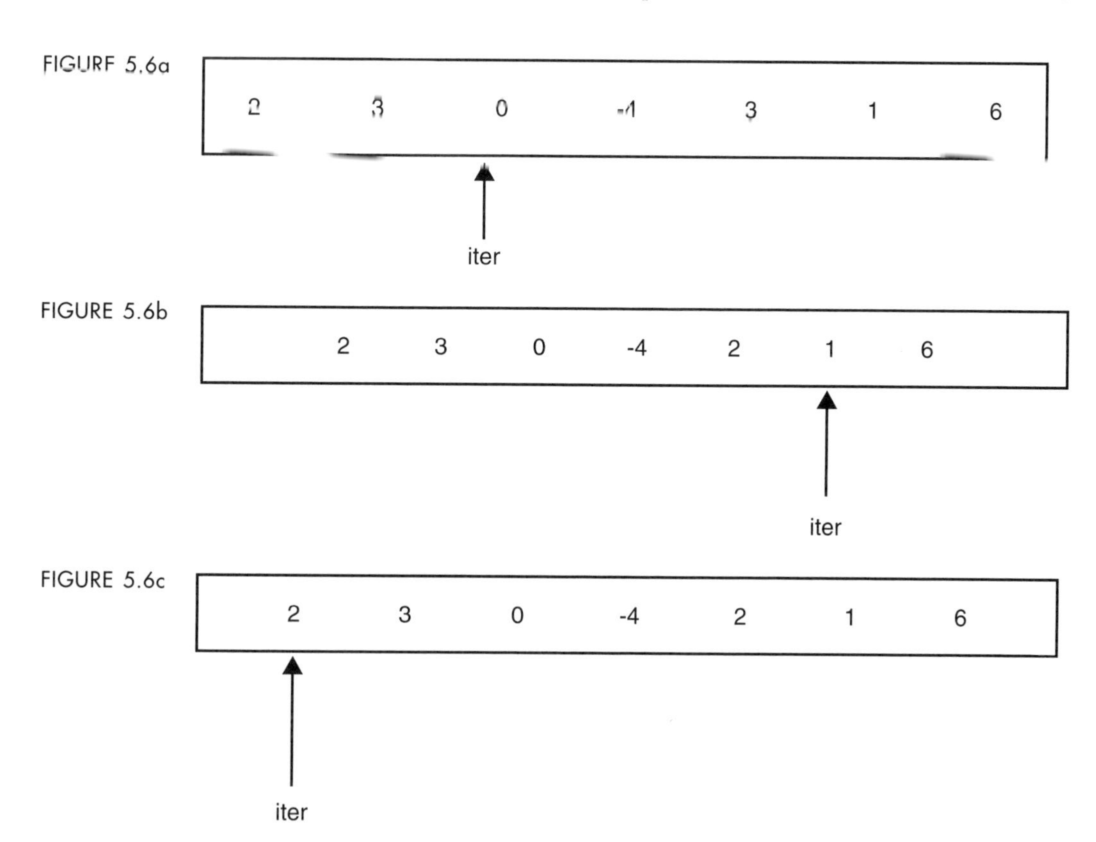

FIGURE 5.6a

FIGURE 5.6b

FIGURE 5.6c

d. The STL also supports the *difference* of two iterators of the same type, returning the *range* of the iterators (the number of positions of the sequence between the two). Thus, if we define

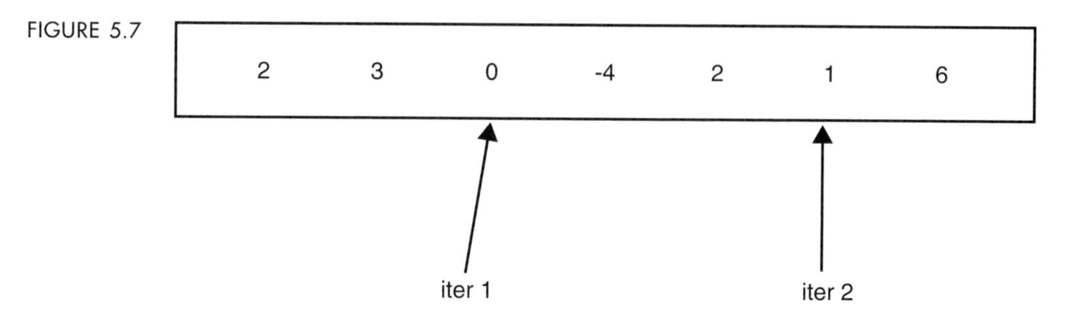

FIGURE 5.7

then the value of the difference `iter2 - iter1` is `3`.

To find the value of the midpoint of a sequence whose initial value is pointed at by `first` and where `last` refers to the location immediately following the last member of the sequence, we use the definition

```
Iter mid = first + ((last - 1) - first)/2;
```

The result is an iterator (constant or mutable) reference to the midpoint value.

EXAMPLE 5.1 The following function template returns the value of the midpoint of the sequence whose boundaries are given as `first` and `last` as just defined.

```
template<class Iter> Iter output_midval(Iter first,Iter last)
// Outputs the middle value of a sequence stored in a container,
// indexed from first to last - 1.
{
  Iter mid = first + ((last - 1) - first)/2;
  return mid;
}
```

If we call `output_midval` for `int_array`, defined as

```
int int_array[] = {-1,5,-9,12,9,6};
```

then the call to `output_midval` given by

```
output_midval(int_array,int_array + 6)
```

results in an iterator reference to `-9`, and if we define `char_array` according to

```
char char_array[] = "michela";
```

then the call to `output_midval` given by

```
output_midval(char_array,char_array + 7)
```

results in an iterator reference to `'h'`.

This iterator version of midpoint allows us to generalize binary search to any STL container supporting the use of random-access iterators. The content of the project described in the Projects section at the end of this chapter is to implement both an iterative and a recursive form of binary search using random-access iterator parameters. In addition, there are several predefined implementations of binary search defined in `<algorithm.h>` called `binary_search` and `lower_bound`. We will be discussing these predefined forms of binary search in some detail in Chapter Eight.

e. Random-access iterators may be compared to one another using any of the `bool`-valued functions `operator<`, `operator<=`, `operator>`, and `operator>=`. For example, if `iter1` and `iter2` are as in Figure 5.7, then each of `iter1 < iter2` and `iter1 <= iter2` is `true`, and each of `iter1 > iter2` and `iter1 >= iter2` is `false`. Intuitively, we may view `iter1 < iter2` as "`iter1` appears before `iter2`" and `iter1 > iter2` as "`iter1` appears after `iter2`."
f. One final basic property of random-access iterators is that they may be indexed using `operator[]`. Specifically, any container type supporting the use of random-access iterators may use the "subscript notation" to

access any value in the container. For example, we may use the subscript notation as an alternative for the successive positions of the iterator reference `int_array` for the ordinary `int`-valued array defined as

```
int int_array[] = {2,3,0,-4,2,1,6};
```

as shown in Figure 5.8.

FIGURE 5.8

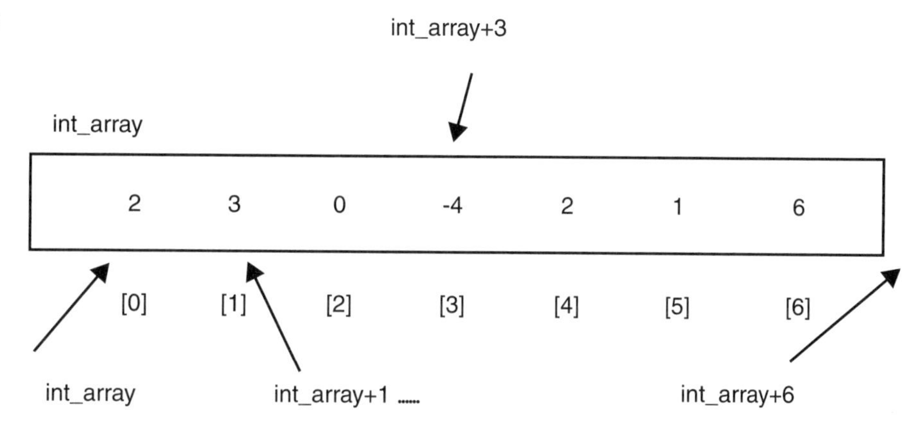

Any value of the array may be accessed using the `int_array` iterator or using subscripts. For example, either `*(int_array + 3)` or `int_array[3]` provides access to the value `-4`. The use of subscript notation as an alternative to iterator access will be used a great deal in Chapter Six.

We may summarize our classification of STL iterators by observing that they form a hierarchy based on their functionality. We describe this hierarchy in Figure. 5.9, where the classification is given in order of decreasing functionality.

Thus, any random-access iterator is also a bidirectional iterator, forward iterator, input iterator, and output iterator; any bidirectional iterator is also a forward iterator, input iterator, output iterator, and so on.

Stream Iterators

Not all of the iterators defined in the STL operate on members of a finite sequence stored in some container. Besides these, there are a number of STL iterators that operate on values in some I/O stream, such as `istream` or `ostream`. These iterators are included in STL classes called `istream_iterator` (for input) and `ostream_iterator` (for output). The inclusion of these classes in the STL permits the implementation of algorithms directly to input and output streams without the need to place the values in these streams in some specific STL container.

FIGURE 5.9

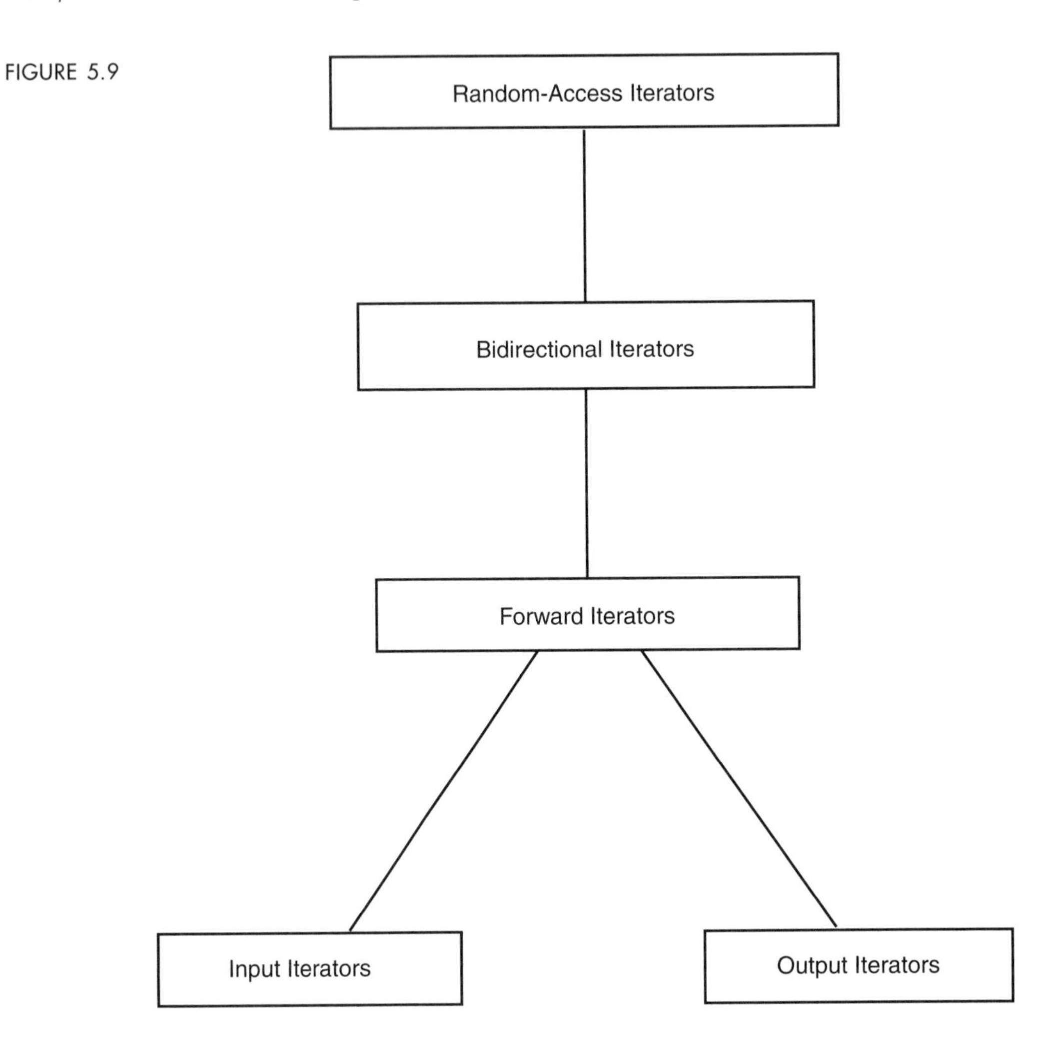

There is an association between `istream_iterator` and input iterators; a similar association exists between `ostream_iterator` and output iterators. Since `istream_iterator` is an STL class template, any object constructed from `istream_iterator` has the functionality of an input iterator. Hence, any such object has the capability of reading data and moving in a single direction. Thus, data cannot be written to a variable using an `istream_iterator` object. A similar association exists between `ostream_iterator` and its objects. In the latter case, the objects constructed from `ostream_iterator` are output iterators whose functionality is limited to the description of output iterators given earlier in this section.

These iterators provide the basic iterator interface for input and output streams. For input, objects constructed from the class `istream_iterator` read values from an input stream. Since one of the member functions of istream_iterator is operator++, any such iterator may be advanced forward to the next available value in istream. However, any such iterator may not be dereferenced for copying because input iterators do not have this functionality. But any istream_iterator object has the capability of becoming equal to the end-of-input-stream iterator value when the end-of-file value is reached. In fact, there is a default constructor in istream_iterator that does nothing more than construct an end-of-input-stream iterator.

The ostream_iterator class template constructs objects with the capability of writing values to an output stream. One constructor for this class involves two parameters: the identity of the output stream and a string whose value will be written after every value in the output stream. Since an ostream_iterator object is an output iterator, its functionality is restricted to that already described for output iterators. Specifically, any such object cannot read new values; it may only write values to a location in the output stream.

The class template ostream_iterator defines three constructors:

1. `ostream_iterator(ostream_type& s);`
2. `ostream_iterator(ostream_type& s,const char* delimiter);`
3. `ostream_iterator(const ostream_iterator<T>& x);`

The first of these creates an ostream_iterator object such that, when it is applied to some value t of the instantiated type T, it has the effect of applying s << t; the second has the effect of an s << T << delimiter; the third is a copy constructor.

As an example of the second form of output_iterator, if we apply

```
ostream_iterator<int> val(cout," ");
```

this constructs an ostream_iterator object val, which writes int-valued members in the standard output, followed by a single horizontal space between these members. We will see another example of this in Section 5.7, when we discuss function objects.

5.6 Algorithms

So far, we have provided a brief overview of STL containers and iterators. In fact, we conclude from these observations that containers are designed to store a finite sequence of values and that iterators allow movement from one of these values to another. But one major question remains: What good are containers and iterators without the capacity to process these values in some specific ways? We may answer this by investigating two possibilities. The first is the application of certain of the member functions defined in the `public` part of the associated container class. The second is the use of generic algorithms.

Most of the algorithms we use do not appear as member functions of some specific container class. Instead, they are *generic:* Each such algorithm is capable of processing data in any one of a number of distinct container classes. We may classify STL algorithms into four major categories:

- *Nonmutating sequence algorithms:* These algorithms process data stored in some container without modifying its contents.
- *Mutating sequence algorithms:* These modify the contents of the container.
- *Algorithms related to sorting data:* These include algorithms for sorting and merging values stored in containers and binary search.
- *Generalized numeric algorithms:* An example of such algorithms are those for generating a random sequence of integers.

Each of these algorithms appears in an STL library called `<algorithm.h>`. Consequently, any user program applying any of these algorithms must use the preprocessor directive

```
#include <algorithm.h>
```

or

```
#include <algorithm>
```

In addition, we use iterators to interface with the implementation of the generic algorithm because these permit many algorithms to be coded only once and to operate correctly on many different kinds of containers.

EXAMPLE 5.2 As an example, look at the generic algorithm `reverse`, requiring two iterator parameters `first` and `last`, with prototype

```
void reverse(BidirectionalIterator first,BidirectionalIterator last);
```

This algorithm reverses the members of a sequence so that the last member becomes the new first member, the first member becomes the new last member, and so on. The following is a sample program driving `reverse` for a `double`-valued array with six members.

```
#include <iostream>
#include <algorithm>

using namespace std;

int main()
{
 double arr[6] = {1.1,2.2,3.3,4.4,5.5,6.6}; // Conformant array.
 cout << "Before applying reverse:" <<endl;
 for(int index = 0; index < 6; ++index)
```

```
  cout << "arr[" << index << "] = " << arr[index] << endl;
 // Apply reverse function from <algorithm>.
 reverse(arr,arr + 6);
 cout << "After applying reverse:" << endl;
 for(int index2 = 0; index2 < 6; ++index2)
  cout << "arr[" << index2 << "] = " << arr[index2] << endl;
 return 0;
}
```

Note that `reverse` uses the iterators `first` and `last`, respectively, as `arr` and `arr + 6` because each of these are pointers (hence, iterators) for one-dimensional array containers that refer to the first member of the sequence and the location just past the last member of the sequence of `int` values stored in `arr`. This program outputs

```
Before applying reverse:
arr[0] = 1.1
arr[1] = 2.2
arr[2] = 3.3
arr[3] = 4.4
arr[4] = 5.5
arr[5] = 6.6
After applying reverse:
arr[0] = 6.6
arr[1] = 5.5
arr[2] = 4.4
arr[3] = 3.3
arr[4] = 2.2
arr[5] = 1.1
```

In later work, we will be able to apply `reverse` to vector, deque, and list containers and will require the use of the class of iterators appropriate for each container. Note that from the description given in the prototype, all that `reverse` requires are bidirectional iterator parameters. From the hierarchy given earlier, each of the categories of one-dimensional arrays, vectors, deques, and lists qualify because the iterators defined on each of these classes of containers are (at least) bidirectional.

Another important observation regarding STL containers is that they perform their operations by connecting algorithms with containers as efficiently as possible. That is to say, iterators represent the "glue" that binds a container holding the data to be processed by a generic algorithm with the assurance that these data will be processed by the underlying algorithm as efficiently as possible. In fact, the iterators defined on the specific class of containers were designed to process the data stored in these containers in as efficient a manner as possible.

For example, the iterators defined on arrays, vectors, and deques are random access. As we have already observed, this permits the movement of an iterator defined on any such container from any one position to any other in a single jump. It is certainly true that, without using the STL, we could have defined a pointer on an ordinary array to move from one position to another *sequentially,* performing an `O(n)` operation, to pass from its current location to its destination (using `operator++`). But this is unnecessary if the purpose of the movement was to reach the destination as quickly as possible (using a single jump—random access).

We now give a brief description of generic algorithms. A more detailed discussion of `<algorithm.h>` will be presented in Chapter Eight.

First, we observe that certain algorithms modify the sequence of values stored in a container. Such algorithms are termed "in-place." An example of an in-place algorithm is `sort`, with prototype

```
template<class RandomAccessIterator>
    void sort(RandomAccessIterator first, RandomAccessIterator last);
```

This version of `sort` sorts the elements in the range `[first,last)` using the (default) comparison operator given by `operator<`. That is, this version sorts the values in the range `[first,last)` in order of increasing size.

EXAMPLE 5.3 The program illustrates how `sort` operates on an ordinary six-component array of `int` values.

```
#include <algorithm>
#include <iostream.h>

using namespace std;

int main()
{
 int int_array[] = {3,-1,7,2,4,5}; // 6-component array.
 cout << "Before the sort:" << endl;
 for(int index1 = 0;index1 < 6;++index1)
  cout << "int_array[" << index1 << "] = " << int_array[index1]
    << endl;
 // Call predefined sort algorithm.
 sort(int_array,int_array + 6);
 cout << "After the sort:" << endl;
 for(int index2 = 0;index2 < 6;++index2)
  cout << "int_array[" << index2 << "] = " << int_array[index2]
    << endl;
 return 0;
}
```

The output derived from this program is

```
Before the sort:
int_array[0] = 3
int_array[1] = -1
int_array[2] = 7
int_array[3] = 2
int_array[4] = 4
int_array[5] = 5
After the sort:
int_array[0] = -1
int_array[1] = 2
int_array[2] = 3
int_array[3] = 4
int_array[4] = 5
int_array[5] = 7
```

In designing the STL, it was decided to omit a version of `sort` in which a copy of the original container holds the sorted sequence, leaving the sequence in the original container unsorted. The reason is that the copying version involves too much processing overhead and, consequently, would be inefficient.

The naming convention of generic algorithms in the STL uses the syntax

algorithm-name`_copy`

to name an algorithm that processes a copy of the original container. As an example, besides the `reverse` function defined in Example 5.2, there is also a copy version whose prototype is

```
template<class BidirectionalIterator,class OutputIterator>
 reverse_copy(BidirectionalIterator first,
              BidirectionalIterator last,OutputIterator result);
```

Here the range of the source container is `[first,last)`, and the container holding the copy, whose elements are the `reverse` of those in the source, begins with the (iterator) value of the third parameter. Specifically, if `int_array` is the `int`-valued array defined in Example 5.3, and if `copy_array` is another `int`-valued array with six components, then the result of the call

```
reverse_copy(int_array,int_array + 6,copy_array);
```

displays the components of `copy_array` as the reverse of those stored in `int_array`, with no change in the order of appearance of the components of `int_array`.

Another version uses an `output_iterator` object in place of `copy_` array. In fact, there is no need to identify the object by name. It may be invoked anonymously, as in

```
reverse_copy(int_array,int_array + 6,ostream_iterator<int>(cout," "));
```

The result of executing this last version on int_array produces the output

```
5 4 2 7 1 -3
```

5.7 Function Objects

A *function object* represent a fourth type of STL component. A function object encapsulates a function in an object so that it may be passed as a parameter to a suitable STL algorithm. When this is done, the algorithm's functionality is extended to include that variation provided by the function object.

For example, in the last section, we introduced the generic algorithm sort which, when applied to two RandomAccessIterator parameters defining the boundaries of some container, sorted the values in that container in order of increasing size. But what if we wish to sort a sequence in order of decreasing size? One option would involve manually rewriting one of the sort algorithms studied in Chapter Three from scratch or instead (if possible) using a generalization of STL's sort using a "greater than" comparison operator between values rather than the default "less than." If the latter were possible, we inherit the efficiency of sort, which is O(n log n), together with the extended functionality of sort to "greater than." This option is indeed possible; in fact, the extended form in the STL has the prototype

```
template<class RandomAccessIterator, class Compare>
  void sort(RandomAccessIterator first,
            RandomAccessIterator last, Compare comp);
```

The last parameter names a comparison operator that either is predefined and appearing in some STL library or is coded by the programmer. The predefined library to which we refer contains a number of class templates such as less<T>, greater<T>, less_equal<T>, greater_equal<T>, and others. Depending on the implementation, these appear either in the predefined <function.h> or <functional>.[4] Thus, to apply these and others defined in this library, we must use either of the directives

```
#include <function.h>
```

[4]In the HP implementation, these appear in <function.h>; according to the C++ standard, these appear in <functional>.

or

```
#include <functional>
```

For example, if we use `int_array` as defined in Example 5.3 and apply

```
sort(int_array,int_array + 6,greater<int>());
```

the result is the sorted array described in Figure 5.10.

FIGURE 5.10

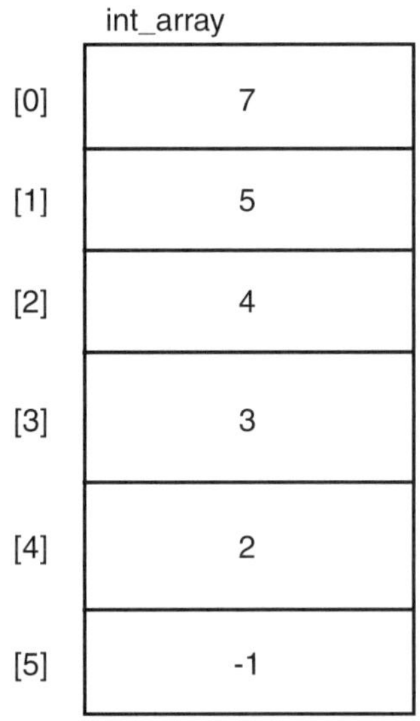

int_array

[0]	7
[1]	5
[2]	4
[3]	3
[4]	2
[5]	-1

The STL provides a small number of function object types for the most commonly used generic algorithms. All of these require the preprocessor directive

```
#include <functional>
```

when applied in the C++ standard. A number of these are in the form of a *binary predicate,* which we define informally as a function of two arguments returning a `bool` value. The `bool` return value expresses the truth or falsehood of some condition involving the two arguments given. These arguments are usually values of some type parameterized by `T`. An example was already given as `greater<T>()`, which we instantiated by substituting `T` by `int`. In more formal terms, the definition of `greater<T>` is given by the `struct` template

```
template<class T> struct greater : binary_function<T,T,bool>
{
 bool operator()(const T& x,const T& y) const
  {
```

```
    return x > y;
  }
};
```

Here we use the fact that a binary function is a function object that is invoked from a calling function just like any ordinary C++ function with exactly two arguments. The "function call operator" `operator()` can be overloaded so that any instance of the type parameter `T` may be used, provided that instance properly defines `operator()`. In the example of `greater` given earlier, we are free to instantiate `T` by any type for which a well-defined concept of `greater` exists. Note also that a subtle application of inheritance is being applied, with `binary_function` as the base class and `greater` as the derived class in the form of a `struct` (Figure 5.11).

FIGURE 5.11

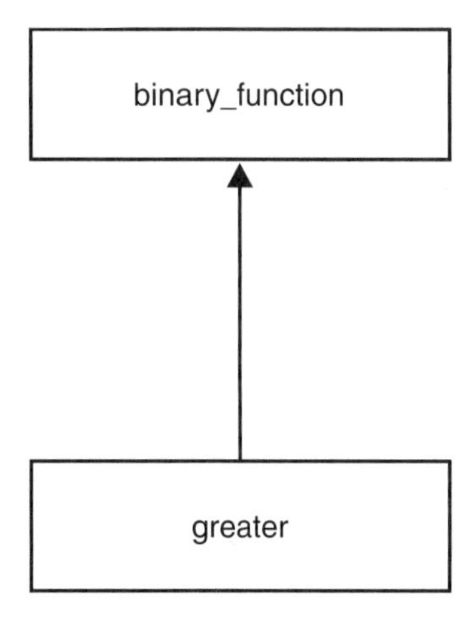

Besides `greater<T>`, the STL supports five other binary predicate classes, each of which is inherited from `binary_function`. These are

```
equal_to<T>
not_equal_to<T>
less<T>
greater_equal<T>
less_equal<T>
```

The STL also supports six derived classes of `function_object`, which encapsulate the most commonly applied arithmetic operations with return value of type parameterized by `T`. As an example, the STL defines the `struct` named `plus` as

```
template<class T> struct plus : binary_function<T,T,T>
{
 T operator() (const T& x,const T& y) const
  {
```

```
  return x + y;
 }
};
```

This operation can be instantiated for any type `T` for which there exists a well-defined version of `operator+`. This includes all of the predefined numeric types supported by C++, as well as the programmer defined types `complex` and `rational` defined in Chapter One.

The other specific arithmetic operations defined in the STL are the binary operators

`minus<T>`
`times<T>`[5]
`divides<T>` (uses `/`)
`modulus<T>` (uses `%`)

whenever applicable, and a unary function `negate<T>`, taking the form of a `unary_function` derived class and defined as

```
template<class T> struct negate : unary_function<T,T>
{
 T operator()(const T& x) const
 {
  return -x;
 }
};
```

In this last case, the base class is `unary_function`. As was the case for binary function objects, `operator()` may be overloaded; thus, any specific numeric type, predefined or otherwise, which supports unary minus, may be used to instantiate `T`.

What is contained in the classes `binary_function` and `unary_function`? Each of these base classes is empty (no objects can be constructed from either of them), but they are not abstract classes in the sense of the definition given in Section 2.8. This is due to the fact that neither class defines a pure virtual function. In fact, each of these classes contains nothing but a finite number of `typedef` descriptions. Their formal coded versions are defined as `struct` templates, given by

```
template<class Arg, class Result>
struct unary_function
{
 typedef Arg argument_type;
 typedef Result result_type;
};
```

[5] This function has been renamed as `multiplies<T>` in the C++ standard.

and

```
template<class Arg1, class Arg2, class Result>
struct binary_function
{
 typedef Arg1 first_argument_type;
 typedef Arg2 second_argument_type;
 typedef Result result_type;
};
```

As a base class, `binary_function` and `unary_function` each establish a number of type definitions for the argument(s) involved in each function and for the return type. Thus, any class template using either of these base classes invoking `operator()` is defined as a class whose objects are function objects with the instantiated types for the arguments and for the return type.

Function objects are important for the efficient use of the generic algorithms as defined in `<algorithm>` because the interface for each allows for an object for which `operator()` is defined—that is, a function object or a reference to an ordinary function. In the former case, efficiency is guaranteed if the function object is predefined in `<functional>`.

Let us illustrate how these function objects are used. For example, there exist two versions of a generic algorithm called `transform`, one version of which is applicable to unary operators and another for binary operators. The purpose of each version is to apply some operation (which may take the form of an appropriate function object) to a range of values stored in STL containers and to copy the result into some appropriate container. The syntax for each form is given by the pair of prototypes

```
template<class InputIterator,
         class InputIterator,
         class OutputIterator,
         class UnaryOperation>
OutputIterator transform(InputIterator first,
                         InputIterator last,
                         OutputIterator result,
                         UnaryOperation op);
```

for unary operators, and

```
template<class InputIterator1,
         class InputIterator2,
         class OutputIterator,
         class BinaryOperation>
OutputIterator transform(InputIterator1 first1,
                         InputIterator1 last1,
```

```
                        InputIterator2 first2,
                        OutputIterator result,
                        BinaryOperation binary_op);
```

for binary operators. The first form applies `op` to each member of a container in the range `[first,last)` and sends the result for each member to a value in the corresponding container `result`. It may occur that `result` names the same container used as the source for input. In this case, an overwriting of the values originally stored in the input container occurs. The version for binary operators applies `binary_op` (in the form of a binary function object) to the corresponding members in the range `[first1, last1)` (for the first argument) and the range beginning at `first2` (for the second argument) and sends the result to a corresponding location in `result`. The algorithm assumes, but does not check, whether the second sequence has at least as many members as those in the range `[first1,last1)`. As before, it is possible that the `result` sequence may be either of the two input sequences. In this case, an overwriting of that sequence occurs.

As an example, suppose `int_array` names an `int`-valued array whose respective components have values `3,-1,4,2,4`. Then the result of applying

```
transform(int_array,int_array + 5,result,negate<int>());
```

produces an `int`-valued array called `result` whose respective components have values `-3,1,-4,-2,-4`.

In addition to the binary predicate classes defined earlier, the STL also defines three logical operators, two of which are binary and one unary. These are useful in combining the values of binary and unary predicate function objects whenever the need arises. They are named

`logical_and<T>` (for conjunction)
`logical_or<T>` (for disjunction)
`logical_not<T>` (for negation)

The first two are binary, and the last is unary. For example, the syntax for `logical_and<T>` is

```
template<class T>
    struct logical_and : binary_function<T,T,bool>
    {
      bool operator()(const T& x,const T& y) const
      {
      return x && y;
     }
};
```

`logical_and` is a binary function object; it returns `true` when both of its arguments are `true` and otherwise returns `false`.

EXAMPLE 5.4 This example illustrates how `transform` may be applied in conjunction with `logical_and<int>` to check two pairs of `int` values input interactively and determine whether the first member of each pair is less than the second and also whether the first value is more than two values smaller than the second member. The code for a driver is given by

```
#include <iostream.h>
#include <algorithm>
#include <functional>

using namespace std;

int main()
{
 cout << "Please input 2 pairs of integers.  The program will" << endl;
 cout << "indicate whether each pair satisfies the following set"
            << endl;
 cout << "of conditions:" << endl;
 cout << "The first member of each pair is strictly less than" << endl;
 cout << "the second, and whether the first member of each" << endl;
 cout << "pair is more than 2 less than the second" << endl;

 cout << "Please input the first pair:" << endl;
 int first1,second1; cin >> first1 >> second1;
 bool arr1[2], arr2[2], result[2];

 // Generate the bool values for component 0.
 arr1[0] = first1 < second1; arr2[0] = first1 + 2 < second1;

 cout << "Please input the second pair:" << endl;
 int first2,second2; cin >> first2 >> second2;

 // Generate the bool values for component 1.
 arr1[1] = first2 < second2; arr2[1] = first2 + 2 < second2;

 transform(arr1,arr1 + 2,arr2, result, logical_and<bool>());

 if(result[0])
  cout << "Both conditions hold for the first pair" << endl;
 else
  cout << "At least one of the conditions fail for the first pair"
    << endl;

 if(result[1])
```

```
  cout << "Both conditions hold for the second pair" << endl;
 else
  cout << "At least one of the conditions fail for the second pair"
    << endl;
 return 0;
}
```

If we run the program for the two sets of input values

```
3 7
-1 0
```

the output is

```
Both conditions hold for the first pair
At least one of the conditions fail for the second pair
```

5.8 Adaptors

Adaptors are STL components that are used to change the interface of another component. Any adaptor is a class template taking a single parameter: the data type of the values to which the operation(s) of the adaptor apply. The STL defines three forms of adaptors: *container adaptors, iterator adaptors,* and *function adaptors.* We give a brief overview of each in this section.

Container Adaptors

There are three forms of container adaptors defined in the STL. These are `stack`, `queue`, and `priority_queue`, each of which is defined as a class template.

In Sections 1.4 through 1.6, we discussed the stack abstraction and provided an implementation as a class template. As an ADT, we defined a stack (of values of some type parameterized by `T`) as a (possibly empty) finite sequence of values permitting the application of four fundamental operations:

- push = inserting a value at one end (the *top*)
- pop = deleting (whenever possible) from the top
- is_empty = testing the current stack as to whether it is empty
- top = retrieving (whenever possible) the current value at the top

This ADT was implemented as an array with an additional `int`-valued variable `top_value`, which keeps track of what portion of the array is common with the stack.

Using container adaptors, we may implement stacks as an adaptation of a fundamental container type (`vector`, `deque`, `list`) with a simpler interface than that defined for any of these fundamental containers. Thus, we may view a stack as a "special" kind of `vector`, `deque`, or `list` object, whose operations are confined to the four fundamental operations defining the stack abstraction.

Similarly, we define the queue ADT as a finite sequence (possibly empty) of values parameterized by `T` that admits the insertion of new values at one end (the *rear*) and removals from the opposite end (the *front*). A queue can also be tested as to whether it is currently empty. In Chapter Seven, we will see that deques and lists are efficient forms of fundamental containers used to implement queues. Vector containers can't be used in this way because there is no efficient way to process values currently at the front of any `vector` object.

A priority queue ADT is defined as a finite sequence (posibly empty) of values parametrized by `T`, in which there is a well-defined comparison operation. Each insertion of a new value in the current priority queue compares that value to those already in the sequence; thus, each new value is "properly placed" according to this comparison operation. For example, if we define an `int`-valued priority queue according to `less<int>`, the current value at the front is the largest `int` value in the sequence. In this case, the value in the sequence having the highest priority is the largest value. On the other hand, if `greater<int>` replaces `less<int>` as the comparison operator, the value in the sequence having the highest priority is the smallest value.

Each of the `stack`, `queue`, and `priority_queue` class templates is defined in the STL as adaptations of fundamental containers because each provides a different and more limited interface to those defined for each of the underlying fundamental containers. As has been mentioned, Chapter Seven is devoted to the detailed treatment of container adaptors.

Iterator Adaptors

Iterator adaptors are STL components used to change the interface of an iterator defined on some fundamental container. There are two basic forms of iterator adaptors: *reverse iterators* and *insert iterators.*

a. Reverse Iterators

There are several forms of reverse iterators depending on the fundamental container involved. For example, if the fundamental container is some `list` object, the underlying iterators are bidirectional. For lists, the STL provides a reverse bidirectional iterator adaptor which, when invoked, transforms (adapts) a given bidirectional iterator into one whose direction of traversal is the reverse of that of the original iterator. In addition, the STL defines reverse iterator adaptors for containers supporting random-access iterators. In each case, these are identified by reverse_iterator.

Each of these container types also provides a pair of member functions called rbegin and rend, which are used to define the boundaries of the reverse iterator traversal. These behave in a manner similar to that described earlier for begin and end in the sense that rbegin and rend define the boundaries of a half-open range. They are distinct from begin and end because they operate in reverse order as follows:

- rbegin() returns the position of the initial member of a reverse iteration—the position of the last member of a sequence.
- rend() returns the position immediately after the last member involved in a reverse iteration—the position immediately before the initial member of the sequence.

As an example, suppose we define each of the following for loops for int_array as it appears in Figure 5.10. Then, for iter1 defined as a const_iterator for int_arr, the result of executing

```
for(iter1 = int_arr.begin(); iter1 != int_arr.end(); ++iter1)
 cout << *iter1 << '\t';
```

is

```
7    5    4    3    2      -1
```

If we define iter2 as a reverse_iterator for int_arr, the result of executing

```
for(iter2 = int_arr.rbegin(); iter2 != int_arr.rend(); ++iter2)
 cout << *iter2 << '\t';
```

is

```
-1   2    3    4    5    7
```

b. Insert Iterators

Ordinarily, when a mutable iterator ptr defined on some STL container is used to change the value currently stored at the position being referenced, the result is an *overwriting* of that value, using an assignment

```
*ptr = expression;
```

In contrast, an *insert iterator* adapts the iterator to a version that instead executes an insertion of the value defined by *expression* at that location. The STL supports three kinds of insert iterators, each of which is a class template:

- Back inserters, causing the container's push_back member function to be invoked, inserting the new value at the back of the container. This causes an increase in the container's size by one for each new value inserted. This form is available to any STL container for which an efficient form of `push_back` is defined (vectors, deques, lists).

- Front inserters, causing the container's `push_front` member function to be invoked. This form is available to those container classes for which such a member function is available (deques, lists).
- A general inserter, available to all STL containers because all of these define a general insert function `insert()`. Since we have not formally treated any of these containers in any detail at this point, we forgo any further discussion of insert iterators here. This treatment will occur in the next two chapters.

Function Adaptors

Just as iterator adaptors extend the functionality of iterators, *function adaptors* permit extensions of the functionality of function objects. We have already observed that by adding an extra parameter in the form of a function object, the functionality of a number of generic algorithms is extended. This was seen for the generic `sort` algorithm, using `greater<T>`. There are three general categories of function adaptors defined in the STL. These are *negators, binders,* and *pointer-to-function adaptors.* Each is defined as a template whose single parameter may be instantiated either by a function or by a function object.

a. Negators

These are used to reverse the values returned by any predicate function object. A negator may assume one of two forms depending on whether the underlying predicate object is unary or binary.

`not1` takes a single unary predicate argument and returns a predicate argument that reverses the truth value of the original. Its syntax is given by

`not1(`*`unary-predicate-name`*`)`

where *`unary-predicate-name`* is an identifier naming the unary predicate object. We illustrate this by creating a class template `is_even`, containing a member function testing whether the current input value is even:

```
template <class T> class is_even : public unary_function<T,bool>
{
 public:
  bool operator()(const T& value) const
   {
```

```
    return value % 2 == 0;
  }
};
```

If we now construct even_test as an object of is_even instantiated for int-valued processing, the result

```
(not1(even_test)(v)?"is even":"is odd")
```

returns is odd if an even integer is input and returns is even if an odd integer is input.

On the other hand, not2 accepts and returns binary function predicate objects, also reversing the truth value of the original. We illustrate this with the next example, where we use the predefined binary predicate object greater<T> instantiated by int. The expression

```
(not2(greater<int>())(u,v)?
"The first is not greater than the second"
     : "The first is greater than the second")
```

returns

The first is not greater than the second

if we input the sequence 3 9, and it returns

The first is greater than the second

if we input the sequence 9 3.

b. Binders

A *binder* is a type of function adaptor that transforms a binary function object into a unary function object. It accomplishes this by applying two arguments: the binary function object and a specific constant of the type defined for the binary function object. We may view this as "binding" one of the arguments of a binary function to a constant, and the result is a unary function. The STL defines two possible binders depending on which of the two arguments is bound to the constant: bind1st and bind2nd. Specifically, bind1st will bind the constant second argument to the binary function object serving as the first argument. Conversely, bind2nd binds the constant first argument to the binary function object serving as the second argument.

We illustrate these ideas using a combination of the transform generic algorithm and bind1st with the function object plus<int> to add 3 to each component of an int-valued array int_array. The result of applying this operation is the array result_array. The operation is coded as

```
transform(int_array,int_array + 4,result_array,bind1st(plus<int>(),3));
```

c. Pointer-to-Function Adaptors

These adaptors are provided by the STL to permit pointers to ordinary unary and binary functions to operate in conjunction with function objects. The STL defines a `pointer_to_unary_function` and `pointer_to_binary_function` adaptor. The first is a function object adaptor that adapts a pointer to a function to work where an object of a derived class of `unary_function` is called for. Similarly, the second is a function object adapting a pointer to an ordinary binary function to work, where an object constructed from a derived class of `binary_function` is required. The adaptors allow ordinary C++ functions, predefined or otherwise, to be used whenever the STL requires the use of an appropriate function object. This is certainly the case when we require that the function be passed as one of the parameters of a generic algorithm.

5.9 Chapter Summary

There are five distinct categories of language features defined in the STL: algorithms, iterators, containers, function objects, and adaptors. Each represents a different and important facility in contemporary software design and implementation.

Algorithms defined in the STL relate to most of the desirable and efficient aspects of data processing: searching, sorting, and general numeric algorithms such as generating a random sequence of values, to name but a few. These are presented in the `<algorithm>` library. These algorithms generally do not appear as member functions in some specific container class; instead, they are capable of being applied to objects constructed in several different container classes. For this reason, they are called *generic algorithms.*

A *container* is a repository of a finite collection of data items of a single fixed type. The STL defines several categories of containers: sequence containers and associative containers. Sequence containers are further subdivided into fundamental containers and container adaptors. The details of fundamental containers and container adaptors will be treated in Chapters Six and Seven, respectively. In contrast, associative containers define a *key* with each item of data stored in the container. The current C++ standard identifies such containers as *sorted associative containers.* These containers were designed primarily for speedy retrieval of any of their values using the associated key as the vehicle for that retrieval.

Iterators provide the important link between algorithms for processing data and the containers storing those data. Intuitively, we may view an iterator as an STL component defined on a specific container, used to refer to values stored in that container, and having the functionality of traversing through a sequence of values stored in such containers. There are several different classifications of iterators. One of these distinguishes between *mutable* and *constant* iterators. The first possesses the capability of writing over a value to which the iterator currently refers, and the second simply possesses "read only" capability. Each container class defined in the STL supports both of these forms. Another classification of iterators refers to a different form of functionality. It is possible to distinguish among input iterators, output iterators, forward iterators, bidirectional iterators, and random-access iterators. These forms are classified in a general hierarchy, with random-access iterators having the functionality of each of its predecessors and more. Besides these, there is a class of iterators not necessarily defined for a specific container; instead, these iterators apply to values stored in some input or output stream, such as `istream` or `ostream`. For this reason, such iterators are called *stream iterators.*

Function objects are defined in the STL to enable functions to be encapsulated in an object so that they may be used as parameters in some algorithm, such as those defined in `<algorithm>`. They are often used to extend the functionality of certain algorithms. For example, we used function objects to extend the functionality of each of the generic algorithms `sort` and `transform`. There are numerous other possibilities, many of which require making a more extensive study of the members of `<algorithm>`, which we undertake in Chapter Eight.

Adaptors take one of three general forms: *container adaptors, iterator adaptors,* and *function adaptors.* Each form is used to change the interface of any one of the respective STL components so as to allow for further flexibility of the component's original form. For an example of a container adaptor, we saw in Chapter One how a stack ADT may be implemented using one-dimensional arrays. One of the Programming Projects in Chapter One describes how the same stack ADT may be implemented as a linear linked list. In Chapter Six, we will extend the concept of one-dimensional arrays to vectors and deques, each of which provides for a dynamic enlargement or reduction of the size of the respective container. We will also observe that the member functions for each of these containers contain forms of the stack operations for pushing, popping, testing whether the current stack is empty, and examining the top of the current stack whenever it is not empty. However, the member functions for each of these containers contain many more member functions than those required to implement stacks. For this reason, a `stack` class template is defined in the STL (and studied in Chapter Seven) as a container adaptor. This means that a vector or a deque is used as a "background" container, with the functionality required only for stacks. Thus, we may view any stack as "sitting on top of" a vector or a deque, showing the user only the interface of member functions defined for stack operations and using nothing else appearing in the list of member functions for the background container.

Similarly, we may define a stack using a linked list implementation. As we will see in the next chapter, the `list` class template also has a functionality extending beyond what is required to implement stacks. Consequently, the role of a `list` object in relation to stacks is identical to that for vectors and deques: It serves as the background for any stack, using lists and list operations to implement the same set of fundamental stack operations. A similar situation occurs for the container adaptor classes `queue` and `priority_queue` and their background classes `deque` and `list`.

Iterator and function adaptors play similar roles in extending the interfaces of their underlying iterators and function objects. Iterator adaptors may assume one of two general forms: reverse iterators and insert iterators. Function adaptors are classified as negators, binders, and pointer-to-function adaptors. There are ample illustrations of these forms of adaptors in the text and in the exercises at the end of this chapter.

EXERCISES

1. a. Trace execution of the program

```
#include <iostream.h>
int main()
{
  int int_array[] = {2,3,8,9,7}; // Conformant array.
  const int *ptr = int_array;
  // Disclose current reference of ptr:
  cout << *ptr << endl;
  // Show that ptr can be moved to reference next
  // sequential array position
  ++ptr;
  // Disclose the new reference in the array:
  cout << *ptr << endl;

  cout << "The array is now given by:" << endl;
  for(int index = 0; index < 5;++index)
   cout << "int_array[" << index << "] = "
     << int_array[index] << endl;
 return 0;
}
```

b. What would be the result of inserting `*ptr = 3;` immediately after `++ptr;` in this program? Explain your answer.

2. a. Trace execution of the program

```
#include <iostream.h>
int main()
{
```

```
int int_array[] = {2,3,8,9,7}; // Conformant array.
int int_val = 2;
int* const ptr = &int_array[0];
// Disclose current reference of ptr:
cout << *ptr << endl;
*ptr = 3;
// Disclose the new reference in the array:
cout << *ptr << endl;
cout << "The array is now given by:" << endl;
for(int index = 0; index < 5;++index)
 cout << "int_array[" << index << "] = "
   << int_array[index] << endl;

return 0;

}
```

b. What would be the result of inserting `++ptr;` immediately after `*ptr = 3;` in this program? Explain your answer.

3. Describe the result of changing the definition of `ptr` given in if Exercise 1 or 2 by

```
const int* const ptr = &int_array[0];
```

4. Show that the following function template gives an alternative form of `linsrch`, where the first parameter refers to the initial position in the array, the second parameter refers to a memory location immediately past the last array location, and the third parameter contains the value sought:

```
template<class T> T* linsrch(T* first,T* last, T& value)
{
 for(; first != last; ++first)
  if(*first == value) return first;
 return NULL;
}
```

a. Write code for a driver for this using `int`-valued arrays.

b. Add a counter variable, which counts the number of cycles of the `for` loop required to arrive at a decision on the linear search.

5. What would be the result of invoking the function template

```
template<class T> void operation(T* first,T* last)
{
 for(; first != last; ++first)
  cout << *first << endl;
}
```

for the same container as that described in (a) of Problem 4?

6. Show that duplicate defined in Section 5.5 may be rewritten as

```
template<class Iter1,class Iter2>
 Iter2 duplicate(Iter1 first,Iter1 last,Iter2 result)
{
 for(;first != last;++first,result++)
   *result = *first;
 // Terminates for-loop
 return result;
} // Terminates duplicate
```

7. Write drivers for look_for, duplicate, substitute, and output_midval as defined in Section 5.5.
8. We propose the following generalization of insertion sort, applicable to all containers supporting bidirectional iterators:

```
template<class Iter,class T>
      void insort(Iter first,Iter last,T v,int& counter)
{
 // Insertion sort.
 for(Iter p = first + 1;p != last;++p){
  // Invariant: values in container in initial segment from
  // position first up to position p-1 are sorted among
  // themselves.
  T temp = *p; // Create temp to hold reference to the next value
               // to be sorted in the new initial segment.
  Iter q = p;
  while(q != first && *(q - 1) > temp){
   // Move larger values in current initial segment down one
   // position to make room for the new value.
   ++counter;
   *q = *(q-1);
   --q;
  } // Terminates inner while-loop.
  // Now place new value in its proper position.
  *q = temp;
 } // Terminates for-loop
} // Terminates insort.
```

Write a driver for this function template using an int-valued array and a char-valued array.

9. Use bind2nd in conjunction with transform and times<int> to multiply each value of an int-valued array of four components by 4.
10. Explain the distinction of the effect on any array of any size between the application of copy_reverse, the application of the generic algorithm reverse, and an application of a reverse_iterator.

11. Using the generic algorithm `transform` and the predefined function object `[illegible]<T>` instantiated for `int`, write a program that determines which values in an `int`-valued array are divisible by 5. Do not use binder function adaptors in this version.

12. Solve Problem 11 using function adaptors and `bind2nd`.

13. Write the complete code for a driver program for the negator function adaptor and the derived class `even_test` as described in Section 5.8.

14. Show that the function object `minus<int>` is not commutative when applied to two `int`-valued arrays `int_array1`, `int_array2` of size 3, executing each of `int_array1 - int_array2` and `int_array2 - int_array1` using the generic algorithm `transform`.

15. Show how the binder function adaptors `bind1st` and `bind2nd` produce different results when performing a subtraction of the value 5 with each component of a three-component `int`-valued array of size 3. Explain why this is so.

16. Use the generic `transform` algorithm, function objects `less<int>`, `greater<int>`, `logical_and<bool>`, and binder function adaptors to test which `int` values of a four-component `int`-valued array lie between `5` and `10`.

17. Solve Problem 16, but now without binder function adaptors or `less<int>` and without `greater<int>`.

18. Define a derived class of `unary_function` called `is_prime<T>` such that each function object constructed from this class, when instantiated to `int`, tests each value greater than or equal to 2 as to whether it is a prime. Demonstrate this for a four-component `int`-valued array, each of whose components is greater than or equal to 2.

PROGRAMMING PROJECT

1. a. Design an iterative version of `binsrch` using a function template whose prototype may be given by

```
template<class Iter, class T> bool binsrch(Iter first,Iter last,
   const T& value,int& counter);
```

where `counter` counts the number of loop cycles required for `binsrch` to decide whether `value` is found in the container whose boundaries are from `first` to just before `last`.

b. Write an alternative iterative version of `binsrch`, but now returning an `Iter` reference to the value located in the container in the case of a successful search and the null reference if not.

c. Write a recursive version of `binsrch` similar to that defined in (a).

CHAPTER 6

Sequence Containers

CHAPTER OBJECTIVES

- To introduce the three types of fundamental sequence containers.
- To describe the implementation of each as a class template.
- To investigate the member functions of each fundamental container class template.
- To compare these classes with respect to their relative functionality.
- To present a number of illustrative examples of the applicability of each container class in efficient problem solving.

6.1 Introduction

An important consideration for the program designer is the choice of the most appropriate form of container to aid in the solution of the specific software problem. For certain problems, the most appropriate choice is to apply `vector` containers; for others, a `deque` or `list` object or a container adaptor or a sorted associative container may be the most convenient. In brief, the choice of the most appropriate container type depends heavily on the underlying functionality required for the solution to the specific problem.

6.2 The `vector` Class Template

A vector is defined as any instance of the class template `vector<T>` for a specific choice of `T`. That is to say, a vector is defined as any object constructed from the `vector` class for a specific data type. As we will see shortly, any vector may be constructed using any one of four possible constructors provided by the `vector` class.

The iterators defined for vector<T> are random access; in fact, iterators defined for vector are actually pointers. In Section 5.4, we distinguished between ordinary (mutable) iterators and constant iterators as applied to vectors. This distinction is based on the intrinsic difference in the behavior of ordinary pointers and constant pointers, as described for arrays in Chapter Five. For example, suppose we have an int-valued vector vect assumed to contain at least one value, and we wish to output the values currently stored in vect in sequence of their appearance from first to last. Our design involves the most appropriate choice of iterator to solve this problem. We choose a constant iterator because no change in any of the current values is involved. In fact, the appropriate solution of this problem occurs as the sequence

```
for(vector<int>::const_iterator ptr = vect.begin(); ptr != vect.end();
     ++ptr)
 cout << *ptr << endl;
```

But suppose our design involves copying the current values of the sequence stored in vect in order of their appearance into a second vect<int> object called vect_copy. Several possible variations of a solution emerge. If vect_copy has not already been constructed, we may invoke the *copy constructor* for vector as described in the next section. This will construct vect_copy as a literal copy of vect in every sense, including the *size.* On the other hand, if vect_copy has already been constructed, we may look for a generic algorithm accomplishing the copying process: This materializes in applying copy as defined in <algorithm.h>. Another possibility will be described in the next section, where we observe that an *assignment operator* operator= is defined for vector objects; in this case, we apply

```
vect_copy = vect;
```

The result of this assignment is that vect_copy is an exact duplicate of vect, up to and including a match of the respective sizes of vect and vect_copy.

Another possibility involves coding the copying process "by hand," which we introduce primarily to show the use of both mutable and constant iterators. Suppose we construct vect_copy with a current size matching that of vect. Then the following code sequence yields vect_copy as an exact duplicate of vect:

```
vector<int> :: iterator qptr = vect_copy.begin();
 for(vector<int> :: const_iterator ptr = vect.begin();
     ptr != vect.end(); ++ptr)
 {
  *qptr = *ptr;
  ++qptr;
}[1]
```

[1]This sequence also works when vect is empty. In that case, the for loop does not execute, producing vect_copy as an empty vector.

Note that qptr is defined as a mutable iterator. This is because the copying process changes the values in vect_copy to those in vect. On the other hand, ptr is properly classified as a constant iterator because its role in the copying process is to refer to each value stored in vect in order of appearance without modifying any such value.

6.3 The Constructors for vector: explicit Declarations

The vector class defines four different versions of constructors:

a. a *default constructor,* which constructs an empty vector of initial size zero.
b. a constructor with a single integer parameter, representing the initial size of the vector. There is an optional second parameter whose type is an instance of T and represents the initial value of each of the vector's components.
c. a *copy constructor,* constructing a new vector as a full copy of some already existing vector.
d. a constructor involving two (constant) iterator parameters, producing a vector whose initial set of values lies in a *range.* This range is specified by the parameters first and last, defining the half-open interval [first,last). In other words, the initial values of the vector lie in the range beginning with and including the value currently pointed at by first up to the value immediately preceding the value referenced by last.

A convenient way of looking at a vector is as a container for a finite sequence of values of some specific type, with random access to these values using iterators, and with efficient insertions and removals occurring at one end only.[2] In this sense, the default constructor initially creates a container for a sequence of zero values. A constructor described as in (b) provides an initial allocation for a sequence of as many places as that given by the value of the (first) parameter. If an additional parameter is supplied, each of the members of the sequence of length defined by the first parameter is a copy of the value of the second parameter. The copy constructor described by (c) produces an exact replica of the vector parameter passed; this includes the size of the vector as well as the complete list of its values. Finally, (d) constructs a vector for that portion of the already existing sequence defined by [first,last). Examples of these are

[2]This description is an oversimplification; vectors contain more functionality than that described here. We will add these features in the next section.

```
vector<int> v1;
vector<double> v2(init_size,0.0);
vector<double> v3(v2);
vector<char> v4(first,last);
vector<vector<int> > v5(init_size);
```

The first of these constructs an int-valued vector of size zero. The second presumes that a preceding declaration

```
int int_size;
```

exists and that int_size has been assigned a nonnegative integer value. If that value is positive, each member of the sequence whose size is given by that value is assigned the initial value of 0.0. The third constructs a copy of the double-valued vector with the same sequence of values as that currently contained in v2. The fourth presumes first and last point at values in a single char-valued sequence,[3] where last points at a location after that referenced by first, causing the initialization of v4 to contain the sequence beginning with the value referenced by first and terminating with the value just before that referenced by last. The final form constructs a vector v5 of size given by the current value of init_size, each of whose components is an initially empty int-valued vector (Figure 6.1).

Recalling the question raised in the last section concerning the definition of vect_copy as a literal copy of vect, note that the use of the copy constructor in the form

```
vector<int> vect_copy(vect);
```

produces the desired result under the assumption that vect_copy was not constructed previously.

The formal description of the prototypes for these constructors in the public section of vector<T> assumes the form

```
explicit vector();
explicit vector(size_type, const T& = T());
vector(const vector<T>&);
template<class InputIterator> vector(InputIterator,InputIterator);
```

where explicit is a new C++ keyword. The reason for using explicit as part of the definition of a constructor is to avoid any "behind-the-scenes" type conversions. The C++ language is somewhat liberal about constructors with respect to implicit type conversions, which ordinarily should flag a "type mismatch" compile error; a specific type cast should be used but is not necessary. This sometimes results in run-time bugs that are very subtle in nature and, consequently, are quite difficult to detect. This is illustrated in Example 6.1.

[3]It is possible for last to point at the location immediately following the last character of the sequence.

FIGURE 6.1 v1

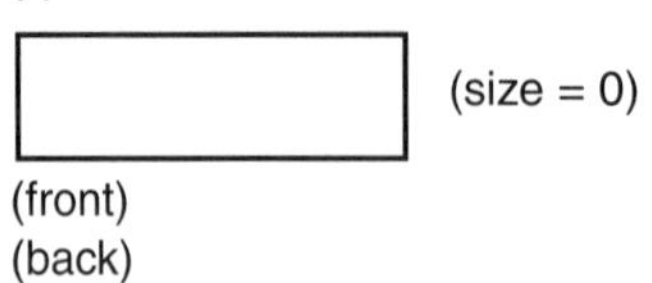

init_size

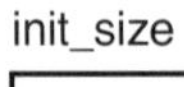

5

v2

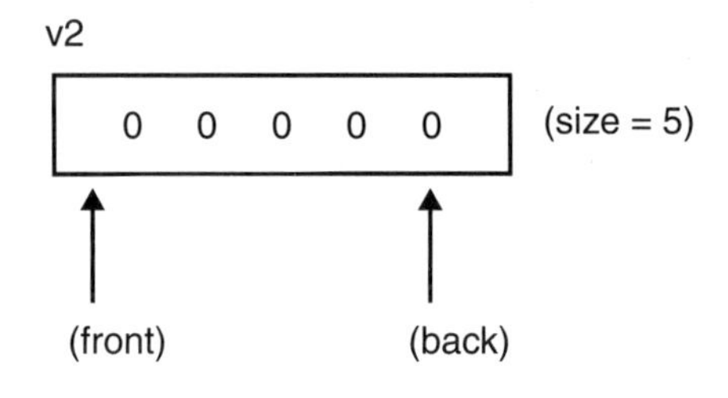

v3

0 0 0 0 0 (size = 5)

v4

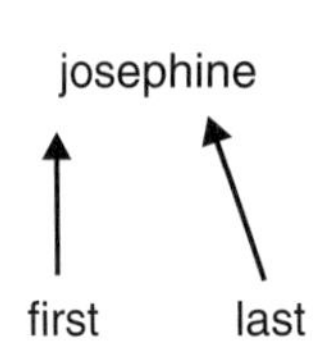

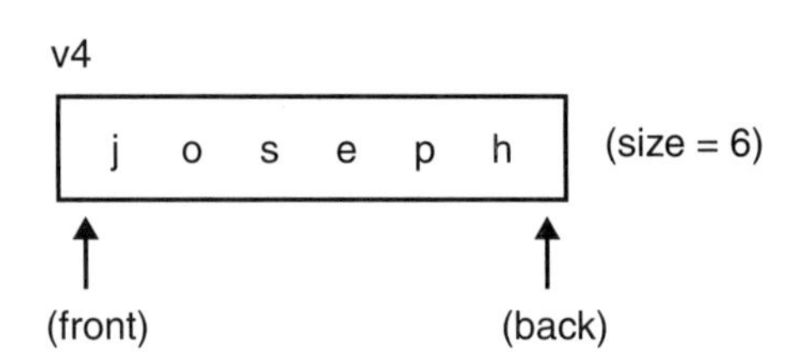

v5 (size = 5)

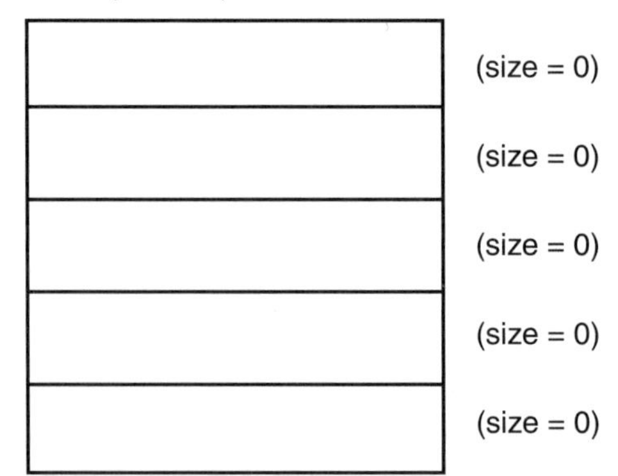

EXAMPLE 6.1 We define a class char_holder whose objects simulate single memory cells containing char values. We divide the definition of char_holder into a user interface and implementation file as follows:

```
class char_holder{ // A class simulating a character
                   // memory component.
public:
 // Explicit form of a constructor with a
 // default parameter value of 'a'.
 explicit char_holder (char = 'a');
 // Returns current char value of object
 char return_value() const;
 // Overwrites current char value of object.
 void write_value(char);
private:
 char data_component;
}; // Completes user interface for char_holder class.
```

The implementation details are

```
// Explicit form of constructor.
// Note "explicit" modifier is not duplicated here.
char_holder :: char_holder(char initial_value)
{
 data_component = initial_value;
}

// Returns current char value of object.
char char_holder :: return_value() const
{
 return data_component;
}

// Overwrites current char value of object
void char_holder :: write_value(char val)
{
 data_component = val;
}
```

Suppose a possible user program contains

```
char_holder cell1;
cell1 = 'c';
```

A compile error is detected in the last assignment as a *type mismatch* because the attempt is being made to cast a char value as a char_holder object.

The `explicit` declaration prevents this. On the other hand, if the user interface instead replaces the `explicit` constructor for `char_holder` by

```
char_holder(char = 'a');
```

and the same code sequence is executed, no compile error is detected. In this case, the cast is performed implicitly, storing `'c'` as the `data_component` value of `cell1`.

6.4 Description of Other Member Functions of `vector`

The `vector` class defines a *destructor* `~vector()` and an *assignment operator* `operator=`, whose behavior is described as follows:

- when applied to any vector, the destructor releases any storage allocated for this object
- if `v1` and `v2` are vectors storing sequences of values of the same type, then the assignment operation is generally written in infix form as

  ```
  v2 = v1;
  ```

  and copies the sequence stored in `v1` into `v2`, and the size of `v2` becomes that of `v1`.

Unlike an ordinary array defined in C++, a vector knows its size because `size()` is a member function defined in `vector`. Thus, for the definitions of the vectors `v1`, `v2`, `v3`, `v4`, and `v5` given in Figure 6.1, the respective sizes (at the point of their definition) are zero, the current value of `init_value`, the current size of `v2`, the value of `last - first`, and the current value of `init_size`. For those situations in processing when it is useful to distinguish nonempty vectors from those that are empty, `vector` provides a `bool`-valued member function `empty()`. Thus, `empty()` is `true` if and only if the vector involved has size equal to zero. For example, referring to the vectors `v1`, `v2`, `v3`, `v4`, and `v5` just defined, `v1.empty()` is `true`, and `v2.empty()`, `v3.empty()`, `v4.empty()`, and `v5.empty()` are `false`.

The `vector` class has a member function `resize` whose syntax is given by

```
resize(int-expression);
```

permitting the user to change the current size of any vector to any number, which may be either larger or smaller than the current size depending on the value of *`int-expression`*. As an example, assuming the current size of `v2` is `5`, and if *`int-expression`* is `2*v2.size()`, then after executing `v2.resize(2*v2.size());` the new size of `v2` is `10`.

Accessors

Accessors are defined as members of a container type that return information about the container without modifying any of the container's current values. In vector, two such accessors are front() and back(), which return references to the values currently at the front and back, respectively, of a vector. They are not iterators but still provide access to these values. front() and back() each appear in two forms: one for any ordinary vector and one for a constant vector.

What is meant by a constant vector and how do we define a constant vector? A constant vector may be created by first constructing an ordinary (mutable) vector and then applying a copy constructor, as in the sequence

```
vector<int> vect1(2); // Constructs a mutable int-valued vector with
                      // two components.
        .
        .
        .
// Code for inputting two int values for the
// components of vect1.
        .
        .
        .
const vector<int> vect2(vect1); // Copy constructor.  Constructs a
                                // constant version of vect1.
```

In a manner similar to that for a constant ordinary int-valued array defined as

```
const int arr[5] = {3,-1,0,0,9};
```

a constant vector does not permit the modification of any of its values.

Let us illustrate how back() may be used for each of these forms. For vect1, we may apply vect1.back() to refer to the int value at the back of the current vector. Since vect1 is mutable, we may apply

```
vect1.back() = int_value;
```

for some int-valued variable int_value (Figure 6.2).

On the other hand, for the constant vector vect2, vect2.back() is invoked as a constant reference. Thus, for example, although we may use back() to access the current value stored at the back of vect2, we cannot modify that value. A similar discussion exists for the accessor front().

Our previous experience with ordinary arrays testifies to the importance of *array indices (subscripts)* for accessing the values of array components. In brief, if arr names some ordinary one-dimensional array with subscripts between 0 and MAX_SIZE - 1 inclusive, and if index names an

FIGURE 6.2

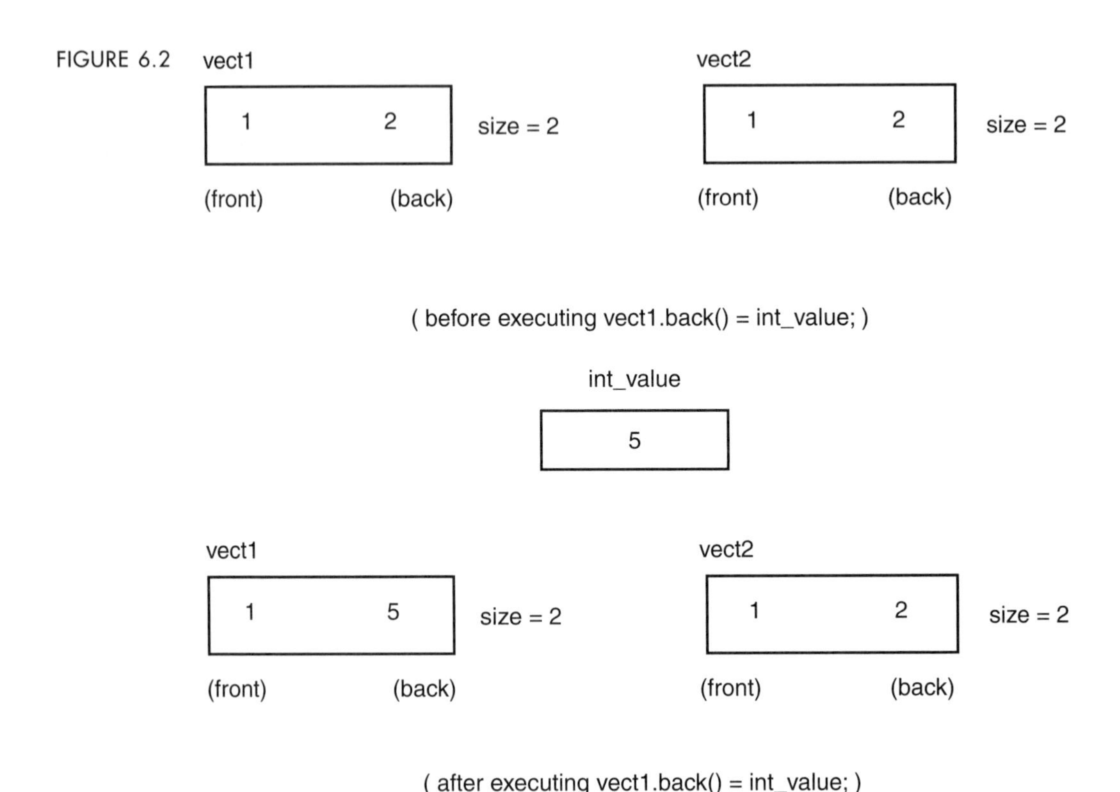

`int`-valued variable in that range, then `arr[index]` accesses the current value of the component of `arr` stored at that position. The `vector` class overloads the `[]` operator by defining a pair of member functions `operator[]`, permitting (random) access to any value stored in a vector using that reference. This was also made evident from our discussion in Section 5.5 on random-access iterators defined for any STL container type. As was the case for `front()` and `back()`, `operator[]` has two versions: one for the mutable reference and one for the constant reference. It is important to state here that if `vect` defines a vector with components of some given type and `index` is an `int`-valued parameter between `0` and `vect.size() - 1` inclusive, then we may access the value currently stored in `vect` at position `index` using either `vect[index]` or the more formally correct `vect.operator[](index)`.

For example, if `vect1` and `vect2` are defined as has been done and we execute

```
vector<int> vect1(2);
vect1[0] = 1; vect1[1] = 2;
const vector<int> vect2(vect1);
```

then, as a result, vect1 and vect2 appear as in the "before" part of Figure 6.2. The values stored in vect1 and vect2 may be output by

```
for(int index1 = 0; index1 < 2; ++index1)
 cout << vect1[index1] << '\t';
cout << endl;
for(int index2 = 0; index2 < 2; ++index2)
 cout << vect2[index2] << '\t';
cout << endl;
```

because it doesn't matter at this point whether a mutable or constant reference is used. However, if we wish to apply operator[] to modify the value of any component, we succeed for vect1 but fail for vect2. Thus,

```
vect1[1] = 5;
```

compiles and executes, but

```
vect2[1] = 5;
```

produces a compile-time error.

An alternative to operator[] offered by vector is the pair of at member functions—one for the mutable reference and the other for the constant reference to the appropriate vector. The key distinction between operator[] and at is that operator[] does not support array-bound checking, whereas at does. Simply stated, if we apply

vector-identifier[*expression*]

to a value of *expression* extending beyond the current limits of the subscripts of *vector-identifier*, no error is detected. However, if we instead apply

vector-identifier.at(*expression*)

under the same conditions, a run-time error is detected.

Modifiers

Another group of member functions are categorized as *modifiers* because they change the state of the current vector. We have already seen an example of a modifier—the *assignment operator*, defined formally as operator=, when applied as v2 = v1; changes the state of v2 to match that of v1.

Unlike ordinary arrays, which maintain a fixed size throughout, the vector class provides member functions push_back and pop_back, which (among other things) permit the size of the vector to increase or decrease. These functions execute *efficiently* (in fact, push_back and pop_back each execute in *constant time*) by pointing directly at the back of the current vector and then performing the insertion or deletion at that end.

`push_back` requires a single parameter whose type matches the type of the components of the underlying vector. The syntax is

vector_identifier`.push_back(`*expression*`);`

where *vector_identifier* names the vector, and *expression* is a well-defined expression whose value is the value to be inserted. When executed, `push_back` inserts the value computed by *expression* at the back of the current vector, increasing its size by one. As an example, suppose that `vec1` is an `int`-valued vector whose current state is as in Figure 6.3a. If `value` is

FIGURE 6.3a vec1

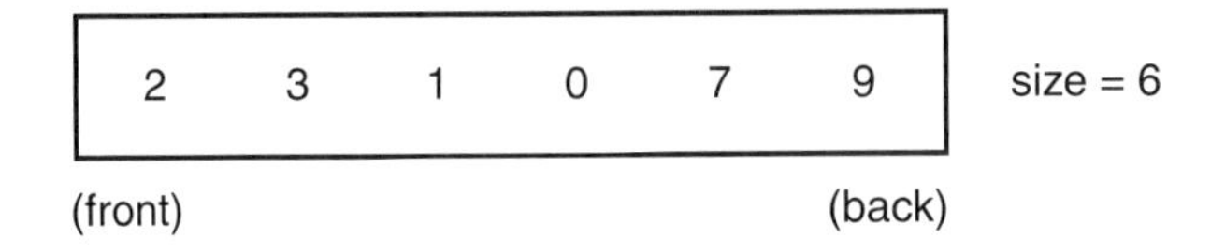

an `int`-valued parameter whose current value is `12`, then the result of executing

```
vec1.push_back(value);
```

is the vector described in Figure 6.3b.

FIGURE 6.3b vec1

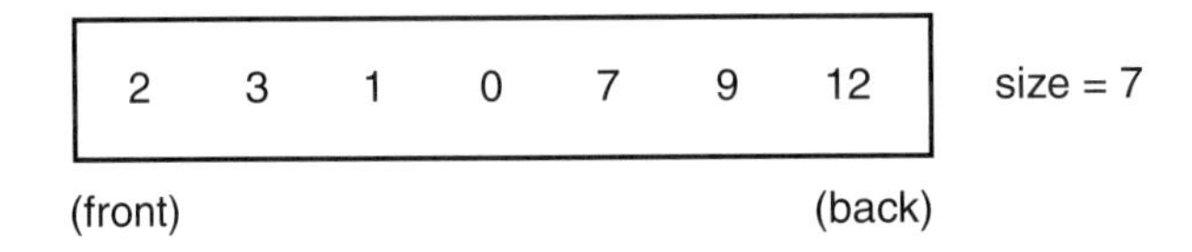

The member function `pop_back` requires no parameters and performs the efficient removal of the value at the back of the current vector whenever that vector is not empty. In addition, the size of the current vector is decreased by one. Its syntax is

vector_identifier`.pop_back();`

with *vector_identifier* defined as it was earlier. For example, if `vec1` is defined as in Figure 6.3a and if we execute

```
vec1.pop_back();
```

the result is as described in Figure 6.3c.

FIGURE 6.3c vec1

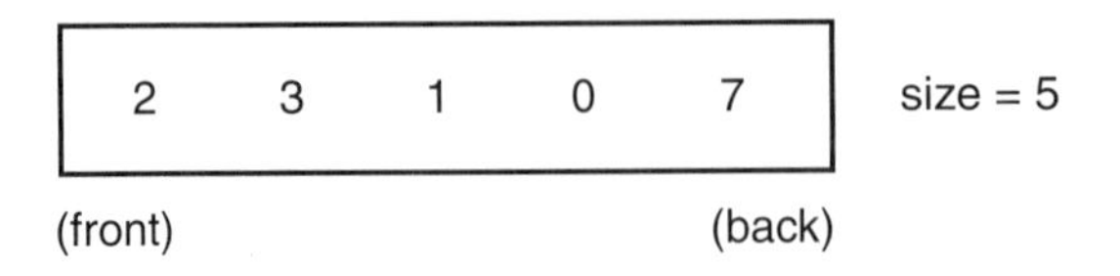

Other modifiers exist among the `public` member functions of `vector`. For example, `insert` is a modifier that inserts a new value at any position in the vector referenced by an iterator, increasing its size by one. But if `insert` is applied to any position other than the back and if the vector contains a relatively large sequence of values, `insert` is not efficient. The reason is that every member of the sequence after the position where the new value is to be inserted has to be moved down one position to make room for that new value.

Two other versions of `insert` are defined in `vector`. The first allows for the insertion of `n` copies of a value at a location directly before that currently referenced by the value of the first parameter. The syntax for this version is given by

```
insert(iterator position,size_type n,const T& value);
```

For example, suppose `vect` is an `int`-valued vector, currently described as in the before version of Figure 6.4. If we then define `mid` by

```
vector<int> :: iterator mid = v.begin() + (v.end() - v.begin())/2;
```

and apply

```
vect.insert(mid,5,7);
```

five copies of the value `7` are inserted into `vect` at the location just before `mid`. The result is described as the after version of Figure 6.4.

FIGURE 6.4

vect

1	3	-5

size = 3

(front) (mid) (back)

(before)

vect

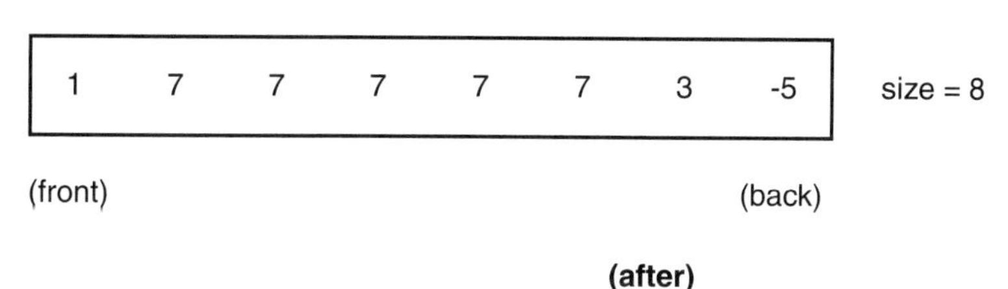

For the insertion to execute properly, the values currently stored in the vector from the location currently referenced by `position` up to and including the back have to be moved `n` locations to the right to make room for the inserted copies of the value of the third parameter.

The last version inserts a range of values `[first,last)` defined by iterators `first` and `last` into the locations immediately before that referenced by the value of the first parameter. The syntax is

```
insert(iterator position,InputIterator first,InputIterator last);
```

As an example, if `vect1` is the `int`-valued vector described in the before version of Figure 6.5 and if `first` and `last` are the respective iterators `arr + 1` and `arr + 5`, then the result of applying

```
vect1.insert(mid,arr + 1,arr + 5);
```

yields the result described in the after version of Figure 6.5.

FIGURE 6.5

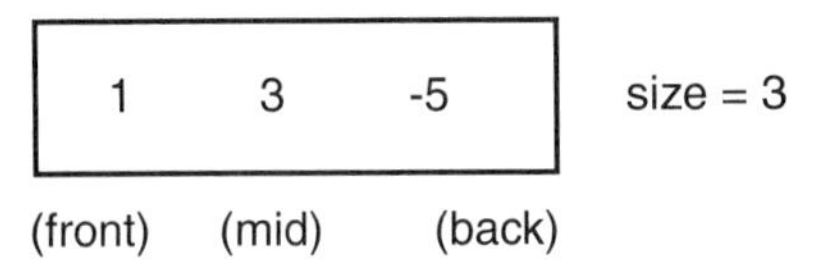

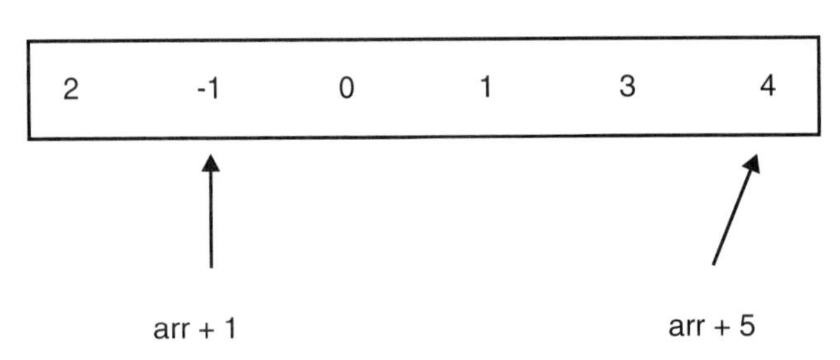

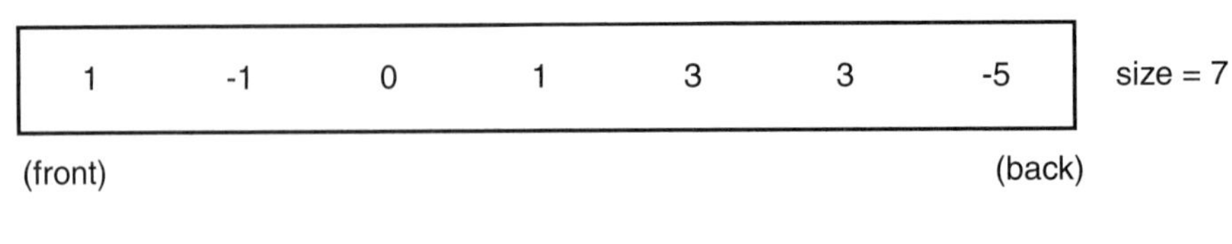

We have already shown how `pop_back` works. This function turns out to be the most efficient form of a deletion function in `vector` because deletion of the value at the back of a vector can be done directly without modifying the position of any of its values. Since `vector` supports efficient insertion and deletion operations only at the back of any of its objects, there is no equally efficient member function for deletion operating on the front. As we will see, the `deque` class supports equally efficient deletion operations at the front (`pop_front`) and at the back (`pop_back`) of any of its objects. Nevertheless, we may mimic `pop_front` for vectors, as well as a general deletion operation for any value occurring in a vector. This general deletion function is called `erase`, and it has two forms: One form takes a single `iterator` parameter and erases the value currently referenced by that parameter; the other is defined using two `iterator` parameters, say, `first` and `last`, as

```
erase(first,last);
```

and removes the values contained in the vector in the range `[first,last)`. Each of these forms applies two operations: the removal of the value(s) and then the shifting of the surviving values to fill the gap caused by the removal. As examples, consider the `int`-valued vector `v` defined as in the before version of Figure 6.6. If we then apply

```
v.erase(mid);
```

the result is described in the after version of Figure 6.6.

FIGURE 6.6

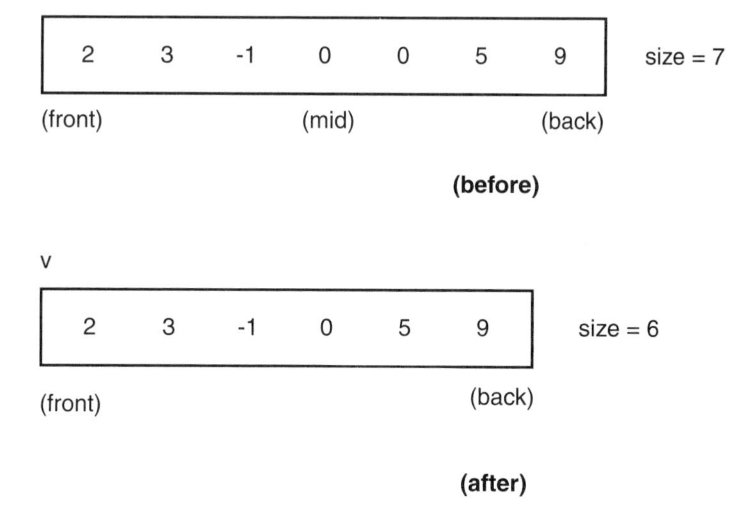

The `erase` function is inefficient because it can be accomplished only by moving all of the members of the sequence past the point of erasure, one at a time and to the left, to fill the gap left by the erasure. This operation executes in linear time—that is, of order `O(n)`.

Suppose `v` is defined as in the before version of Figure 6.7, and we now apply

```
v.erase(first,mid);
```

The result is described as in the after version of Figure 6.7.

FIGURE 6.7

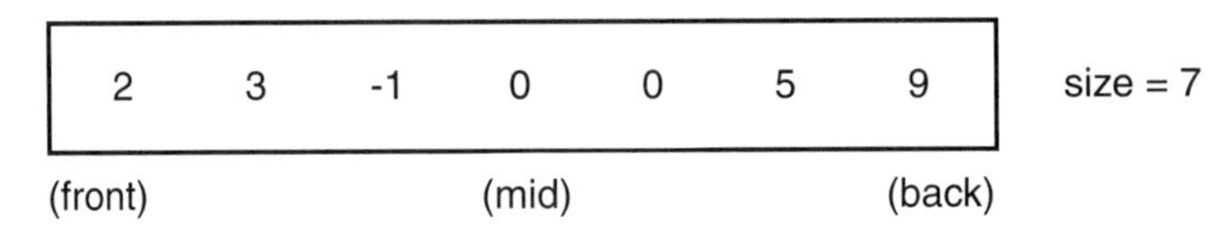

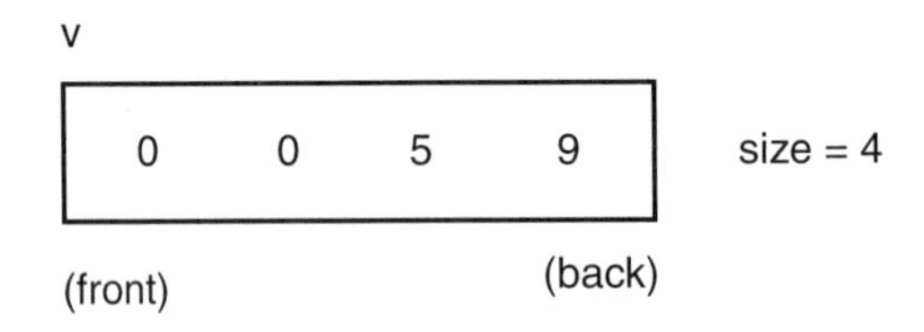

The final modifier is the `swap` member function. Its syntax is

```
swap(vector<T>& x);
```

This function is applied to a `vector` object `v1` using a single `vector` parameter `v2` whose sequence values are the same as those of `v1`. The result of applying

```
v1.swap(v2);
```

is that the vectors `v1`, `v2` are interchanged. That is, if `v1`, `v2` appear as the `char`-valued vectors in the before version of Figure 6.8, then the result of applying

```
v1.swap(v2);
```

is the after version of the figure.

Storage Allocators

We have already discussed the possibility of considerable processing overhead when `insert` or `erase` is applied to a vector containing a large sequence of values. In fact, a reallocation of storage may be necessary, even

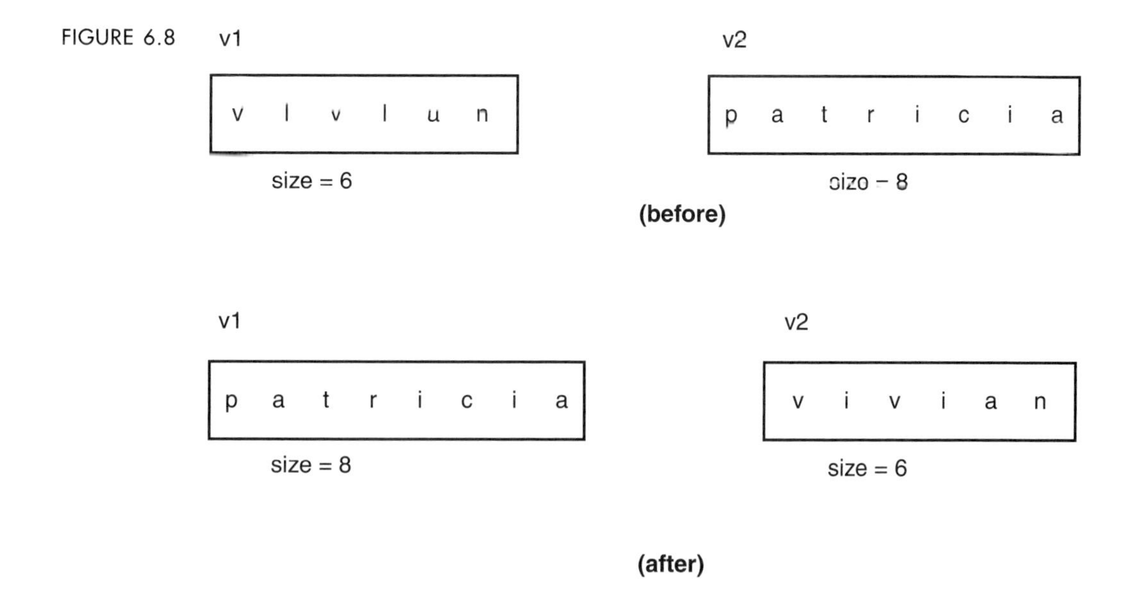

FIGURE 6.8

if we apply `push_back`. In the case of `insert` or `push_back`, a new data item is to be added, and the reason for the possible extra processing is that such data are generally stored in a contiguous block of real memory. If that block is currently filled to capacity, then each insertion operation must involve a request for additional storage, after which all of the old values, as well as the value to be inserted, must be copied into that new storage. Consequently, a simple act such as pushing an additional value onto the back of a vector may not be as efficient as we expect. For this reason, `vector` contains a pair of member functions called `capacity` and `reserve`, which respectively return the current amount of storage allocated to the vector and a request for a specified amount of storage for that vector. This gives the programmer a measure of control over storage reallocation whenever deemed necessary. For example, if the programmer anticipates performing a long sequence of insertion operations (using either `push_back` or `insert`), the processing time can be speeded up by executing `reserve` prior to the insertions, rather than suffering through repetitions of reallocation. If this is done, there is the guarantee that no reallocations will occur until the insertions fill up the vector to its new capacity. The syntax for these is given by

```
vector_identifier.capacity();
```

and

```
vector_identifier.reserve(expression);
```

where *expression* yields an integer value.

Comparisons

In certain instances, it may be necessary to compare two vectors containing values of a common type and then choosing some action depending on the result of the comparison. To this end, `vector` defines two comparison functions (as nonmembers), `operator==` and `operator<`, best applied in infix form, between two `vector` operands `v1` and `v2`. Each of these returns a `bool` value, and each is extendible to other containers besides vectors. Indeed, suppose `v1` and `v2` are vectors containing values of some common type. Then `v1` and `v2` are judged to be equal; that is, `v1 == v2` is `true` if and only if the size of `v1` is the same as the size of `v2` and the sequence members of `v1` are identical with those of `v2` term by term (Figure 6.9).

FIGURE 6.9

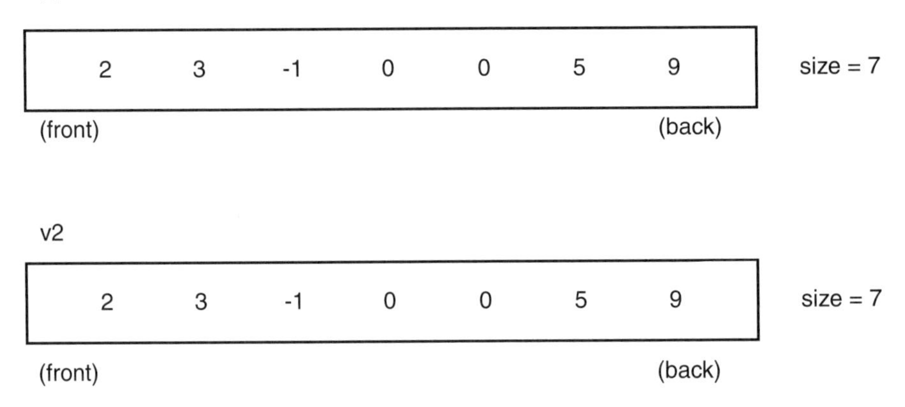

The definition of `operator<` for vectors uses lexicographic ordering in the following sense: Assume there is a well-defined order relation < for values in the underlying type of the members of each of the vectors `v1`, `v2`. Then `v1` is less than `v2`; that is, `v1 < v2` is true if and only if either of the following occurs:

1. Begin comparing the values contained in the respective vectors `v1` and `v2`, starting from `v1.front()` and `v2.front()`. If the first instance of inequality between the respective *`ith`* components of `v1` and `v2` is because the *`ith`* component of `v1 <` *`ith`* component of `v2`, or
2. If all of the corresponding components of `v1` and `v2` match, and there are leftover members of `v2` (occurring because `v1.size()` is strictly less than `v2.size()`) (Figure 6.10).

As an example, suppose `v1` and `v2` are `int`-valued vectors, and the following code segment appears in some user program:

```
if(v1 == v2) cout << "v1 and v2 are equal" << endl;
else if(v1 < v2) cout << "v1 is strictly smaller than v2" << endl;
else cout << "v1 is strictly larger than v2" << endl;
```

FIGURE 6.10

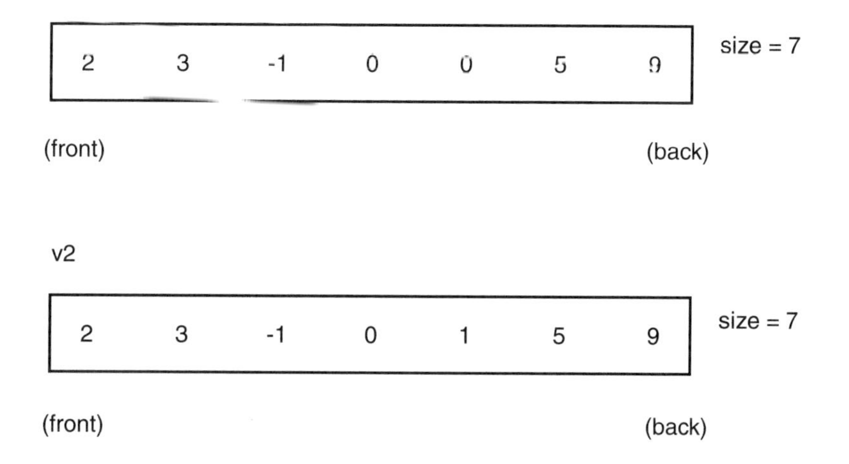

If `v1` and `v2` happen to be equal (in the sense just described), then the message

```
v1 and v2 are equal
```

is output. On the other hand, if `v1` is less than `v2` at this point, then

```
v1 is strictly less than v2
```

is output. Finally, if neither `v1` and `v2` are equal or `v1` is not strictly less than `v2`, then

```
v1 is strictly larger than v2
```

is output.

We may now define other comparisons `operator>`, `operator<=`, `operator>=`, and `operator!=` as `bool`-valued combinations of the primitive forms `operator==` and `operator<`. For example, for any vectors `v1`, `v2` constructed from the same class,

`v1 <= v2` if and only if `v1 == v2 || v1 < v2`
`v1 > v2` if and only if `v2 < v1`
`v1 >= v2` if and only if `v1 == v2 || v2 < v1`
`v1 != v2` if and only if `!(v1 == v2).`

The `vector` class supports both constant and mutable reverse iterators, as well as both constant and mutable forms of iterator member functions called `rbegin` and `rend`. Their behavior was described in Section 5.8. As an example, suppose `vect` is the `int`-valued `vector` described in Figure 6.11 and suppose we execute

```
for(vector<int> :: reverse_iterator iter = vect.rbegin();
iter != vect.rend(); ++iter)
 cout << *iter << '\t';
```

FIGURE 6.11

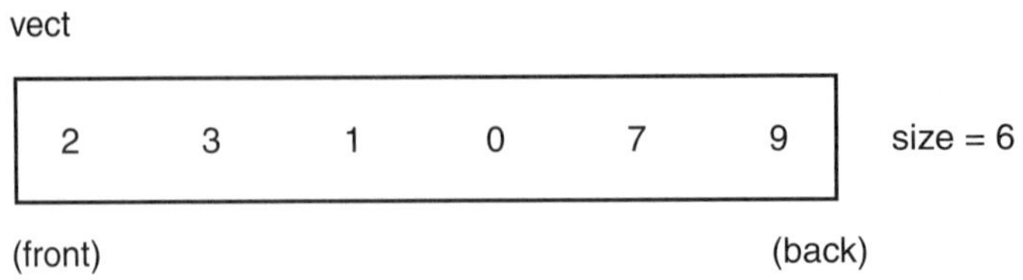

This outputs the sequence

```
9 7 0 1 3 2
```

6.5 An Application of the `vector` Class

Example 6.2 shows how the `vector` class is used to solve the following problem:

> *Given any finite sequence of integers and any selected positive integer (called the* modulus*), classify the remainders of each of the members of the sequence when divided by the chosen modulus.*

For example, suppose we select `7` as the modulus and input the sequence

```
343  119  43  12  601  120  1134  215
```

Our algorithm classifies the values of the sequence as follows:

```
343   119   1134  have remainder 0
43    120  have remainder 1
none have remainder 2
none have remainder 3
12   215  have remainder 5
601  has remainder 6
```

Our algorithm first prompts the user for the value of the modulus and then prompts for the length of the sequence of input integer values. Once this is done, the user supplies the values of the sequence. Since the modulus can be any positive integer, a vector `vect` is the most efficient data structure to hold the sequence members sharing the same remainder. Its initial size is the value of the chosen modulus, and its components are initially empty. Second, since the sequence of input integers may be of any finite length, we use a vector `v` to hold these values. Also, each component of `vect` must be an `int`-valued vector because any number of the values of the input sequence may have the same remainder when divided by the modulus. Thus, we define `vect` using the constructor

```
vector<vector<int> > vect(modulus);
```

where modulus is an int-valued variable holding the current choice for the modulus. The function accomplishing the insertion of the values of the input sequence into the appropriate components of vect is given by the function compute_remainders:

```
void compute_remainders(vector<int>& v,int modulus,
                             vector<vector<int> >& vect)
{
 // Insert each value of the input sequence into its
 // appropriate component of vect.
 for(vector<int> :: const_iterator p = v.begin(); p != v.end(); ++p)
 {
  int value = (*p)%modulus;
  vect[value].push_back(*p);
 } // terminates for-loop
} // terminates compute_remainders
```

EXAMPLE 6.2 A driver program for compute_remainders is

```
int main()
{
 // Prompt user for a value for the modulus:
 int modulus;
 cout << "Which modulus do you wish to apply?" << endl;
 cout << "Modulus: ";
 cin >> modulus;
 // Construct vector to hold the remainders
 vector<vector<int> > vect(modulus);
 // Prompt user for the size of the input sequence
 cout << "How many integer values do you wish to process?" << endl;
 cout << "Size: ";
 int size; cin >> size;
 // Construct int-valued vector v holding input values.
 vector<int> v(size);
 // Prompt user for the values of the input sequence.
 cout << "Input " << v.size() << " integers:" << endl;
 for(int index = 0; index < v.size() ; ++index)
  cin >> v[index];

 // Invoke compute_remainders.
 compute_remainders(v,modulus,vect);

 // Output the final form of the components of vect.
 for(int index2 = 0;index2 < modulus; ++index2)
```

```
  if(vect[index2].empty()) // Current component is empty
   cout << "Component " << index2 << " has no entries." << endl;
    else // nonvoid vect component
  {
   cout << "Component " << index2 << " has entries" << endl;
   for(vector<int>:: const_iterator p = vect[index2].begin();
     p != vect[index2].end(); ++p)
    cout << *p << '\t';
   cout << endl;
  } // Terminates else-clause and for-loop
 return 0;
}
```

If this program is run with the input list given earlier, the output is

```
Component 0 has entries
343     119     1134
Component 1 has entries
43      120
Component 2 has no entries.
Component 3 has no entries.
Component 4 has no entries.
Component 5 has entries
12      215
Component 6 has entries
601
```

The final form of `vect` is shown in Figure 6.12.

FIGURE 6.12

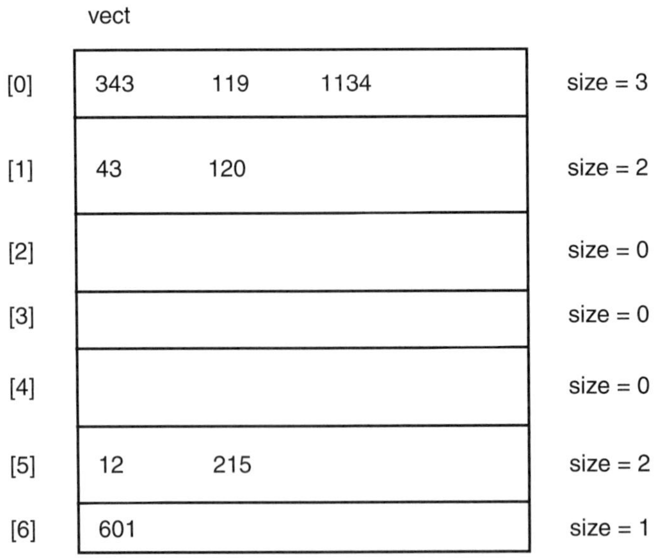

vect

[0]	343 119 1134	size = 3
[1]	43 120	size = 2
[2]		size = 0
[3]		size = 0
[4]		size = 0
[5]	12 215	size = 2
[6]	601	size = 1

6.6 An Introduction to Deques

A *deque* is any sequence container that supports random-access iterators and permits efficient insertions and removals of values from both ends. In essence, deques possess a functionality very similar to that of vectors. The key difference is that deques allow for constant-time insertions and removals at the front of the container as well as from the back. Since vectors, deques, and lists are the three fundamental sequence containers in the Standard Library, it is useful to examine their similarities as well as their differences. For example, we may note that, like vectors, deques are *indexed collections:* Deques permit the use of `operator[]` to access any value of the sequence. In direct contrast, values contained in any `list` object cannot be accessed by `operator[]` because `list` iterators are bidirectional, not random access. However, deques are similar in functionality to lists to the extent that both permit constant-time insertions and deletions at either end.

One distinction between deques and vectors lies in the choice of the appropriate preprocessor directive for the client function. To invoke operations of `deque`, we use

```
#include <deque>
```

`deque` and `vector` each have the same set of constructors, a similar destructor, similar constant and mutable random-access iterators, as well as constant and mutable reverse iterators. The `deque` class uses `begin()` and `end()` in the same way as `vector`, as well as *accessors* `operator[]`, `at()`, `front()`, and `back()`, *comparison operators* `operator==` and `operator<`, *modifiers* `push_back()`, `pop_back()`, `push_front()`, `pop_front()`, `insert()`, and `erase()`, *capacity operators* `size()`, `max_size()`, `resize()`, and `empty()`, and an *assignment operator* `operator=`.

There are many other striking similarities between `deque` and `vector` extending beyond the description of their respective member functions. For example, in Section 5.4, we defined the function `duplicate` as a generic application for copying a finite sequence of values stored in one sequence container into another. In fact, it is possible to apply `duplicate` when we wish to copy values stored in one type of sequence container into another of a different type. Specifically, suppose `int_vector` is an integer-valued vector and suppose we wish to copy this sequence into the integer-valued deque `int_deque`. We may accomplish this by invoking

```
duplicate(int_vector.begin(),int_vector.end(),int_deque.begin());
```

In addition, the version of `selsort` with iterator parameters described in Section 5.5 works just as well for vectors and deques. In fact, invoking `selsort` for `int_vector` is done by

```
selsort(int_vector.begin(),int_vector.end(),0,swap_counter);
```

and invoking `selsort` for `int_deque` takes the form

```
selsort(int_deque.begin(),int_deque.end(),0,swap_counter);
```

There are some subtle differences in the listing of member functions for `vector` and `deque`. For example, `vector` contains the member functions `capacity` and `reserve`, but `deque` does not provide either of these. The reason lies in the internal reorganization of storage done automatically for deques. This reorganization also affects the implementation of iterators. The details are quite involved and are not critical to our treatment. For our purposes, it is enough to indicate that `vector` uses these functions to improve performance, which are viewed as unnecessary for deque processing. (For more on this topic, see Musser & Saini, 1996, Plauger, 1996, and Plauger, 1997a in the References of this chapter.)

6.7 An Application of the `deque` Class: Pseudorandom and Random Numbers

We consider a very simply stated problem whose solution varies in complexity with the choice of the container. Its statement is

Given any finite sequence of positive integers, we wish to "sift" its members so that the even values precede the odd members.

It is not necessary that the sequence is sorted. For example, if our sequence is

```
15514  29530  9846  27983  9085  22060
```

then the result of sifting these values is

```
22060  9846  29530  15514  27983  9085
```

The algorithm for solving this problem is quite straightforward:

Input the size of the random sequence of integers;
Construct the container to be used for the sifting process;
Generate the random sequence;
`for` *each sequence member:*
    `if`*(member is even) insert it at the front of the container;*
    `else` *insert it at the back of the container;*

How do we generate the random sequence? We cannot use any algorithm for this purpose because an algorithm is *deterministic* by its very definition. That is, each step of an algorithm determines exactly one successor. Thus, in generating any sequence of random numbers, the next random number cannot depend in any combinatorial way on the value of any of its predecessors. Conceding this, we can accomplish the next best thing: generate a *pseudorandom sequence* of integers, applying functions whose output gives the appearance of random sequences. (A very thorough and comprehensive discussion of generating pseudorandom sequences is found in Knuth in the References at the end of this chapter.)

`<stdlib.h>` is a C++ library containing two functions `rand()` and `srand()`, which are instrumental in generating random number sequences. `rand()` and `srand()` are parameterless; `rand()` returns a new random number each time it is called, whose value depends on the value of the random number that was generated last.[4] But what about the first such random number? How is its value generated? This is done by providing an implementation-dependent initial value (called the *seed*) to the random number generator.

Having conceded this, it seems plausible that any random sequence of length `RANDOM_LENGTH`, where `RANDOM_LENGTH` is assumed to be a programmer-defined positive integer constant, can be generated using

```
for(int index = 0; index < RANDOM_LENGTH; ++index)
cout << rand() << endl;
```

But this is only partly true. The fact is that each time this loop executes, the same random number sequence is generated. This was intentially designed for testing purposes. The function `srand()` is used to generate a different random number each time this loop executes. Unlike `rand()`, a single `unsigned` parameter is passed to establish the seed. Once this is done, `rand()` is used to generate the random number sequence.

A common method for establishing the seed is to use the *internal clock* present in any computer system. Each C++ implementation contains a predefined library `<time.h>` enabling an interface to be created with the client program using the preprocessor directive

```
#include <time.h>
```

This library contains a function `time()` returning values from a specially designed integer type predefined in `<time.h>`. If we evaluate `time(0)`—that is, evaluate the time at zero—the return value is an integer from that type. The seed is established using `srand` and a cast operation, expressed as

```
srand((unsigned) time(0));
```

When executed, the compiler converts the seed from this internal integer type to an `unsigned` value. To illustrate this, observe that the sequence

```
srand((unsigned) time(0));
for(int index = 0; index < RANDOM_LENGTH; ++index)
cout << rand() << endl;
```

[4]The value returned by `rand()` is a nonnegative integer in the range from `0` to `RAND_MAX` inclusive, where `RAND_MAX` is an implementation-dependent positive integer predefined in `<stdlib.h>`.

will generate a completely different random number sequence each time it executes.

Implementing the Sifting Algorithm

We seek an efficient solution to the sifting problem that is independent of the size of the sequence. This necessarily rules out the choice of an ordinary one-dimensional array as a candidate for the container used to store the sifted randomly generated integers because the size of the array would have to conform to the size of this input sequence. As a matter of fact, even if we were to agree to a maximum possible size for the random sequence and then "overdimension" the size of the array to this maximum size, the resulting solution would involve an array that, in most situations, contains needless extra components. This results in a proposed solution that is space inefficient. Even if we were to concede this factor of space inefficiency, the shifting of the array subscripts down one additional position to make room at one end for the next value of the sequence to be placed properly involves this shifting operation, which is `O(n)`. We then conclude for these reasons, as well as others, that arrays are not the best choice of the underlying container.

What about vectors? This is a better choice than arrays because vectors have a size whose value may change during the course of execution. But vectors are not the best possible choice because the insertions to be performed at the front of the vector are inefficient `O(n)` operations. A deque is the best possible choice because it permits equally efficient insertions at both front and rear. This is exactly what we require to implement this algorithm.

The solution begins by prompting the user for the number of random integers to be generated. As these numbers are generated, we store them in a container (we choose an `int`-valued vector) called `input_vector`. We use the constructor

```
deque<int> sifter;
```

to define the deque that will ultimately contain the sifted random sequence. The sifting operation is done by

```
template<class Iter> void sift(Iter first, Iter last,
                               deque<int>& sifter)
{
 for(Iter ptr = first; ptr != last; ++ptr)
  if((*ptr)%2 == 0)  // value is even
   sifter.push_front((*ptr));
  else
   sifter.push_back((*ptr));
}
```

and is invoked from the user function by

```
sift(input_vector.begin(),input_vector.end(),sifter);
```

EXAMPLE 6.2 Suppose `input_vector` is as illustrated in Figure 6.13. If we trace the execution of the `for` loop in `sift`, we observe that initially `sifter` is empty

FIGURE 6.13 input_vector

15514	29530	9846	27983	9085	22060

(Figure 6.14a). The next sequence of figures displays the progress of the sifting process as it applies to the values in `input_vector`, scanned rightward from `input_vector.front()`. This trace can be done by inserting code in the text of the loop displaying the current contents of `sifter` after completing execution of each cycle. This is left as an exercise.

FIGURE 6.14a sifter

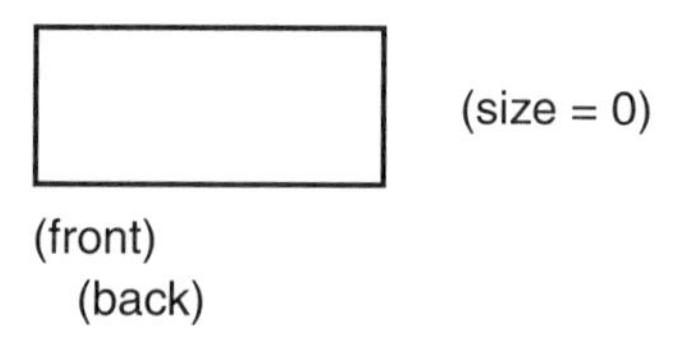

FIGURE 6.14b sifter

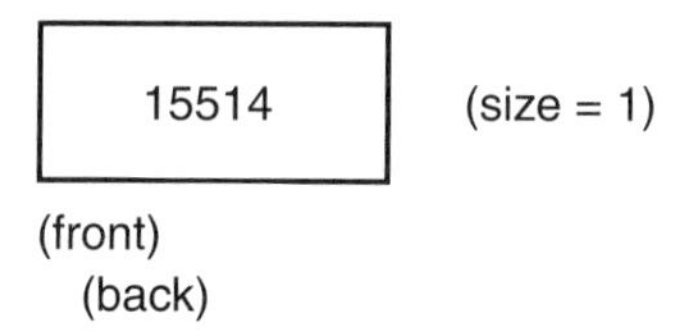

FIGURE 6.14c sifter

29530	15514

(size = 2)

(front) (back)

FIGURE 6.14d sifter

9846	29530	15514

(size = 3)

(front) (back)

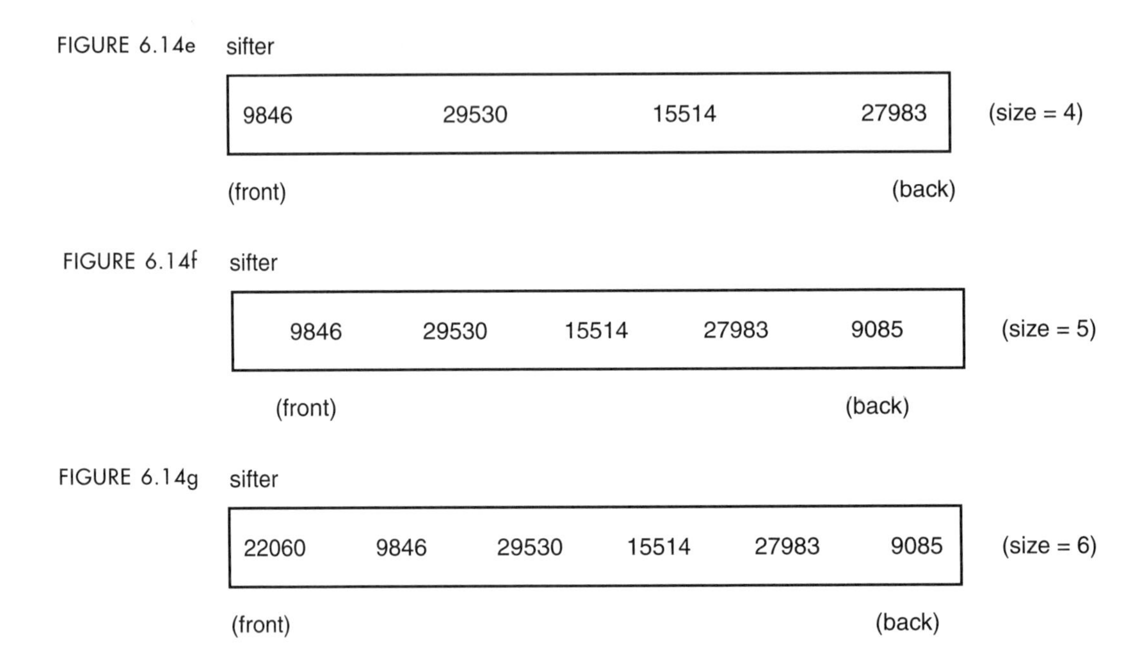

6.8 An Introduction to STL Lists

We begin by describing the concept of *linked storage* and how it differs from storage maintained in an array. When defining an array, the programmer must specify its size and the type of data to be stored in its components.[5] Even when defining a vector or a deque, an initial size is assigned to the object either explicitly or by default depending on the constructor. In the conventional case, the original size allotted to the array is fixed, and the only way to change it is left to the programmer. He or she must define a new array of a different size and then copy the contents of the original into the new array. In using `vector` or `deque` container objects, the new allocation is automatic and applied when needed, as already described.

For the moment, we will be content with enumerating key distinctions between ordinary arrays and linked storage. In an array, any value is accessed using an *index* or *pointer.* This provides *random access* in the sense that passage from any component to another is done in constant time. In linked storage, no such indexing is available: The array (or vector or deque) is replaced by a different data structure in which each component stores the location of the previous and next value along with the value. This combination of a value stored along with references to the location of the

[5]Arrays can be defined as *conformant arrays* whose size is specified by the number of initial values.

previous and next values is defined as a *node*. A typical node has the structure shown in Figure 6.15 and may be formally defined by

```
template<class T> struct node
{
 node *previous;
 T data;
 node* next;
};
```

FIGURE 6.15

As an example, the sequence of integers 3,-1,6,8 can then be represented as shown in Figure 6.16a. Here any pointer referring to any node

FIGURE 6.16a

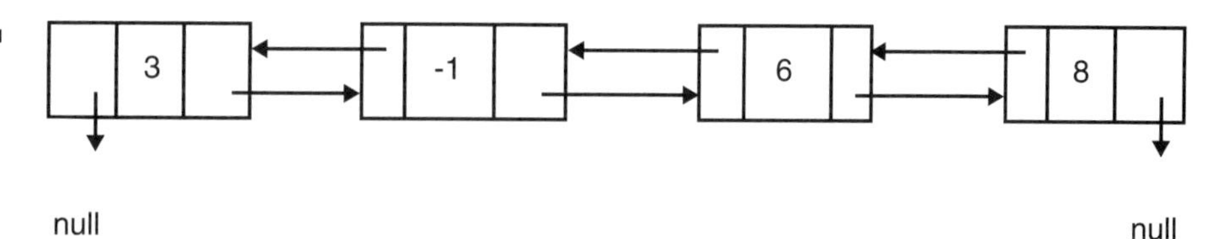

may move either forward or backward, one node at a time, until either end of the list is reached. A linked list with nodes constructed in this way is called a *doubly linked list,* and a pointer to any node in this list is called *bidirectional.* For convenience, we will use the less formal alternative description as pictured in Figure 6.16b.

FIGURE 6.16b

6.9 The Standard Class Template list: Basic Member Functions

In this section, we describe the member functions of list that are used for the more basic operations associated with linked lists in the STL. In describing these, we will note that similar names for many of the member functions exist in vector and in deque. Nevertheless, we should be aware from the outset that a very different type of container is being defined here.

Because of this, we will see that many of these member functions apply in very different ways.

Constructors, Destructors, Iterators

What should be included in a class whose objects are (doubly) linked lists? Certainly, we expect to see a number of *constructors* for creating lists. In fact, the `list` class template defines the same four constructors defined for `vector` objects as in Section 6.3 and for `deque` objects as in Section 6.6.

The definition of *iterator* is interpreted as *bidirectional iterator,* as described by the doubly linked list abstraction of the preceding section. In effect, iterators defined on lists[6] behave exactly like pointers to list nodes. For example, this implies that we can't apply `operator[]` as we could for vectors and deques. Nevertheless, other operations (such as autoincrement `operator++` and autodecrement `operator--`) are overloaded to apply to `list` objects.

For constructors, we may apply constructors similar to those described in Section 6.3 for vectors:

```
list<int> lis1;
list<double> lis1(init_size,0.0);
list<double> lis3(lis2);
list<char> lis4(first,last);
list<vector<int> >lis5(init_size);
```

The significant change here is that, in each case, a list is constructed instead of a vector. The first of these constructs `lis1` as an empty `int`-valued list. The second assumes a prior declaration

```
int init_size;
```

with a current value for `init_size` stored at the point of invoking the constructor for `lis2`. The third applies the copy constructor with `lis3` constructed as a literal copy of `lis2`. The fourth presumes the iterators `first` and `last` refer to locations in a `char`-valued sequence, where `last` refers to a later position in the sequence than that currently pointed at by `first` or is pointing to the first position directly after that of the last character in the sequence. This causes `lis4` to contain the sequence beginning with the value pointed at by `first` and terminating with the value immediately preceding that currently pointed at by `last`. The last of these constructs `lis5` initially of size `init_size`, each of whose components contains an `int`-valued vector whose initial size is zero.

The `list` class template defines the destructor `~list()` whose behavior is identical with that defined for vectors and deques; `~list()` frees away storage allocated to the `list` object being destroyed.

[6]Unless we specify otherwise, list will refer to doubly linked list.

A useful tool in working with lists is the ability to copy one currently existing list into another. This operation is available in the form of an overloaded assignment operator operator=, whose behavior mimics that for vectors and deques. Indeed, if lis1 and lis2 name two list objects whose components are of the same data type, then

```
lis2 = lis1;
```

copies the sequence currently stored in lis1 into lis2 and modifies lis2.size() to match that of lis1.size().

There are two versions of bidirectional iterators defined for list:

1. *mutable iterators,* which permit the data component as well as either of the previous or next components to change value[7]
2. *constant iterators,* which point at constants, prohibiting any change in the data component

The list class template continues to use iterator when referring to a mutable iterator and const_iterator when referring to a constant iterator. In addition, when referring to any specific list, the list class template defines two forms of begin() and end(), one pair for mutable iterators and the other for constant iterators. Their behavior is similar to that defined for their counterpart in vector and in deque.

list also contains a member function resize, with a single integer-valued parameter, whose behavior is similar to that described for its vector counterpart with several noteworthy changes. When applied to a specific list object, the current size of that object is changed to the value passed by the parameter. If the new size is less than the current size, then the new object is truncated at the back by removing the last *current_size - new_size* values. To illustrate this, suppose lis is an int-valued list whose current size is 5, as illustrated in the before part of Figure 6.17.

FIGURE 6.17

lis

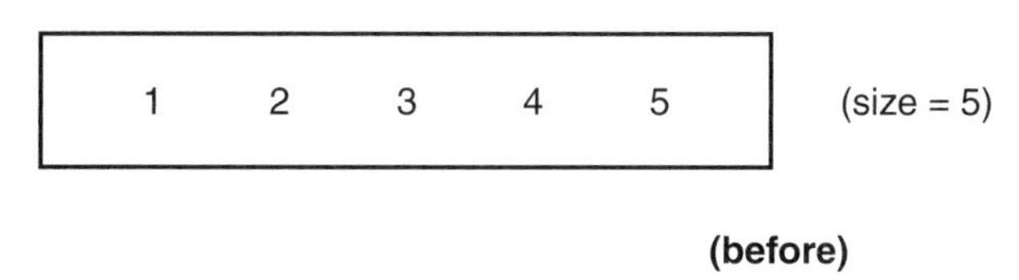

Suppose we apply lis.resize(val), where val is an int-valued variable whose current value is 3. Then the result is given by the after 1 part of Figure 6.17, and lis.size() is now 3.

[7]In our applications, we will never have any occasions to change the values of previous or next manually. This will be done by using the appropriate member function of list.

FIGURE 6.17 lis

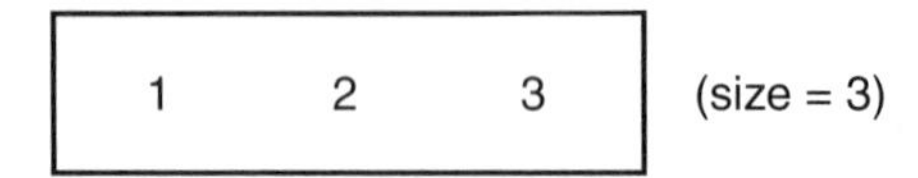

(after 1)

On the other hand, if *new_size* is greater than *current_size*, then the new list grows by appending *new_size - current_size* copies of the value stored in `val` at the back of the current list. For example, suppose the value currently stored in `val` is `9`. Then the result of executing `lis.resize(val)` is given in the after 2 part of Figure 6.17, with the new value of `lis.size()` equal to `9`. When applying `resize` to a `char`-valued list in the case where *new_size* is greater than *current_size*, then *new_size - current_size* "blanks" are appended.

FIGURE 6.17 lis

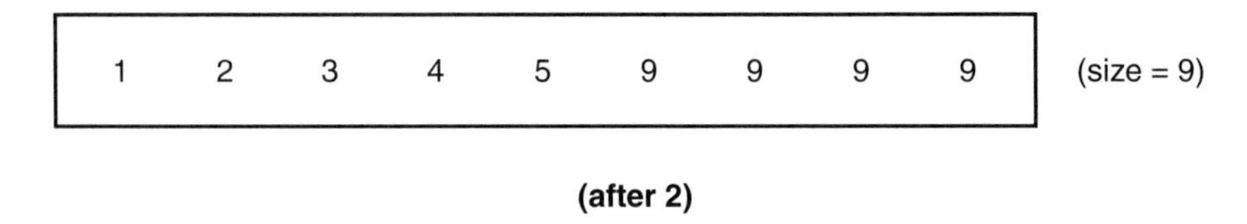

(after 2)

Accessors

The counterpart for `empty()` and `size()` exists for lists. As examples, `lis1.empty()` is `true` and `lis3.empty()` is `true` if and only if `lis2.empty()` is `true`. In addition, `lis1.size()` is zero, while `lis2.size()` is the current value of `init_size`, and `lis3.size()` is the current value of `lis2.size()`.

What about references to nodes in the list? In this case, `list` provides a number of member functions similar to those seen in `vector` and `deque`. These are the member functions `front()` and `back()`, which return either a reference or a constant reference to the respective first and last members of a list. In addition, we don't have to maintain a reference to some designated head node: If `lis` denotes some `list` object, then `lis.front()` refers to the initial node, and `lis.back()` refers to the last node. For example, the list described in Figure 6.16a or Figure 6.16b may be represented as shown in Figure 6.18.

FIGURE 6.18 lis

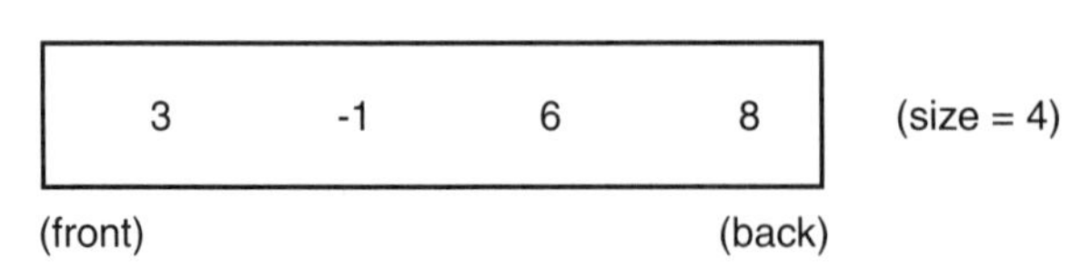

Modifiers

There are two characteristics that distinguish lists from the other fundamental sequence containers. These are the ability to make insertions at any position in the list and to delete a value at any position. Certainly, these operations are possible for vectors and deques, but the emphasis here is on efficiency. In `vector` and `deque`, these operations are of order `O(n)` because the sequence must first be traversed to find the proper location for the insertion or deletion. However, if the container is a `list` object, there are several member functions for inserting and removing values that execute in constant time.

We begin with insertions at the front and back. The `list` class template defines some familiar functions, `push_front` and `push_back`, now applicable to `list` objects. If this were to be done manually, it would require an `O(n)` operation to locate either the front or back of the list prior to executing the insert operation. But insertion goes beyond these special cases. In fact, `list` supports three possible forms of the member function `insert`. These are

1. `insert(position,value);`
2. `insert(position,n,value);`
3. `insert(position,first,last);`

Here `position` is an iterator value referring to a specific position in the list, `value` defines a value of the specific data type of the values in the container, `n` is some (positive) integer value, and `first` and `last` define a range `[first,last)`. When version 1 is applied, the data item stored in `value` is inserted into the list immediately before the location referenced by `position`; version 2 inserts `n` copies of the contents of `value` immediately before `position`; and version 3 inserts the values in `[first,last)` immediately before `position`.

A key observation here is that each version of `insert` has a counterpart as a member function in `vector` and `deque`. That is to say, each of the insertion functions for `list`, `vector`, and `deque` has essentially the same user interface but with significant differences in functionality. The insertion operations for `list` execute in constant time at any position, whereas insertions for `vector` execute in constant time only when the insertion is at the back and insertions for deques execute in constant time only when those insertions are performed at either end.

The `list` class template supports several versions of member functions dedicated to the removal of values from any `list` object, each of which is `O(1)`. The first two are the familiar `pop_front()` and `pop_back()`, and consistent with their counterpart in `vector` and `deque`. For removals at any position in a list, `list` supports two variations of the member function erase, assuming the forms

1. `erase(position);`
2. `erase(first,last);`

When applied to a nonempty `list` object, the first of these removes the value pointed at by `position`; the second removes the sequence of values in the range `[first,last)`.

Unlike vectors or deques, insertions in a `list` object never invalidate any iterators. In the case of the removal of a value from a list, the only iterator that is invalidated is the iterator pointing to the value to be removed. Since these insertions and deletions can be performed at any position in the list in constant time, a `list` object is by far the best choice of a fundamental sequence container, especially when a large number of insertions and deletions are anticipated, with a large proportion of these occurring at interior positions. In addition, a `list` object should be the fundamental container of choice if there is virtually no need for the random jumping of references in the container from one position to any other.

More on Iterators

`list` also supports reverse iterators, and defined member functions `rbegin()` and `rend()`, with the same underlying behavior as for `vector` and `deque`. The only distinction is that now these iterators are bidirectional instead of random access.

There are other changes, already mentioned in Section 5.5, between bidirectional and random-access iterators that deserve repetition here. There are distinctions inherent in the possible arithmetic operations available for these iterators. For example, suppose `v` names either a `vector` or a `deque` object. Then we may define a random-access iterator of the form

```
v.begin() + ((v.end() - 1) - v.begin())/2
```

pointing to the midpoint of the sequence currently stored in `v`. This is not possible if `v` is a `list` object. However, as described in Section 5.5, autoincrement (`operator++`) and autodecrement (`operator--`) are applicable for iterators defined for each of the fundamental sequence container types. In the case of `list`, these are interpreted as referring to the respective `next` and `previous` components of a typical list node.

Comparative Operators

We conclude this section by describing two comparative operators for `list` objects for which a similar counterpart exists for both `vector` and `deque`. The first of these is `operator==`, most often applied infixed between two list operands lis1 and lis2, whose values come from a common data type. The bool value true is returned if and only if lis1 and lis2 are identical. The second is operator<, implementing lexicographical ordering for list objects in exactly the same way as for vectors and deques.

6.10 The Standard Class Template list: More Specialized Member Functions

In the preceding section, we gave an overview of the basic member functions of list. In contrast, this section describes other member functions of list stemming from the observations that lists have a significantly different functionality from the other fundamental sequence containers.

Merging Two Sorted Lists

Suppose lis1 and lis2 are sorted lists with data components of the same type. Then list defines a member function merge which, when applied to any one of these with the other as a single parameter, produces a sorted list merging lis1 and lis2. Thus, if we apply

```
lis1.merge(lis2);
```

then lis1 is the merged result, and lis2 becomes empty. We illustrate this with the merging of two sorted int-valued lists. Suppose that lis1 is originally the list described in Figure 6.19a and lis2 is originally as in

FIGURE 6.19a lis1

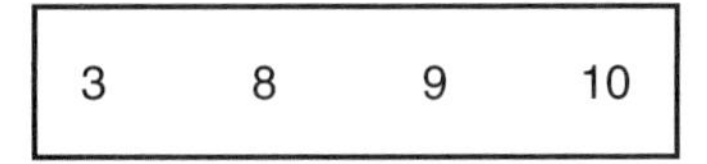

Figure 6.19b. Then after executing lis1.merge(lis2), lis1 becomes the list in Figure 6.19c, and lis2 becomes empty.

FIGURE 6.19b lis2

-2 0 3 12 16

FIGURE 6.19c lis1

-2 0 3 3 8 9 10 12 16

We should also note that `merge` defines a *stable sort:* When the same value appears in both lists, the values in the list being acted on by `merge` always precede those carried in the parameter. In our example, the value `3` appearing in `lis1` precedes the `3` appearing in `lis2`.

There is a more general version of `merge` supported by `list`. This version permits the changing of the default ordering, `operator<`, to any other well-defined ordering of list values. This is very similar to the idea of function objects defined in Section 5.7, now applied to member functions of `list`. All that has to be done is to pass the definition of the ordering you wish to apply as a second parameter and then apply `merge` as earlier.

As it turns out, `merge` plays a dual role in the STL. Not only is it defined as one of the specific member functions of `list`, but it also appears as one of the generic algorithms of `<algorithm>`. In this second form, it does not appear as a member function of some fundamental container class. Thus, the compiler "knows" the version being applied by its context. Furthermore, in this generic form, `merge` may be applied to two sorted sequences of values of the same data type appearing in any two containers (not necessarily from the same container type) and produces a single merged sorted sequence in a third container. We will say more about this generic version of `merge` in Chapter Eight.

Splicing Two Lists

Linked storage allows for a level of flexibility that is not available for contiguous storage data structures such as ordinary arrays, vectors, and deques. In particular, it is not a simple operation to insert another finite sequence of values inside an already existing array or, in the case of vectors or deques, somewhere besides the back or at either end, respectively. On the other hand, if both sequences are stored as lists, the process of inserting one of the sequences inside of the other at any position (that is, *splicing* one list inside the other) becomes a simple matter of repositioning several pointers. For example, if we intend to splice `lis2` at a position in `lis1` immediately following the node in `lis1` currently pointed at by `ptr`, we first find the last node in `lis2` and point to it using `qptr`. Then we assign the value of `qptr -> next` to the current value of `ptr -> next`. The resulting list splices the entire list referenced by `lis2` inside `lis1` directly after the position in `lis1` immediately after that referenced by `ptr`.

The `list` class template defines three versions of the `splice` member function. These are listed as

1. `splice(position,lis_value);`
2. `splice(position,lis_value,ptr);`
3. `splice(position,lis_value,first,last);`

where lis_value is an already existing list and position is an iterator parameter currently pointing at some specific value in the list where the splice is to be made. To illustrate these, suppose lis1 names the list object where the splice is to be made and suppose we apply version 1 in the form

```
lis1.splice(position,lis_value);
```

The result causes the insertion of values in lis_value to occur in lis1 just before the location referenced by position, after which lis_value becomes empty. We illustrate this for char-valued lists. Figure 6.20a refers to the current version of lis1 and Figure 6.20b refers to the current version of lis_value. Also suppose the value of position is ++lis1.begin(). Then Figure 6.20c shows the newly spliced form of lis1 using version 1.

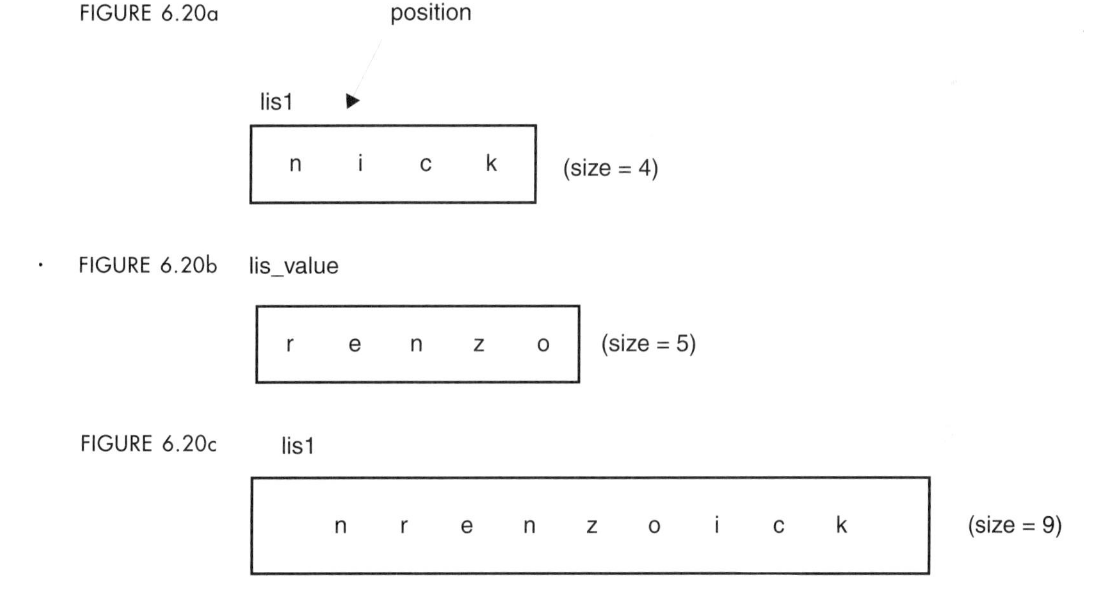

FIGURE 6.20a

FIGURE 6.20b

FIGURE 6.20c

Version 2 may take the form

```
lis1.splice(position,lis_value,ptr);
```

where position, lis_value, and lis1 are the same as in version 1, and where ptr is an iterator parameter that we assume is currently pointing at some value in lis_value. The result of applying this version places the value pointed at by ptr directly in front of the value currently pointed at by position. Unlike the first version, lis_value does not become empty; instead, it loses only the value pointed at by ptr. For example, suppose lis1 and position are defined as in Figure 6.20a and suppose lis_value and ptr currently appear as in Figure 6.20d. Then the result of applying this version yields lis1 as it appears in Figure 6.20e and lis_value as it appears in Figure 6.20f.

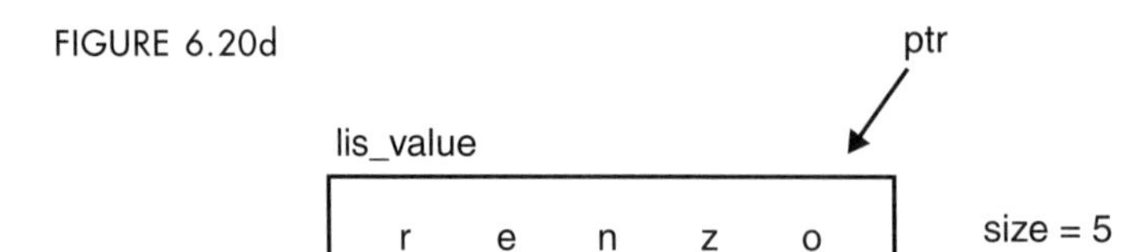

FIGURE 6.20d

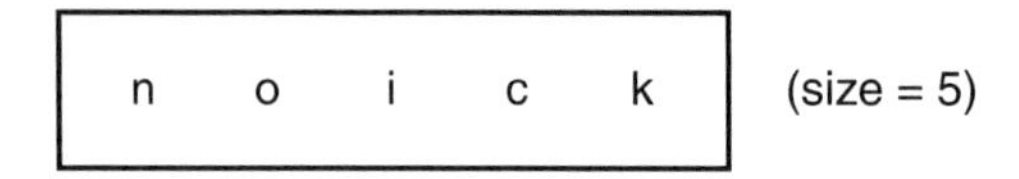

FIGURE 6.20e

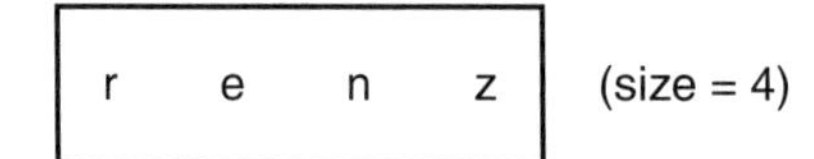

FIGURE 6.20f

We illustrate version 3 in the form

```
lis1.splice(position,lis_value,first,last);
```

where `position`, `lis1`, and `lis_value` are as in version 1 and where `first` and `last` are iterator parameters pointing at values in `lis_value` in the range `[first,last)`. In this case, the sequence of values in `lis_value` in the range `[first,last)` are spliced in front of the value currently pointed at by `position` in `lis1`, and `lis_value` loses those values. Indeed, suppose `first` is `++lis_value.begin()` and `last` is `--lis_value.end()`, as in Figure 6.20g. Then executing this version results in `lis1` appearing as in Figure 6.20h and `lis_value` appearing as in Figure 6.20i.

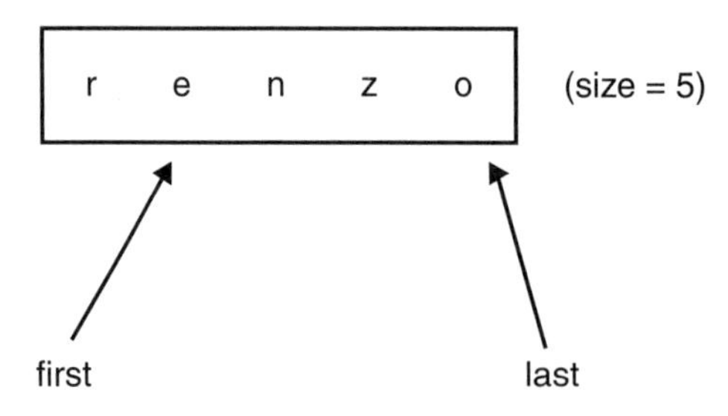

FIGURE 6.20g

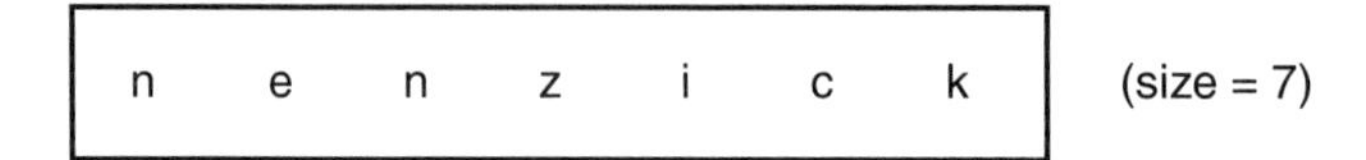

FIGURE 6.20h

FIGURE 6.20i

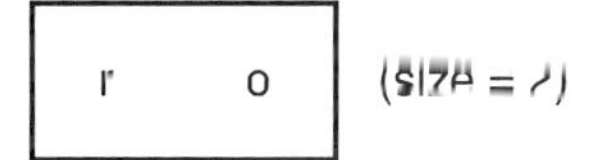

Reversing a List

The `list` class template defines a special member function `reverse()` which, when applied to any specific (nonempty) `list` object, reverses the order of appearance of the sequence of values contained there. We illustrate this with the next example. Suppose `lis1` identifies an `int`-valued list whose contents are given as in Figure 6.21a. Then the result of applying

```
lis1.reverse();
```

is the list described in Figure 6.21b.

FIGURE 6.21a lis1

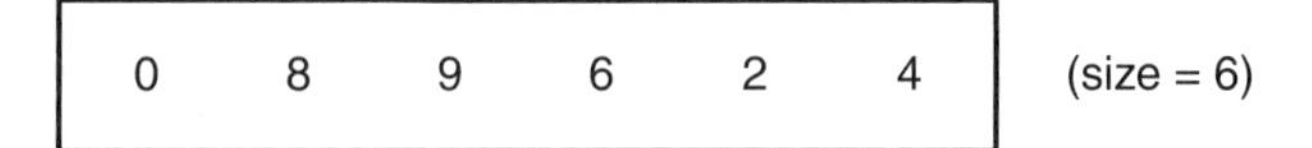

FIGURE 6.21b lis1

4	2	6	9	8	0

(size = 6)

Besides this, the Standard Library supports a generic `reverse` function in `<algorithm>`, which is applicable to any fundamental sequence container. This generic form may be applied to lists as well as vectors, deques, or arrays. It requires two parameters: iterators that point to the first and last values, respectively, of any range `[first,last)`. Applying this form to `lis1` as

```
reverse(lis1.begin(),lis1.end());
```

the result would be identical to that already described. This raises a very interesting dilemma: Which version is more suitable for lists? Since `vector` and `deque` do not have a `reverse` member function, there is no issue as to what to do. This is not the case for lists. However, there may be a difference in performance between the generic form and the member function that favors the latter. In particular, this happens when sequences with increasingly large numbers of terms have to be reversed. Our justification for favoring the member function version lies in the observation that the design for the member function uses special algorithms exploiting the specific features of pointers and their efficient use on doubly linked lists.

Sorting a List

The generic `sort` function defined in Section 5.6 cannot be applied to lists because it requires and uses random-access iterators. Consequently, a different approach is necessary to sort any nonempty list of values. Accordingly, `list` defines a member function `sort` that performs this task. To illustrate, suppose `lis1` is a nonempty `list` object whose values come from some data type, any two of whose values are comparable (by `operator<`). Then the result of applying

```
lis1.sort();
```

converts `lis1` to its sorted form. For example, suppose `lis1` is as in Figure 6.21a. Then the result of applying `lis1.sort()` is given in Figure 6.22. Note also that, unlike the generic version, the member function `sort` defined in `list` is stable.

FIGURE 6.22 lis1

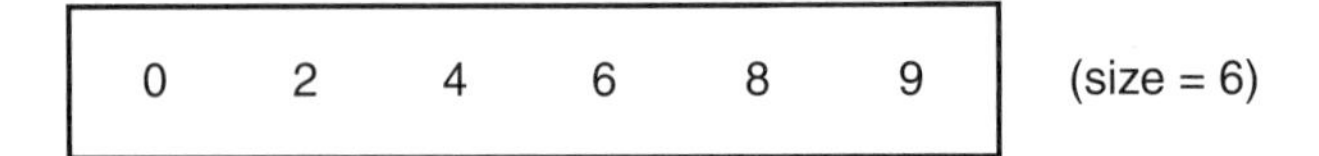

We have presented the "default form" of the `sort` member function, which assumes that the order relation is `operator<`. Besides this, using function objects, there is another version permitting the user to include any other well-defined binary order relation as a parameter. This version is also stable.

Removing Consecutive Duplicate List Values

`unique()` is a useful member function. When applied, it removes copies of consecutive repeated values in any list, leaving only the initial occurrence of each such value. This operation works only when consecutive duplicate values are involved; it does not remove repeated occurrences of values appearing singly and scattered throughout the list. We illustrate this with the following example. Suppose `lis1` is the `int`-valued list given in Figure 6.23a. Then the result of applying

```
lis1.unique();
```

is the list of Figure 6.23b.

FIGURE 6.23a lis1

2	3	3	3	1	1

(size = 6)

FIGURE 6.23b lis1

Removing a Value from a List

There is a member function available in `list` which removes a value specified by the user, provided that value appears in the current list. If the value does not appear, then no action is performed, and the current list remains intact. If the value to be removed occurs more than once in the current list, then all such values are removed, and the list automatically decreases to the smaller size. To illustrate, suppose `lis2` is the `int`-valued list given in Figure 6.24a and `v` is the `int`-valued variable whose current value is `3`. Then the result of applying

```
lis2.remove(v);
```

is the list of Figure 6.24b.

FIGURE 6.24a lis2

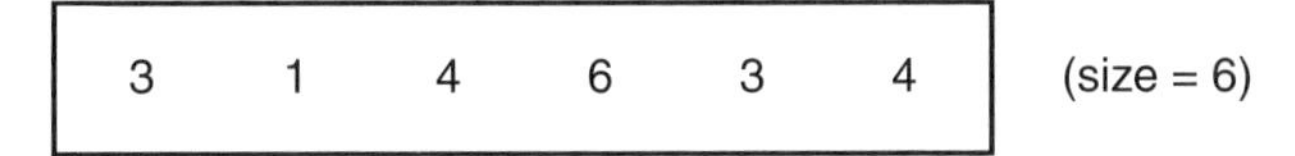

FIGURE 6.24b lis2

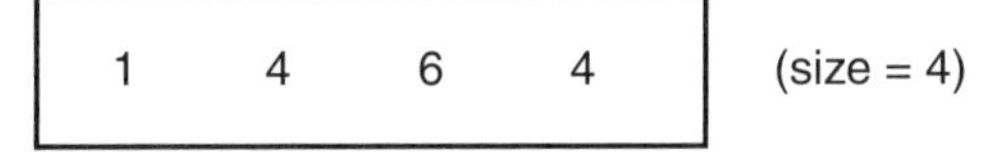

The `list` class template also has a member function `remove_if` whose single parameter is some predicate `pred`.[8] Thus, `pred` is some `bool`-valued function defined on values whose type is the same as those contained in the list. When applied, `remove_if` removes all values in the list satisfying `pred`—that is, all values for which `pred` is `true`. In fact, this member function is stable: The relative order of the surviving list values is preserved. As an example, suppose we define the predicate `is_even` for a single `int`-valued parameter as

```
bool is_even(int v)
{
```

[8]Not all current implementations provide this member function. Some implement only the generic version `remove_if` appearing in `<algorithm>`.

```
    return v%2 == 0;
}
```

and suppose our original list is `lis3`, as in Figure 6.25a. If we then apply

```
lis3.remove_if(is_even);
```

the result is the version of `lis3` appearing in Figure 6.25b.

FIGURE 6.25a lis3

3631	18182	13058	30831	19605

(size = 5)

FIGURE 6.25b lis3

6.11 Application of the `list` Class Template: Sorting Randomly Generated Odd and Even Positive Integers

This section describes a problem involving some of the ideas first discussed for deques. Its proposed solution uses `list` objects and some of its member functions. The problem to be solved is

> *Given any finite sequence of positive integers, we wish to convert it into a sequence beginning with the odd integers in the sequence, sorted in order of increasing size, and ending with the even numbers in the sequence, also sorted in order of increasing size.*

To illustrate this, suppose we generate the following random sequence:

208 10564 26370 5783 6400 11610 21483

Our solution would then involve rearranging the sequence as

5783 21483 208 6400 10564 11610 26370

How do we design an algorithm for solving this? The algorithm would begin by constructing two `list` objects, called `odds` and `evens`, the first of which will store the odd randomly generated numbers and the second the even randomly generated numbers. As each new random number is generated, it is determined whether it is odd or even and then inserted into the appropriate list. The insertion is a matter of choice: It does not matter with respect to efficiency in `list` operations whether it is more efficient to use push_front, insert, or push_back because each executes in constant time.

After generating these numbers and inserting each in some way into the appropriate list, we then apply

```
odds.sort();
```

and

```
evens.sort();
```

to sort each list. The final step is to splice the list evens after the list odds.

A number of the programming details, especially those involved with generating random integers, are the same as those already discussed in Section 6.7. For instance, the use of the predefined library <time>, as well as the use of srand and rand, are exactly as they were in Section 6.7.

A preliminary form of the formal algorithm used to solve this problem is then given as

Begin by determining the number of random integers to generate;
Construct two initially empty lists of integers: one for storing the odd integers generated, and the other for storing the even numbers generated, in some order.
Generate the values of the random sequence:
for *each sequence member generated:*
Decide whether that number is even or odd;
if*(number is odd) insert that number in the list* odds;
else *insert that number in the list* evens;
// *this concludes execution of the* for-loop
Sort each of the lists odds *and* evens *in order of increasing size;*
Splice the list evens *at the end of* odds;
// *The result of this splicing operation produces* odds *as the list beginning with*
// *the sorted odd numbers, followed by the sorted even numbers.*
Display the contents of the list odds;

We will insert newly generated random values using push_front on each of odds and evens. Besides this, we will employ traces of the progress of the computation by outputting the value of each new random number generated and the decision as to whether that number is odd or even. In addition, we will display first the unsorted list of the odd and even numbers generated followed by their sorted versions. Finally, we will display the final solution by first invoking the appropriate form of splice and then invoking

```
display(odds.begin(),odds.end());
```

where display is defined for any fundamental container object as

```
template<class Iter> void display(Iter first, Iter last)
{
```

```
    // Outputs current contents of container, from position first
     // to position just before last.
    for(Iter p = first; p != last; ++p)
     cout << *p << '\t';
    cout << endl;
   }
```

The programmed solution to this problem may then be given by

```
#include <iostream>
#include <list>
#include <time>

using namespace std;

int main(){
// Establish the random generator seed
srand((unsigned) time(0));
// Prompt user for the number of random integers to generate
cout << "Please indicate the number of random integers to generate:"
   << endl;
int number;
cin >> number;
// Define the list to be used to hold the odd and even numbers
list<int> odds, evens;
// Now perform the generating and inserting operations.
for(int index = 0;index < number;++index){
 // Generate a new random integer
 int v = rand();
 // Decide whether that number is even or odd
 // and take appropriate action
 if(v % 2 == 0){ // integer is even
  cout << v << " is even" << endl;
  evens.push_front(v);
 }
 else { // integer is odd
  cout << v << " is odd" << endl;
  odds.push_front(v);
 }
} // ends for-loop

// At this point, the generated integers have all been classified as
// even or odd, and have been placed in the appropriate list.

// Display each unsorted list
```

```
cout << "After generating " << number << " integers, and" << endl;
cout << "prior to sorting, the list of odd numbers is: " << endl;
display(odds.begin(),odds.end());
cout << "and the list of even numbers is:" << endl;
display(evens.begin(),evens.end());

// Now sort each list
odds.sort();
evens.sort();

// Display contents of each sorted list
cout << "After sorting, the list of odd integers is" << endl;
display(odds.begin(),odds.end());
cout << "and the list of even integers is" << endl;
display(evens.begin(),evens.end());

// Now splice the even numbers after the odd numbers.
odds.splice(odds.end(),evens);

// Display the final result
cout << "The final sorted list is:" << endl;
display(odds.begin(),odds.end());

return 0;
}
```

Here is a sample run of this program:

```
Please indicate the number of random integers to generate:
7
208 is even
10564 is even
26370 is even
5783 is odd
6400 is even
11610 is even
21483 is odd
After generating 7 integers, and
prior to sorting, the list of odd numbers is:
21483   5783
and the list of even numbers is:
11610   6400   26370   10564   208
After sorting, the list of odd integers is
5783   21483
and the list of even integers is
```

```
208    6400    10564    11610    26370
The final sorted list is:
5783    21483    208    6400    10564    11610    26370
```

Could we solve this problem using vectors or deques? If we use vectors, we would have to construct initially empty vectors called `odds` and `evens` and proceed as before, but now each odd number generated would be pushed at the back of `odds` and each even number generated would be pushed at the back of `evens`. Once this is done, we would invoke the generic `sort` function from `<algorithm>` on each of `odds` and `evens`. This would result in sorted forms of `odds` and `evens`. But now the tricky part is to create one vector with all the values in the sorted order as described. This would have to be done either by systematically removing the values from `evens` from the front and then pushing each such value at the rear of `odds` to create the desired result or by using the generic `reverse` function on `evens` to obtain the vector of even numbers sorted in reverse order, then popping each value in `evens` from its rear, and then pushing each such value at the rear of `odds`. To say the least, the operations involved are much more complex than when the fundamental containers were lists. Similarly, using deques instead of vectors does not represent a significant improvement. There are several exercises at the end of this section that ask you to explore these alternatives.

6.12 Chapter Summary

This chapter introduced the `vector` class template, defining what is perhaps the most elementary of the container classes in the Standard Library, the others being `deque` and `list`. Briefly stated, a vector is an object capable of storing a finite sequence of values of some fixed data type, whose size is permitted to change while the application program is executing. In addition, insertions of new values and removals of current values occur in constant time from one end only, known as the *back* of the vector.

We may think of a vector as a generalization of an ordinary one-dimensional array, except that the array has a size that is fixed when compiled and cannot vary at any time during the course of execution. In fact, we observed that a number of key processing problems in searching and sorting, originally applied to arrays in Chapter Three, work equally well for vectors.

Besides introducing vectors as fundamental sequence containers, `vector` introduces a category of iterators known as *random-access iterators*, which allow access to any value stored in a vector in constant time. As it turns out for `vector` and `deque`, iterators are implemented as ordinary pointers.

Deques and vectors have very few differences in functionality. The most obvious difference is with respect to insertion and removal operations at the front of the respective containers: For deques, these operations are performed in constant time, whereas they require linear time for vectors.

Since deques support random-access iterators, and thus also support such operations as indexing, the algorithms for searching and sorting described in Chapter Three apply as well to deques. We also presented an example in which deques were the most suitable container for the solution to the underlying software problem. This had to do with "sifting" a finite sequence of randomly generated positive integers. The choice of a `deque` in this case stemmed from the viewpoint of performance because this problem made heavy use of processing activity at the front of the container as well as the back.

The Standard Library provides a fundamental class template called `list` implementing the abstraction of doubly linked lists and their properties. The iterators defined by `list` are bidirectional, and its member functions reflect this basic change in functionality. For instance, bidirectional iterators permit constant-time insertions and deletions of values at any position in the list. However, without random-access iterators, some of the important generic algorithms, such as those for sorting, cannot be applied to lists. In many such situations, these operations are provided as member functions instead. The linked implementation inherent in lists provides a number of member functions such as the merging of two sorted lists, splicing one list inside another, and sorting the values in a list, among others.

We gave an example of how lists are used as the container of choice for solving a specific software problem. This involved sorting any number of randomly generated odd and even positive integers, illustrating the ability of lists in situations where any number of insertions and/or deletions are performed at any position and where other forms of sequence containers either fail altogether or provide inefficient alternatives. In addition, a key difference between `list` iterators and those defined for `vector` and `deque` is that list insertions never invalidate any iterators, and deletions invalidate only those referring to any of the values deleted. The Appendix describes a lengthier and major application of lists to the design of local network simulators.

EXERCISES

1. Show that the code sequence described in Section 6.2 for copying `vect` into `vect_copy` may also be coded as

```
vector<int> :: iterator qptr = vect_copy.begin();
 for(vector<int> :: const_iterator ptr = vect.begin();
```

```
    ptr != vect.end(); ++ptr,++qptr)
  *qptr = *ptr;
```

Explain why this is the case.

2. Write a user program illustrating the difference between the ordinary constructor for `char_holder` and the `explicit` version, as described in Example 6.1.
3. What happens in the compilation of the code sequence

```
char_holder cell1;
cell1 = 'c';
```

if the constructor defined for `char_holder` in Example 6.1 is replaced by the default constructor

```
char_holder();
```

4. Show that the loop

```
for(int index = 0;index < n;++index)
  vect.insert(position,value);
```

produces the same result as

```
vect.insert(position,n,value);
```

Also show that the `for` loop version requires `n * m` moves, while the latter requires `n + m` moves, where `m` is the number of values in the sequence from `position` to the last position in the vector.

5. Another storage allocator member function of the `vector` class is `max_size()`, which returns the size of the largest possible `vector` object supported by your implementation. Compare the values returned by `vect.size()` and `vect.max_size()` by your implementation for an `int`-valued vector constructed using

```
vector<int> vect;
```

What happens if you attempt to output the value of `vect.size()` after executing `vect.reserve(vect.max_size() + 1);`?

6. Show that the function `compute_remainders` described in Section 6.5 can be generalized to

```
template<class Iter> void compute_remainders(Iter first,Iter last,
                        int mod,vector<vector<int> >& vect)
{
 // Insert each value of the input sequence into its
 // appropriate component of vect.
 for(Iter p = first; p != last; ++p)
 {
  int value = (*p)%mod;
  vect[value].push_back(*p);
 }
}
```

Then show that this form accommodates any fundamental container (vector, array, deque, list) storing the input sequence whose remainders are stored in `vect`.

7. In Problem 8 of the Exercises at the end of Chapter Five, we presented a generalization of Insertion sort called `insort`. This version uses iterator parameters. Show that this version applies to `vector` and `deque` containers, using

```
insort(int_vector.begin(),int_vector.end(),0,swap_counter);
```

for `int`-valued vectors and

```
insort(int_deque.begin(),int_deque.end(),0,swap_counter);
```

for `int`-valued deques.

8. Show that the following program generates a sequence of random numbers using a seed input by the user:

```
#include <iostream.h>
#include <stdlib.h>

int main()
{
 // Prompt user for a seed.
 cout << "Please input an integer seed:" << endl;
 unsigned int seed; cin >> seed;
 srand(seed); // Starts the random number sequence
 const int RANDOM_LENGTH = 5;
 for(int index = 0; index < RANDOM_LENGTH; ++index)
  cout << rand() << '\t';
 cout << endl;

 return 0;
}
```

9. Use `srand()` and `rand()` to generate random sequences of any length of lowercase alphabet letters. The length of the string is supplied by the user.

10. Use `srand()` and `rand()` to generate random sequences of integers of any length in the range `0 . . . n-1` for `n`, any positive integer supplied by the user. The length of the sequence is also supplied by the user.

11. Show that the code for `mergesort` originally applied to ordinary arrays in Section 3.16 works equally well for `vector` and `deque` containers.

12. Similar to Exercise 11, show that the code for `quicksort` originally applied to ordinary arrays in Section 3.14 works equally well for `vector` and `deque` containers.

13. Design a version of the `sifter` function to rearrange any string of lowercase alphabet letters so that all vowels appearing in the string precede all consonants. For example, if the input string is `"alphabet"`, then sifter rearranges this to `"eaalphbt"`.

14. Design a version of `sifter` to rearrange any list of randomly generated positive integers, placing all primes in the sequence before any nonprimes.

15. Consider the following function:

```
list<char> ch_list(char* str)
{
 list<char> lst;
 while(*str != '\0')
 {
  lst.push_back(*str);
  ++str;
 }
 return lst;
}
```

and the definitions

```
list<char> lst1, lst2;
```

a. Describe the result of applying each of

```
lst1 = ch_list("Hello, there!");
lst2 = ch_list("Celeste Aida, forma divina.");
```

b. What would be the result of replacing `lst.push_back(*str)` in the preceding `while` loop by `lst.push_front(*str)`?

16. Describe the storage allocated by invoking each of the following `list` constructors:

```
a. list<int> lst1;
b. list<vector<float> > lst2(3);
c. list<list<char> > lst3;
d. list<int> lst4(5);
e. list<int> lst5(lst4);
f. list<int> lst6(++lst1.begin(),–lst1.end());
```

17. a. Suppose we are given

```
#include <list>
#include <vector>
#include <iostream.h>

using namespace std;

template<class Iter> void display(Iter first,Iter last)
// Displays contents of current container.
{
 for(Iter p = first; p != last; ++p)
```

```
    cout << *p << '\t';
  cout << endl;
}

template<class T> void input_vector(vector<T>& v)
{
  int value;
  for(int index = 0; index < v.size(); ++index)
  {
    cin >> value; v[index] = value;
  }
}

template<class Iter1, class T>
 void duplicate(Iter1 first,Iter1 last,list<T>& lis)
{
  for(;first!= last; ++first)
    lis.push_back(*first);
}

int main()
{
  cout << "Working with int-valued vectors and lists:" << endl;
  int size;
  cout << "What will be the size of the vector?" << endl;
  cin >> size;
  vector<int> v1(size);
  cout << "Input " << v1.size() << " integers:" << endl;
  input_vector(v1);
  cout << "The vector contains the values:" << endl;
  display(v1.begin(),v1.end());
  list<int> lis1;
  duplicate(v1.begin(),v1.end(),lis1);
  cout << "The list has size " << lis1.size() << endl;
  cout << "and has the corresponding values" << endl;
  display(lis1.begin(),lis1.end());
  cout << "Operation terminated!" << endl;

  return 0;
}
```

Describe the result of executing this program.

b. Suppose we replaced

```
duplicate(v1.begin(),v1.end(),lis1);
```

in the program by

```
duplicate lis1(v1.begin(),v1.begin() + (v1.end() - v1.begin())/2,lis1);
```

Would the resulting program compile? Explain why or why not.

18. a. Test the code for sequential search, namely,

```
template<class Iter,class T> bool seq_search(Iter first, Iter last, T value)
// Performs sequential search on container from first to last for value.
{
 bool UNSUCCESSFUL_SEARCH = false;
 for(Iter p = first;p != last;++p)
 // Invariant: the values in the container up to and including position
 // immediately preceding p have already been inspected, if p != first.
 if(*p == value)
  return true;
 return UNSUCCESSFUL_SEARCH;
}
```

for list objects.

b. Test whether the generic algorithm `find` can be used for `list` objects.

19. a. Use the `list` class to test character strings for palindromes. Also use the `reverse()` member function defined in `list` to test for palindromes.

b. Test whether we can accomplish the same task as in part (a), but now using the generic function `reverse` supplied in `<algorithm>`.

c. Test whether we can replace `list` objects in (b) by vectors or deques.

20. a. Solve the problem described in Section 6.11 using vectors instead of lists.

b. Solve the problem described in Section 6.11 using deques instead of lists.

21. a. What list would result in Section 6.11 if we attempted to solve the original problem by first sorting `odds` and `evens`, using

```
odds.sort();
```

and

```
evens.sort();
```

and then applying

```
odds.merge(evens);
```

b. What list would result in Section 6.11 if we attempted to solve the original problem by first applying

```
odds.splice(odds.end(),evens);
```

and then applying

```
odds.sort();
```

22. Write a function that uses `remove` in any list so that the second value in the sequence is removed. What would happen if that value is repeated at least once more in the list?

23. Explain the result of applying the following code sequence on any `int`-valued `list` object constructed with the name `lis` and where `v` is an `int`-valued variable whose value is known at the point where that sequence executes.

```
list<int> :: iterator p = lis.begin();
while(*p != v)
  ++p;
lis.remove(*p);
```

If you believe there exist several cases that have to be considered, explain the result of applying the sequence to each case.

PROGRAMMING PROJECT

1. In the Programming Project at the end of Chapter Four, we designed and implemented the `hash_table` class template using separate chaining. Now implement this once again using the class templates `vector` and `list`.

REFERENCES

Knuth, Donald E., *The Art of Computer Programming, Volume 2, Seminumerical Algorithms,* (Reading, MA: Addison-Wesley, 1981).

Musser, D. R. and Saini, Atul, *STL Tutorial and Reference Guide* (Reading, MA: Addison-Wesley, 1996).

Plauger, P. J., "Containers," *C/C++ Users Journal,* December 1996.

Plauger, P. J., "The Header <vector>," *C/C++ Users Journal,* January 1997a.

Plauger, P. J., "The Header <list>," *C/C++ Users Journal,* February 1997b.

Plauger, P. J., "The Header <deque>," *C/C++ Users Journal,* March 1997c.

CHAPTER 7

Container Adaptors

CHAPTER OBJECTIVES

- To introduce the concept of container adaptors and the use of the underlying fundamental sequence container in this respect.
- To define and classify the three container adaptors supported by the Standard Library.
- To investigate several key uses of container adaptors in important application areas, such as language analysis, compiler design, and operating systems.

7.1 Introduction

In Chapter Six, we studied the properties of the fundamental container class templates `vector`, `deque`, and `list` provided by the Standard Template Library. Along with ordinary one-dimensional arrays, these form a category of STL container types known as *sequence containers*. They are characterized as containers whose structure permits any finite collection of values of any single type to be stored in a strictly linear arrangement. In Chapter Five, we defined a *container adaptor* as an STL component used to change the interface of another sequence container. The STL defines three forms of container adaptors: `stack`, `queue`, and `priority_queue`, each of which is implemented as a class template. In each case, the container adaptor defines a new data structure whose implementation uses a limited form of the internal structure of one of the three fundamental sequence containers.

7.2 The Stack Abstraction

In Section 1.2, we defined a stack (of values of some type `T`) as a data structure that is either empty or consists of a finite sequence of values of type `T`, upon which we define the finite collection of admissible operations

- `push`, which inserts a new value onto the stack
- `pop`, which removes a value from the current stack (whenever possible)
- `top`, which retrieves the value currently at the top of the stack (whenever possible)
- `is_empty`, which tests whether the current stack is empty

We observed that a stack is an example of an *abstract data type* (ADT), which is an aggregate consisting of a (nonempty) collection of entities, together with a finite collection of well-defined admissible operations on these entities. Other examples of ADTs we have already studied are hash tables, vectors, deques, and lists. Implementing an ADT in C++ involves defining a class whose member functions implement the admissible operations, along with constructors and destructors for creating and destroying specific instances of that type. If we use fundamental container classes from the Standard Library, much of the internal structural details of the abstraction are already defined as implementation details. This is one of the key advantages in using container adaptors: We bypass the burden of having to provide code for the implementation of the structure manually and are assured of the optimal level of efficiency attached to that implementation.

In any case, we wish to use the abstraction in applications without having to be concerned about how it is implemented. Thus, for example, when we use stacks in a specific application, we must be able to apply any of the admissible operations for stacks without any concern as to whether the stack is being implemented using arrays (as in Sections 1.4 through 1.6), vectors, deques, lists, or some other underlying structure. These implementation details are hidden from the user by applying encapsulation and information hiding.

Examples of stacks abound in everyday life. However, each example has a common characteristic: We allow items to "stack up" on top of one another in such a way that, when we need one of the stacked items, we gain access to the item that was placed last. In addition, there is no permitted access to the items currently on the stack except for the one currently on top—the one most recently placed ("pushed") onto the stack. Further, the only item eligible to be removed ("popped") from the current stack (if not empty) is the item on top. For example, if we allow newspapers to be "stacked" in this manner, we'll gain access to the most recently placed one (although the stack may contain some very old newspapers). The key idea is that stacks allow access to the data items they store in a *last-in, first-out* (LIFO) manner.

7.3 Implementation of Stacks Using the `stack` Container Adaptor

In Sections 1.4 through 1.6 and in Programming Project 2 at the end of Chapter One, we described two "conventional" implementations of the stack ADT. In each case, the implementation was designed and coded "by hand." In doing so, we become vulnerable to several shortcomings, some of which were stated earlier, such as the *overflow condition* in the array implementation. In addition to these, another set of potential shortcomings exist: the lack of *portability* and compromising the *efficiency* of the underlying code. Portability refers to the ability to use the same code in a wide variety of different programming platforms. In an industrial setting, where the processing of large chunks of data is more the rule than the exception and where processing speed is a major consideration, it is critical to have the best implementation possible in the widest variety of environments. These were key considerations in the design of function and class templates comprising the Standard Library.

If we examine each of these fundamental sequence containers described in Chapter Six, we see that each has the necessary functionality to implement the stack ADT. For example, each contains the necessary constructors to create stacks and destructors and contains implementations closely associated with `push`, `pop`, `top`, and `is_empty`. For each of these fundamental containers, we have `push_back`, `pop_back`, `erase`, and `empty`, respectively. The only problem with each of the implementations using `vector`, `deque`, and `list` directly (that is, without adaptors) is that each such implementation has substantially more member functions than the four admissible operations described in the stack ADT!

The view taken by the designers of the Standard Library was not to create a completely new fundamental sequence container category for stacks. Thus, the resulting design did not have a completely new class template at the same level as those created for `vector`, `deque`, and `list`. Instead, since each of these fundamental container types can serve as a suitable environment for stacks, the idea was to "adapt" any one of these fundamental containers to the much simpler interface provided by stacks. That is to say, the stack container adaptor designed using the STL causes any one of the three fundamental containers to behave as though it were a stack, limiting the operations of the container class simply to constructors, destructors, and `empty`, `top`, `push`, and `pop` operations.[1] Thus, the fundamental container (be it a `vector`, `deque`, or `list`) sits in the background, providing the necessary storage medium for the values on the stack, but using only the operations available for the stack and not those for the underlying fundamental container.

How do we define a `stack` object in this context? Suppose we wish to construct an `int`-valued stack called `i_stack` using a `vector` container. First, we must provide two preprocessor directives:

[1]The STL `stack` container adaptor contains an additional member function `size()`, returning the number of values currently on the stack.

```
#include <vector>
#include <stack>
```

The stack object is then constructed using

```
stack<int,vector<int> >;
```
[2]

Note that two parameters are passed: the data type of the values to be stored on the stack (int in this case) and the type of fundamental container used to implement the stack (vector<int> in this case).[3]

The member functions for the stack class contain no specific constructors or destructor. These are inherited from the underlying fundamental container class. From the viewpoint of stack applications, the constructor chosen will be the default because the theory supports initializations using initially empty stacks. The public member functions are

- a bool-valued member function empty, testing whether the current stack object is empty
- an int-valued parameterless function size, returning the number of values presently on the stack and 0 if the current stack is empty
- two versions of the top function, one of which is mutable and the other not
- a push function, requiring a single parameter of the type describing the type of values to be stored on the stack
- a parameterless pop function, which pops the current stack (whenever possible) without returning the value

The mutable form of top permits the programmer to change the current value at the top of the stack. For example, assuming st identifies an int-valued stack object that is currently nonempty and *expression* is some int-valued expression, the mutable form of top permits either

```
st.top() = expression;
```

or

```
++st.top();
```

Besides these, the stack class template contains two infixed relational operators operator== and operator<, each of which compares two stacks lexicographically in a manner similar to that for vector, deque, and list. We give no further details here about either of these except to say that their

[2] It is customary to leave at least one blank space between two consecutive occurrences of '>'—some implementations view the presence of >> without a blank separator as a compile-time error.

[3] Some implementations support a default container type, such as deque<T>, for the stack object. In this case, we only have to code the constructor as

```
stack<int> i_stack;
```

instead of

```
stack<int, deque<int> > i_stack;
```

behavior is very similar to that defined for each of the three fundamental container classes.

7.4 Applications of the Stack ADT

We present several key applications of the stack ADT, using stack from the Standard Library. We should note, however, that each of the problems we investigate here is also solvable by any implementation of stacks, including the array and list implementations seen in Chapter One.

Application 1: Balanced Parentheses, Brackets, and Braces

The first application involves testing any character string of finite length for the occurrence of balanced parentheses `(` and `)`, brackets `[` and `]`, and braces `{` and `}`. Let `str` be a character string of finite length. We say `str` is *balanced* (with respect to parentheses, brackets, and braces) if

1. `str` is empty (that is, it has no characters and is of length zero) or has no occurrences of `(` and `)`, or `[` and `]`, or `{` and `}`, or
2. `str` contains as many occurrences of right parentheses `)` as there are left parentheses `(`, as many occurrences of right brackets `]` as there are left brackets `[`, and as many occurrences of right braces `}` as there are left braces `{`, and
3. the occurrence of the corresponding right parenthesis, right bracket, or right brace occurs later in `str` than its matching left parenthesis, left bracket, or left brace, and
4. a right parenthesis matches only a left parenthesis, a right bracket matches only a left bracket, and a right brace matches only a left brace, and
5. any right parenthesis, bracket, or brace must match the closest corresponding left parenthesis, bracket, or brace occurring earlier in `str`.

Thus, each of the following character strings is balanced:

```
((a+b)+c)+[d+(e)]
a+(b*c)
({})
```

and each of the following is not balanced:

```
([a+b]+c
{a+{b+c
({)}
```

The ability to detect balanced parentheses, brackets, and braces is critical in the design of compilers for the most popular high-level programming languages (such as C, C++, Scheme, Ada, Java) because each of the underlying syntax structures defined in these requires balanced characters of this type. Therefore, one of the components used in writing a compiler for any of these languages is a test for balanced parentheses, brackets, and braces. Character-valued stacks are particularly useful in this regard because they represent a relatively simple tool for testing any such string for balance.

The efficiency of `push`, `pop`, `top`, and `empty` depends on the implementation of the underlying fundamental sequence container; thus, we may affirm that each of these functions executes in constant time, assuming that a form of the `stack` container adaptor is used. Accordingly, we design a `stack`-based solution to this problem. We will therefore define a `char`-valued stack called `c_stack` for the solution and execute the steps described in the followed proposed algorithm:

Scan the input string character by character from left to right;
If a left parenthesis, left bracket, or left brace is scanned, push it onto `c_stack`*;*
If a right parenthesis, right bracket, or right brace is scanned, compare it to the character currently at the top of `c_stack` *(if such exists);*
`if`*(the character currently at the top of* `c_stack` *is a left parenthesis, left bracket, or left brace matching the right character currently being scanned)*
  apply `c_stack.pop();`
`else`
  signal a "mismatch" error;
In the case of a "mismatch" error, reject the input string as unbalanced;
`if`*(the entire character string is scanned and the final stack is empty)*
  accept the input string as balanced;
`else`
  reject the input string as unbalanced;

Mismatches also occur if `c_stack` is empty before the entire input string is scanned and that string has a further occurrence of a right parenthesis, right bracket, or right brace before an occurrence of a left parenthesis, left bracket, or left brace. This happens as a consequence of an oversupply of right characters. A mismatch also occurs by an attempt to pop from a currently empty stack, occurring by scanning a right character before a left character, or if the entire character string is scanned and the final stack is not empty. This last situation occurs when there is an oversupply of left characters. Finally, if the string contains other characters besides parentheses, brackets, or braces, scan that character but perform no action on `c_stack`.

Let us test the algorithm on several input strings. Suppose the input string is `((a+b)+c)+[d+(e)]`. Each of the first two characters scanned is pushed onto `c_stack` and then `a`, `+`, and `b` are scanned, with no action taken on `c_stack`. The next character scanned is `)`, which is the right character corresponding to the character (currently at the top of c_stack; accordingly c_stack is popped once, leaving c_stack with a single character (. Each of the characters + then c is scanned, with no action taken on c_stack. The next character scanned is), prompting a pop action on c_stack because its current top is (. At this point, c_stack is empty. The + is scanned, with no action taken on c_stack. The next character scanned is [, which is pushed onto c_stack. The next two characters d and + are scanned, with no action performed on c_stack. Then a left parenthesis is scanned and pushed onto c_stack. The next character scanned is e, prompting no action on c_stack. The next character scanned is a right parenthesis, which is a match with the left parenthesis currently at the top of c_stack; thus, c_stack is popped, leaving c_stack with the single character [. The final character (which is]) is scanned, matching the left bracket currently at the top of c_stack. Therefore, c_stack is popped, and because the entire input string has been scanned, the algorithm accepts the original input string as balanced.

Look at the input string ({)}. Push the first two characters (, { onto c_stack. The next character scanned is a right parenthesis. Since) is not the matching right symbol for the left brace currently at the top of c_stack, the decision is to reject the input string as unbalanced.

Finally, suppose the input string is ([a+b]+c. The first two characters (and [are scanned and pushed in that order onto c_stack. The next three characters a, +, and b are scanned, with no change in c_stack. The next character scanned is], matching the [currently at the top of c_stack. Consequently, c_stack is popped once, leaving it holding a single character (. The remaining characters of the input string are scanned, with no further action performed on c_stack. Since c_stack is not empty after the entire input string is scanned, it is unbalanced.

The following bool-valued function, called check_balance, implements this algorithm using a char-valued vector and a char-valued stack:

```
bool check_balance(vector<char>& v,stack<char,vector<char> >& st)
{
 bool running = true;  // Signals that the scan is still active.
 for(vector<char> :: iterator p = v.begin(); p != v.end(); ++p)
 {
  if(*p == '(' || *p == '[' || *p == '{')
   st.push(*p);
  else if(!st.empty() && *p == ')' && st.top() == '(')
   st.pop();
  else if(!st.empty() && *p == ']' && st.top() == '[')
   st.pop();
  else if(!st.empty() && *p == '}' && st.top() == '{')
   st.pop();
```

```
    else if(st.empty() && (*p == '(' || *p == '[' || *p == '{'))
    {
     running = false;
     break;
    }
    else if(st.empty() && (*p == ')' || (*p == ']' || (*p == '}'))
    {
     running = false;
     break;
    }
  } // ends for-loop
  return (running && st.empty());
} // ends check_balance
```

The `vector<char>` formal parameter `v` holds the current input string, and `st` is the formal parameter playing the role of `c_stack`. The user function invokes `check_balance` using

```
check_balance(input_string,c_stack);
```

The coding of the user function is left as an exercise. (See Problem 1 of the Exercises at the end of this chapter.)

Application 2: Evaluating Postfix Expressions

When we write arithmetic expressions, we usually use *infix form;* that is, we place a binary operator symbol between its two operands. With *postfix form,*

TABLE 7.1 **Prefix and Postfix Forms for Some Arithmetic Expressions**

Infix	Prefix	Postfix
a+b	+ab	ab+
a+b*c	+a*bc	abc*+
(a+b)*c	*+abc	ab+c*
(a+b)*(c−d)	*+ab−cd	ab+cd−*
(b*b − 4*a*c)/(2*a)	/−*bb**4ac*2a	bb*4ac*−2a*/

the operator immediately follows its two operands. Conversely, in *prefix form,* the operator immediately precedes its two operands. Table 7.1 shows the prefix and postfix forms for several arithmetic expressions.

Table 7.1 shows that prefix and postfix expressions do not require parentheses. Instead, the order of appearance of the symbols in each of these expressions dictates the order of application of the underlying operations. This is particularly valuable in automating the evaluation of arithmetic expressions, as is done in language compilers.

Many hand-held calculators perform their computations by first converting the expression into postfix form and then evaluating the resulting postfix expression. Furthermore, compilers for the conventional high-level programming languages convert arithmetic expressions in the source code into their equivalent postfix form before generating lower-level code to evaluate the expression. This section describes how the Standard Library, particularly with respect to vector containers and stacks, is useful in evaluating postfix expressions. The result will be a function designed to evaluate such expressions with single-digit arguments (operands).

We look at several examples. Suppose we wish to evaluate `23+7*`. This is the postfix equivalent of the infix expression `(2+3)*7`. The parentheses are needed because this calls for the `+` operation to be performed before `*`. Indeed, if we consider `2+3*7` instead with the usual precedence rules in effect, the multiplication of `3` and `7` is performed first, followed by the sum of that product with `2`, yielding an answer of `23`. The equivalent postfix form for `2+3*7` is `237*+`.

How do we evaluate `23+7*`? We first scan `2`, then `3`, and push these values in succession onto an empty `int`-valued stack `st`, resulting in Figure 7.1a. Then we scan the operator symbol `+`. This prompts a popping of `st` twice, producing the values of the two operands `opnd1` and `opnd2`, in that order. In this case, `opnd1` has value `3` and `opnd2` has value `2`. Then `+` is applied to `opnd1` and `opnd2`, producing an answer of `5`, which is now pushed onto `st`, as in Figure 7.1b. The next step is to scan the next character in the postfix expression. This character is the digit `7`, which is now pushed onto `st`, as in Figure 7.1c. The next character `*` is scanned, prompting two successive pops of `st`, with `opnd1` now storing `7` and `opnd2` now storing `5`. Then `opnd1*opnd2` is computed, yielding `35`, which is now pushed onto the stack, as in Figure 7.1d. The entire postfix has been scanned at this point, prompting a final popping of `st`, whose only value (`35`) represents the value of the postfix expression.

FIGURE 7.1

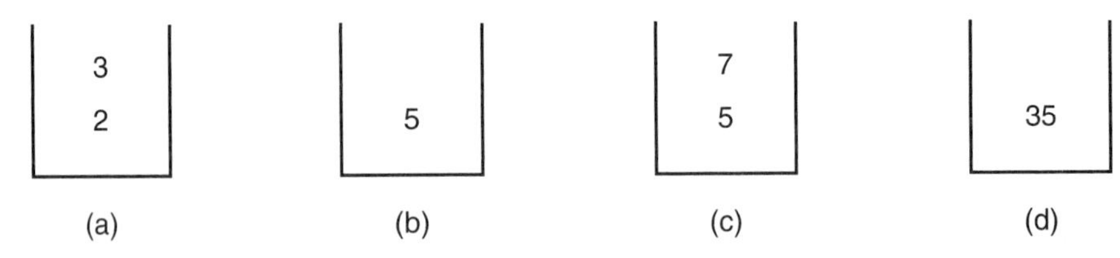

We compare this to the result of evaluating `237*+`. We trace this evaluation as well, observing the changes in `st` viewed in the various forms of Figure 7.2. The first three characters, each a single numeric digit, are scanned and pushed onto `st` in order, as in Figure 7.2a. Then the operator symbol `*` is scanned, prompting two successive pops of `st`, with `opnd1` holding `7` and `opnd2` holding `3`. Their product is computed and pushed onto

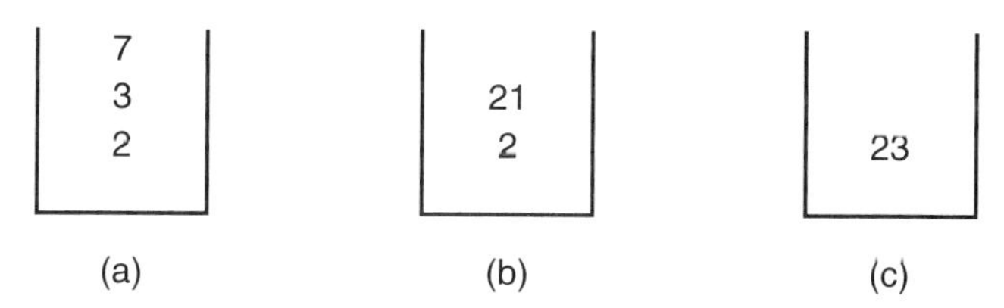

FIGURE 7.2

`st`, as displayed in Figure 7.2b. Then the operator + is scanned, once again causing two successive pops of `st`, with `opnd1` now holding `21` and `opnd2` now holding `2`. The sum `opnd1 + opnd2` is computed, and the result `(23)` is pushed onto `st`, as in Figure 7.2c. This result is popped, and because there are no further characters to scan, the value popped is the value of the postfix expression.

We wish to design a formal algorithm for evaluating postfix expressions. We note first that any postfix expression serving as input to this algorithm is simply a special form of a character string. Hence, any numeric digit appearing in the string is a character that must be converted to its integer-valued equivalent so as to enable arithmetic computations to be performed. These converted integer values are pushed onto the operand stack. Similarly, even if we restrict the computations to involve five integer-valued binary operations `+`, `-`, `*`, `/`, and `%`, each of these symbols appears as a character value in the postfix expression. When any one of these operator symbols is scanned, it prompts the popping of the operand stack twice and then the application of the operation to these operands. For `-`, `/`, and `%`, it is particularly important to observe that the operation is not commutative; hence, the proper order of operands must be observed. In each such case, the second value popped (`opnd2`) appears in front of the operator, and the first value popped (`opnd1`) appears after the operator. Thus, we have

- `opnd2 - opnd1` when `'-'` is scanned
- `opnd2 / opnd1` when `'/'` is scanned
- `opnd2 % opnd1` when `'%'` is scanned

If the original postfix string is well-defined, the scanning process terminates with the entire postfix string scanned and with a final operand stack containing a single integer value. This value is popped from the final stack and represents the value of the original postfix string.

The algorithm may then be expressed as

```
for(each character in postfix string scanned successively from left to right)
{
 if(the character is a numeric digit)
  push the corresponding integer onto st;
 else
 {
 pop st for the value of opnd1;
 pop st for the value of opnd2;
```

```
switch(operator symbol currently scanned)
{
 case '+': push opnd1 + opnd2 onto st and exit;
 case '-': push opnd2 - opnd1 onto st and exit;
 case '*': push opnd1 * opnd2 onto st and exit;
 case '/': push opnd2 / opnd1 onto st and exit;
 case '%': push opnd2 % opnd2 onto st and exit;
} // ends switch
} // ends for-loop
// At this point, there should be a single integer value on st
// if the postfix string is well defined. Pop that value and return it
// as the value of the original postfix expression.
return the result of popping st;
```

The code for converting an integer character to its equivalent `int` value is straightforward.

```
// Convert character digit to corresponding integer value
int convert(char ch_value)
{
 switch(ch_value){
  case '0': return 0;
  case '1': return 1;
  case '2': return 2;
  case '3': return 3;
  case '4': return 4;
  case '5': return 5;
  case '6': return 6;
  case '7': return 7;
  case '8': return 8;
  case '9': return 9;
  default: {
   error();
   return -1;
  }
 } // terminates switch
} // terminates text of convert
```

The error handler `error()` simply returns an error message:

```
// Error handler
void error()
{
 cout << "Error in evaluation." << endl;
}
```

Finally, to implement the algorithm, we code an `int`-valued function `eval_postfix` with two parameters. The first parameter is `v`, a `char`-

valued vector whose successive characters are those of the postfix expression to be evaluated, and the second is an int-valued stack st used to store the operands as the evaluation process progresses. The return value is the result of the evaluation of the postfix expression passed as the value of the first parameter v. The code for eval_postfix is

```
// Code for postfix evaluator
int eval_postfix(vector<char>& v,stack<int,vector<int> >& st)
{
 for(vector<char>::iterator ptr = v.begin();ptr != v.end();++ptr)
 {
  if('0' <= *ptr && *ptr <= '9') // if *ptr is a character digit
      st.push(convert(*ptr));  // push int value onto operand stack
  else
  {
      int opnd1 = st.top();
      st.pop();
      int opnd2 = st.top();
      st.pop();
      switch(*ptr){
      case '+': {st.push(opnd1 + opnd2); break;}
      case '-': {st.push(opnd2 - opnd1); break;}
      case '*': {st.push(opnd1 * opnd2); break;}
      case '/': {st.push(opnd2 / opnd1); break;}
      case '%': {st.push(opnd2 % opnd1); break;}
      } // terminates text of switch
  } // terminates else-clause
   // Monitoring stack action by disclosing top of stack
   // value during each loop cycle.
   cout << "Top of stack is now: " << st.top() << endl;
  } // terminates for-loop
  int result = st.top();
  st.pop();
  return result;

} // terminates eval_postfix
```

This version of eval_postfix also monitors the activity of the operand stack as the evaluation progresses by outputting the value at the top of the stack for each cycle of the for loop. The results obtained are consistent with our design. To illustrate, suppose we apply eval_postfix to 23+7*. The execution of eval_postfix then produces

```
Top of stack is now: 2
Top of stack is now: 3
Top of stack is now: 5
```

```
Top of stack is now: 7
Top of stack is now: 35
```

If we input the postfix string `237*+` instead, `eval_postfix` yields

```
Top of stack is now: 2
Top of stack is now: 3
Top of stack is now: 7
Top of stack is now: 21
Top of stack is now: 23
```

Application 3: Converting Infix Expressions to Postfix

We may view the evaluation of postfix expressions in Application 2 as the second step of a two-step process performed in the compilation of higher-level source code into lower-level code. The first step of the process is the translation of any arithmetic expression written in infix form to its postfix equivalent. This application provides that step.

Again, stacks provide the necessary computational tool for this translation. However, there are several key differences in the stacks used for this step. Here the stacks are `char`-valued, and binary operator symbols as well as left parentheses are capable of being pushed onto the stack. Other members of the infix string will either be single-digit numeric characters or (possibly) right parentheses. The binary operator symbols will be the same as in Application 2.

Let us consider several applications before formulating a general conversion algorithm. Suppose we begin with the infix expression `2+3`. Its corresponding postfix form is clearly `23+`. But how do we automate this translation process? We define three objects:

1. a `char`-valued stack of operators, initially empty, called `operator_stack`
2. a `char`-valued vector, initially empty, called `postfix_vector`
3. a `char`-valued vector, initially holding the infix expression, called `infix_vector`

We scan the input string contained in `infix_vector` from the leftmost character to the end, as usual. Referring to the infix expression `2+3`, the first character (`'2'`) is scanned; since it is an operand, we push that value at the back of `postfix_vector` and continue by scanning the next character. This is the operator symbol `'+'`, which we push onto `operator_stack` and scan the next (and final) character. This is the numeric character `'3'`, which is pushed at the back of `postfix_vector`. Since this completes the scan of the infix string, the computation completes by popping `operator_stack` until empty and pushing each value popped at the back of `postfix_vector`. This results in the final version of `postfix_vector` as `23+`, the desired postfix string. We trace this sequence of actions in Figure 7.3a.

FIGURE 7.3a

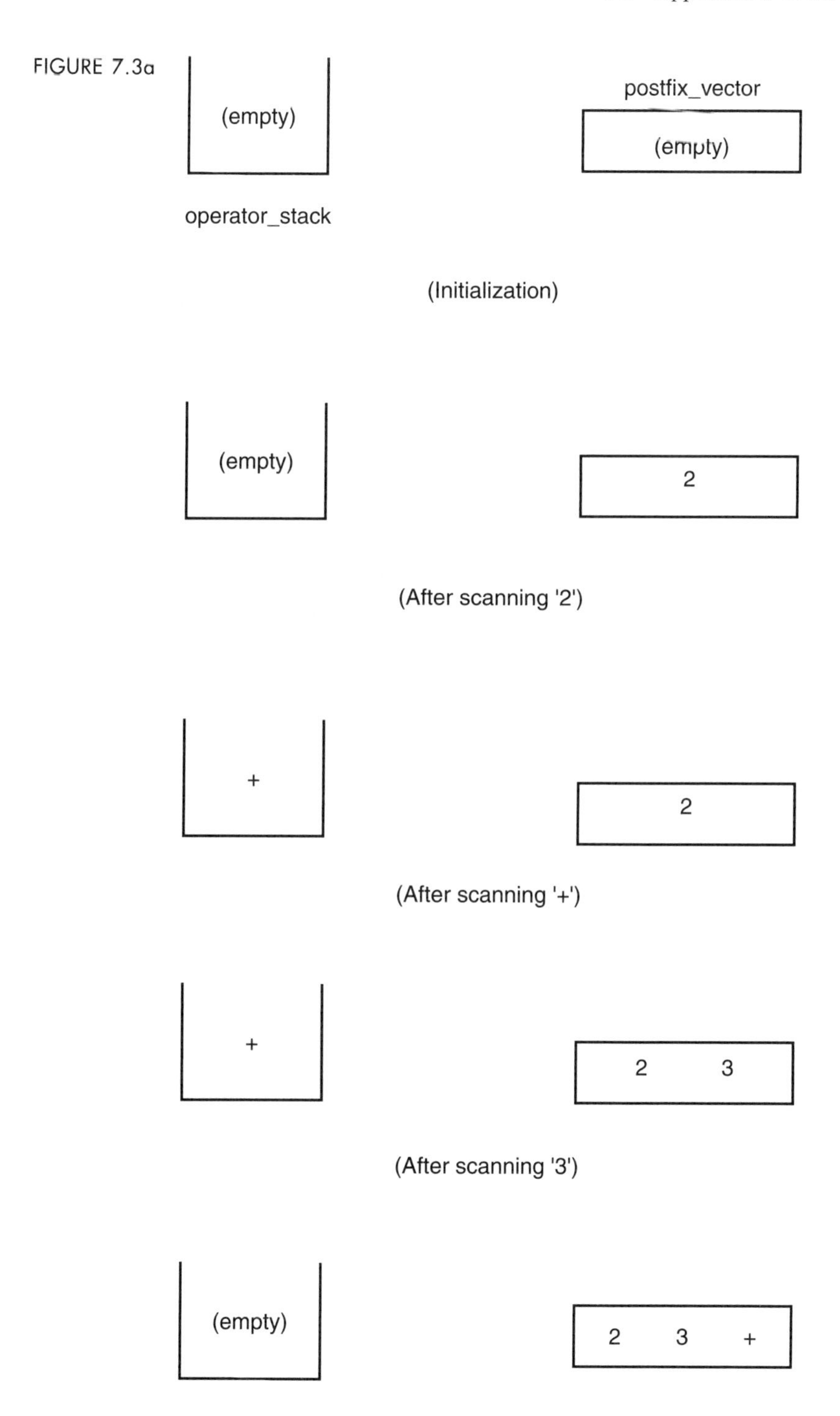
postfix_vector
(empty)
(empty)
operator_stack
(Initialization)
(empty)
2
(After scanning '2')
+
2
(After scanning '+')
+
2 3
(After scanning '3')
(empty)
2 3 +
(After popping operator_stack)

What about `2+3*7`? Here we have two operators `'+'` and `'*'`, with `'*'` having a higher precedence than `'+'`. We begin as before, pushing `'2'` at the back of `postfix_vector` and continue by scanning `'+'`. As before, `'+'` is pushed onto `operator_stack`, and we resume by scanning `'3'`, which is again pushed at the back of `postfix_vector`. Now `'*'` is scanned. At this point, we examine the current status of `operator_stack`. If this stack contains other operator symbols whose precedence is the same as `'*'`, such as `'*'`, `'/'`, or `'%'`, we systematically pop `operator_stack` and push each such operator symbol at the back of `postfix_vector` until either `operator_stack` empties or the top of `operator_stack` contains either `'+'` or `'-'`, of lower precedence. Then the current operator symbol being scanned (`'*'` in this case) is pushed onto `operator_stack` because no such operator symbols of equal precedence to `'*'` appear at the top of `operator_stack` (recall that `operator_stack` currently contains the single symbol `'+'`). At this point, `operator_stack` is read from bottom to `top` as `'+'`, `'*'`. We then scan the final character `'7'` of the infix string and push it at the back of `postfix_vector`. Since this completes the scan of the entire infix expression, we systematically pop `operator_stack` and push each such character at the back of `postfix_vector`, producing the result `237*+`. These steps are illustrated in Figure 7.3b.

How are enclosing parentheses handled, as in `(2+3)*7`? Here the enclosing parentheses emphasize that the usual precedence between operators is to be superseded and that the evaluation of the expression `2+3` is to be done before operating on the result with `'7'` using `'*'`. We begin by pushing `'('` onto `operator_stack` and continue by scanning `'2'`. As usual, `'2'` is pushed at the back of `postfix_vector`, and `'+'` is now scanned. This is pushed onto `operator_stack`, and `'3'` is scanned next and pushed at the back of `postfix_vector`. Then `')'` is scanned. This prompts a sequence of pops of `operator_stack` and pushing at the back of `postfix_vector` up to but not including the first occurrence of `'('`. The symbol `'('` is popped from `operator_stack` but not pushed at the back of `postfix_vector`. Scanning the infix expression resumes by pushing `'*'` onto `operator_stack`. The character `'7'` is then scanned and is pushed at the back of `postfix_vector`. Since this completes the scan of the infix string, the remaining characters on `operator_stack` (only `'*'` in this case) are popped and pushed at the back of `postfix_vector`, yielding `23+7*`. This sequence of actions is traced in Figure 7.3c.

We may now state the algorithm for infix-to-postfix conversion under the assumption that the current infix expression is well defined with operators `+`, `-`, `*`, `/`, `%`, and (possibly) `(` and `)`.

Initialize `operator_stack` *and* `postfix_vector` *as empty;*
`for`*(each character in* `infix_string` *scanned successively from left to right)*

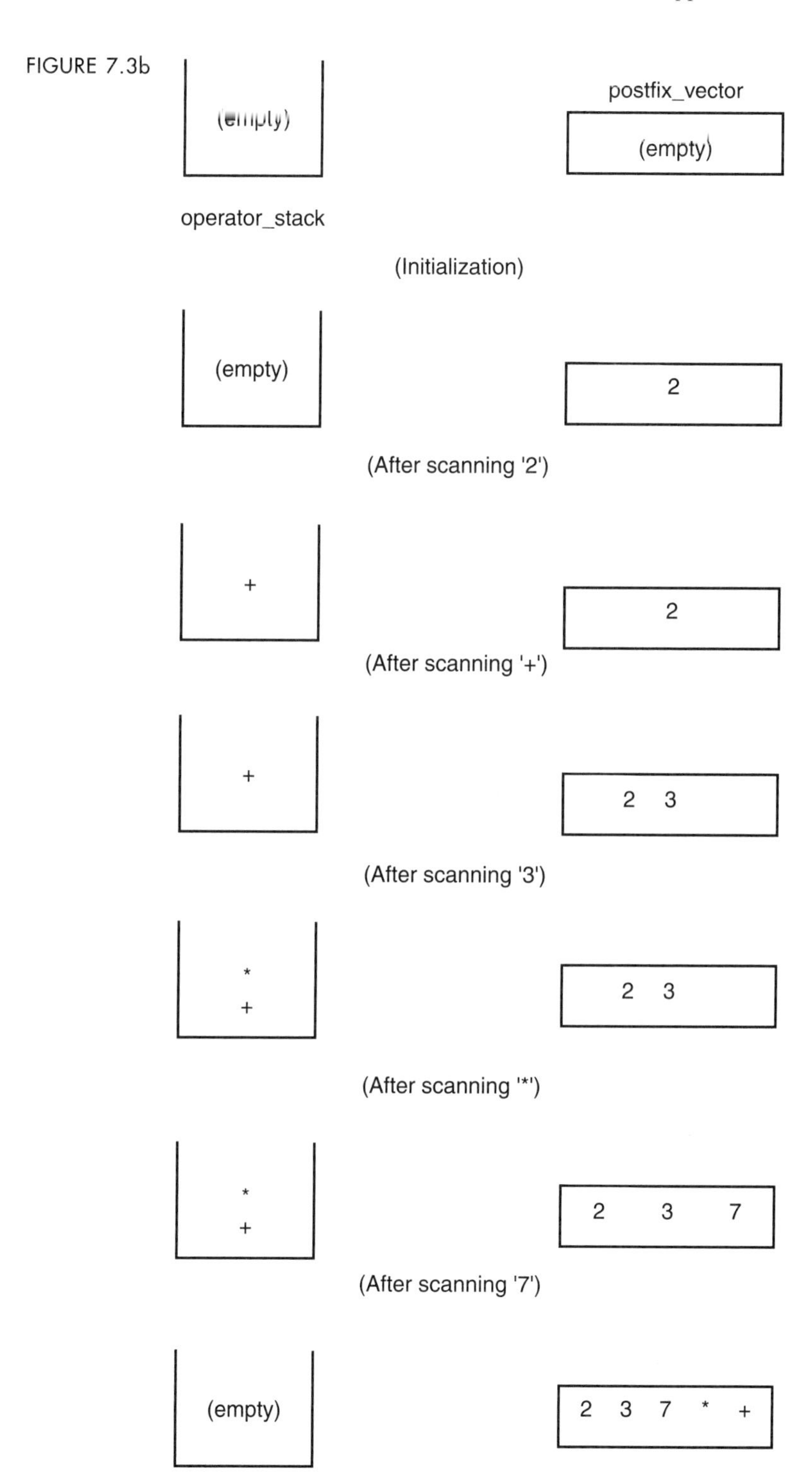

(empty)
postfix_vector
(empty)
operator_stack
(Initialization)
(empty)
2
(After scanning '2')
+
2
(After scanning '+')
+
2 3
(After scanning '3')
*
+
2 3
(After scanning '*')
*
+
2 3 7
(After scanning '7')
(empty)
2 3 7 * +
(After popping operator_stack until empty)

FIGURE 7.3b

FIGURE 7.3c

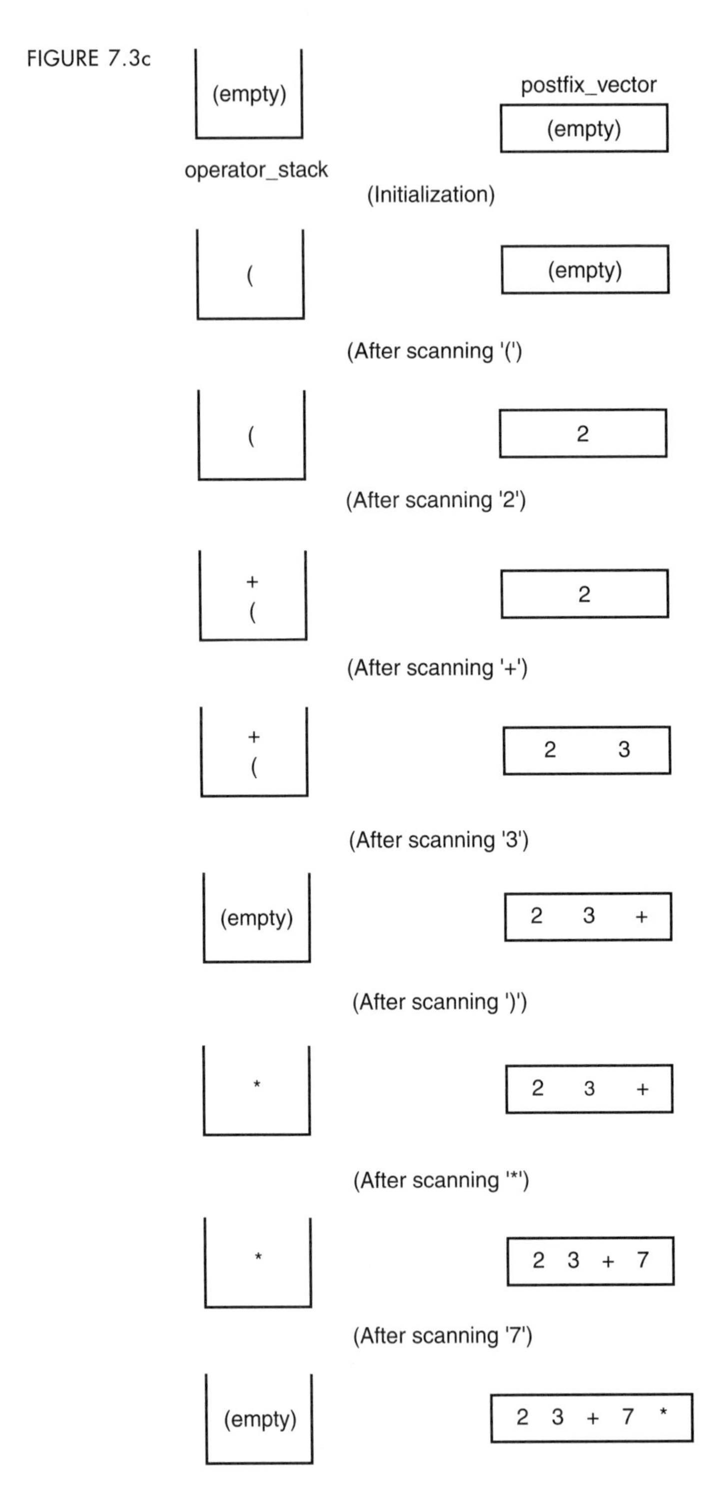
(empty)
postfix_vector
(empty)
operator_stack
(Initialization)
(
(empty)
(After scanning '(')
(
2
(After scanning '2')
+
(
2
(After scanning '+')
+
(
2 3
(After scanning '3')
(empty)
2 3 +
(After scanning ')')
*
2 3 +
(After scanning '*')
*
2 3 + 7
(After scanning '7')
(empty)
2 3 + 7 *
(After popping operator_stack until empty)

```
{
 if(character is a numeric digit)
  apply postfix vector.push_back(that digit);
 else if(the character is '(')
  apply operator_stack.push('(');
 else if(the character is ')')
  pop operator_stack of each operator symbol and push each such symbol
  at the back of postfix_vector until the first occurrence of '(' is located
  on operator_stack;
  pop operator_stack (but do not push '(' at the back of postfix_vector;
 else if(the character is '*', '/', or '%')
  pop operator_stack of all '*', '/', or '%' up to but not including (if such
  exist) the first occurrence of '+' or '-';
  push the character scanned onto operator_stack;
 else if(the character is either '+' or '-')
  pop operator_stack of all symbols down to (but not including) the first
  occurrence of '(' (if it appears at all) and push each such symbol at the
  back of postfix_vector. Then push the current operator symbol onto
 operator_stack.
} // terminates for-loop.
// At this point the current infix expression has been completely scanned.
// If current operator_stack is not empty, pop this stack and push each
// value popped at the back of postfix_vector until operator_stack is empty.
while(!operator_stack.empty())
{
pop operator_stack of each remaining symbol;
push that symbol at the back of postfix_vector;
}
output contents of postfix_vector;
```

The implementation of this algorithm in C++ uses a `void` function called `infix_to_postfix`, with three reference formal parameters

- `in_vector`, holding the current infix string
- `op_stack`, initially empty
- `post_vector`, initially empty, where the final translated postfix string will be stored

The prototype for this function may be given as

```
infix_to_postfix(vector<char>& in_vector,
                 stack<char,vector<char> >& op_stack,
                 vector<char>& post_vector);
```

The formal code implements the preceding algorithm. Thus, if we assume a call of the form

```
infix_to_postfix(infix_vector,operator_stack,postfix_vector);
```

with `infix_vector` containing the infix form of the arithmetic expression, say, `(2+3)*7`, and with `operator_stack` and `postfix_vector` initially empty, then the result returned to the caller produces a value for `postfix_vector` of the form `23+7*`. We leave the formal coding details of `infix_to_postfix` as an exercise. (See Programming Project 1 at the end of this chapter.)

7.5 The Queue Abstraction

A *queue* is a data structure that differs from a stack in that values are inserted at one end (called the *back*) and removed from the other end (called the *front*). Instead of the last-in, first-out (LIFO) behavior characterizing a stack, a queue stores and processes its contents in a first-in, first-out (FIFO) manner.

As an ADT, queues are generally identified by the following list of admissible operations:

- an insertion operator, inserting a new value at one end: a `push` operation[4]
- a removal operator, removing (whenever possible) the value currently at the front of the queue: a `pop` operation
- a `bool`-valued function testing whether the current queue is empty: an `empty` operation
- functions retrieving (whenever possible) the values stored at the front and back of the current queue: `front` and `back` functions, respectively

There are many instances of queues in our everyday experience. Examples include a group of individuals waiting to enter a theater for a performance, a group of customers waiting in a bank for teller services, or a group of individuals waiting to renew their driver's licenses. There are a number of key applications of queues in computer science. One is the use of queues either in a timesharing system or in a local network of jobs waiting to acquire the services of a shared line printer. A second application used in timesharing systems involves a queue of processes waiting on a queue to be executed by a single shared multiprogrammed CPU.

[4]Here we use the terminology of the STL implementation. This does not necessarily coincide with that used by many computer scientists. The variation in terminology is particularly true in the case of queues. For example, many call the push operation "insert," "add," or "enqueue," and the pop operation is often called "remove" or "dequeue."

7.6 Implementation of Queues Using STL's queue Container Adaptor

The Standard Library provides a queue container adaptor that is applicable to any fundamental sequence container supporting the functions empty, push_back, pop_front, size, front, and back. In particular, each of the fundamental container classes deque and list represent highly efficient implementations as fundamental containers for the queue ADT because each defines a version of push_back() and pop_front() that executes in constant time. The queue container adaptor allows an eligible container to behave as a queue, since each of the operations empty, push, pop, front, and back are definable using the fundamental container operations listed earlier. In addition, STL includes the size attribute, which for any queue object returns the number of values currently stored in the queue.

The construction of queue objects using a suitable fundamental sequence container follows a syntax very similar to that already described for stacks in Section 7.3. Indeed, suppose we wish to construct an int-valued queue object called i_queue, where we assume that deque has been chosen as the underlying fundamental container class. We must then include the preprocessor directives

```
#include <deque>
#include <queue>
```

The constructor for i_queue is then coded as

```
queue<int,deque<int> > i_queue;
```

You should check your implementation once again for the possibility of default fundamental containers. If such exist (assuming the default fundamental container class template is deque), the constructor could then be expressed as

```
queue<int> i_queue;
```

In the STL implementation, and in a manner similar to that seen for the top() member function for stacks in Section 7.3, queue supports both a constant and mutable form for each of the member functions front() and back(). These then allow for the value(s) at the front and the back of the current queue object to be assigned new values without requiring the use of any push and pop operations.

7.7 Applications of the Queue ADT

Application 1: Simulating a Finite Sequence of Processes on the Ready Queue in a Multiprogrammed Environment

From its earliest days up through the mid-1960s, computing was performed using *single-stream batch processing,* which simply means that data and programs were submitted for execution in groups called *batches,* with a single job submitted for processing at any given time. All other jobs were delayed until the current job completed execution. Of course, this represented a highly inefficient way to operate because it is rarely the case that any single job uses all of the resources of the system. Even at this early stage of development, it was observed by operating systems programmers that when a given job in execution is waiting for the completion of the execution of an external service, such as acquiring new input data or depositing newly computed data in a permanent storage device (a segment of magnetic tape or a sector of a disk), the central processor (CPU) remained idle. It would therefore be extremely important for a process to better utilize this "idle time" by having a second process submitted to the CPU to begin executing. In fact, the outcome of this analysis was the observation that submitting more than one job to the CPU at any given time, with the mixture of submitted jobs representing a diversity of computing activities, was the best way to minimize the idle time of the processor. This also had the very desirable side effect of optimizing the active time of the CPU and increasing system *throughput,* defined as the amount of data generated by the computer for a fixed and given period of time.

As a consequence, operating system designers developed the concept of *multiprogramming,* in which several jobs are kept in main memory at once. The processor then switches from one job to another as is necessary to minimize the processor's idle time. More advanced operating systems followed in the early 1970s that were designed to serve a number of *interactive users,* namely, those who communicate with the computer via terminals. Since the user is present and interacting directly with the computer, the operating system must be designed with the objective of responding as quickly as possible to the users' requests. The fulfillment of this objective optimized the system's productivity. Thus, *timesharing systems* were designed as a response to this, where "timesharing" refers to the fact that several processes are permitted to share processing time in the CPU, with one process currently executing and the rest in a state of "readiness" waiting to execute.[5]

The first example we present shows how queues are used to simulate a multiprogrammed system in a very elementary setting. The version offered here is one in which a fixed number of processes are submitted for execution by a single timeshared CPU, with the first of these being the only one in the "running" state. This form maintains a process queue in which each entry is an integer value representing the number of processing steps required for that job to complete its execution. Every process runs to

[5]We distinguish between a *job* and a *process* by observing that when a job is admitted to the CPU for execution, it assumes the internal form of a process. The queue then holds a finite sequence of processes in the ready state awaiting execution by the CPU.

completion, and its execution begins when its predecessor in the queue completes execution. As that process completes execution, it is purged (popped) from the queue, with its successor in the queue being the next process to execute. This version does not allow any new process to be added during the course of execution; only those processes submitted originally are permitted to execute in the order of their submission into the queue. Thus, these processed execute in a first-in, first-out (FIFO) order.

How do we design the simulator? We will design an *interactive* version, which first prompts the user for the number of processes to be monitored. The `int` value returned will be stored in a variable called `size`. We also construct an `int`-valued queue called `process_queue`, initially empty, to store the number of execution steps for each process. At this point, the user is prompted to supply the number of such steps for each process. The values are pushed into `process_queue` using the sequence

```
cin >>  steps;
process_queue.push(steps);
```

where steps is an `int`-valued variable storing the number of execution steps for any single process. This sequence is actually the body of a `for` loop that cycles `size` times. When this loop completes execution, `process_queue` holds `size` values in the order of their appearance in the input sequence.

The following discussion describes the key steps of the simulation. We begin by describing the execution, one step at a time, of the processes whose steps are stored in `process_queue` beginning at the front, since this describes an FIFO environment. In our simulator, this is done by invoking `monitor_queue`, whose prototype is given by

```
void monitor_queue(queue<int,deque<int> >& proc_queue, int& cntr);
```

The first step initializes `cntr` at `1`, and we use `cntr` to keep track of the number of the process, from `1` to `size`, present initially in `process_queue`. Control of execution now transfers to a `while` loop whose entry condition depends on whether the current contents of `process_queue` are empty. If `process_queue` is not empty, this signifies that there are processes remaining to be monitored; consequently, the `while` loop is reentered. On the other hand, if `process_queue` is empty, entry into the `while` loop is blocked and represents the termination of the monitoring process. The monitoring process itself consists of a description of the number of the process currently executing (that is, in the running state) and the step number in that process. After the process completes execution, the value of `cntr` is incremented, and `process_queue` is popped. This loop terminates when `process_queue` eventually becomes empty.

The complete code for `monitor_queue` is given by

```
void monitor_queue(queue<int,deque<int> >& proc_queue,
            int& cntr)
```

```
{
 cntr = 1;
 while(!proc_queue.empty())
 {
  cout << "Process " << cntr << " is executing." << endl;
  for(int index = 0; index < proc_queue.front();++index)
   cout << "Process " << cntr << " is executing step"
     << index + 1 << endl;
  cout << "Process " << cntr << " terminates execution." << endl;
  ++cntr; // Go to the next process
  proc_queue.pop(); // Purge proc_queue of completed process.
 } // terminates while-loop
 // At this point, simulation process terminates.
 // Prepare to exit.
 cout << "Entire execution shuts down." << endl;
} // terminates text of monitor_queue.
```

The driver is used primarily to set up `process_queue` by prompting the user for the number of processes to be pushed onto `process_queue` and the number of execution steps for each such process:

```
// Driver
int main()
{
 int counter, // stores the process number
     size,    // stores the number of processes
     steps;   // stores the number of executable steps of any
              // process.
 // Prompt user for the number of processes:
 cout << "Input the number of processes:" << endl;
 cin >> size;
 // Create queue holding processing steps for each process:
 queue<int,deque<int> > process_queue;
 // Prompt user for contents of process_queue:
 cout << "Input " << size << " integers, representing the execution"
       << endl;
 cout << "steps of the " << size << " processes:" << endl;
 // Input these values into process_queue
 for(int index1 = 0; index1 < size; ++index1)
 {
  cin >> steps;
  process_queue.push(steps);
 } // ends for-loop

 // Echo the initial size of process_queue after loading
```

```
 cout << "The queue now has " << process_queue.size()
    << " members." << endl;

 // Monitor the action of process_queue:
 monitor_queue(process_queue,counter);

 return 0;
} // terminates main code
```

The following represents the result of a test run of this program:

```
Input the number of processes:
4
Input 4 integers, representing the execution
steps of each of the 4 processes:
3 3 4 2
The queue now has 4 members.
Process 1 is executing.
Process 1 is executing step1
Process 1 is executing step2
Process 1 is executing step3
Process 1 terminates execution.
Process 2 is executing.
Process 2 is executing step1
Process 2 is executing step2
Process 2 is executing step3
Process 2 terminates execution.
Process 3 is executing.
Process 3 is executing step1
Process 3 is executing step2
Process 3 is executing step3
Process 3 is executing step4
Process 3 terminates execution.
Process 4 is executing.
Process 4 is executing step1
Process 4 is executing step2
Process 4 terminates execution.
Entire execution shuts down
```

Application 2: Simulating a Finite Sequence of Processes in a Multiprogrammed Environment Using a Time Quantum

In Application 1, we simulated the activity of a multiprogrammed system of processes residing simultaneously in main memory, which executes in sequence until completion. In that setting, once a specific process begins executing, it continues executing until completion, regardless of the number of processing steps required. Thus, for example, if Processes `1,2,3` currently reside in main memory with respective steps `7,2048,5`, these complete execution in the order presented. Consequently, Process `3`, having only `5` steps, must wait until Process `1` and Process `2` terminate to begin executing. We may not judge this as a major hardship, but it certainly represents a significant delay in the presence of Process `2`. This is particularly emphasized if Process `3` is "time critical"—that is, if it must execute as soon as possible.

Our simulation in Application 1 makes no accommodation for such a situation. However, in practice, there are several ways for multiprogrammed operating systems to cope with this situation. One way is to place a *priority* on each process submitted for execution, with those of highest priority placed in the ready queue before those of any lower priority to ensure their rapid completion. The container adaptor used to implement this is a *priority queue,* discussed in the next section. Another method commonly used to cope with such situations employs ordinary queues and is the method described in this application. It is often used in conjunction with priorities and involves the implementation of a *quantum.* Each process is pushed initially on the queue of ready processes and gradually moves to the front of that queue. When the process arrives at the front and when the CPU becomes available, the state of the process is changed from ready to running, and the CPU begins executing the steps of that process. The act of assigning the CPU to the process currently at the front of the queue is known as *dispatching* and is performed by special operating systems software called the *dispatcher.* To prevent any lengthy process from monopolizing the CPU for any significant amount of time, such as that just described for the processes `1,2,` and `3,` it is possible for the hardware to set an *interval timer* to allow this process to execute during a preset time interval (or *quantum*). If the number of steps of the process does not surpass the quantum, the process completes execution and is purged from the system. Otherwise, the process executes as many steps as the value of the quantum permits, is then popped from the queue, going from the running to the ready state, after which it is pushed onto the queue once again, with the remaining steps required for it to complete execution. It again moves gradually to the front, gains the CPU once again, and continues in this way until it finally completes execution.

We will design software to simulate this situation using a queue to store the sequence of ready processes. Our first task is to design a method of identifying the distinct processes. Unlike the situation in the simulator described in Application 1, it is no longer necessarily true that a process, once executing, goes to completion. Therefore, we must include the process number in our naming convention, along with the number of execution steps remaining for that process to complete. Thus, the queue will not contain single `int` values as it did before, but will instead consist of pairs of `int` values: one for the process number and the second for the remaining steps. It also follows that, in this case, a process cannot be identified simply by locating its position in the queue. It could be the case at some point of execution of the simulator that a process in the queue has a smaller process number than a predecessor.

We then define the `struct`

```
struct process {
 int proc_number;
 int steps;
};
```

as the means of describing any process. Our contact with this applies only at initialization. All that is required from the user is the number of processes to be simulated and the number of steps involved initially in each. The initial queue will still be in the usual sequential order so far as the naming of processes is concerned. We illustrate these ideas with the following example. Suppose `size` is an `int`-valued variable whose value is input by the user and represents the number of ready processes originally submitted to the system. Our version will prompt the user for the value of `size`. Assume that value is `4`. Then the user will be prompted for four `int` values representing the respective number of processing steps involved initially for each of these processes. Suppose in response the user inputs the sequence

5 2 12 4

The result is that the initial number of steps is `5` for Process `1`, `2` for Process `2`, `12` for Process `3`, and `4` for Process `4`. These pairs of values will be placed in order into the queue constructed as

```
queue<process,deque<process> > process_queue;
```
[6]

as described in Figure 7.4.

The inputting of initial data into `process_queue` is accomplished using the declaration

```
int size;
```

whose value represents the number of processes submitted to the system, prompting the user for its value:

```
Input the number of processes
```

We also assume the declaration

```
process proc;
```

[6]Here we adopt the convention of representing each member of `process_queue` as a pair of integers, with the first member representing the value of `proc_number` and the second representing the value of `steps`.

FIGURE 7.4 process_queue

(1,5)	(2,2)	(3,12)	(4,4)	(size = 4)
(front)			(back)	

This input operation is accomplished using

```
for(int k = 0; k < size; ++k) {
  proc.proc_number = k + 1;
  cin >> proc.steps;
  process_queue.push(proc);
}  // ends for-loop
```

We fix the value of the quantum by

```
const int quantum = some positive integer;
```

If the number of remaining steps does not exceed the value of `quantum`, the process completes execution and is popped from `process_queue`. Otherwise, the value of `steps` is adjusted to reflect the fact that another cycle has terminated without completing the execution of the process. In its adjusted form, it is pushed onto `process_queue` and begins moving to the front. This key processing step is implemented as the major segment of the function `monitor_quantum_queue` whose prototype is

```
void monitor_quantum_queue(
            queue<process,deque<process> >& proc_queue,
            process& proc;
            const int& quantum);
```

with the actual parameter `process_queue` passed by reference to the formal parameter `proc_queue`.

The segment of `monitor_quantum_queue` to which we refer is the loop coded as

```
while(!proc_queue.empty()) {
  cout << "Process " << proc_queue.front().proc_number
   << " is executing" << endl;
  counter = proc_queue.front().steps;
  if(counter > quantum){ // Process does not complete on this cycle
    cout << "Process " << proc_queue.front().proc_number
     << " executes for the complete quantum of " << quantum << " steps"
     << endl;
    cout << "and does not terminate on this cycle." << endl;
    counter = counter - quantum;
```

```
    proc.proc_number = proc_queue.front().proc_number;
    proc.steps = counter;
    proc_queue.push(proc);
  } //  completes if clause
  else { // Process at front of proc_queue completes execution
         // on this cycle because counter <= quantum.
    cout << "Process " << proc_queue.front().proc_number
     << " completes execution in this cycle in " << counter
     << " steps" << endl;
  } // completes else clause
  proc_queue.pop();
 } // Completes while-loop
```

At the point of completion of execution of the `while` loop, all processes have executed to completion, `proc_queue` is empty, and our monitor terminates with the message

```
Entire execution shuts down.
```

The main function is a driver for `monitor_process_queue` and supplies the necessary initialization information. The version we present assumes a value of `3` for `quantum`.

```
int main() {
 int size,    // number of processes
   counter;   // holds number of remaining steps to execute
 const int quantum = 3;  // duration of quantum
 queue<process, deque<process> > process_queue;  // queue holding
                                                  // sequence

 process proc;

 // Prompt user for number of processes to monitor
 cout << "Input the number of processes:" << endl;
 cin >> size;
 cout << "Input " << size << " integers, representing the execution"
      << endl;
 cout << "steps of each of the " << size << " processes:" << endl;

 // Input initial data for each process.
 for(int k = 0; k < size; ++k) {
  proc.proc_number = k + 1;
  cin >> proc.steps;
  process_queue.push(proc);
 }  // ends for-loop
```

```
 // Describe activity of execution sequence
 monitor_quantum_queue(process_queue,proc,quantum);

 return 0;
}
```

The complete code for `monitor_quantum_queue` is

```
void monitor_quantum_queue(
            queue<process,deque<process> >& proc_queue,
            process& proc,
            const int& quantum)
{
  while(!proc_queue.empty()) {
  cout << "Process " << proc_queue.front().proc_number
   << " is executing" << endl;
  counter = proc_queue.front().steps;
  if(counter > quantum){ // Process does not complete on this cycle
    cout << "Process " << proc_queue.front().proc_number
     << " executes for the complete quantum of " << quantum << " steps"
     << endl;
    cout << "and does not terminate on this cycle." << endl;
    counter = counter - quantum;
    proc.proc_number = proc_queue.front().proc_number;
    proc.steps = counter;
    proc_queue.push(proc);
  } //  completes if-clause
  else { // Process at front of proc_queue completes execution
        // on this cycle because counter <= quantum.
    cout << "Process " << proc_queue.front().proc_number
     << " completes execution in this cycle in " << counter
     << " steps." << endl;
  } // completes else-clause
  proc_queue.pop();
 } // Completes while-loop

  // At this point proc_queue is empty.
  // Indicate that this signifies shutdown.
  cout << "Entire execution shuts down." << endl;
} // completes monitor_quantum_queue
```

Let us look at a trace of the execution of the `while` loop of `monitor_quantum_queue`. Using the input information and initial description of `process_queue` as described in Figure 7.4, Process `1` executes for the entire quantum without completion, leaving the number of steps left to complete at 2. Then Process 1 is popped and pushed back onto proc_queue, as described in Figure 7.5a. Now Process 2 is at the front of proc_queue. It executes to completion and is then popped from proc_queue, as in Figure 7.5b. Process 3 then begins execution, using the entire span of the quantum without completion, and is popped and then pushed once again onto proc_queue with 9 remaining steps, as in Figure 7.5c.

Process 4 then begins execution for the first time, running for the entire quantum without completion, and is popped and then pushed onto proc_queue once again with one remaining processing step, as in Figure 7.5d. Process 1 then returns to the front of proc_queue, completing its execution, and is then popped from proc_queue, as in Figure 7.5e. Process 3 then executes for the entire time quantum without completing and is popped and once again pushed onto proc_queue as in Figure 7.5f.

Process 4 completes its final execution step and is popped from proc_queue, resulting in the situation described in Figure 7.5g. Once again, Process 3 does not complete execution on this cycle. It is then popped and again pushed onto proc_queue, as in Figure 7.5h. Finally, Process 3 executes to completion and is popped from proc_queue. Because proc_queue now is empty, execution terminates.

FIGURE 7.5a proc_queue

(2,2)	(3,12)	(4,4)	(1,2)	(size = 4)
(front)			(back)	

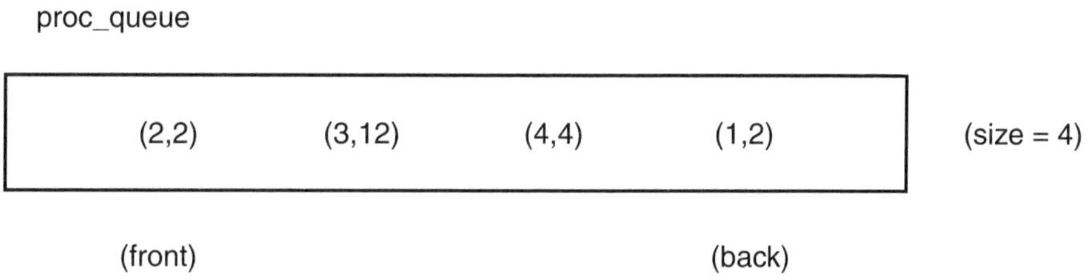

FIGURE 7.5b proc_queue

(3,12)	(4,4)	(1,2)	(size = 3)
(front)		(back)	

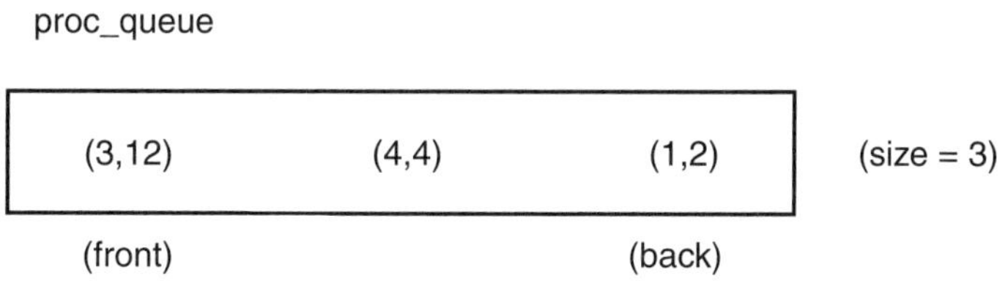

FIGURE 7.5c proc_queue

(4,4)	(1,2)	(3,9)	(size = 3)
(front)		(back)	

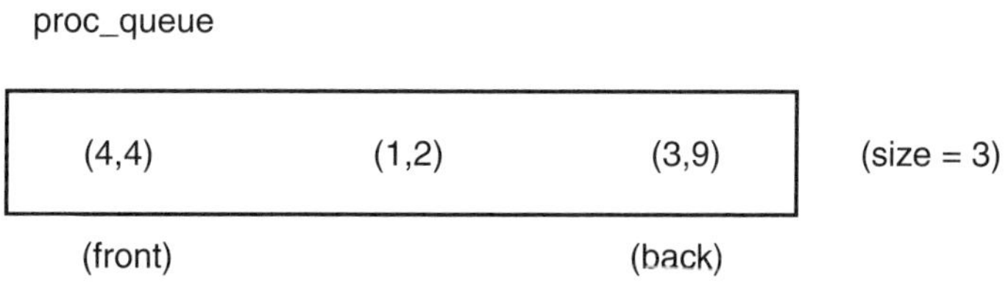

FIGURE 7.5d proc_queue

(1,2) (3,9) (4,1) (size = 3)

(front) (back)

FIGURE 7.5e proc_queue

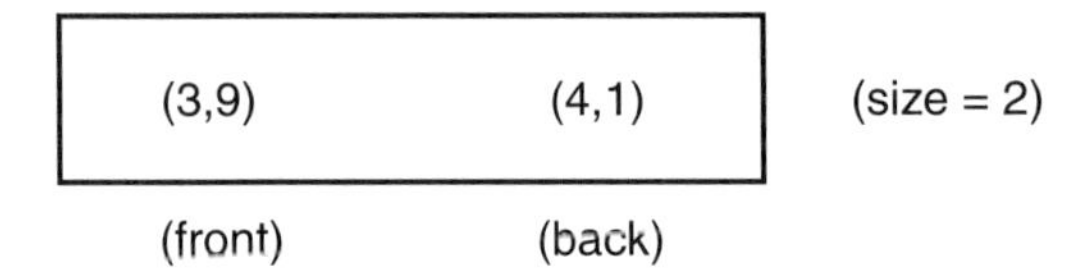

FIGURE 7.5f proc_queue

(4,1) (3,6) (size = 2)

(front) (back)

FIGURE 7.5g proc_queue

(3,6) (size = 1)

(front)
(back)

FIGURE 7.5h proc_queue

(3,3) (size = 1)

(front)
(back)

The output for this sample run is

```
Input the number of processes:
4
Input 4 integers, representing the execution
steps of each of the 4 processes:
5 2 12 4
Process 1 is executing
Process 1 executes for the complete quantum of 3 steps
```

```
and does not terminate on this cycle.
Process 2 is executing
Process 2 completes execution in this cycle in 2 steps
Process 3 is executing
Process 3 executes for the complete quantum of 3 steps
and does not terminate on this cycle.
Process 4 is executing
Process 4 executes for the complete quantum of 3 steps
and does not terminate on this cycle.
Process 1 is executing
Process 1 completes execution in this cycle in 2 steps.
Process 3 is executing
Process 3 executes for the complete quantum of 3 steps
and does not terminate on this cycle.
Process 4 is executing
Process 4 completes execution in this cycle in 1 steps.
Process 3 is executing
Process 3 executes for the complete quantum of 3 steps
and does not terminate on this cycle.
Process 3 is executing
Process 3 completes execution in this cycle in 3 steps.
Entire execution shuts down.
```

A more complicated case involves a simulator that is not only initialized with a finite number of processes going to completion but also allows for new processes to enter the queue later as they are spawned and at random times. This simulates a more realistic situation than those already described because most contemporary multiprogrammed operating systems perform in this manner. Using deques, queues, and priority queues to simulate such situations is perhaps the best design choice because their implementation involves dynamic storage allocation with predefined member functions designed for efficiency of execution.

7.8 The Priority Queue Abstraction

A *priority queue* is a data structure differing from stacks and ordinary queues in that the value to be popped next is the "largest" value in the container. Thus, we may characterize a priority queue either as empty or, if not, as a finite sequence of values of some fixed type `T` where

a. a relational operator < is defined for any two members of `T` and
b. the value in the sequence immediately available for removal (or retrieval) is the value of "highest priority" in the sense of <

In this sense, a priority queue does not classify either as an LIFO or FIFO container. As an ADT, priority queues are identified by the following list of admissible operations:

- a `push` operation, admitting a new value `v` into the priority queue
- a `pop` operation, removing (whenever possible) the value of highest priority currently in the priority queue
- a Boolean-valued operation `empty`, testing whether the current priority queue is empty—returning `true` if so and `false` if not
- a `top` operation, retrieving (whenever possible) the value of highest priority currently in the priority queue

The Standard Library supports the `priority_queue` class template. In fact, any object constructed from `priority_queue` is a container adaptor that allows the object to behave as a priority queue in the sense of its description given earlier as an ADT. This implies that the value currently stored in the priority queue of highest priority (as defined either by the default comparison operator `operator<` or any other well-defined comparison operator existing in the underlying data type of the members stored in the priority queue) is at the *top* (or *front*) of the priority queue. As a consequence, pushing a new value on any priority queue may cause a rearrangement of the previously stored members of the sequence and this new value so as to ensure that the value of highest priority is the value at the top. We illustrate this with the following example of integer-valued priority queues.

EXAMPLE 7.1 Assume the priority queue `pr_queue` is currently empty and suppose we push the following sequence into `pr_queue`:

```
2 3 -1 7 9
```

If we then pop `pr_queue` until it is empty, the resulting output sequence is

```
9 7 3 2 -1
```

How are priority queues implemented in the STL? These are defined as container adaptors whose underlying fundamental sequence container is any fundamental container supporting random-access iterators and the functions `empty`, `size`, `push_back`, `pop_back`, and `front` (or `top`) operators. Therefore, any `vector` or `deque` container is adaptable to a priority queue. Further, any user function employing priority queues requires the following sequence of preprocessor directives:

```
#include <deque> (or #include <vector>)
#include <queue>
```

Note the following curiosity: The "directive"

```
#include <priority_queue>
```

is not defined in the STL. The attitude of the Standard Library in this regard is that priority queues are viewed as special kinds of queues. In fact, according to the C++ standard, the class template priority_queue is declared in the header <queue>.

How do we distinguish between the construction of a priority_queue object and a queue object? More precisely, how do we tell C++ that pr_queue is an int-valued priority_queue object? This is accomplished using

```
priority_queue<int,vector<int>,less<int> > pr_queue;
```

or

```
priority_queue<int,deque<int>,less<int> > pr_queue;
```
[7]

There are some key distinctions among the member functions of the three container adaptor classes described in this chapter. For example, stack, queue, and priority_queue each define default constructors and copy constructors. But priority_queue objects may also be constructed that initially copy values in a sequence defined by the iterator range [first,last). In addition, we have already seen that stack supports both mutable and constant forms of the member function top(). Similarly, queue supports both mutable and constant versions of front() and back(). However, only the constant version of top() is supported for priority_queue. This is perfectly sensible because top() refers to the value of highest priority present in the priority queue, allowing only the constant form of top() to prevent the user from tampering with that value.

7.9 Applications of the Priority Queue ADT

Priority queues have many useful applications. For example, we may observe that priority queues are often used in designing operating systems to choose the next process in the ready queue to obtain services of the CPU.

Application 1: Simulating the Ready Queue of Processes in a Multiprogrammed Environment

In practice, the ready queue of processes awaiting the services of the CPU takes the form of a priority queue because these processes are generally classified according to several possibly different levels of priority. Usually, processes initiated by a member of the group of systems programmers whose primary duty is to monitor and improve the efficiency of operations of the system have a significantly higher priority than those of other

[7] Certain implementations allow the default less<T> to be dropped.

members of the staff. Therefore, such processes execute earlier than those of other users. This is accomplished by implementing the ready queue of processes as a priority queue.

We begin the simulation by prompting the user for the number of processes to be pushed onto the priority queue and then prompt for the priority of each such process. We assume the priority of each process will be a positive integer, with larger integers indicating processes of higher priority. As before, we will not allow any new processes to be pushed onto the priority queue after the initial input, and in this particular case, we will not output the number of processing steps nor involve a quantum. These additional attributes will be treated in later applications. (See Application 2 and Programming Project 2 at the end of this chapter.)

The simulator may be designed with a main function prompting the user for the number of processes and the priority of each. The activity of the priority queue will be handled by a `void` function called `monitor_priority_queue`, with prototype

```
void monitor_priority_queue(
    priority_queue<int,deque<int>,less<int> >& pr_queue);
```

The main function is

```
int main()
{
 int size,   // stores the number of processes
  priority; // stores the priority of each process

 // Prompt user for the number of processes.
 cout << "Input the number of processes:" << endl;
 cin >> size;

 // Construct priority queue storing the priority of each process.
 priority_queue<int,deque<int>,less<int> > process_queue;

 // Prompt user for contents of process_queue:
 cout << "Input " << size << " integers, representing the" << endl;
 cout << "respective priorities of the " << size << " processes:"
  << endl;

 // Input these values into process_queue:
 for(int index1 = 0; index1 < size; ++index1)
 {
  cin >> priority;
  process_queue.push(priority);
 } // ends for-loop
```

```
 // Echo initial size of process_queue after loading.
 cout << "The priority queue now has " << process_queue.size()
   << " members." << endl;

 // Monitor the activities of process_queue:
 monitor_priority_queue(process_queue);

 return 0;
}
```

What about the monitor function? Our design calls for `monitor_priority_queue` to provide a step-by-step account of the progress of execution of the processes with the designated priority values. Its coding may be given by

```
// Function monitoring the process queue.
void monitor_priority_queue(
   priority_queue<int,deque<int>,less<int> >& pr_queue)
{
 while(!pr_queue.empty())
 {
  cout << "Process with priority " << pr_queue.top()
    << " is executing." << endl;
  cout << "This process terminates execution." << endl;
  pr_queue.pop();
 } // terminates while-loop
 // At this point, simulation process terminates
 // Prepare to exit.
 cout << "Entire execution shuts down." << endl;
} // terminates text of monitor_priority_queue
```

We illustrate these ideas with a sample run of the program.

```
Input the number of processes:
5
Input 5 integers, representing the
respective priorities of the 5 processes:
 7  6  3  4  7
The priority queue now has 5 members.
Process with priority 7 is executing.
This process terminates execution.
Process with priority 7 is executing.
This process terminates execution.
Process with priority 6 is executing.
This process terminates execution.
Process with priority 4 is executing.
```

```
This process terminates execution.
Process with priority 3 is executing.
This process terminates execution.
Entire execution shuts down.
```

Thus, the output indicates that five processes were pushed onto the priority queue with the respective priorities 7, 6, 3, 4, 7, and the activity of the priority queue is to execute the two processes with priority 7 first, followed in order by those of priorities 6, 4, and 3.

Application 2: Simulating for the Ready Queue of Processes in a Multiprogrammed Environment, Counting Processing Steps

The simulator for the priority queue of ready processes described in Application 1 of this section is fine for as far as it goes, but it does not provide a description of the number of steps executed by the process currently in the running state. To do so, we must give a more detailed description of each process, defining its process number, number of executable steps, and its priority. Part of the description includes a definition of the less relation between two such processes. Thus, we will design a class for processes, including a description of a `friend` function defining the (binary) relation < between any two objects of this class. Thus, we define

```
class process  // User interface
{
 public:
  // Comparison operator for process objects.
  // Prototype only in here.
  friend bool operator<(const process& p1,const process& p2);
  // Data members:
  int process_number;
  int steps;
  int priority;
}; // terminates user interface for process class
```

The only remaining implementation detail is the formal coding of the binary relation < for any two distinct objects constructed from the `process` class. We do so by defining `p1 < p2` if and only if the process number of `p1` is less than that of `p2` whenever the priorities of `p1` and `p2` are the same or otherwise whenever the priority of `p1` is strictly less than that of `p2`. This is coded as

```
bool operator<(const process& p1,const process& p2)
{
 if(p1.priority == p2.priority)
  return p1.process_number > p2.process_number;
```

```
    else
      return p1.priority < p2.priority;
    }
```

Once the processes are pushed onto the priority queue, its behavior is monitored by the following function, which indicates which process is currently executing, its priority, and the current execution step. The code for this monitor is given by

```
// Void function monitoring the activity of the processes
void monitor_priority_queue(
  priority_queue<process,deque<process>,less<process> >& proc_queue)
{
 while(!proc_queue.empty())
 {
  cout << "Process " << proc_queue.top().process_number
   << " is executing." << endl;
  cout << "This process has priority " << proc_queue.top().priority
   << endl;
  for(int index1 = 1;index1 <= proc_queue.top().steps;++index1)
   cout << "Process " << proc_queue.top().process_number
    << " is executing step: " << index1 << endl;
   // Terminates for-loop.
  cout << "Process " << proc_queue.top().process_number
   << " terminates execution." << endl;
  // Go to the next process
  proc_queue.pop();
 } // ends while-loop
 // At this point, simulation process terminates.
 // Prepare to exit.
 cout << "Entire execution shuts down" << endl;
} // Terminates text of monitor_priority_queue
```

Finally, the main function drives the monitor, after it has prompted the user for the necessary input information and after the priority queue has been constructed.

```
// Main driver function.
int main()
{
 priority_queue<process,deque<process>,less<process> > process_queue;
 int size;
 process proc; // Constructs object proc from process class.

 cout << "Input the number of processes to be monitored:" << endl;
 cin >> size;
```

```
 cout << "Input the number of executions of each of the "
  << size << " processes," << endl;
 cout << "followed by the priority of each of the "
  << size << " processes" << endl;

 for(int index = 0; index < size; ++index)
 {
  proc.process_number = index + 1;
  cout << "Process Number " << proc.process_number << endl;
  cout << "------------------" << endl;
  cout << "Number of steps:";
  cin >> proc.steps;
  cout << "Priority:";
  cin >> proc.priority; cout << endl;
  process_queue.push(proc);
 }

 monitor_priority_queue(process_queue);

 return 0;
} // end main.
```

We describe a sample run of this program, with diagrams illustrating the current form of the priority queue during the progress of execution.

```
Input the number of processes to be monitored:
4
Input the number of executions of each of the 4 processes,
followed by the priority of each of the 4 processes
Process Number 1
------------------
Number of steps: 5
Priority: 4
Process Number 2
------------------
Number of steps: 3
Priority: 6
Process Number 3
------------------
Number of steps: 4
Priority: 4
Process Number 4
------------------
Number of steps: 6
Priority: 3
```

FIGURE 7.6a process_queue

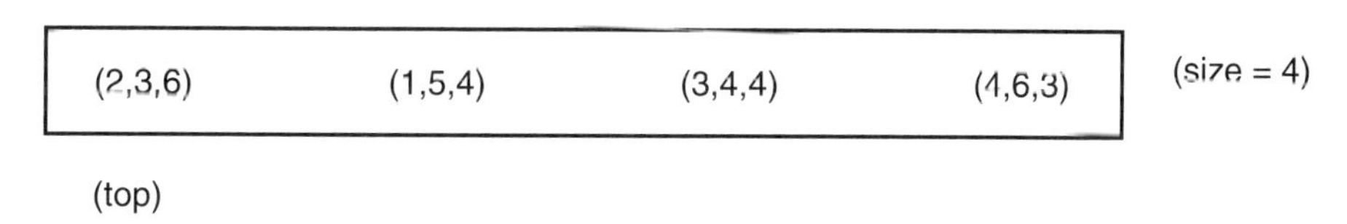

After pushing these processes onto `process_queue`, that priority queue may be pictured as in Figure 7.6a. Here each process is described by an ordered triple, whose first component is the process number, with the second component describing the number of executable steps, and whose third component gives the priority. Execution of the simulator continues with the output

```
Process 2 is executing.
This process has priority 6
Process 2 is executing step: 1
Process 2 is executing step: 2
Process 2 is executing step: 3
Process 2 terminates execution
```

At this point, `process_queue` is popped, producing the result described in Figure 7.6b. The steps of execution of the monitor continue as

```
Process 1 is executing.
This process has priority 4
Process 1 is executing step: 1
Process 1 is executing step: 2
Process 1 is executing step: 3
Process 1 is executing step: 4
Process 1 is executing step: 5
Process 1 terminates execution
```

FIGURE 7.6b process_queue

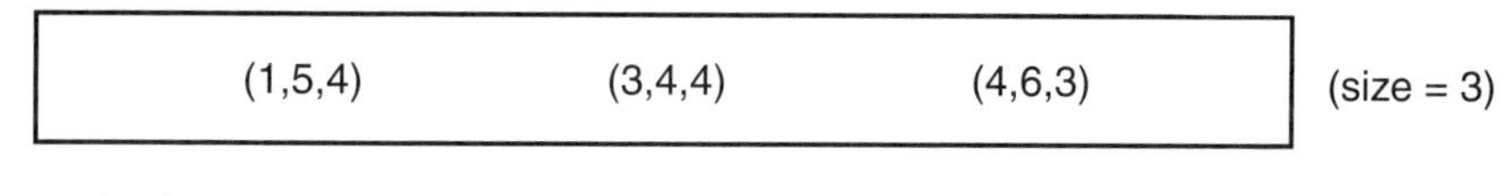

At this point, `process_queue` is popped once again, yielding the description given by Figure 7.6c. The output of the monitor program continues as

```
Process 3 is executing.
This process has priority 4
```

FIGURE 7.6c process_queue

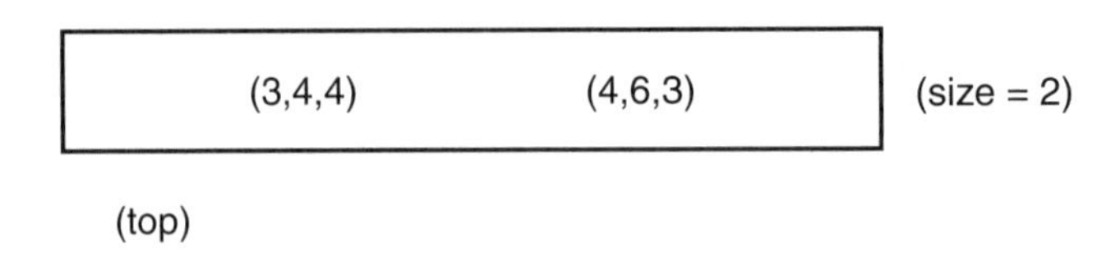


```
Process 3 is executing step: 1
Process 3 is executing step: 2
Process 3 is executing step: 3
Process 3 is executing step: 4
Process 3 terminates execution
```

`process_queue` is popped once again, yielding the description given by Figure 7.6d. Processing in the monitor continues with the output

```
Process 4 is executing.
This process has priority 3
Process 4 is executing step: 1
Process 4 is executing step: 2
Process 4 is executing step: 3
Process 4 is executing step: 4
Process 4 is executing step: 5
Process 4 is executing step: 6
Process 4 terminates execution
```

FIGURE 7.6d process_queue

(4,6,3) (size = 1)

(top)

`process_queue` is popped once again, which causes `process_queue` to become empty. This terminates the `while` loop in `monitor_priority_queue`, causing execution of the final output statement

```
Entire execution shuts down
```

7.10 Chapter Summary

This chapter extends ideas first presented in Chapter Five, where adaptors were introduced as one of the five major categories of language features of the Standard Library. There are three forms of container adaptors defined in the STL: `stack`, `queue`, and `priority_queue`, and each requires an appropriate fundamental sequence container to "sit in the background." In each case, the operations of the fundamental sequence container are adapted to those defined by the ADT of the adaptor.

For stacks, the fundamental container may be chosen to be any one of `vector`, `deque`, or `list`. Our applications of stacks solve a number of key problems in several distinct application areas:

- balanced parentheses, brackets, and braces: useful in formal languages and compiler construction
- evaluating an arithmetic expression in postfix form: useful in syntax analysis for compiler construction
- converting an arithmetic expression from infix form to its equivalent in postfix form: useful in compiler construction.

Although each of these problems requires the application of stacks, whether predefined by the implementation (as is the case with STL's container adaptors) or designed by the programmer, our solutions use the former approach. The advantage is that we are relieved of the further burden of having to design and implement the fundamental stack operations. We are also assured of the highest level of efficiency of these underlying operations because optimizing efficiency was a major goal of the design of all tools supplied by the Standard Library.

For queues, the fundamental container of choice is either `deque` or `list` because pushing values from one end of the container and popping values from the other end are most efficient for deques and `list`s. Our applications of queues concentrated on some fundamental ideas coming from the theory of operating systems. We used queues as the basic container for the problem of monitoring a finite sequence of ready processes waiting to execute in a timeshared CPU in a multiprogrammed operating system. Similar simulators may be designed for processes in a local area network waiting to acquire the services of a single line printer attached to that network.

Priority queues were first introduced as an ADT and then implemented in the Standard Library as a container adaptor. The corresponding fundamental sequence container is generally a `vector` or a `deque`, since priority queues are implemented using a fundamental container supporting the use of random-access iterators. Our applications of priority queues concentrated on their use in monitoring the activity of processes in a multiprogrammed timesharing operating system. The use of priority queues in this application area provides a more realistic simulation because processes submitted for execution in real life involve a priority system depending on the position of the individual submitting the process for execution. Certain personnel, such as system programmers or network operators, submit processes of the highest possible priority because these processes are generally intended to upgrade and/or improve the quality of system performance.

EXERCISES

1. Write a driver for `check_balance` as described in Section 7.4.
2. Write a driver for `eval_postfix` as described in Section 7.4.
3. Test each of the following for balanced parentheses, brackets, and braces. Show your results in two ways: by hand and by use of `check_balance`.
   a. `(x + {y - (z + w))]`
   b. `x + (y - (z * {w + u}))`
   c. `x + (y - [z + (w + u)]])}`
   d. `x * y /(z + w)`
4. Evaluate each of the following postfix expressions. Establish the result in two ways: by hand and by use of `eval_postfix`.
   a. `xy+zw-*pr-/` with `x = 6, y = 4, z = 3, w = 1, p = 2, r = 1`
   b. `xyzw+-*` with `x = 4, y = 3, z = 3, w = 2`
5. Convert each of the following to its equivalent postfix form. Establish the result in two ways: by hand and by use of `infix_to_postfix`.
   a. `(x + y) * (c - d/e) % f`
   b. `(((x + y) - (z + w)) * u`
6. Implement the following algorithm using `char`-valued stacks to test for palindromes:

   Construct three `char`*-valued stacks* `stack1, stack2, stack3`. *Push the character string to be tested onto each of* `stack1` *and* `stack2`. *Pop the contents of* `stack2`, *and push each of the characters popped from* `stack2` *onto* `stack3`. *If the contents of* `stack1` *and* `stack3` *are identical, then the original input string is a palindrome; otherwise, it is not a palindrome.*
7. Design and write code for a `void` function template that swaps the two topmost values on a stack.
8. Design and write code for a `void` function that appends the contents of one stack at the top of a second stack of values of the same data type. The appended stack begins with its bottom value directly on top of the top value of the second stack.
9. Write a `void` function template sorting the values currently on the stack. Use a `list` container into which the initial stack values are poured; then sort the list and push these sorted values back onto the stack.
10. Redo Problem 9, but now pour the unsorted values into a vector and a deque, and sort using the generic function `sort` appearing in `<algorithm>`.
11. Write a `bool`-valued function template that tests whether two queues of values of the same type are equal. Code this as an overloaded version of `operator==`.
12. Write a function that adds `1` to each prime positive integer on an `int`-valued queue and adds `5` to each nonprime.

13. Write a function template that reverses the sequence of values currently stored on a queue.
14. Write a function template that tests for palindromes using queues.
15. Change the value of quantum from 3 to 4 and then to 6 in Application 2 of Section 7.7. Compare the results of each simulator. Is any general conclusion derivable from these observations?
16. Observe that iterators of any kind are not defined for any of the container adaptor classes. Discuss ways of defining iterators for these adaptors by copying their values into a corresponding fundamental container. Then process the results on that fundamental container. After this completes, pour the results back into the adaptor. Which form(s) of fundamental containers appear to be the most appropriate for these actions?
17. Describe the output obtained by executing

```
#include <iostream>
#include <vector>
#include <stack>
#include <queue>

using namespace std;

class pairing
{
 public:
  // Constructor
  pairing(char c,int v):ch_val(c),int_val(v){}
  // Prototypes
  friend bool operator<(const pairing&,const pairing&);
  friend bool operator==(const pairing&,const pairing&);

  char ch_val;
  int int_val;
}; // Terminates user interface

// Implementation details
bool operator<(const pairing& p1,const pairing& p2)
{
 if(p1.ch_val == p2.ch_val)
  return p1.int_val < p2.int_val;
 else
  return p1.ch_val < p2.ch_val;
}
```

```
bool operator==(const pairing& p1,const pairing& p2)
{
 return p1.ch_val == p2.ch_val;
}

// Driver
int main()
{
 priority_queue<pairing,vector<pairing>,less<pairing> > p_queue;
 p_queue.push(pairing('r',4));
 p_queue.push(pairing('t',7));
 p_queue.push(pairing('a',12));
 p_queue.push(pairing('c',10));
 while(!p_queue.empty())
 {
  cout << p_queue.top().int_val << "," << p_queue.top().ch_val
   << endl;
  p_queue.pop();
 } // ends while

 return 0;
} // ends main
```

PROGRAMMING PROJECTS

1. Write the formal code for `infix_to_postfix` and then test this function by writing a driver using several different versions of `infix_vector` as input.
2. Extend the simulation of Application 2 of Section 7.9 to include the use of a time quantum of three processing steps.
3. Extend the simulator for Programming Project 2 by adding different quanta to each priority as follows: Assume a process may have a priority value from `1` to `3` inclusive, with the higher priority value attached to the process of higher priority. Assume any process of priority `3` has a quantum of `12` processing steps, a process of priority `2` has a quantum of `6` steps, and a process of priority `1` has a quantum of `3` steps. Experiment with a number of processes of differing priorities and different numbers of processing steps.

CHAPTER 8

Generic Algorithms

CHAPTER OBJECTIVES

- To describe the concept and purpose of generic algorithms and their use in the problem-solving environment.
- To classify generic algorithms into categories reflecting their functionality.
- To investigate each generic algorithm from the standpoint of efficiency.
- To provide specific examples of their use in a number of applications areas.

8.1 Introduction

Chapters Six and Seven provided detailed discussions of two important categories of containers: fundamental sequence containers and container adaptors. The fundamental sequence container classes defined in Chapter Six also define classes of iterators applicable to these containers. In this chapter, we study a number of general-purpose algorithms used regularly by commercial software designers and programmers. These algorithms are *generic* in the sense that their implementation is not necessarily restricted to any single container class. In fact, such algorithms may be implemented in any container class defined in the Standard Library (or possibly, ordinary one-dimensional arrays) supporting the appropriate category of iterators. This implies that programmers using these generic algorithms no longer are required to redesign and encode these algorithms. The programmer need only choose the appropriate algorithm from `<algorithm.h>` with the assurance that the algorithm has been designed for correctness and efficiency. This assurance was one of the major objectives in the design of all STL components.

8.2 A General Overview of the Generic Algorithms in the Standard Library

As stated in Section 5.6, STL generic algorithms may be classified into four main categories:

- nonmutating sequence algorithms
- mutating sequence algorithms
- sorting-related algorithms
- generalized numeric algorithms

We consider each of these in turn in this chapter. However, before we do so, it is important to consider some important facts that are applicable to each category of generic algorithms:

a. When a pair of iterator parameters is defined in an algorithm to specify the boundaries of a finite sequence to be processed, the first iterator value ordinarily refers to the initial value of the sequence, and the second ordinarily refers to the position immediately following the last value in the sequence.
b. Many generic algorithms have an *in-place version* and a *copying version.* The in-place version processes a sequence in its original location, whereas the copying version copies the values of the sequence into a new set of contiguous locations, performing the computation on the copy and thus leaving the values of the original sequence unchanged. The convention adopted by the designers of the Standard Library is to name the copying version of the algorithm with the same name as the in-place form and then add the suffix `_copy` to the copying version. For example, `reverse` and `reverse_copy` represent two versions of the generic algorithm for reversing the members of a sequence, as seen in Example 5.2. The first names the in-place version, and the second names the copying version. We should also note at this point that the sorting algorithms provided by the Standard Library do not have two versions. The sorting is done exclusively as an in-place algorithm.
c. A number of generic algorithms are presented in both an *unconditional version* and a *conditional* (or *predicate*) *version.* The unconditional version executes on every member of a sequence, whereas the conditional version performs its computation on just those members of the sequence satisfying the specified condition (or predicate). The naming convention used in the STL to distinguish these forms uses the suffix `_if` for the conditional form. As an example, we will see later in this chapter that the Standard Library provides an unconditional and a predicate version of the implementation of the linear search algorithm first discussed in Section 3.7. The unconditional version is called `find`, and the predicate version is called `find_if`.

d. The type of iterator (whether bidirectional, random access, or other) required for the generic algorithm to successfully complete its computation is specified in its prototype appearing in <algorithm.h>. The idea is that any container whose iterators satisfy at least the properties specified by the prototype allows the algorithm to execute successfully on that container; otherwise, a compile error is reported. As an example, the generic sort algorithm operates successfully on ordinary arrays, vectors, and deques because each of these containers supports random-access iterators (see Section 5.6). The sort algorithm therefore cannot be applied successfully to any list container, since the iterators are bidirectional, not random access. This is one of the reasons the collection of member functions for the list class template includes a sort function (see Section 6.10).

e. A user program using any generic algorithm must include the preprocessor directive

```
#include <algorithm.h>
```

or

```
#include <algorithm>
```
[1]

8.3 Nonmutating Sequence Algorithms

Nonmutating sequence algorithms were defined as those for which the contents of the container on which they operate are not changed as a result of their application. Such algorithms include those used for searching for members of a sequence, checking for equality, and counting members of a sequence equal to a specific value.

The find Algorithm and Its Variations: Helper Functions

In Section 5.5, we coded the function template look_for and noted that it implements a generic version of linear search. We noted that there exists a version of the same function template in <algorithm> called find. In fact, its formal code is given by

```
template <class InputIterator, class T>
InputIterator find (InputIterator first, InputIterator last, const T& value)
{
    while (first != last && *first != value)
```

[1] #include <algorithm.h> is used in the Hewlett-Packard (HP) implementation; the standard implementation uses #include algorithm>.

```
        ++first;
    return first;
}
```

As was the case for `look_for`, `find` returns an `InputIterator` value. In the case of a successful search, the value returned is the reference to the first value of the sequence where a match occurs. In the case of an unsuccessful search, the value returned is the reference to the first location past the end of the sequence.

EXAMPLE 8.1 We illustrate `find` for a sequence of `int` values stored in a deque.

```
#include <iostream>
#include <deque>
#include <algorithm>
using namespace std;
int main()
{
 // Construct and initialize int-valued deque.
 deque<int> deq(6);
 deq[0] = 3; deq[1] = 7; deq[2] = -2; deq[3] = 4; deq[4] = 0;
 deq[5] = -12;
 // Echo back the contents of deq:
 cout << "The current sequence is given by:" << endl;
 for(int index = 0; index < deq.size(); ++index)
  cout << "deq[" << index << "] = " << deq[index] << endl;
 // Prompt user for search value:
 cout << "Input a value to search for in the deque:" << endl;
 int value; cin >> value;
 // Use find function to arrive at a conclusion:
 if(find(deq.begin(),deq.end(),value) != deq.end())
  cout << value << " appears in the container" << endl;
 else
  cout << value << " does not appear in the container" << endl;
 return 0;
}
```

There is also a predicate version of `find` called `find_if`. Its code appears in `<algorithm>` and is given as

```
template <class InputIterator, class Predicate>
InputIterator find_if (InputIterator first, InputIterator last,
Predicate pred)
{
    while (first != last && !pred(*first)) ++first;
    return first;
}
```

This version also conducts a linear search through a finite sequence of values. However, unlike `find`, this version does not search the sequence for a particular value; instead, it searches for a sequence member satisfying the condition satisfying `pred`. Again, if the search is successful, the value returned is the first reference to a sequence member satisfying `pred`; otherwise, the return value is `last`. As was the case for `linsrch` in Section 3.7, `find` and `find_if` are of complexity `O(n)`.

In Section 5.7, we described how a function object (a number of which take the form of *binary predicates*) may be passed as parameters to generic algorithms. Whenever a parameter of this type is used, the user program must include the directive

```
#include <functional>
```

Note that the last parameter passed to `find_if` is a predicate. In C++, there are several ways for such predicates to materialize. We illustrate this with an example. Suppose we wish to process a list of `int` values of a specific size, searching for the first value (if it exists) in the list greater than `6`. Our design calls for an application of `find_if` for which the last parameter is a unary predicate returning `true` if the `int` value is greater than `6` and otherwise returning `false`.

There are several ways to proceed. One approach is to observe that the Standard Library provides two predefined unary function adaptors `binder1st` and `binder2nd`, each of which transforms a binary predicate function object to a corresponding unary form. Informally, if we assume a fixed binary predicate `F` and a fixed (`int`-valued) constant `c`, then to say `f`, a unary predicate, is an object of the class `binder1st` means that for any `int` value `x`, `f(x)` is `true` if and only if `F(c,x)` is `true`. Similarly, `f` is an object of the class `binder2nd` means that for any `int` value `x`, `f(x)` is `true` if and only if `F(x,c)` is `true`. In the first case, we may view `binder1st` as "binding" the first argument passed to a binary predicate object to a specific constant. Similarly, `binder2nd` binds the second argument to a constant, resulting in a corresponding unary predicate object.

Since `binder1st` and `binder2nd` represent classes, and since `f` is an object of one of these classes, `f` arises as the result of invoking the appropriate constructor. This constructor requires that both `F` and `c` are passed as arguments, and in fact, `f` is constructed in this way. However, the STL also provides a useful and relatively simple alternative in the form of a *helper function* without any loss of efficiency. The predefined helper function attached to `binder1st` is called `bind1st`, and the corresponding helper function for `binder2nd` is called `bind2nd`. The next program solves the problem stated earlier using one of these helper functions.

EXAMPLE 8.2 We wish to write an application that processes a finite sequence of `int` values, returning the first value of the finite sequence greater than `6`, if such a value exists. The user is prompted for the values in the sequence, and the sequence is stored in a `list` container. Since we will be applying the generic function `find_if` and a binary (and unary) predicate object, we require both `<algorithm>` and `<functional>` as well as `<list>`. The program is then coded as

```
#include <iostream>
#include <list>
#include <algorithm>
#include <functional>
using namespace std;
// Driver for find_if
int main()
{
 list<int> int_list;
 // Prompt user for list values:
 cout << "Please input six values into list:" << endl;
 int value;
 for(int index = 0;index < 6;++index)
 {
  cin >> value;
  int_list.push_back(value);
 }
 // Echo current contents of int_list
 cout << "The values currently in int_list are:" << endl;
 for(list<int>::const_iterator ptr = int_list.begin();
      ptr != int_list.end();++ptr)
  cout << *ptr << " ";
 cout << endl;
 // Conduct the search:
 cout << "We search for the first value in int_list bigger than 6."
  << endl;
 list<int>::iterator qptr = find_if(int_list.begin(),
              int_list.end(),bind2nd(greater<int>(),6));
 if(qptr != int_list.end())
  cout << "The first value in int_list bigger than 6 is:"
   << *qptr << endl;
 else
  cout << "No value in the list is bigger than 6" << endl;
 return 0;
}
```

Recall from Section 5.7 that `greater<T>` is given by

```
template<class T> struct greater : binary_function<T,T,bool>
```

```
{
 bool operator()(const T& x,const T& y) const
 {
  return x > y;
 }
};
```

In our example, the role of `F` is played by `greater<int>()`, `c` is `6`, and `f` is `bind2nd(greater<int>(),6)`. Informally, the unary predicate object represented by `f` is "`x > 6`". Thus, in invoking this predicate on the sequence of `int` values currently stored in `int_list`, the return value is a reference to the first location in `int_list` of a value greater than `6`, if such a value exists. Otherwise, the reference returned by `find_if` is to `int_list.end()`, signifying that the current `int_list` contains no such value.

Another approach to solving this problem is to define the class whose constructor is the third parameter passed to `find_if`. This class may be coded as

```
// Class greater_than_six.
class greater_than_six
{
 public:
  bool operator()(int x) const
  {
    return x > 6;
  }
}; // terminates class definition
```

We then apply

```
find_if(int_list.begin(),int_list.end(),greater_than_six())
```

The advantage here is that no predefined predicate objects such as `bind1st`, `bind2nd` are used; consequently, there is no need for `<functional>`. The coding details are left as an exercise. (See the problems in the Exercises at the end of this chapter.)

The Standard Library also supports an `adjacent_find` algorithm given in two versions. The first searches a sequence for a consecutive pair of equal values. When two such values are found, it returns an iterator reference to the first of these values. If no such pair exists, the reference returned is to the position immediately following the last value in the sequence. This version is coded as

```
template <class ForwardIterator> ForwardIterator adjacent_find
        (ForwardIterator first, ForwardIterator last)
{
  if (first == last) return last;
  ForwardIterator next = first;
```

```
  while (++next != last)
  {
   if (*first == *next) return first;
   first = next;
  }
  return last;
}
```

Suppose a user program contains the code sequence

```
vector<int> :: const_iterator qptr
   = adjacent_find(int_vector.begin(),int_vector.end());
if(qptr != int_vector.end())
 cout << "First duplicate value is: " << *qptr << endl;
else
 cout << "No consecutive duplicate values appear" << endl;
```

This will produce the output

First duplicate value is: 3

for the sequence

2 7 0 3 3 2 -9

and will produce the output

No consecutive duplicate values appear

for the sequence

2 7 0 3 2 3 -9

The second version uses a third parameter in the form of a binary predicate object `pred`. It searches the sequence for a consecutive pair of values making `pred` true when this pair is passed as arguments. If such a pair exists, the return value is an iterator reference to the first member of the pair; the return value is a reference to the position immediately following that of the last member of the sequence if no such pair satisfies `pred`. The formal code for this version is given by

```
template <class ForwardIterator , class BinaryPredicate>
ForwardIterator adjacent_find (ForwardIterator first,
ForwardIterator last, BinaryPredicate binary_pred)
{
 if (first == last) return last;
 ForwardIterator next = first;
 while (++next != last)
 {
  if (binary_pred(*first, *next)) return first;
  first = next;
 }
```

```
 return last;
}
```

A very useful application of this version tests whether a given sequence is *strictly increasing*. We say a sequence of values

$a_0, a_1, \ldots, a_{n-1}$

of type `T` is strictly increasing if each of the following inequalities holds:

$a_0 < a_1,\ a_1 < a_2,\ \ldots,\ a_{n-2} < a_{n-1}$

We will do this by designing a function template called `monotone_test`:

```
 template<class T> bool monotone_test(vector<T>& vect)
{
 vector<T>:: const_iterator qptr =
        adjacent_find(vect.begin(),vect.end(),greater<T>());
 if(qptr == vect.end()) return true;
 else return false;
}
```

Thus, `monotone_test` searches the sequence for the first location `j` in the sequence where $a_j \geq a_{j+1}$—namely, the first instance where the sequence is no longer strictly increasing. If no such reference exists—that is, if `qptr == vect.end()` is `true`—then the sequence is strictly increasing; otherwise, the sequence is not strictly increasing. The user program stores the sequence in a vector, and that vector is passed as the parameter to `monotone_test`.

The last variation of the `find` algorithm is called `find_first_of`. It searches through a sequence, and unlike `find` or `adjacent_find`, it searches for the first occurrence in the sequence given by `[first1,last1)` for any member of a second sequence given by `[first2,last2)`. This variation is very useful for any application that seeks an occurrence of any one of a finite sequence of values. The return value is an iterator reference to the first possible match of a value in `[first1,last1)` to a value in `[first2,last2)`. The code appearing in `<algorithm>` for this variation is

```
template <class ForwardIterator1, class ForwardIterator2>
ForwardIterator1 find_first_of
 (ForwardIterator1 first1, ForwardIterator1 last1,
  ForwardIterator2 first2, ForwardIterator2 last2)
{
    ForwardIterator1 next = first1;
    while (next != last1)
    {
        if (find(first2,last2,*next) != last2)
            return next;
        next++;
```

```
    }
    return last1;
}
```

A useful application of `find_first_of` is to list every vowel appearing in a character string input by the user. We choose `char`-valued vectors for the input string and the list of vowels, represented in both upper and lower cases. Assume that the vowels are stored in a 10-component vector called `vowels`, and the input string is stored in `char_vector`. The following code sequence implements the search:

```
vector<char>::iterator ptr;
ptr = find_first_of(char_vector.begin(),char_vector.end(),
                    vowels.begin(),vowels.end());
 while(ptr < char_vector.end())
 {
  cout << *ptr << " ";
  ptr = find_first_of(ptr + 1,char_vector.end(),vowels.begin(),
                      vowels.end());
 }
 cout << endl;
```

The first call to `find_first_of` finds the first occurrence of a vowel in the input string, and the call to `find_first_of` in the scope of the `while` loop finds the next such occurrence, and so on, until all of the contents of `char_vector` are scanned. As an example, suppose the contents of `char_vector` are as in Figure 8.1. Then the output produced from the preceding code sequence is

```
A e a
```

A predicate version of `find_first_of` exists. We leave it as an exercise to provide illustrative examples of its use.

FIGURE 8.1 char_vector

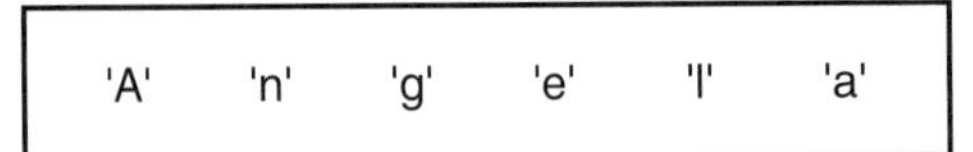

The `count` Algorithm and Its Variations

The `count` algorithm searches a sequence and counts the number of sequence members equal to a value specified by the programmer. Its code is given by

```
template <class InputIterator, class T, class Size>
void count (InputIterator first, InputIterator last, const T& value,
Size& n)
```

```
{
    while (first != last)
        if (*first++ -- value) ++n;
}
```

There is a corresponding predicate form called `count_if`, whose code is given by

```
template <class InputIterator, class Predicate, class Size>
void count_if (InputIterator first, InputIterator last, Predicate pred,
               Size& n)
{
    while (first != last)
    if (pred(*first++)) ++n;
}
```
[2]

The `count` algorithm compares `value` to members of the sequence defined by `[first,last)` and increments `n` each time there is a member of the sequence whose content matches that of `value`. For example, the code sequence

```
int counter = 0;
count(arr,arr + 10,5,counter);
cout << "There are " << counter << " values in the sequence" << endl;
cout << "equal to 5" << endl;
```

counts the number of occurrences of the value `5` appearing in a 10-component `int`-valued array `arr` and outputs that result.

The predicate version `count_if` allows the programmer to specify some unary predicate object `pred` and increments `n` each time a member of the sequence satisfies `pred`. The next example illustrates the predicate version.

The following code sequence counts all members of an `int`-valued sequence that are greater than `6`:

```
// Display the number of values of the sequence greater than 6.
  int counter = 0;
  count_if(int_vector.begin(),int_vector.end(),
        bind2nd(greater<int>(),6),counter);
  cout << "The number of sequence members greater than 6 is: "
       << counter << endl;
```

If we assume `int_vector` is an `int`-valued vector whose contents are displayed in Figure 8.2, the output produced from this last code sequence is

```
The number of sequence members greater than 6 is: 4
```

[2]The version described in the text is defined in Borland C++, Version 5.0. There is a similar version whose return value is `int` and involves three parameters, defined in Microsoft Visual C++, Version 5.0.

FIGURE 8.2 int_vector

9	8	2	6	4	-12	10	-3	5	7

The Generic `for_each` Algorithm

Suppose your application calls for a function to be applied to each member of a sequence specified by the range `[first,last)`. The Standard Library supports a generic function `for_each` to handle such a situation. The code for this algorithm may be given by

```
template<class InputIterator,class Function>
void for_each(InputIterator first,InputIterator last,Function f)
{
 while(first != last)
   f(*first++);
}
```

Since this is a nonmutating algorithm, the values of the sequence remain unchanged after its application. But then how does `for_each` obtain its result? It does so by working with "side effects," such as outputting its work, as Example 8.3 shows.

EXAMPLE 8.3 We wish to apply the function `f(value) = value`^{2} `+ 1` to each value stored in an `int`-valued deque called `int_deque`. Suppose the current state of `int_deque` is as shown in Figure 8.3 and suppose the function is coded as

```
void output_values(int value)
{
 cout << value*value + 1 << " ";
}
```

FIGURE 8.3 int_deque

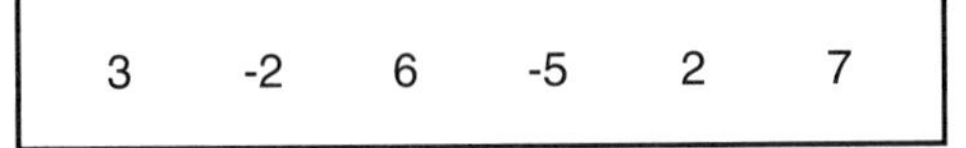

Then the following code sequence

```
for_each(int_deque.begin(),int_deque.end(),output_values);
```

produces output

```
10 5 37 26 5 50
```

Comparing Two Ranges: The <pair> Template

The Standard Library supports two generic algorithms for comparing two ranges `[first1,last1)` and `[first2,last2)` of values from a common data type. The first of these is called `equal` and uses three iterator parameters `first1`, `last1`, and `first2`. The algorithm is `bool`-valued and returns `true` just when the values `*(first1 + ptr)` and `*(first2 + ptr)` are equal for all values in `[first1,last1)` and is `false` otherwise. We may use two different types of containers in the comparison, as Example 8.4 shows.

EXAMPLE 8.4 Suppose the values in an `int`-valued vector and an `int`-valued list are described as in Figure 8.4. Then the statement

```
if(equal(int_vector.begin(),int_vector.end(),int_list.begin()))
   cout << "The ranges are identical" << endl;
else
   cout << "The ranges disagree" << endl;
```

FIGURE 8.4 int_vector

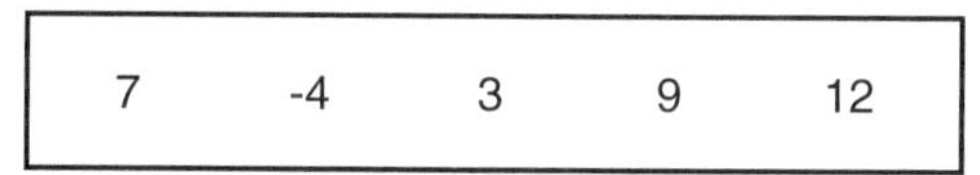

int_list

produces the output

```
The ranges are identical
```

There are a number of generic algorithms that return a pair of values instead of a single value. Since this occurs frequently, the Standard Library defines a data structure implemented as a class template for handling such situations. This template is called `pair` and involves two parameters `T1` and `T2`. Its formal definition appears in the header `<utility>` in the C++ standard. The class `pair` defines two `public` parameters `first` and `second` of the respective types `T1` and `T2`, allowing access to each component of a `pair` return value. The `pair` class is very useful in that it provides a template for encapsulating pairs of values coming from different data types. As a return type for certain generic algorithms, it returns a single value containing two values within it. To gain each value in a pair, we employ qualified references to the pair, using `first` and `second`.

The `pair` class represents the return type of the generic algorithm `mismatch`, which may assume one of two possible forms. The first of these is given by the prototype

```
template<class InputIterator1, class InputIterator2>
 pair<InputIterator1,InputIterator2>
 mismatch(InputIterator first1, InputIterator1 last1,
          InputIterator2 first2);
```

This form returns a pair of iterator references, one for each container for which the corresponding iterators are defined. The value returned is a `pair` of iterator components; the first we will call `ptr` and the second `qptr`. The value returned is the pair (if it exists) for which `*ptr != *qptr` holds, whenever `ptr` is in `[first1,last1)` and `qptr` is in `[first2,first2 + (last1 - first1))`. The reference to the first mismatch (should such a mismatch occur) is output as the `pair` object `p`; the values occurring in the mismatch may then be output using `*p.first` and `*p.second`. Example 8.5 illustrates this.

EXAMPLE 8.5 Suppose `int_vector` is an `int`-valued vector whose current state is as in Figure 8.5a, and `int_list` is an `int`-valued list whose current state is pictured in Figure 8.5b. The result obtained by applying the code sequence

```
pair<vector<int>::iterator,list<int>::iterator>
  p1 = mismatch(int_vector.begin(),int_vector.end(),int_list.begin());

 cout << "A mismatch occurs at the pair" << endl;
 cout << "int_vector value = " << *p1.first << " and "
      << "int_list value = " << *p1.second << endl;
```

FIGURE 8.5a int_vector

2	4	6	8

FIGURE 8.5b int_list

2	4	7	8

is

```
A mismatch occurs at the pair
int_vector value = 6 and int_list value = 7
```

The second version has the prototype

```
template<class InputIterator1, class InputIterator2,
         class BinaryPredicate>
pair<InputIterator1,InputIterator2>
mismatch(InputIterator1 first1,InputIterator1 last1,
```

```
        InputIterator2 first2,
        BinaryPredicate binary_pred);
```

This version finds the first iterator reference `ptr` in `[first1,last1)` with corresponding `qptr` in `[first2,first2 + (last1 - first1))` for which the value of `binary_pred(*ptr,*qptr)` is `false`. Again, if no such pair exists, the return value is a pair `ptr,<qptr` where `ptr` refers to `last1` and `qptr` refers to `first2 + (last1 - first1)`.

EXAMPLE 8.6 To illustrate this version, suppose `int_vector` is the `int`-valued vector described in Figure 8.5a and suppose `int_list` is given by Figure 8.5c. If we execute the code sequence

```
pair<vector<int>::iterator,list<int>::iterator>
  p1 = mismatch(int_vector.begin(),int_vector.end(),int_list.begin(),
                greater_equal<int>());

cout << "A mismatch occurs for greater_equal at the pair" << endl;
cout << "int_vector value = " << *p1.first << " and "
     << "int_list value = " << *p1.second << endl;
```

FIGURE 8.5c int_list

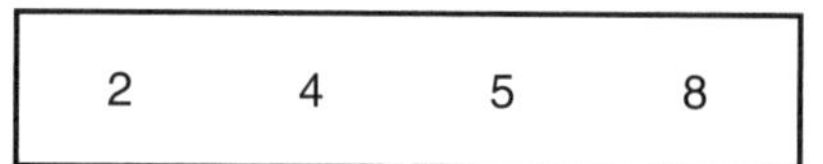

the output is given by

```
A mismatch occurs for greater_equal at the pair
int_vector value = 6 and int_list value = 5
```

The Generic `search` Algorithm

We have observed that the `find` and `find_if` algorithms search a sequence for the first occurrence of a single value. The Standard Library supports the implementation of a generic algorithm called `search`, which goes one step further. The `search` algorithm attempts to find the first occurrence of an entire subsequence delimited by `[first2,last2)` within the sequence `[first1,last1)`. This is equivalent to searching for a substring enclosed within a given string. The return value is an iterator reference to the first occurrence of the substring (if it exists). In case the string contains no such occurrence of the substring, the value returned is `last1`. That is to say, the iterator value returned is a reference to the first location following the end of the original string. Unlike the other algorithms described in this section, each of whose complexity is O(n), the search algorithm has complexity $O(n^2)$.

There is both a default form (using operator==) and a predicate form defined for search. We list the prototype for the default version here:

```
template<class ForwardIterator1, class ForwardIterator2>
ForwardIterator1 search(ForwardIterator first1, ForwardIterator last1,
                        ForwardIterator first2, ForwardIterator last2);
```

Example 8.7 illustrates a useful application of search used in word processing. The function counts the number of occurrences of a designated substring within a given string.

EXAMPLE 8.7

```
// Program which attempts to count the number of occurrences
// of a substring contained in a given character string.
// This version uses char-valued vectors.

#include <iostream>
#include <algorithm>
#include <vector>

using namespace std;
int main()
{
 // Initialize a vector character sequence and
 // a vector subsequence.
 char sequ[37] = "Look for a substring within a string";
 char subsequ[7] = "string";
 vector<char> vect_sequ(sequ,sequ+36);
 vector<char> vect_subsequ(subsequ,subsequ+6);

// Output the original sequence and subsequence:
cout << "The original sequence is: " << sequ << endl;
cout << "The subsequence is: " << subsequ << endl;

// Declare and initialize count.
int count = 0;

// Create an iterator to identify location of
// subsequ within sequ.
vector<char>::iterator
 ptr = search(vect_sequ.begin(),vect_sequ.end(),
              vect_subsequ.begin(),vect_subsequ.end());

// Perform search
```

```
while(ptr != vect_sequ.end())
{
 count++;
 ptr = search(ptr+1,vect_sequ.end(),vect_subsequ.begin(),
              vect_subsequ.end());
 }

 cout << "There were " << count << " occurrences of "
  << subsequ << " inside of" << endl;
 cout << sequ << endl;

 return 0;
}
```

The output of this function is

```
The original sequence is: Look for a substring within a string
The subsequence is: string
There were 2 occurrences of string inside of
Look for a substring within a string
```

There are a number of other generic nonmutating sequence algorithms defined in `<algorithm>`. Some of these appear in the Exercises at the end of this chapter.

8.4 Mutating Sequence Algorithms

Mutating sequence algorithms are characterized as those that, in some way, modify the members of the sequence to which they are applied. This may involve changing the order of appearance of the values in the sequence or changing one or more values to another value. Some of these are in-place algorithms, whereas others operate on a copy of the sequence.

All mutating sequence algorithms share a common property: They modify the values in a sequence referenced by a range of iterators rather than modifying the iterators. Thus, after applying any algorithm described in this section, the positions referenced by the iterators remain unchanged; however, one or more of the sequence values to which these refer may have changed.

The Generic `copy` and `copy_backward` Algorithms

The generic algorithms `copy` and `copy_backward` are used to copy elements from one range to another. The code is

```
template <class InputIterator, class OutputIterator>
OutputIterator copy (InputIterator first, InputIterator last,
                    OutputIterator result)
```

```
{
    while (first != last) *result++ = *first++;
    return result;
}
```

This algorithm copies the members of a sequence in the range `[first,last)` to a range defined as `[result,result + (last - first))`. In effect, the algorithm executes each of the assignments

```
*result = *first;
*(result + 1) = *(first + 1);
          .
          .
          .
*(result + (last - first)) = *last;
```

Example 8.8 illustrates the functionality of the `copy` algorithm. The `copy` algorithm copies the members of an `int`-valued vector called `int_vector` to the standard output using `ostream_iterator<int>`, as defined in Section 5.5.

EXAMPLE 8.8

```
// Illustration of the use of the generic "copy" algorithm.
// This example copies the contents of an int-valued
// vector directly into ostream, using ostream_iterator.
#include <iostream>
#include <algorithm>
#include <vector>
using namespace std;
int main()
{
 // Initialize and echo initial state of int_vector.
 vector<int> int_vector(4);
 int_vector[0] = 3; int_vector[1] = 4; int_vector[2] = 7;
 int_vector[3] = 8;
 cout << "Currently, int_vector has size " << int_vector.size()
   << " and has the following components:" << endl;
 for(int index1 = 0; index1 < int_vector.size(); ++index1)
  cout << "int_vector[" << index1 << "] = " << int_vector[index1]
   << endl;
 // Now apply copy algorithm.
  // Echo final results
 cout << "After applying copy:" << endl;
 copy(int_vector.begin(),int_vector.end(),
       ostream_iterator<int>(cout," "));
```

```
 cout << endl;
 return 0;
}
```

The output is

```
Currently, int_vector has size 4 and has the following components:
int_vector[0] = 3
int_vector[1] = 4
int_vector[2] = 7
int_vector[3] = 8
After applying copy:
3  4  7  8
```

The complexity of `copy` is `O(n)` because `last - first` assignments are performed.

The `copy_backward` algorithm is coded as

```
template <class BidirectionalIterator1, class BidirectionalIterator2>
BidirectionalIterator2 copy_backward (BidirectionalIterator1 first,
                                      BidirectionalIterator1 last,
                                      BidirectionalIterator2 result)
{
    while (first != last) *--result = *--last;
    return result;
}
```

Note that, unlike `copy`, `copy_backward` requires the presence of (at least) bidirectional iterators due to the backward motion of `last` and `result`. In addition, `copy` performs its assignment operations from front to back, whereas `copy_backward` executes the following assignments in the order presented:

```
*(result - 1) = *(last - 1);
*(result - 2) = *(last - 2);
              .
              .
              .
```

In summary, `copy_backward` executes the assignments

```
*(result - n - 1) = *(last - n - 1);
```

in order of increasing values of `n` starting at `0` up to (but not including) `last - first`.

A more subtle difference between `copy` and `copy_backward` is that in `copy`, the iterator reference returned is to the beginning of the output range, but the iterator value returned by `copy_backward` is a reference to the end of the output range. Example 8.9 illustrates these ideas.

EXAMPLE 8.9 We apply `copy_backward` to the same `int`-valued `int_vector` defined in Example 8.8 in the form of the code sequence

```
copy_backward(int_vector.begin(),int_vector.begin() + 2,
                    int_vector.end());
copy(int_vector.begin(),int_vector.end(),
                    ostream_iterator<int>(cout," "));
```

Initially, `int_vector` appears as in Figure 8.6a. Then `copy_backward` is applied, and the first assignment takes the form

```
*(int_vector.end() - 1) = *(int_vector.begin() + 1);
```

resulting in the version of `int_vector` pictured in Figure 8.6b. Next a final assignment

```
*(int_vector.end() - 2) = *(int_vector.begin());
```

is executed, resulting in `int_vector` as in Figure 8.6c. Then `copy` is applied, resulting in the output

```
3 4 3 4
```

FIGURE 8.6a int_vector

3	4	7	8

FIGURE 8.6b int_vector

FIGURE 8.6c int_vector

The Generic `fill` and `fill_n` Algorithms

The generic algorithms `fill` and `fill_n` assign a given value to members in a range `[first,last)`. `fill` assigns that value to all of the elements in `[first,last)` and is coded as

```
template <class ForwardIterator, class T>
void fill (ForwardIterator first, ForwardIterator last, const T& value)
{
    while (first != last) *first++ = value;
}
```

As an example of how this is used, let `int_vector` be defined as in Example 8.8. Then the result of executing `fill(int_vector.begin(), int_vector.end(),26);` is the version of `int_vector` given in Figure 8.7.

FIGURE 8.7 int_vector

26	26	26	26

`fill_n` assigns the same value to every element in the first `n` positions of a sequence, where `n` is some fixed nonnegative integer. In other words, `fill_n` assigns the value to each member of the sequence in the range `[first,first + n)`. Unlike `fill`, `fill_n` returns an iterator value equal to `first + n`. Its formal code is

```
template <class OutputIterator, class Size, class T>
OutputIterator fill_n (OutputIterator first, Size n, const T& value)
{
    while (n-- > 0) *first++ = value;
    return first;
}
```

If we again assume `int_vector` is defined and initialized as in Example 8.8, then executing `fill_n(int_vector.begin(),2,26);` converts `int_vector` to the version described in Figure 8.8.

FIGURE 8.8 int_vector

The `generate` Algorithm

Like the `fill` algorithm, `generate` assigns values to all or some of the members of a sequence. The difference lies in the fact that `generate` fills these positions with values obtained by applying a function object. Depending on the nature of the function object, this may result in different sequence members receiving different values.

The underlying code for `generate` is

```
template <class ForwardIterator, class Generator>
void generate (ForwardIterator first, ForwardIterator last, Generator
gen)
```

```
{
    while (first != last) *first++ = gen();
}
```

Here `gen` denotes the function object. Simply put, `gen` is the name of a function object applied to each iterator reference in the range `[first,last)`. Unlike `fill`, this implies that `gen` need not return the same value each time it is invoked.

EXAMPLE 8.10 Suppose we design the class

```
class sumsqplus1{
 public:
  sumsqplus1() : valuc(0) {}
  int operator()(){++value; return value*value + 1;}
 private:
  int value;
};
```

Any object constructed from this class is a function object not predefined in `<functional>`. Besides this, any such object has a data member `value` initialized as zero and has a single member function described using `oper-ator()()`. This last may be interpreted as meaning that any object constructed from this class may invoke this member function using `sumsqplus1()`. Suppose we apply

```
generate(int_vector.begin(),int_vector.end(),sumsqplus1());
```

where we assume the construction

```
vector<int> int_vector(4);
```

The functionality of the member function `sumsqplus1()` is that it begins operation using `value`'s current contents of `0`, first incrementing it to `1` and then applying `1*1 + 1 = 2` and storing this result as the initial component of `int_vector`. Since `value` was incremented to `1`, it increments once more to `2` and then computes `2*2 + 1 = 5`, storing that result as the value of the next component of `int_vector`, and so on, completing execution when the value of `int_vector.size()` is exceeded. In summary, the result of applying

```
generate(int_vector.begin(),int_vector.end(),sumsqplus1());
```

is the version of `int_vector` appearing in Figure 8.9. The complexity of `generate` is linear because `generate` executes `last - first` times whenever it is invoked.

FIGURE 8.9

int_vector

2	5	10	17

The `partition` and `stable_partition` Algorithms

The Standard Library supports two generic algorithms `partition` and `stable_partition`, whose functionality is essentially the same. Each operates on a sequence defined by the range `[first,last)` and uses a unary predicate object `pred`. When either `partition` or `stable_partition` is applied, the original sequence is subdivided into two smaller subsequences `subseq_1` and `subseq_2`. All of the values in the sequence satisfying `pred` are placed in `subseq_1`, and those values that do not satisfy `pred` are placed in `subseq_2`. The distinction between these two algorithms is that `stable_partition` guarantees that within `subseq_1` and `subseq_2`, the relative positions of the original values are preserved. Each version returns an iterator referring to the end of `subseq_1` (and the beginning of `subseq_2`). The prototype for `partition` is

```
template <class BidirectionalIterator, class Predicate>
BidirectionalIterator partition (BidirectionalIterator first,
                                 BidirectionalIterator last,
                                 Predicate pred);
```

and the prototype for `stable_partition` is essentially the same, although the positioning of values in the sequence may be different.

EXAMPLE 8.11 We apply `partition` to solve the "sifting" problem first introduced for deques in Section 6.7. Recall that the problem required that a sequence of randomly generated positive integers be sifted in such a way that the even numbers in the sequence precede the odd numbers. In the earlier situation, we chose `int`-valued deques for purposes of efficiency. Here we use a combination of generic algorithms: The first is `generate`, allowing the generation of a fixed number of random integers, followed by an application of `partition`, using the unary predicate `is_even`, defined as

```
bool is_even(int n){ return n % 2 == 0;}
```

The `main` function constructs an `int`-valued deque of some fixed size (we chose `6`):

```
deque<int> int_deque(6);
```

Then we apply `generate(int_deque.begin(),int_deque.end(),rand);` to initialize `int_deque`. Finally, we sift `int_deque` using

```
partition(int_deque.begin(),int_deque.end(),is_even);
```

In the Exercises at the end of this chapter, you are asked to compare the result obtained by executing the foregoing code with that of changing the call to `partition` to

```
stable_partition(int_deque.begin(),int_deque.end(),is_even);
```

The `random_shuffle` Algorithm

The `random_shuffle` generic algorithm rearranges the existing members appearing in a sequence `[first,last)` using pseudorandom sequences. There are a pair of `random_shuffle` algorithms. The first version uses a random number generator, which is part of the Standard Library, and the second uses a random function generator passed as an additional parameter, which represents the user's choice. We discuss only the first of these, whose prototype is given as

```
template<class RandomAccessIterator>
void random_shuffle(
                    RandomAccessIterator first,
                    RandomAccessIterator last);
```

Note that `random_shuffle` is applicable to any container type supporting random-access iterators, such as ordinary arrays, vectors, and deques.

EXAMPLE 8.12 We will apply `random_shuffle` to a character string using a `char`-valued vector as the underlying container. The following code sequence

```
char char_string[8] = "rosalie";
vector<char> char_vector(char_string,char_string + 7);
random_shuffle(char_vector.begin(),char_vector.end());
```

produces the output

```
l a r s e o i
```

The `remove` Algorithm and Its Variations

The `remove` algorithm has prototype

```
template <class ForwardIterator, class T>
ForwardIterator remove (ForwardIterator first,
                        ForwardIterator last,
                        const T& value);
```

`remove` eliminates all of the members of a sequence `[first,last)` referenced by the iterator `ptr` for which `*ptr == value` holds. The return value is an iterator referencing the end of the range of sequence values resulting after `remove` completes execution. In addition, `remove` is a *stable* algorithm: The relative order of the members of the surviving sequence is the same as their relative order in the sequence before invoking the algorithm.

An interesting fact about applying `remove` is that the size of the resulting sequence is unchanged. The reason is that `remove` performs only the following two operations:

1. the values of the sequence not removed are copied into the positions at the front of the sequence
2. an iterator value is returned, referring to the position in the sequence where the retained values end

Elements appearing after the position provided by this return value are not defined. Further, `remove` has complexity `O(n)` becausee exactly `last - first` applications of `*ptr = value` are performed. As a matter of fact, all versions of this algorithm have complexity `O(n)`.

EXAMPLE 8.13 Suppose the `int`-valued `int_list` has the form described in Figure 8.10. Then the code sequence

```
list<int>::iterator qptr = remove(int_list.begin(),int_list.end(),6);
for(list<int>::iterator ptr2 = int_list.begin();
        ptr2 != int_list.end(); ++ptr2)
 cout << *ptr2 << " ";
cout << endl;
```

FIGURE 8.10 int_list

2	3	6	7	8	6	3	6

produces the output

```
2 3 7 8 3
```

A variation of `remove` is the predicate form `remove_if`, with prototype

```
template <class ForwardIterator, class Predicate>
ForwardIterator remove_if (ForwardIterator first,
                           ForwardIterator last,
                           Predicate pred);
```

The main difference between this version and `remove` is that `remove_if` eliminates all members of the sequence for which `pred(*ptr)` is `true`. If we replace the call to `remove` in the last code sequence by

```
list<int>::iterator qptr = remove_if(int_list.begin(),int_list.end(),
                                bind2nd(less<int>(),5));
```

the resulting output is

```
6 7 8 6 6
```

Both `remove` and `remove_if` are examples of in-place algorithms. Besides these, the Standard Library also provides copying versions of each. The copying version of `remove` is `remove_copy`, with prototype

```
template <class InputIterator, class OutputIterator, class T>
OutputIterator remove_copy (InputIterator first, InputIterator last,
                            OutputIterator result, const T& value);
```

For example, the result of executing

```
remove_copy(int_list.begin(),int_list.end(),
            ostream_iterator<int>(cout," "),6);
```

produces the output

```
2 3 7 8 3
```

while `int_list` retains the form described in Figure 8.10.

The copy version of `remove_if` is `remove_copy_if`, with prototype

```
template <class InputIterator, class OutputIterator, class Predicate>
OutputIterator remove_copy_if (InputIterator first, InputIterator last,
                               OutputIterator result, Predicate pred);
```

The result of executing

```
remove_copy_if(int_list.begin(),int_list.end(),
               ostream_iterator<int>(cout," "),
               bind2nd(less<int>(),5));
```

on `int_list` as described in Figure 8.10 outputs

```
6 7 8 6 6
```

to the standard output, while `int_list` retains its original form.

The `replace` Algorithm and Its Variations

The generic `replace` algorithm replaces all members of a sequence equal to a specific value with another value. The entire sequence is scanned, implying that each version of the algorithm executes in linear time—that is, of complexity `O(n)`.

The in-place versions are identified as `replace` and its predicate form `replace_if`. The prototype for `replace` is given by

```
template<class ForwardIterator, class T>
void replace(ForwardIterator first, ForwardIterator last,
             const T& old_value, const T& new_value);
```

As stated, the execution of `replace` involves traversing the entire sequence defined by the range `[first,last)`, replacing all occurrences of `old_value` with `new_value`. We illustrate the functionality of `replace` using an `int`-valued vector `int_vector` with contents as described in Figure 8.11a.

FIGURE 8.11a int_vector

3	2	7	8	2	8	4	8

After executing `replace(int_vector.begin(),int_vector.end(), 8,10)`, each occurrence of the value `8` is replaced by `10`, yielding the contents shown in Figure 8.11b.

FIGURE 8.11b int_vector

3	2	7	10	2	10	4	10

The predicate and copy versions of `replace` are left as exercises. (See the Exercises at the end of this chapter.)

The `reverse` and `reverse_copy` Algorithms

In Section 5.5, we designed a "generic" form of a function template called `copy_reverse` for copying the values of a sequence defined by a range of iterators in reverse order. In Section 5.6, we spoke of the `reverse` algorithm defined in `<algorithm>`, with prototype

```
template<class BidirectionalIterator>
void reverse(BidirectionalIterator first, BidirectionalIterator last);
```

`reverse` is an in-place algorithm, which can be verified by displaying the values of the sequence in order before applying `reverse` and then comparing them to the values of the sequence after applying `reverse`. We leave this as an exercise. Since the iterator parameters passed to `reverse` are bidirectional, it is applicable to all forms of fundamental containers discussed earlier in the text. Its complexity is linear because `reverse` involves `(last - first)/2` swap operations to complete its execution.

The copy form of `reverse` is `reverse_copy`, coded as

```
template <class BidirectionalIterator, class OutputIterator>
OutputIterator reverse_copy (BidirectionalIterator first,
                             BidirectionalIterator last,
                             OutputIterator result)
{
    while (first != last) *result++ = *—last;
    return result;
}
```

This is a simple rewriting of our version of `copy_reverse`, presented in Section 5.5. The advantage in using `reverse_copy` is that we needn't bother coding the algorithm; all we need to do is invoke it from `<algorithm>`, with the additional assurance that it is the most efficient form.

If we apply

```
reverse_copy(int_vector.begin(),int_vector.end(),
                output_iterator<int>(cout," "));
```

to `int_vector` as described in Figure 8.11a, the output resulting from this call is

```
8 4 8 2 8 7 2 3
```

However, the contents of `int_vector` do not change.

The `rotate` Algorithm

The generic `rotate` algorithm "rotates" the elements in a sequence whose range is `[first,last)`. Its prototype is

```
template <class ForwardIterator>
void rotate (ForwardIterator first, ForwardIterator middle,
             ForwardIterator last);
```

`rotate` moves the sequence member referenced by `middle` to position `first`, then moves the member referenced by `middle + 1` to position `first + 1`, and so on, for every choice of an integer `n` in `0 <= n < last - first`. It is understood that the value passed to `middle` must be in the range `[first,last)`. The result obtained by executing `rotate` is that the sequence members originally in `[middle,last)` now appear in the range `[first,first + (last - middle))`; further, the sequence members originally in `[first,middle)` now appear in `[first + (last - middle),last)`. Example 8.14 illustrates these ideas.

EXAMPLE 8.14 Look at the `int`-valued sequence originally appearing as the contents of `int_vector` in Figure 8.11a. Suppose we then execute

```
rotate(int_vector.begin(),int_vector.begin() + 4,int_vector.end());
```

The result is pictured in Figure 8.12.

FIGURE 8.12 int_vector

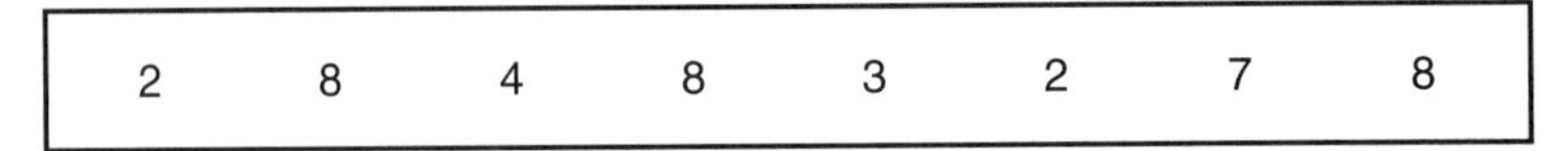

This was accomplished by swapping the values `*middle` and `*first`, then `*(middle + 1)` and `*(first + 1)`, then `*(middle + 2)` and `*(first + 2)`, and finally `*(middle + 3)` and `*(first + 3)`, where `middle = int_vector.begin() + 3` and `first = int_vector.begin()`. In fact, at most `last - first` swaps are involved, and since each swap is `O(1)`, it follows that `rotate` is an `O(n)` algorithm. Note also that `rotate` is an in-place algorithm.

There is a copy version called `rotate_copy`, with prototype

```
template <class ForwardIterator, class OutputIterator>
OutputIterator rotate_copy (ForwardIterator first,
                            ForwardIterator middle,
                            ForwardIterator last,
                            OutputIterator result);
```

The complexity of rotate_copy is also O(n). There is an example of the use of rotate_copy in the Exercises at the end of this chapter.

Generic Swapping Algorithms

We have designed mechanisms for swapping values as early as Section 1.6. In Chapter Three, swapping values in a sequence was seen to be a critical part of both selection sort and quicksort. In fact, the idea of swapping values is so critical in general data processing that the designers of the Standard Library decided to include a number of generic swapping algorithms. These are called swap, iter_swap, and swap_ranges.

The prototype for swap is

```
template<class T> void swap(T& a,T& b);
```

swap does the usual work described earlier for swap_values: It simply interchanges two values and is therefore O(1). The only condition imposed on these values is that they must be "assignable." That is to say, the data type instantiated for T supports operator= for any two of its values. In addition, swap is a rare example of a generic algorithm operating on individual values rather than on ranges of values. We will go no further here about swap; however, a useful exercise is to replace the call to swap_values in selsort from Section 3.12 to the generic version given earlier as well as the calls to swap_values in place_pivot in Section 3.14.

The prototype for iter_swap is

```
template <class ForwardIterator1, class ForwardIterator2>
 void iter_swap (ForwardIterator1 a, ForwardIterator2 b);
```

The iter_swap function swaps two values referenced by the two iterator parameters listed.

EXAMPLE 8.15 Suppose int_list and int_vector are pictured in their respective initial forms in Figure 8.13a and Figure 8.14a and suppose the following version of iter_swap is executed:

```
iter_swap(int_list.begin(),int_vector.begin());
```

FIGURE 8.13a int_list

3	2	7	8	2	8	4	9

FIGURE 8.14a int_vector

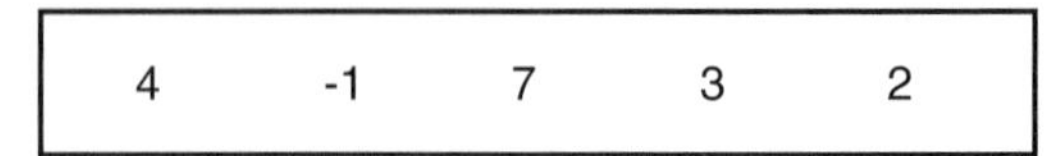

The results are seen in Figure 8.13b and Figure 8.14b. Note that the initial value of each sequence was swapped because `iter_swap` interchanges the references given by `int_list.begin()` and `int_vector.begin()`. Also

FIGURE 8.13b int_list

4 2 7 8 2 8 1 9

FIGURE 8.14b int_vector

3 -1 7 3 2

note that the swap involved two different kinds of iterators: the bidirectional iterator at `int_list.begin()` and the random-access iterator `int_vector.begin()`. The algorithm executes in amortized constant time; that is, it is essentially `O(1)`.

The prototype for `swap_ranges` is

```
template <class ForwardIterator1, class ForwardIterator2>
ForwardIterator2 swap_ranges (ForwardIterator1 first1,
                              ForwardIterator1 last1,
                              ForwardIterator2 first2);
```

This algorithm exchanges the contents of two ranges of equal size, described by `[first1,last1)` and `[first2,first2 + (last1 - first1))`. It is assumed that these two ranges do not overlap. In executing `swap_ranges`, the following pairs of values are swapped in the order presented:

`*first1` and `*first2`,
`*(first1 + 1)` and `*(first2 + 1)`,

.
.
.

`*last1` and `*(first2 + (last1 - first1))`.

The iterator value returned is `first2 + (last1 - first1)`. The algorithm has complexity `O(n)` because exactly `last1 - first1` swaps are executed.

EXAMPLE 8.16 Suppose `int_list` and `int_vector` currently are described as in Figure 8.13a and Figure 8.14a, respectively, and suppose

```
swap_ranges(int_vector.begin(),int_vector.begin() + 3,
                    int_list.begin());
```

The corresponding results are described in Figure 8.13c and Figure 8.14c.

FIGURE 8.13c int_list

4	-1	7	8	2	8	4	9

FIGURE 8.14c int_vector

3	2	7	3	2

We should observe that `rotate` and `swap_ranges` perform essentially the same work, but with one major difference: `rotate` allows for the swapping of ranges of different lengths, whereas `swap_ranges` applies only to ranges of equal length.

The `transform` Algorithm

This algorithm was introduced in Section 5.7 and applied to a specific problem illustrated in Example 5.4. In addition, a number of problems in the Exercises at the end of Chapter Five dealt with specific applications of `transform`; consequently, we do not discuss `transform` at any great length here. Instead, we simply repeat the observation that each version of the algorithm applies some function object to a range `[first,last)` and stores the result in some appropriate range. Therefore, the complexity of the algorithm in each of its forms is linear.

The `unique` Algorithm and Its Variations

The generic `unique` algorithm removes all consecutive duplicate values from a given range `{first,last)`. This algorithm also has predicate and copy forms, and each executes with complexity `O(n)`. The `unique` version is an in-place algorithm, with prototype

```
template<class ForwardIterator>
ForwardIterator unique(ForwardIterator first, ForwardIterator last);
```

The algorithm traverses the sequence given by `[first,last)` and deletes all copies of consecutive equal values. Since the algorithm locates only adjacent duplicate values, the most effective way to apply `unique` is after sorting the sequence. Example 8.17 shows how `unique` operates on an `int`-valued list.

EXAMPLE 8.17 Suppose `int_list` is given initially as in Figure 8.15a. Then the result of applying `unique(int_list.begin(),int_list.end());` is described in Figure 8.15b. As the result shows, `unique` does not change the size of the

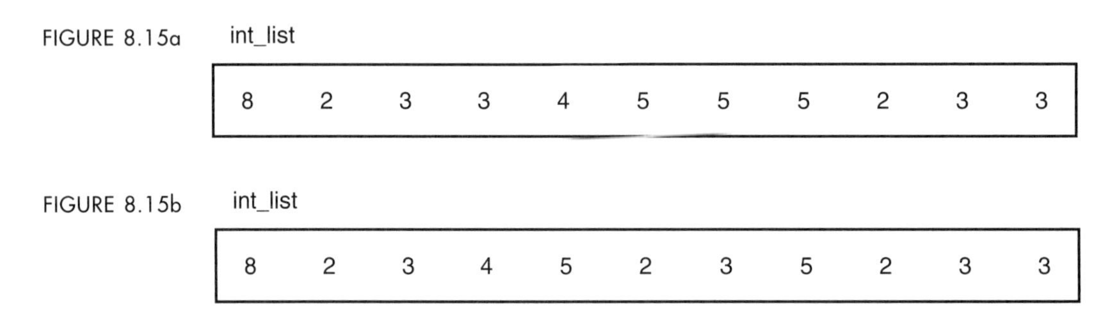

FIGURE 8.15a

FIGURE 8.15b

container to which it is applied. Instead, it copies the elements that are not consecutive duplicates in a smaller range and returns an iterator reference to the end of the smaller range. To show this, compare the output obtained from executing `unique` as described earlier to the output obtained by replacing that call by the sequence

```
list<int>::iterator iter = unique(int_list.begin(),int_list.end());
for(list<int>::iterator qptr = int_list.begin(); qptr != iter; ++qptr)
  cout << *qptr << " ";
cout << endl;
```

The copy version of `unique` is `unique_copy`, with prototype

```
template<class InputIterator,class OutputIterator>
OutputIterator unique_copy(InputIterator first,
                           InputIterator last,
                           OutputIterator result);
```

Although there are predicate versions for `unique` and `unique_copy`, the suffix `_if` is not used. Instead, the predicate forms of each are recognized by the presence of an extra parameter taking the form of a binary predicate object. These will be explored in the Exercises at the end of this chapter.

8.5 Sorting-Related Algorithms

As early as Chapter Three, the problem of sorting a range of values was described as one of the most important activities performed in computing. In fact, a major portion of that chapter is devoted to the discussion, implementation, and analysis of a number of different sorting algorithms. Each of the algorithms was designed and coded with special emphasis on efficiency of execution. Further, in Section 5.6, we introduced the concept of STL's generic algorithms and noted that a number of these were devoted to sorting. In that earlier section, we looked at one such specific algorithm called `sort`, applicable to all container-supporting random-access iterators. In Section 5.7, we gave a preliminary discussion concerning the possibility of extending `sort` to other binary comparison predicates beyond the default version `operator<`.

We will assume that the algorithms described in this section are applicable to a "sorted" range, which we define as a range whose values are arranged in order of ascending size according to the order relation chosen. In the default case, ascending means ascending with respect to `operator<`, as in

```
-1  2  3  4  5  7
```

for ordinary integers. But in the case of, say, `operator>`, ascending order would be interpreted as

```
7  5  4  3  2  -1
```

Since a range may contain duplicates, it is more appropriate to describe the range as one whose values are comparable using a *strict weak ordering*. This is an important consideration, particularly for programmers designing their own special order relation for use in sorting because, as we have already observed for `sort` in Chapter Five, the generic `sort` algorithms contain a version with an additional parameter allowing the programmer to replace the "default" version `operator<` by the version designed for the purposes of the problem at hand. We should note at this point that all of the predefined numeric types in C++ contain order relations `operator<` and `operator>` satisfying the conditions of a strict weak ordering.

What is meant by a strict weak ordering? A binary predicate `P` defined for all pairs `value1`, `value2` from some fixed type `T` is a strict weak ordering of `T` if each of the following conditions hold:

1. For any pair `value1`, `value2`, if `P(value1,value2)` is `true`, then `P(value2,value1)` is `false`.
2. For any `value1`, `value2`, `value3`, if both of `P(value1,value2)` and `P(value2,value3)` are `true`, then `P(value1,value3)` is `true`.
3. For any pair `value1`, `value2`, we say `value1` "is equivalent to" `value2` if and only if both of `P(value1,value2)` and `P(value2,value1)` are `false`.[3]

[3]Actually, we assume this sense of "equivalence" defines an *equivalence relation* among the values present in `T`. This means that for any `value1`, `value2`, `value3` in `T`, each of the following conditions holds: (a) `value1` is equivalent to itself; (b) if `value1` is equivalent to `value2`, then `value2` is equivalent to `value1` for all `value1`, `value2`; (c) if `value1` is equivalent to `value2`, and if `value2` is equivalent to `value3`, then `value1` is equivalent to `value3`.

Not all binary order relations defined on a type `T` are strict weak orderings of their values. As an example, suppose you wish to arrange a list of individuals by surname. There may exist two or more individuals in the list with the same surname. These individuals would be classified as "equivalent," although they certainly are not equal.

This is the sense of equivalence that applies to `sort` algorithms described in this section, and it is presented here as a design consideration. We will use this idea very infrequently because we will usually concentrate either on the default case or some simple variation thereof. Nevertheless, one important consideration remains: The sorting-related algorithms described here make no direct use of equality. For example, we will not use such predefined binary predicate objects as `greater_equal<T>` or `less_equal<T>`. The reason is that each permits the possibility of equality for which both of `P(value1,value2)` and `P(value2,value1)` are `true`, violating strict weak ordering. In fact, if we were to attempt to invoke `"sort"` in the form

```
"sort"(first,last,less_equal<int>());
```

where we use `"sort"` to name any one of the generic `sort` algorithms described in this section, the possibility exists that a run-time error occurs.

The Generic `sort`, `stable_sort`, and `partial_sort` Algorithms

The STL provides several generic sorting functions, each of which has complexity `O(n log n)` and sort a sequence `[first,last)` defined using random-access iterators.

In Section 5.6, we introduced the generic algorithm `sort`, with prototype

```
template<class RandomAccessIterator>
void sort(RandomAccessIterator first, RandomAccessIterator last);
```

This version sorts the members of the sequence defined by `[first,last)` in ascending order. As an example, we may apply `sort(int_vector.begin(),int_vector.end())` to `int_vector` as described in Figure 8.11a to yield the result described in Figure 8.16.

FIGURE 8.16 int_vector

2	2	3	4	7	8	8	8

A more general version of `sort` includes an additional parameter `comp` of type `Compare`, indicating the possible option of applying a comparative operator other than the default. Its prototype was described in Section 5.7 as

```
template<class RandomAccessIterator, class Compare>
void sort(RandomAccessIterator first,
          RandomAccessIterator last,
          Compare comp);
```

If we apply `sort(int_vector.begin(),int_vector.end(),greater<int>())` to the same `int_vector`, the result of executing this extended version is as shown in Figure 8.17.

FIGURE 8.17 int_vector

8	8	8	7	4	3	2	2

Is sort a stable operation? That is to say, when applied to sequences such as the integer values of `int_vector`, do the repeated values retain their original order? For example, in sorting `int_vector` as it appears in Figure 8.11a, which "2" appears first, and where does each "8" appear in the sorted sequence? There is no indication that `sort` is an example of a stable sorting operation. However, there is a generic sort algorithm called `stable_sort` which guarantees that the relative positions of equal values in the original sequence are maintained in the sorted sequence. The two versions of `stable_sort` have the prototypes

```
template<class RandomAccessIterator>
void stable_sort(RandomAccessIterator first,
                 RandomAccessIterator last);
```

and

```
template<class RandomAccessIterator>
void stable_sort(RandomAccessIterator first,
                 RandomAccessIterator last,
                 Compare comp);
```

The result of applying `stable_sort` to the `int`-valued vector `int_vector` in Figure 8.11a produces the same result as `sort`. If we also investigate the result obtained by applying `stable_sort` to `int_vector` for the case where the additional parameter is `greater<int>()`, again the result shows no difference from the same application using sort.

What differences exist between `sort` and `stable_sort`? The differences between the two are subtle. First, it is usually the case that `sort` executes slightly faster than `stable_sort`. Second, `stable_sort` preserves the relative ordering of equivalent elements in the sense of equivalence as defined earlier. That is to say, if `value1` and `value2` are members of the sequence defined by [first,last) and if value1 appears before value2 prior to applying stable_sort, then stable_sort preserves that precedence: After applying stable_sort, value1 still appears before value2. (Recall the ordering of individuals by surname).

The generic algorithm partial_sort permits the sorting of a smaller segment of a sequence, leaving the remaining members of the sequence unsorted. Two forms of partial_sort exist. The default form has the prototype

```
template<class RandomAccessIterator>
void partial_sort(RandomAccessIterator first,
                  RandomAccessIterator middle,
                  RandomAccessIterator last);
```

partial_sort rearranges the sequence in the range [first,last) so that the smaller middle - first members are sorted in ascending order.

Suppose int_vector is as in Figure 8.11a, and we want to sort only the three smallest values, placing these in the first three positions in int_vector. This is accomplished by invoking

```
partial_sort(int_vector.begin(),int_vector.begin()+3,int_vector.end());
```

The result appears in Figure 8.18.

FIGURE 8.18 int_vector

The second version is the more general form, allowing for an extra parameter of type Compare. Its prototype is

```
template<class RandomAccessIterator, class Compare>
void partial_sort(RandomAccessIterator first,
                  RandomAccessIterator middle,
                  RandomAccessIterator last,
                  Compare comp);
```

For example, suppose we begin with int_vector as in Figure 8.11a, and we wish to sort its three largest values, placing these in the first three positions. This may be accomplished by

```
partial_sort(int_vector.begin(),int_vector.begin()+3,int_vector.end(),
        greater<int>());
```

partial_sort is useful in solving many data processing problems, such as listing last week's top 20 best-selling nonfiction books or sorting the highest 50 grades on the latest bar examination in some specific state in the United States.

We now describe some specific properties inherent in the functionality of `partial_sort`. First, we may observe that applying

```
partial_sort(first,middle,last);
```

places the `k = middle - first` smallest members of the entire range `[first,last)` into `[first,middle)`. The entire range is not sorted because the remaining part `[middle,last)` contains the "leftover" members of the sequence in no specific order. This is evident by examining all of the members of `int_vector` as shown in Figure 8.18: Only the first three members are sorted in order of increasing size, while the remaining `last - middle` members are in no specific order. Second, we observe that the complexity of either version of `partial_sort` is approximately `O(n log n)` because approximately `k log k` comparisons of the sequence members are performed. This is because the values are placed in a nonlinear data structure (called a *heap*), and the sort operation coming from this emulates *heapsort*, a sorting strategy studied later in this chapter.

There are also two copy versions of `partial_sort`, called `partial_sort_copy`, described by the prototypes

```
template<class InputIterator, class RandomAccessIterator>
 RandomAccessIterator partial_sort_copy(
                                 InputIterator first,
                                 InputIterator last,
                                 RandomAccessIterator result_first,
                                 RandomAccessIterator result_last);
```

and

```
template<class InputIterator, class RandomAccessIterator>
 RandomAccessIterator partial_sort_copy(
                                 InputIterator first,
                                 InputIterator last,
                                 RandomAccessIterator result_first,
                                 RandomAccessIterator result_last,
                                 Compare comp);
```

The first of these sorts the number of elements equal to the smaller of the lengths `last - first`, `result_last - result_first` of the respective ranges `[first,last)` and `[result_first,result_last)` and places these elements in a sequence beginning at the location given by the value of the iterator `result_first`. The value returned is a reference to `result_last`. The idea is to view `[first,last)` as an *input range* and `[result_first,result_last)` as an *output range*. If the output range has smaller size than the input range, then `[result_first,result_last)` contains exactly as many of the sorted values from `[first,last)` as fit into `[result_first,result_last)`. On the other hand, if `[result_first,` `result_last)` is larger than `[first,last)`, then the sorted form of the entire sequence contained in `[first,last)` is placed into the initial `last - first` positions of `[result_first,result_last)`, with the remaining positions padded with zeros (in the case of numeric types).

EXAMPLE 8.18 Suppose `input_vector` is an `int`-valued vector described as in Figure 8.19 and `output_vector` is defined by

```
vector<int> output_vector(6);
```

FIGURE 8.19 int_vector

7	3	6	4	11	9	3	20	12	5

Then the result of executing

```
partial_sort_copy(input_vector.begin(),input_vector.end(),
                  output_vector.begin(),output_vector.end());
```

does not change the contents of `input_vector`, but `output_vector` becomes the vector displayed in Figure 8.20.

FIGURE 8.20 output_vector

The result obtained by applying the same call to `partial_sort_copy` with `output_vector` defined by

```
vector<int> output_vector(14);
```

is left as an exercise. (See the Exercises at the end of this chapter.)

The Generic `nth_element` Algorithm

This is an algorithm with complexity `O(n)`, with prototypes

```
template<class RandomAccessIterator>
 void nth_element(RandomAccessIterator first,
                  RandomAccessIterator nth,
                  RandomAccessIterator last);
```

and

```
template<class RandomAccessIterator>
 void nth_element(RandomAccessIterator first,
                  RandomAccessIterator nth,
```

```
                RandomAccessIterator last,
                Compare comp);
```

For the default case, the algorithm rearranges the values in the sequence in such a way that the following conditions prevail (similar to the partition algorithm of quicksort):

1. the element that would ordinarily be in the `nth` position if the sequence were sorted is in the `nth` position
2. all sequence members before the `nth` position are those that would ordinarily precede that value in the converted sequence (but these sequence members are not necessarily sorted among themselves)
3. all sequence members after the `nth` position are those that would ordinarily follow that value in the sequence (but these members are not necessarily sorted among themselves)

For example, suppose `char_vector` is a `char`-valued vector whose current contents are seen in Figure 8.21a. Then the result of applying

```
nth_element(char_vector.begin(), char_vector.begin() + 3,
                char_vector.end());
```

is as shown in Figure 8.21b.

FIGURE 8.21a

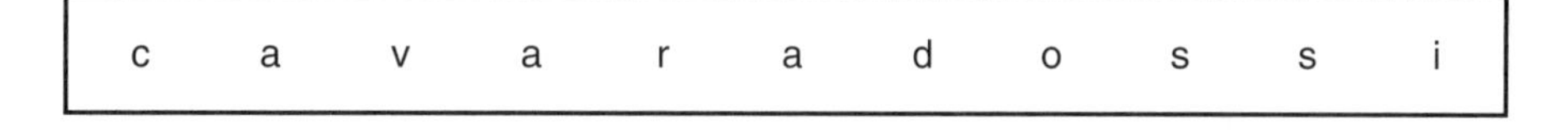

FIGURE 8.21b

Generic Binary Search Algorithms

In Section 3.10, we studied and designed code for the binary search algorithm. In Section 3.11, we analyzed binary search and showed that its complexity is `O(log n)`. Since binary search assumes the precondition that the sequence is sorted, either using the default less than comparison operator or some other supplied by the programmer, any generic algorithm related to binary search is properly classified as one among those related to sorting.

There are four generic algorithms related to binary search. These are `binary_search`, `lower_bound`, `upper_bound`, and `equal_range`. In each case, we assume that the range `[first,last)` is sorted. The generic `binary_search` algorithm is `bool`-valued, returning `true` if and only if the value sought is found in the sequence. The prototypes for `binary_search` are

```
template <class ForwardIterator, class T>
bool binary_search (ForwardIterator first, ForwardIterator last,
                    const T& value);
```

for the default case, and

```
template <class ForwardIterator, class T, class Compare>
bool binary_search (ForwardIterator first, ForwardIterator last,
                    const T& value, Compare comp);
```

for the general case.

Each version of `binary_search` searches the sequence from `first` up to but not including `last` for `value`. The second version passes a comparative operator `comp` as the fourth parameter, comparing members of the sequence to `value` using `comp`.

The following is an example of how `binary_search` is applied to an `int`-valued list. Since `binary_search` requires only that `[first,last)` be specified by forward iterators, we may apply the algorithm to `int_list`, defined as the `int`-valued list given by Figure 8.22. If the user program contains the conditional statement

```
if(binary_search(int_list.begin(),int_list.end(),value))
 cout << value << " was found in int_list" << endl;
else
cout << value << " does not appear in int_list" << endl;
```

FIGURE 8.22 int_list

and if the user is prompted for an integer to be stored in `value`, then the conditional executes the appropriate response.

The advantage in using this version of `binary_search` over `binsrch` in Chapter Three is that we no longer have to supply the code for the binary search algorithm; it is supplied free of charge simply by invoking the generic algorithm. In addition, the efficiency is not compromised by invoking one version over the other because each has complexity `O(log n)`.

The generic algorithm `lower_bound` searches a sorted sequence for the first member greater than or equal to a `value` supplied by the user. There are the usual two prototypes for `lower_bound`; the prototype for the default is

```
template <class ForwardIterator, class T>
ForwardIterator lower_bound (ForwardIterator first,
                             ForwardIterator last,
                             const T& value);
```

and

```
template <class ForwardIterator, class T>
ForwardIterator lower_bound (ForwardIterator first,
                             ForwardIterator last,
                             const T& value,
                             Compare comp);
```

for the general version.

This algorithm searches a sorted sequence for the first member greater than or equal to `value`. This is the first position into which that value can be inserted without destroying the sorted sequence. The value returned references this member or returns `last` if the kind of sequence member that has been described does not exist.

We may apply `lower_bound` for the same binary search of `int_list` in place of `binary_search`. We accomplish this by replacing the preceding code sequence by

```
if(lower_bound(int_list.begin(),int_list.end(),value) ==
                                              int_list.end())
 cout << value << " does not appear in int_list" << endl;
else
 cout << value << " appears in int_list" << endl;
```

We can go further for fundamental sequence containers supporting random-access iterators. For such containers, we may use the "bracket" operator `operator[]` to access any value. Rather than merely stating the qualitative result that the value sought appears in the container or not, we may output the location of the value sought (in the case of a successful search). The underlying code applied to the sorted `int`-valued vector `int_vector` of Figure 8.16, where `value` is an `int`-valued variable holding the value sought, is

```
int *ptr = lower_bound(int_vector.begin(),int_vector.end(),value);
 if(binary_search(int_vector.begin(),int_vector.end(),value))
  cout << value << " appears in position " << ptr - int_vector.begin()
      << endl;
 else
  cout << value << " does not appear in int_vector" << endl;
```

As an example, if we search for `8` using this code sequence, the output returned is

```
8 appears in position 5
```

but if we instead search for `5`, the output is

```
5 does not appear in int_vector
```

The generic `upper_bound` algorithm finds the first value in any sorted sequence that is greater than the value supplied by the user. Potentially, this is the last position in the sequence into which that value may be inserted without violating the integrity of the sorting of the sequence. The two versions of the prototypes for `upper_bound` are virtually the same as those listed for `lower_bound`, but now "`upper_bound`" replaces "`lower_bound`".

Example 8.19 illustrates how `upper_bound` is used to find a suitable location to insert a new value into a sorted `int`-valued list, preserving the integrity of the sorting.

EXAMPLE 8.19

```
#include <iostream>
#include <algorithm>
#include <list>
using namespace std;

int main()
{
 // Initialize int_list.
 int int_array[8] = {-3,-1,0,2,5,7,9,23};
 list<int> int_list; // Initially empty.
 for(int index = 0; index < 8; ++index)
  int_list.push_back(int_array[index]);
 cout << "int_list has size " << int_list.size() << endl;
 cout <"and has the respective values:" << endl;
 for(list<int>::iterator ptr = int_list.begin();
      ptr != int_list.end(); ++ptr)
      cout << *ptr << " ";
 cout << endl;

 // Now locate the position where 6 should be put in order
 // to preserve the integrity of the sorted list:
 list<int>::iterator qptr =
   upper_bound(int_list.begin(),int_list.end(),6);

 // Output the components of the list before 6:
 cout << "The components in int_list before 6 are:" << endl;
 for(list<int>::iterator ptr1 = int_list.begin();
```

```
        ptr1 != qptr; ++ptr1)
        cout << *ptr1 << " ";
  cout << endl;
  // Then output the components after the 6:
  cout << "The values in int_list after 6 are:" << endl;
  for(list<int>::iterator ptr2 = qptr; ptr2 != int_list.end();
        ++ptr2)
        cout << *ptr2 << " ";
  cout << endl;

  // Now insert 6 in its proper position:
  cout << "Inserting 6 in its proper sorted position:" << endl;
  int_list.insert(qptr,6);

  cout << "The result of the insertion produces the list:" << endl;
  for(list<int>::iterator ptr3 = int_list.begin();
        ptr3 != int_list.end(); ++ptr3)
   cout << *ptr3 << " ";
  cout << endl;
  return 0;
}
```

This program outputs

```
int_list has size 8
and has the respective values:
-3 -1 0 2 5 7 9 23
The components in int_list before 6 are:
-3 -1 0 2 5
The values in int_list after 6 are:
7 9 23
Inserting 6 in its proper sorted position:
The result of the insertion produces the list:
-3 -1 0 2 5 6 7 9 23
```

The `equal_range` algorithm searches a sorted sequence `[first,last)` for a range of values, each of which is equal to a value input by the user. The purpose of `equal_range` is to supply the programmer with a range of candidates into which the input value may be inserted without destroying the sorting of the sequence.

The prototypes for `equal_range` are

```
template <class ForwardIterator, class T>
pair<ForwardIterator, ForwardIterator>
equal_range (ForwardIterator first, ForwardIterator last,
             const T& value);
```

and

```
template <class ForwardIterator, class T>
pair<ForwardIterator, ForwardIterator>
equal_range (ForwardIterator first, ForwardIterator last,
             const T& value, Compare comp);
```

In either form, the algorithm searches `[first,last)` for a range of elements equal to `value`. If such a range exists, it returns a pair of iterators `[ptr,qptr)` specifying the range. If no such range exists—since `value` is not in `[first,last)`—the pair returned consists of two iterators, each of which is equal to `first`. In this case, something like `upper_bound` is applied to implement the insertion.

EXAMPLE 8.20 Suppose we look at `char_vector` defined as in Figure 8.21b and execute the code sequence

```
pair<vector<char>::iterator,vector<char>::iterator>
 letters = equal_range(char_vector.begin(),char_vector.end(),'a');
cout << "The subrange is:" << endl;
for(vector<char>::iterator qptr = letters.first;
     qptr != letters.second; ++qptr)
 cout << *qptr << " ";
cout << endl;
```

This program outputs

```
The subrange is
a  a  a
```

Algorithms for Merging Two Sorted Sequences

The Standard Library supports two generic algorithms that merge two sorted ranges, which results in a single sorted range called `merge` and `inplace_merge`. The `merge` algorithm places the result in a range that does not overlap either of the two input ranges; consequently, it is not an in-place algorithm. This version extends the `merge` member function for `list` objects, as defined in Section 6.10. The generic versions may apply to any two sorted sequences, even if the sequences are stored in different types of containers. For example, if one sequence `[first1,last1)` is stored in a `list` object and `[first2,last2)` is stored in a vector, we may apply the generic `merge` function to `merge` these sequences in a third container or output the result directly using `ostream_iterator`.

The two prototypes for `merge` are given by

```
template <class InputIterator1, class InputIterator2,
        class OutputIterator>
```

```
OutputIterator merge (InputIterator1 first1, InputIterator1 last1,
                      InputIterator2 first2, InputIterator2 last2,
                      OutputIterator result);
```

and

```
template <class InputIterator1, class InputIterator2,
          class OutputIterator, class Compare>
OutputIterator merge (InputIterator1 first1, InputIterator1 last1,
                      InputIterator2 first2, InputIterator2 last2,
                      OutputIterator result, Compare comp);
```

The `OutputIterator` value returned in this case is a reference to the first location after the last value in the output sequence.

The complexity of either form of `merge` is linear. The algorithm is modeled after the `merge` function template described in Section 3.16; consequently, `(last1 - first1) + (last2 - first2) -1` comparisons among the values of the sequences are required for its execution. In addition, both versions of `merge` and `inplace_merge` are examples of stable algorithms.

EXAMPLE 8.21 Suppose `int_list` is given as in Figure 8.22 and `int_vector` is given as in Figure 8.16. If we apply

```
merge(int_list.begin(),int_list.end(),int_vector.begin(),
      int_vector.end(),ostream_iterator<int>(cout," "));
```

its execution produces the output

```
-3 -1 0 2 2 2 3 4 5 7 7 8 8 8 9 23
```

The `inplace_merge` algorithm merges two consecutive ranges `[first,middle)` and `[middle,last)` and combines these into a single sorted range. The two versions of its prototype are

```
template <class BidirectionalIterator>
void inplace_merge (BidirectionalIterator first,
                    BidirectionalIterator middle,
                    BidirectionalIterator last);
```

and

```
template <class BidirectionalIterator, class Compare>
void inplace_merge (BidirectionalIterator first,
                    BidirectionalIterator middle,
                    BidirectionalIterator last, Compare comp);
```

To illustrate `inplace_merge`, suppose the `int`-valued vector `vec` appears as in Figure 8.23a. If we apply

```
inplace_merge(vec.begin(),vec.begin() + 3,vec.end());
```

the result is described in Figure 8.23b.

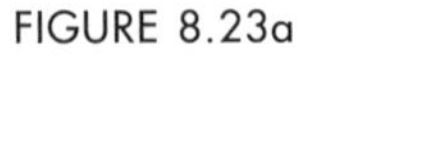

FIGURE 8.23a

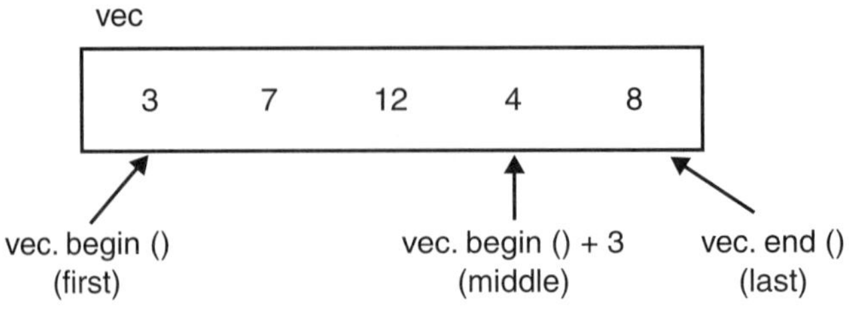

FIGURE 8.23b

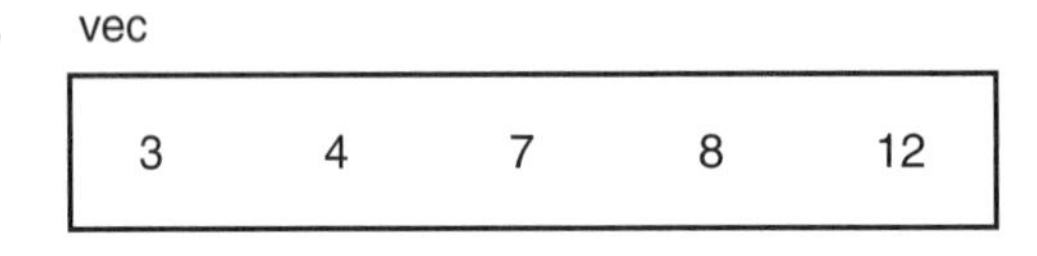

Generic Algorithms for Heaps[4]

A *heap* is a binary tree in which every node has the property that its value is greater than or equal to the value assigned to each of its children. Since this property is defined recursively, it prevails throughout the entire tree. Thus, the largest value contained in the heap is found at its root. A simple example of an integer-valued heap (assuming the default less than relation) is given in Figure 8.24a.

FIGURE 8.24a

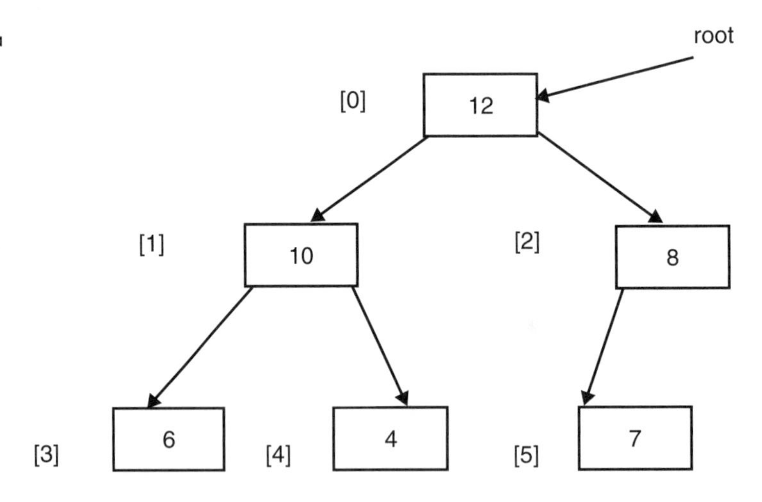

The heap may also be represented by a sequence of values defined by the range `[first,last)`, where the iterators are random access. For example, if `heap_vector` is an `int`-valued vector used to represent the heap pictured in Figure 8.24a, it assumes the form pictured in Figure 8.24b.

[4]This section assumes some background in nonlinear data structures, particularly the rudiments of binary trees.

FIGURE 8.24b heap_vector

12	10	8	6	4	7

Heaps are efficient data structures commonly used in commercial data processing, especially to solve the problem for finding the largest value in a sequence. In addition, if the root is removed, a new heap can be re-formed from the surviving values by moving nodes (using a finite sequence of swap operations) from lower levels of the heap upward. This upward movement (known as "trickle up") has complexity `O(log n)`. Therefore, the re-forming of the heap using this technique is very efficient.

If new values are to be inserted into the heap (a "push" operation), they are first inserted as new leaf nodes and are then trickled upward to re-form the heap with the new value properly situated. Deletions ("pop" operations) of values from a heap are accomplished by removing the current root and then re-forming the two surviving subtrees into a single heap. This technique is used in sorting a sequence of values `[first,last)` by first inserting each member, from `first` to immediately before `last`, to form the initial heap and then deleting the root each time and inserting each value removed at the right end of the sequence until the heap becomes empty. At that point, the resulting sequence is a sorted version of the original sequence. These operations can be performed without using any generic algorithms from the Standard Library. (See the Programming Project at the end of this chapter.)

The Standard Library contains a number of generic functions used to create and manipulate heaps, represented as sequences defined by ranges `[first,last)` of random-access iterators. The first of these is `make_heap`, which is used to build a heap from a given unsorted sequence. Its prototype appears in two versions:

```
template <class RandomAccessIterator>
void make_heap (RandomAccessIterator first, RandomAccessIterator last);
```

for the default case, and

```
template <class RandomAccessIterator, class Compare>
void make_heap (RandomAccessIterator first, RandomAccessIterator last,
                Compare comp);
```

for the general case. In either version, this function rearranges the values in `[first,last)` so that they form a heap. This operation is of complexity `O(n)` and must be implemented before any sorting operation on the heap is performed.

The next two generic heap operations are called `pop_heap` and `push_heap`. We describe their functionality without formally displaying their prototypes, leaving that as an exercise. The pop_heap function removes the current root and places that value at the end of the current sequence. The resulting sequence is one value shorter than its predecessor, and the value referencing the end of the current sequence must be shifted back one position to continue. The resulting sequence [first,last-1) is also a heap, and the operations needed to re-form the heap have complexity O(log n).

The push_heap operation permits a new value to be inserted into an already existing heap, and the resulting structure is re-formed into a new heap with one more node than its predecessor. In this case, the resulting sequence is represented by [first,last+1) to accommodate the new node. The complete push_heap operation has complexity O(log n).

The last heap-related algorithm is sort_heap, with prototypes

```
template <class RandomAccessIterator>
void sort_heap (RandomAccessIterator first,RandomAccessIterator last);
```

and

```
template <class RandomAccessIterator, class Compare>
void sort_heap (RandomAccessIterator first, RandomAccessIterator last,
                Compare comp);
```

sort_heap applies pop_heap as many times as necessary to remove nodes from the heap to form the resulting sorted sequence, where each cycle of the underlying loop fills in the next highest value. Since each execution of pop_heap is of complexity O(log n) and the sequence contains n values, the sort_heap has complexity O(n log n).

EXAMPLE 8.22 Suppose we execute the following code sequence on int_vector as described in Figure 8.11a:

```
make_heap(int_vector.begin(),int_vector.end());
sort_heap(int_vector.begin(),int_vector.end());
```

After executing make_heap, the components of int_vector are as pictured in Figure 8.25a. This implies that the underlying heap constructed using make_heap has the form shown in Figure 8.25b. After executing sort_heap, the resulting vector is sorted as in Figure 8.25c. int_vector can be sorted using heapsort by invoking iterations of push_heap and pop_heap. (See the Exercises at the end of this chapter.)

FIGURE 8.25a int_vector

8	8	7	8	2	3	4	2

FIGURE 8.25b

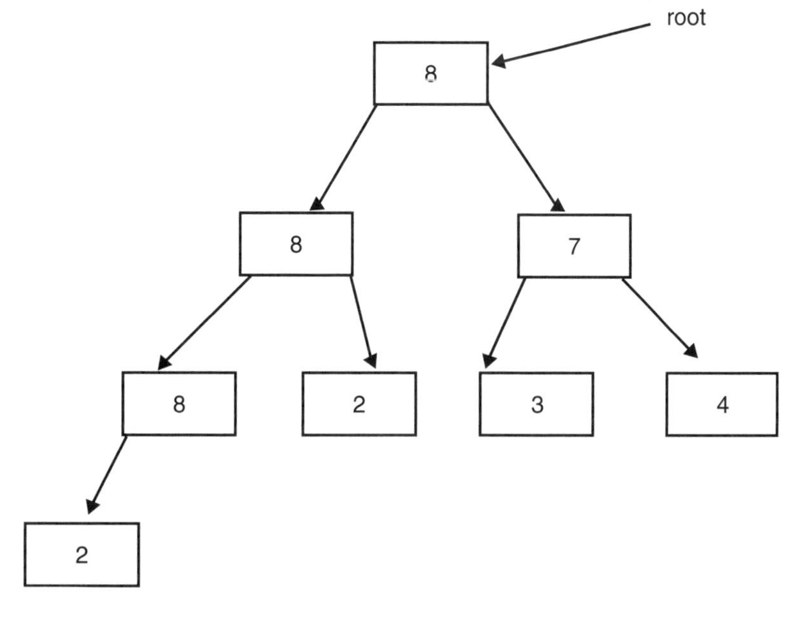

FIGURE 8.23c int_vector

2	2	3	4	7	8	8	8

8.6 Generalized Numeric Algorithms

The Standard Library provides a group of algorithms that are characterized as generalized numeric algorithms because they refer to a number of useful arithmetic operations in various areas of specialization. There are four such algorithms, all applicable to numeric sequences, and they include computing subtotals, inner products, accumulation, and differences of adjacent values. Although generic, these are stored in a separate library called <numeric>; consequently, a user program invoking any of these must add the preprocessor directive

#include <numeric>[5]

The accumulate Function

The generic accumulate algorithm takes a sequence [first,last) and, when not applying the default version, an operator. It applies the operator to every member in the sequence, accumulating and outputting the total. The algorithm has a default version described by the prototype

[5]In the HP implementation, these algorithms appear in <algo.h>.

```
template <class InputIterator, class T>
T accumulate (InputIterator first, InputIterator last, T init);
```

The default version assumes that the operator is addition—`plus<T>()`—and a general version has the prototype

```
template <class InputIterator, class T, class BinaryOperation>
T accumulate (InputIterator first, InputIterator last, T init,
              BinaryOperation binary_op);
```

The binary operator object is passed to this version as the value of `binary_op`.

Each version requires an initial value `init`. If we wish to accumulate a sum, the value passed to `init` is zero; if we wish to accumulate a product, that value will be one. The purpose of including an `init` parameter is to guarantee a return value for `accumulate`, even when the range is empty. The operator passed as `binary_op` need not be associative or commutative because `accumulate` assumes a grouping of the sequence $a_0, a_1, a_2, \ldots, a_{n-1}$ referenced by `[first,last)` using the binary operator `op` as $(\ldots(((a_0 \text{ op } a_1) \text{ op } a_2) \text{ op } \ldots) \text{ op } a_{n-1}$. Thus, first $a_0 \text{ op } a_1 = s_1$ is computed, then $s_1 \text{ op } a_2 = s_2$, and so on, ending with $s_{n-2} \text{ op } a_{n-1} = s_{n-1}$. This algorithm has a complexity of $O(n)$.

Suppose we apply the default and general versions of `accumulate`, using `multiplies<int>()`, to the `int`-valued vector int_vector of Figure 8.11a:

```
int sum = accumulate(int_vector.begin(),int_vector.end(),0);
int product = accumulate(int_vector.begin(),int_vector.end(),1,
                         multiplies<int>());
```

The result is

```
42
172032
```

The Inner Product Function

The generic `inner_product` algorithm is an important computational tool in elementary vector analysis. We first illustrate the idea from a theoretical standpoint. Suppose `vec1` and `vec2` are three-dimensional `double`-valued vectors, as in Figure 8.26. Then the *inner product* of `vec1` and `vec2` is given by `(2.1)*(-4.1) + (-7.3)*(3.1) + (5.5)*(6.2) = 2.86.`

FIGURE 8.26

vec1		
2.1	-7.3	5.5

vec2		
-4.1	3.1	6.2

The Standard Library implements two versions of inner_product. We will consider only the default version, which implements inner products as just shown. Its prototype is

```
template <class InputIterator1, class InputIterator2, class T>
T inner_product (InputIterator1 first1, InputIterator1 last1,
                  InputIterator2 first2, T init);
```

The general version allows the addition and multiplication operations to be replaced by binary operators chosen by the programmer. This represents a situation whose application goes beyond the scope of this text, and so we leave its investigation as an exercise.

The inner_product algorithm has complexity O(n) because it operates in a linear fashion on two ranges [first1,last1) and [first2,last2), where we assume [first2,last2) is at least as long as [first1,last1). The sum of last1 - first1 products of the corresponding components of the two ranges [first1,last1) and [first2,first2 + (last1 - first1)) are accumulated, beginning with an init value of zero. It is also important to note that the sequences [first1,last1) and [first2,last2) need not be stored in the same kind of container.

For example, if we assume vec1 is implemented as a double-valued vector and vec2 is implemented as a double-valued list, and we execute

```
double result =
   inner_product(vec1.begin(),vec1.end(),vec2.begin(),0.0);
```
[6]

the value of result is 2.86.

The partial_sum Algorithm

Suppose the sequence $a_0, a_1, a_2, \ldots, a_{n-1}$ is defined by the range [first1,last1). Then the generic algorithm partial_sum generates a sequence $b_0, b_1, b_2, \ldots, b_{n-1}$ defined by a range beginning with result, where *result = b_0, and such that

```
*result = *first,
*(result + 1) = *first + *(first + 1),
                .
                .
                .
```

that is, where $b_0 = a_0$,

[6]In computing the inner product of any double-valued or float-valued sequences, the programmer must supply the initial value of 0.0, not 0; otherwise, a run-time error occurs.

$$b_1 = a_0 + a_1,$$
$$b_2 = a_0 + a_1 + a_2,$$
$$\vdots$$

for the default version, whose prototype is given by

```
template <class InputIterator, class OutputIterator>
 OutputIterator partial_sum (InputIterator first, InputIterator last,
                              OutputIterator result);
```

The default version presumes that the binary operator applied to consecutive sequence values is addition; however, the STL supports a more general version in which an additional `BinaryOperation` parameter named `binary_op` is given, so that

```
*result = *first,
*(result + 1) = binary_op(*first,*(first + 1)),
              = binary_op(*result,*(first + 1)),
*(result + 2) = binary_op(*(result + 1),*(first + 2)),
```

and so on. The prototype for the general form is

```
template <class InputIterator, class OutputIterator,
          class BinaryOperation>
 OutputIterator partial_sum (InputIterator first, InputIterator last,
                                  OutputIterator result,
                                  BinaryOperation binary_op);
```

The complexity of either version of `partial_sum` is `O(n)`, and the return value is a reference to the end of the output range, `result + (last - first)`.

To illustrate the default form of `partial_sum`, suppose we apply

```
partial_sum(int_list.begin(),int_list.end(),
              ostream_iterator<int>(cout," "));
```

to `int_list` as defined in Figure 8.22. Then the result of this call is the output

```
-3 -4 -4 -2 3 10 19 42
```

The `adjacent_difference` Algorithm

The default version of the generic `adjacent_difference` algorithm computes the (signed) difference of adjacent members in a sequence by subtracting the second value of any adjacent pair from the first. That is, if $a_0, a_1, a_2, \ldots, a_{n-1}$ represents the sequence, then `adjacent_difference` generates the sequence $b_0, b_1, b_2, \ldots, b_{n-1}$, where $b_0 = a_0$, $b_1 = a_1 - a_0$, $b_2 = a_2 - a_1$, $\ldots$, $b_{n-1} = a_{n-1} - a_{n-2}$.

The default version presumes ordinary subtraction and has the prototype

```
template <class InputIterator, class OutputIterator>
 OutputIterator adjacent_difference (InputIterator first,
                                     InputIterator last,
                                     OutputIterator result);
```

The general form is not discussed in any detail in this text. If the range is empty, zero subtractions are performed; if not, `(last - first) - 1` subtractions are done because the first member of the result sequence is a copy of the first member of the original sequence. This implies that the complexity of `adjacent_difference` is `O(n)`.

To illustrate how `adjacent_difference` works, suppose we apply the function to `int_list` as described in Figure 8.22 using `ostream_iterator<int>(cout," ")` to reference values in the result sequence. Specifically, suppose we invoke

```
adjacent_difference(int_list.begin(),int_list.end(),
                    ostream_iterator<int>(cout," "));
```

The result of this execution is the output

```
-3 2 1 2 3 2 2 14
```

8.7 Chapter Summary

This chapter is devoted to a detailed treatment of a major component of the Standard Library: generic algorithms. These algorithms are characterized as generic because they are applicable to a wide variety of sequences stored in different containers and to a wide scope of application domains.

The C++ standard places these generic algorithms into two separate libraries, `<algorithm>` and `<numeric>`, and the algorithms have been designed for flexibility and efficiency. They are classified into four main categories:

- nonmutating sequence algorithms
- mutating sequence algorithms
- sorting-related algorithms
- generalized numeric algorithms

Except for a very limited number of exceptions, each such algorithm is applicable to a sequence of values defined by a range `[first,last)` of iterators. The majority of such algorithms have several versions: (a) a default version, which assumes the presence of a specific operator; (b) a general version, in which the programmer supplies the operator to be used; (c) a copy version, in which the algorithm executes on a copy of the original sequence; and (d) a predicate version, which applies only if the members of the sequence satisfy a given predicate. Copy versions usually use a naming convention with a suffix _copy, as in the case of reverse_copy and remove_copy, and predicate versions involve the suffix _if, as seen in find_if and count_if. Besides these, certain algorithms combine both the copy and predicate forms and involve the suffix _copy_if, as in remove_copy_if.

The design objective for including generic algorithms is to provide a predefined and highly efficient version of a number of frequently used algorithms in the commercial software application area. This relieves the burden, to a large extent, of coding such algorithms from the shoulders of the programmer: All the programmer has to do is tailor the existing members of <algorithm> and <numeric> to suit the purpose of the specific problem to be solved. The fact that such libraries are available in C++ makes the choice of that language as a candidate for coding the underlying solution a significant design decision.

A number of generic algorithms were omitted from this chapter. Those relating to set operations will be considered and used in Chapter Nine. Others, such as permutation generators, were not discussed in this text because they were judged less important than those that were included. However, these can be found in a number of references devoted to the Standard Library. (See the References at the end of this chapter.)

EXERCISES

1. Show that the same result obtained in Example 8.2 may also be obtained by invoking

```
find_if(int_list.begin(),int_list.end(),bind1st(less<int>(),6))
```

2. Complete the coding of the user function driving

```
find_if(int_list.begin(),int_list.end(),greater_than_six())
```

   from Example 8.2.

3. Write a driver for the first version of adjacent_find. Note that this version is the same as the predicate version, with the third parameter given as equal_to<T>().
4. Write a driver for the function template monotone_test, using both int-valued and char-valued sequences as input.
5. Write a program using find_first_of that counts the number of vowels appearing in any input character string.
6. Show that it is possible to redesign the application of find_first_of listing all of the vowels appearing in any character string using a list container.
7. Show that for any int-valued constant c, count(arr,arr + 10,c, counter) produces the same output as

```
count_if(arr,arr + 10,bind2nd(equal_to<int>(),c),counter)
```

where `arr` is some 10-component `int`-valued array.

8. Show that `search` works for `int`-valued vectors by designing a function similar to that described in Example 8.7, counting the number of occurrences of the sequence `9, 3` appearing in the sequence `9, 3, 5, 9, 3, 7, 9, 3`.

9. Write the entire program used as a driver for the application of `mismatch` described in Example 8.5.

10. Redo Exercise 9, except that now the function drives the version of `mismatch` described in Example 8.6.

11. The generic algorithm `lexicographical_compare` has two versions. The default version has the prototype

```
template <class InputIterator1, class InputIterator2>
bool lexicographical_compare (InputIterator1 first1,
                              InputIterator1 last1,
                              InputIterator2 first2,
                              InputIterator2 last2);
```

The algorithm returns `true` if the range `[first1,last1)` is lexicographically less than the range `[first2,last2)` and is `false` otherwise. Test this algorithm on the following two pairs of sequences:

a. the `int`-valued sequences `2,3,7,1,8` and `2,3,8,1,8`

b. the `char`-valued sequences `'j','a','n','e','y'` and `'j','a','n','e'`

12. The Standard Library supports a generic nonmutating sequence algorithm `max_element`, whose default version has the prototype

```
template <class ForwardIterator>
ForwardIterator max_element (ForwardIterator first,
ForwardIterator last);
```

The algorithm returns an iterator reference to the maximum element in a sequence defined by `[first,last)`. The default involves the comparison operator `operator<`. If the sequence contains more than one copy of the maximum element, the iterator refers to its first occurrence. Apply this algorithm to each of the following:

a. the `int`-valued sequence `2,3,7,8,1,8`, stored in a vector

b. the `char`-valued sequence 'a','n','t','h','o','n','y', stored in a list

c. the `double`-valued sequence `2.7,5.94,3.081,4.7,-6.3`, stored in an ordinary one-dimensional array

Show that `max_element` is an `O(n)` algorithm.

13. There is a generic nonmutating sequence algorithm `min_element` similar to `max_element` described in Exercise 12, except that now `min_element` returns an iterator reference to the first occurrence of the minimum element occurring in `[first,last)`. Apply `min_element` to each of the three sequences defined in Exercise 12.

14. Given an `int`-valued array `int_array` defined and initialized by

```
int int_array[4] = {7,3,2,1};
```

explain the result obtained by applying

```
copy(int_array,int_array + 4,int_array + 2);
```

Also explain how the output justifies the in-place nature of the `copy` algorithm.

15. Compare the results obtained by executing

```
copy(int_vector.begin(),int_vector.end(),vector_copy.begin());
```

for `int_vector` constructed and initialized as in Example 8.8 and `vector_copy` constructed as

a. `vector<int> vector_copy;`

b. `vector<int> vector_copy(4);`

c. `vector<int> vector_copy(8);`

16. a. Show that `fill_n(int_vector.negin(),int_vector.size(),26)` produces the same result as `fill(int_vector.begin(),int_vector.end(),26)`.

b. What is the result of applying `fill_n(int_vector.begin(),0,26)`?

17. Suppose we declare

```
deque<int> int_deque(10);
```

and then apply

```
generate(int_deque.begin(),int_deque.end(),rand);
```

Describe the result obtained.

18. Apply `stable_partition` instead of `partition` to solve the sifting problem of Example 8.11. Compare the results of each version.

19. Sift any sequence of positive integers so that the prime numbers appearing in any sequence of positive integers input by the user are placed in front of all of the nonprimes.

20. Iterate `random_shuffle` five times to the character string `"rosalie"` and derive conclusions from the comparative ouputs.

21. Show that the result of applying

```
remove(int_list.begin(),int_list.end(),6);
```

in Example 8.13 is identical to the result of applying

```
remove_if(int_list.begin(),int_list.end(),
        bind2nd(equal_to<int>(),6));
```

22. Similarly, show the result of applying

```
remove_copy(int_list.begin(),int_list.end(),
          ostream_iterator<int>(cout," "),6);
```

is identical with the result of applying

```
remove_copy_if(int_list.begin(),int_list.end(),
```

```
ostream_iterator<int>(cout," "),
bind2nd(equal_to<int>(),5));
```

23. Apply

```
replace_copy(int_vector.begin(),int_vector.end(),
             ostream_iterator<int>(cout," "),8,10);
```

to int_vector with components given initially as in Figure 8.11a.

24. Apply

```
replace_copy_if(int_list.begin(), int_list.end(),
                ostream_iterator<int>(cout," "),
                bind2nd(less<int>(),6),12);
```

to int_list as described in Problem 22.

25. Apply reverse to int_list as defined in Example 8.13 and to char_vector as described in Example 8.12. Show the before and after listings of each sequence.

26. Apply rotate_copy to int_vector as described in Figure 8.11a. Show that int_vector remains the same after applying the function.

27. Apply unique_copy to int_list as described in Figure 8.15a in the form

```
unique_copy(int_list.begin(),int_list.end(),
            ostream_iterator<int>(cout," "));
```

28. Show that

```
list<int>::iterator iter =
unique(int_list.begin(),int_list.end(),equal_to<int>());
```

produces the same result as

```
list<int>::iterator iter =
    unique(int_list.begin(),int_list.end());
```

Test this using int_list as described in Figure 8.15a.

29. a. Show, using int_vector as described in Figure 8.11a, that

```
sort(int_vector.begin(),int_vector.end())
```

produces the same result as

```
sort(int_vector.begin(),int_vector.end(),less<int>())
```

b. Show the same equivalence as (a) when "sort" is replaced by "stable_sort."

30. Show that

```
partial_sort(int_vector.begin(),int_vector.begin()+k,int_vector.end())
```

yields the same result as

```
partial_sort(int_vector.begin(),int_vector.begin()+k,int_vector.end(),
        less<int>())
```

for any integer k, where 0 <= k < int_vector.size(), for int_vector as described in Figure 8.11a.

31. a. Show that `partial_sort(first,last,last)` sorts the entire sequence in the range `[first,last)` in order of increasing size.
b. Show that `partial_sort(first,first,last)` leaves all of the members of the sequence in their original position.

32. Execute `partial_sort_copy(input_vector.begin(),input_vector.end(), output_vector.begin(),output_vector.end())` for `input_vector` as described in Example 8.18 and with `output_vector` defined by `vector<int>output_vector(14);`

33. Apply

```
nth_element(input_vector.begin(),input_vector.begin()+5,
                input_vector.end());
```

to `input_vector` given initially as in Example 8.18.

34. Suppose the members of `int_list` of Figure 8.22 are now described in descending order. Apply the general version of each of `binary_search` and `lower_bound` using the additional parameter `greater<int>()`.

35. Design a program similar to that of Example 8.19, but now the value to be inserted into its proper position is input interactively.

36. Write a program that first sorts the characters in the string `"raskolnikov"` and then applies `equal_range` with a `char` value that is input interactively.

37. Show that heapsort may be accomplished on the same `int_vector` as described in Example 8.22 by using the alternative code sequence

```
for(int index1 = 2;index1 < 8;++index1)
 push_heap(int_vector.begin(),int_vector.begin()+index1);
for(int index2 = 8;index2 > 1;—index2)
 pop_heap(int_vector.begin(),int_vector.begin()+index2);
```

38. Apply

```
int difference = accumulate(int_vector.begin(),int_vector.end(),0,
                                         minus<int>());
```

to `int_vector` as defined in Figure 8.11a and explain how the value is computed.

PROGRAMMING PROJECT

Create a class template (using parameter `T`) for heaps with `public` parts consisting of the default constructor, constructing an initially empty heap of values of type `T`, and with two additional member functions called `reheap_down` and `reheap_up`, simulating the "trickle down" and "trickle up" operations, respectively. The class also contains two other `public` data members: the original array of values and the size of the current heap. After doing this, apply the `heap` class to sort the `int`-valued array whose members, in order, are `381, 224, 363, 114, 220, -71, -90, 116, 2429, 606, 2294, 612, 933.`

REFERENCES

Austern, Matthew H., *Generic Programming and the STL* (Reading, MA: Addison-Wesley, 1999).

Josuttis, Nicolai M., *The C++ Standard Library* (Reading, MA: Addison-Wesley, 1999).

Musser, David R., and Saini, Atul, *STL Tutorial and Reference Guide* (Reading, MA: Addison-Wesley, 1996).

Robson, Robert, *Using the STL* (2nd ed.). (New York: Springer-Verlag, 1999).

CHAPTER 9

Sorted Associative Containers

CHAPTER OBJECTIVES

- To introduce the concept of sorted associative containers.
- To distinguish between the various forms of such containers and to describe the advantages inherent in their use in a number of problem-solving situations.
- To introduce the concept of associative arrays.
- To present specific applications of the use of sorted associative containers in hashing and the implementation of graph ADTs.

9.1 Introduction

Beginning with Chapter Six, we studied various types of sequence containers and container adaptors provided by the Standard Template Library. With the exception of priority queues, each of these container types and their adaptors share a common property: When values are inserted into or removed from the underlying containers, they appear in the same relative order.

In addition to these, the Standard Library provides another category of container abstractions whose primary concern is not to maintain the relative order of appearance of its values as these values are inserted or removed from the container. The reason is that the sequence containers studied in Chapter Six and their adaptors store their values in a linear arrangement, whereas this new category does not. In fact, this new category aims primarily at the ability of the containers involved to retrieve data as quickly and efficiently as possible. For each class of new containers studied in this chapter, the retrieval is based on the use of *keys,* which may be either the values themselves or one component of a finite collection of data items to be stored. Each such class supports efficient insertion and removal of its values but differs from sequence containers and their adaptors in that no specific member functions exist for inserting or removing a value at a position in the designated container.

We discussed some of these ideas in Chapter Four. In that earlier treatment, it was up to the programmer to code the retrieval mechanisms by hand using hash tables and hash functions. In this chapter, we study facilities predefined in the Standard Library by looking at a new category of containers, collectively called *sorted associative containers.* These containers are named in this manner because they are designed to store their values in sorted order rather than in the order in which these values were inserted. For the case where the key and value coincide, the STL defines two class templates: `set` and `multiset`; for the case where the key is part of, but not all of the data, the STL defines the class templates `map` and `multimap`.

The distinction between `set` and `multiset` is that the former supports unique keys: If a `set` object contains a specific value `val`, then `val` appears only once. But in the case of `multiset` objects, duplicate keys are allowed: `val` appears as many times as it is inserted into the `multiset` object. A similar distinction exists between `map` and `multimap` objects: `map` objects support unique keys, whereas `multimap` objects support duplicate keys.

One principal reason for including sorted associative containers in the STL is in response to the following question:

What methods exist for optimizing the speed and efficiency of the retrieval of data stored in some container?

One method is to sort the keys in some specific order, such as ascending numeric order if the keys are numeric or ascending lexicographic order if the keys are strings. Another method is to use some form of a hash function, as treated initially in Chapter Four. The Standard Library responds to the first method by providing sorted associative containers, which are the topic of this chapter. The second method is handled by defining a category of associative containers called *hashed associative containers.* As of the writing of this text, the current standard for the C++ programming language does not provide for predefined hashed associative containers. However, there are implementations of the language in which appropriate class templates exist for hashed associative objects. We do not treat this topic in this text.[1]

9.2 Sets and Multisets

We begin this section by describing the `set` interface. Recall that with any `set` or `multiset` object, the values stored in the object are the keys. In

[1]For a more detailed treatment of hashed associative containers, see the site on the World Wide Web from Silicon Graphics, Inc. (www.sgi.com/STL/*.*).

addition, any user function requiring the use of set objects must include the directive

```
#include <set>
```

The template parameters for each of the set and multiset class templates are

```
template<class Key, class Compare = less<Key>,
               class Allocator = allocator>
```

The first parameter is the type of keys to be stored, the second is the type of comparison function defined for ordering the values, and the third is the type of storage allocator implemented.[2] The second parameter defines a specific relational operator on the keys and is used to establish their order when traversing the values in the container by some appropriate form of an iterator. The set and multiset iterator types are bidirectional and constant, implying that some of the generic algorithms studied in Chapter Eight are not applicable to set and multiset objects—namely, those that specify the use of random-access iterators. In addition, since these iterators are constant, no value may be modified through their use, for a very good reason: The application of any mutable iterator might spoil the sorting of the values stored in the container.

Three constructors are defined for set:

- the default constructor, with interface

  ```
  explicit set(const Compare& = Compare());
  ```

- a constructor initializing a set object by specifying some predefined range:

```
template<class InputIterator>
  set(InputIterator,InputIterator,const Compare& = Compare());
```

- a copy constructor, with prototype[3]

  ```
  set(const set<Key,Compare>&);
  ```

For example, suppose we wish to construct an int-valued set object called set_value using the default constructor. We can do this using

```
set<int,less<int> > set_value;
```

Since set describes a class (template) of sorted associative containers, the input values presented for insertion into any such object need not appear in sorted order, but when the appropriate object is constructed, these values are stored and output in ascending order (assuming the default

[2]In each of the Borland C++ and Visual C++ implementations, the Allocator parameter may be dropped for the default. Neither version permits less<Key> to be dropped.

[3]In the Borland C++ and Visual C++ implementations, the Compare parameter may be dropped when the default comparison less<Key> is assumed.

comparison operator). Second, although the input stream may contain duplicate values, the associated `set` object does not. To illustrate, consider the `int`-valued vector `vec`, currently as in Figure 9.1. Suppose we apply the constructor

```
set<int,less<int> > set_value(vec.begin(),vec.end());
```

FIGURE 9.1

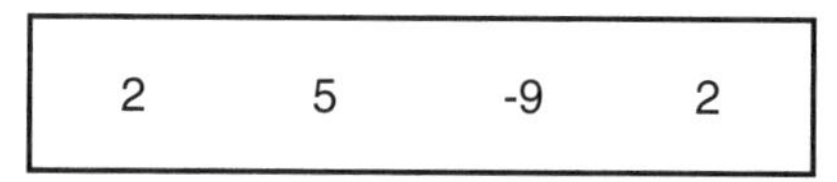

Then the contents of `set_value` are output as

```
-9 2 5
```

If we then apply the copy constructor

```
set<int,less<int> > set_value2(set_value);
```

then the contents of `set_value2` are output as

```
-9 2 5
```

There are a number of member functions of `set` that are characterized as *capacity operators* because they deal with the number of values contained in any `set` object. The first of these is `empty()`, whose behavior is identical with its counterpart for other containers: The `bool` value returned is `true` or `false` depending on whether the current `set` object is empty or not. In addition, the `size()` member function returns the number of (distinct) values in the set, whereas `max_size()` returns the maximum number of possible values that can be stored in any `set` object. The last of these depends on the underlying implementation of the language.

The next collection of member functions is identified as *modifiers* because they change the current contents of the set to which they are applied. The first of these is `insert`, appearing in three different versions. The first version is perhaps the simplest, with prototype

```
pair<iterator,bool> insert(const value_type& x);
```

where `value_type` names the data type of the values stored in the set. To implement this, we require a single `value_type` parameter—namely, the specific value to be inserted into the set.

What purpose is served by the `pair` value returned?[4] The first component of the return value refers to the position of the newly inserted member if the insertion is successful; otherwise, the `first` component refers to the value already present in the `set` object. As we will see later, this version of `insert` is invalid for `multiset` objects because these allow for

[4]The `pair` template was discussed in Section 8.3.

repeated occurrences of values. The `second` component of the return value is either `true` or `false` according to whether the value stored in the parameter was actually inserted into the set. Using this version of `insert`, we may also confirm that the insertion was performed. For example, suppose `set_value` is constructed as earlier, and we then apply the conditional

```
if(set_value.insert(4).second)
  cout << "4 successfully inserted into set_value" << endl;
else
  cout << "4 was not inserted into set_value" << endl;
```

Thus, if the value `4` is not already in `set_value` at the point of execution of this conditional, then it is inserted, and the message

```
4 successfully inserted into set_value
```

is returned. Otherwise, the message

```
4 was not inserted into set_value
```

is returned.

The C++ standard also allows the return value to be omitted. Thus, the insertion may be accomplished simply by invoking

```
set_value.insert(4);
```

No iterator value need be supplied by the programmer. This is unlike any form of insert operator studied in Chapter Six for fundamental sequence containers. In those earlier versions, the location in the sequence where the value is to be inserted is critical, but in the case of sets (or for that matter, for any form of sorted associative container), the position of the newly inserted value is that which maintains the sorted order of its values.

In the face of this last observation, the syntax for the second version of `insert` is rather curious:

```
iterator insert(iterator position, const value_type& x);
```

What role is played by the first parameter? After all, executing this version still places the value of the second parameter in the appropriate position in the `set` object, maintaining the sorted order. The actual role of the first parameter is as a "hint" to the processor as to where execution should begin to search for the appropriate location for placing the new value, and it may be omitted. If the value of this parameter aids in the search, the complexity of `insert` speeds up to almost constant time; otherwise, the complexity is of order `O(log n)`, where `n` is the number of values already stored in the set.

The third version is given by

```
template<class InputIterator>
 void insert(iterator position, InputIterator first,
                                InputIterator last);
```

which inserts a copy of the entire set of values in the sequence defined by the range [first,last) into the set. The first parameter may again be ignored, but if present, it hints at the proper location where the values in [first,last) may be stored.

A second group of modifiers represents three forms of erase, each of which executes a form of removal of values in a set. The first of these is

```
void erase(iterator position);
```

This form removes the value currently referenced by the value of the iterator parameter. To apply this version, the position of the value to be removed must be provided.

The next version is

```
size_type erase(const key_type& x);
```

which removes the value x from the set if x appears in the set; otherwise, the set is not changed. The return value is the number of occurrences of x that are removed. For a set object, this value is either 1 or 0 depending on whether x was in the set or not.

The last form is given by

```
void erase(iterator first,iterator last);
```

where iterator defines a valid iterator for a set object. This version removes all values in a set lying in the range [first,last).

As stated earlier, both set and multiset support bidirectional constant iterators. As with other containers, it is possible to reference the first value in a nonempty set object using begin() and the value just past the last component using end(). Consequently, it is possible to output the current components of the set object set_value described earlier using

```
for(set<int,less<int> >::const_iterator ptr = set_value.begin();
      ptr != set_value.end(); ++ptr)
 cout << *ptr << endl;
```

In addition, we can define reverse iterators referencing set objects using rbegin() and rend(). Example 9.1 illustrates many of these ideas.

EXAMPLE 9.1

```
// Program illustrating various forms of insert and erase
// member functions for set objects.  Also includes
// the range form of insert and a copy constructor.

#include <iostream>
#include <set>
using namespace std;
int main()
{
```

```
int int_array[] = {3,2,7,-1,8,2,8}; // Conformant array
// Apply default constructor for sets:
set<int,less<int> > set_value;
// Apply range form of insert to set_value:
set_value.insert(int_array,int_array + 7);
// Display output for set_value:
cout << "The components of set_value are:" << endl;
for(set<int,less<int> >::const_iterator ptr = set_value.begin();
     ptr != set_value.end(); ++ptr)
 cout << *ptr << " ";
cout << endl;
// Now apply the copy constructor for sets:
set<int,less<int> > set_value2(set_value);
// Apply size() to each of set_value and set_value2:
cout << "The current size of set_value is: " << set_value.size()
  << endl;
cout << "and the current size of set_value2 is: "
 << set_value2.size() << endl;
// Apply various forms of erase to set_value and set_value2:
set_value.erase(2);
set_value.erase(0);  // 0 not in current set_value
cout << "After applying first form of erase to set_value:" << endl;
cout << "attempting to erase 2 and 0, the size of set_value is"
 << endl;
cout << set_value.size() << " and its components are" << endl;
for(set<int,less<int> >::const_iterator qptr = set_value.begin();
     qptr != set_value.end(); ++qptr)
 cout << *qptr << " ";
cout << endl;
set<int,less<int> >::const_iterator iter = ++set_value2.begin();
cout << "Now apply the range version of erase to " << endl;
cout << "[set_value2.begin(),++iter):" << endl;
set_value2.erase(set_value2.begin(),++iter);
cout << "After performing this erasure on set_value2,its" << endl;
cout << "components are:" << endl;
for(set<int,less<int> >::const_iterator ptr1 = set_value2.begin();
     ptr1 != set_value2.end(); ++ptr1)
 cout << *ptr1 << " ";
cout << endl;
// Finally, apply reverse interators on current set_value2
cout << "Apply reverse iterators to last form of set_value2:"
      << endl;
for(set<int,less<int> >::reverse_iterator ptr2
```

```
        = set_value2.rbegin(); ptr2 != set_value2.rend(); ++ptr2)
    cout << *ptr2 << " ";
  cout << endl;
  return 0;
}
```

The output obtained by executing this program is

```
The components of set_value are:
-1 2 3 7 8
The current size of set_value is: 5
and the current size of set_value2 is: 5
After applying first form of erase to set_value:
attempting to erase 2 and 0, the size of set_value is
4 and its components are:
-1 3 7 8
Now apply the range version of erase to
[set_value2.begin(),++iter);
After performing this erasure on set_value2,its
components are:
3 7 8
Apply reverse iterators to last form of set_value2:
8 7 3
```

The set class template also defines a modifier member function `swap`, with prototype

```
void swap(set<Key,Compare>&);
```

Thus, `swap` requires a single `set` parameter storing values of the same type as the object to which it is being applied. The result of applying `swap` is that the parameter and the object to which `swap` is applied are interchanged. This behavior is identical to `swap` member functions for the sequence containers defined in Chapter Six. For example, suppose we construct and initialize two `int`-valued sets `set_value1` and `set_value2`. Then the result of executing

```
set_value1.swap(set_value2);
```

is that the contents of `set_value1` and `set_value2` are interchanged.

Both `set` and `multiset` contain a number of member functions that can be characterized as *set operations,* most of which have a counterpart in `<algorithm>`. The first of these is `count`, with prototype

```
size_type count(const key_type&) const;
```

The parameter is a reference to a value of type `key_type`, returning a value of type `size_type` (we will assume `size_type` is `int`) representing the number of occurrences of the value of the key (the value of the parameter) in the associated `set` (`multiset`) object. In the case of `set` objects, this return value will be either 1 (if the key appears in the set) or 0 (if not). This is not necessarily the case for a multiset, which permits repeated occurrences of any key. In the case of set_value as it appears initially in Example 9.1, set_value.count(8) is 1, and set_value.count(0) is 0.

In addition, each of set and multiset support member functions find, lower_bound, upper_bound, and equal_range . Why present these as member functions, since the generic forms of each exist and apply to these objects? The answer is the efficiency of the member functions over their generic counterparts. The member functions are optimized versions of their generic counterparts because each member function has complexity O(log n), whereas its corresponding generic version has complexity O(n). The reason is that, internally, values stored in any set or multiset object are stored as nodes of a binary tree (to be discussed later in this chapter), but the generic forms assume a linear arrangement of these values. In designing software for commercial use, if correctness is not sacrificed and if several options for containers are available, the design decision should always favor optimized efficiency.

The prototypes of each of these are as follows:

```
pair<iterator,iterator> equal_range(const key_type&) const;
iterator find(const key_type&) const;
iterator lower_bound(const key_type&) const;
iterator upper_bound(const key_type&) const;
```

We illustrate each of these on int-valued set objects. Suppose the current contents of set_value are -1,2,3,7,8. If value is an int-valued variable, and we apply

```
if(set_value.find(value) != set_value.end())
 cout << value << " appears in set_value." << endl;
else
 cout << value << " does not appear in set_value." << endl;
```

and if the current contents of value are 2, executing the conditional produces

```
2 appears in set_value.
```

If we now apply

```
pair<set<int,less<int> >::iterator,set<int,less<int> >::iterator>
 result = set_value.equal_range(value);
```

and set_value and value are as before, the output obtained by executing

```
for(set<int,less<int> >::const_iterator qptr = result.first;
     qptr != result.second; ++qptr)
 cout << *qptr << " ";
```

is **2.**

In addition, applying the respective member functions lower_bound and upper_bound produces

2 (for lower_bound)
3 (for upper_bound)

set also defines two member functions described as "observers." These are key_comp() and value_comp(). We will use these very sparingly, if at all. Nevertheless, they have the respective prototypes

```
key_compare key_comp() const;
```

and

```
value_compare value_comp() const;
```

For sets and multisets, there is no distinction between these; each is parameterless, and each returns the appropriate comparison operator applied to the two arguments to which it is applied. To illustrate, suppose we assume the int-valued set object set_value with current contents -1,2,3,7,8 and suppose we apply

```
set_value.key_comp()(2,8);
```

The value returned is the bit value 1, indicating that less<int>(2,8) is true. Instead, if we construct

```
set<int,greater<int> > set_value;
```

and then insert -1,2,3,7,8 and apply

```
set_value.key_comp()(2,8);
```

the return value is 0, indicating that greater<int>(2,8) is false.

To complete the list of member functions for set, we note that there is a well-defined assignment operator operator=, with prototype

```
set<Key,Compare>& operator=(const set<Key,Compare>&);
```

with behavior similar to its counterpart for each of the fundamental sequence containers. Thus, if set_value1 and set_value2 are both already constructed set objects containing values of the same type, with the same comparison operator defined for both, then

```
set_value2 = set_value1;
```

copies the current contents of set_value1 into set_value2.

In contrast to set, characterized as a *unique sorted associative container*—that is, sorted associative containers having the property that no two or more of their members are identical—multiset may be characterized as a multiple sorted associative container, meaning that two or more of its members may be identical. In standard C++, there is no special preprocessor directive for multisets. That is, to apply multiset objects in a C++ program, the needed preprocessor directive remains

```
#include <set>
```

The member functions for `multiset` are virtually identical to those for `set`, with a number of noteworthy exceptions. For example, the group of `insert` member functions for `multiset` has prototypes

```
iterator insert(const value_type& x);
iterator insert(iterator position, const value_type& x);
template<class InputIterator>
 void insert(InputIterator first, InputIterator last);
```

The distinction in syntax lies with the last version because `multiset` objects permit the existence of duplicate keys, whereas `set` objects do not. Specifically, insertion of a value in a `set` object may fail if that value already appears in that object. This is the reason for the `pair` return value in the case of a `set` insertion. Other distinctions are more subtle. For example, applying `count()` to a `multiset` object may produce a value greater than `1` if that value has duplicate keys.

EXAMPLE 9.2 The program illustrated here is simply the version of Example 9.1 with `multiset` arguments.

```
#include <iostream>
#include <set>
using namespace std;
int main()
{
 int int_array[] = {3,2,7,-1,8,2,8}; // Conformant array
 // Apply default constructor for sets:
 multiset<int,less<int> > set_value;
 // Apply range form of insert to set_value:
 set_value.insert(int_array,int_array + 7);
 // Display output for set_value:
 cout << "The components of set_value are:" << endl;
 for(multiset<int,less<int> >::const_iterator ptr = set_value.begin();
      ptr != set_value.end(); ++ptr)
  cout << *ptr << " ";
 cout << endl;
 // Now apply the copy constructor for sets:
 multiset<int,less<int> > set_value2(set_value);
 // Apply size() to each of set_value and set_value2:
 cout << "The current size of set_value is: " << set_value.size()
   << endl;
 cout << "and the current size of set_value2 is: "
  << set_value2.size() << endl;
 // Apply various forms of erase to set_value and set_value2:
 set_value.erase(2);
```

```
set_value.erase(0);  // 0 not in current set_value
cout << "After applying first form of erase to set_value:" << endl;
cout << "attempting to erase 2 and 0, the size of set_value is"
 << endl;
cout << set_value.size() << " and its components are" << endl;
for(multiset<int,less<int> >::const_iterator qptr = set_value.begin();
     qptr != set_value.end(); ++qptr)
 cout << *qptr << " ";
cout << endl;
multiset<int,less<int> >::const_iterator iter = ++set_value2.begin();
cout << "Now apply the range version of erase to " << endl;
cout << "[set_value2.begin(),++iter):" << endl;
set_value2.erase(set_value2.begin(),++iter);
cout << "After performing this erasure on set_value2,its" << endl;
cout << "components are:" << endl;
for(multiset<int,less<int> >::const_iterator ptr1 =
    set_value2.begin(); ptr1 != set_value2.end(); ++ptr1)
 cout << *ptr1 << " ";
cout << endl;
// Finally, apply reverse interators on current set_value2
cout << "Apply reverse iterators to last form of set_value2:"
      << endl;
for(multiset<int,less<int> >::reverse_iterator ptr2
           = set_value2.rbegin(); ptr2 != set_value2.rend(); ++ptr2)
 cout << *ptr2 << " ";
cout << endl;
return 0;
}
```

The output of this program is

```
The components of set_value are:
-1 2 2 3 7 8 8
The current size of set_value is: 7
and the current size of set_value2 is: 7
After applying first form of erase to set_value:
attempting to erase 2 and 0, the size of set_value is
5 and its components are
-1 3 7 8 8
Now apply the range version of erase to
[set_value2.begin(),++iter);
After performing this erasure on set_value2,its
components are:
2 3 7 8 8
Apply reverse iterators to last form of set_value2:
8 8 7 3 2
```

There are several changes for `find`, `equal_range`, `lower_bound`, and `upper_bound` when applied to `multiset` objects. For example, although the syntax for `find` is exactly the same for `multiset` objects, the `iterator` value returned refers to the first member of the `multiset` object with the value of the parameter (if the value appears at all); otherwise, the value returned is exactly that of a `set` object: a reference to the `end()` location.

The prototype for `equal_range` is similar to that for `set`, but now multiple keys are allowed:

```
pair<iterator,iterator> equal_range(const key_type& x);
```

The return value is the pair `(lower_bound(x),upper_bound(x))`. The syntax for the prototypes for `lower_bound` and `upper_bound` is exactly the same as those for `set` objects. Indeed, if we apply `equal_range` to the `int`-valued `multiset` object `set_value` constructed as in Example 9.2, using the parameter value **2**, in the form

```
pair<multiset<int,less<int> >::iterator,
     multiset<int,less<int> >::iterator>
 result = set_value.equal_range(value);
```

the result is

```
2 2
```

If we now apply `lower_bound` and `upper_bound`, respectively, to `set_value`, the results are

```
2
3
```

9.3 Set Operations

`set` objects share a behavior similar to finite sets in a number of ways. In fact, if not empty, any `set` object stores a finite collection of values of some given type that are output in sorted order. These objects are also subject to a number of predefined algorithms defined in `<algorithm>` and mimic the fundamental mathematical operations of set inclusion, union, intersection, difference, and symmetric difference. Since these operations are generic, they are also applicable to arrays, vectors, multisets, and other containers, although this section treats these operations for `set` objects only.

Set Inclusion

`<algorithm>` contains a `bool`-valued `includes` function involving four iterator parameters: `first1`, `last1`, `first2`, and `last2`. There are two versions: the "default" version, using the "includes" comparison operator, and a general form, allowing the programmer to define his or her own comparison operator. We treat the default form only, whose prototype is given by

```
template <class InputIterator1, class InputIterator2>
bool includes (InputIterator1 first1, InputIterator1 last1,
               InputIterator2 first2, InputIterator2 last2);
```

This function returns `true` if the members of the set (or multiset) represented by the sequence `[first1,last1)` contain all of the members of the set (or multiset) represented by `[first2,last2)` and returns `false` otherwise. As an illustration, consider the `int`-valued `set` objects `set_value1` and `set_value2`, represented abstractly by `set_value1 = {2,3,7,9,15}` and `set_value2 = {-4,0,2,3,6,7,8,9,14,15,20}`. If we then apply

```
if(includes(set2.begin(),set2.end(),set1.begin(),set1.end()))
 cout << "set_value1 is included in set_value2" << endl;
else
 cout << "set_value1 is not included in set_value2" << endl;
```

the output is

`set_value1 is included in set_value2`

Set Union

The generic function `set_union` implements the set-theoretic operation of union applied to two finite sets. More precisely, `set_union` constructs the sorted union of values coming from two ranges of values of the same type and returns an iterator reference to the end of the range constructed from that union. There are two versions of `set_union`, and we treat only the default version. The prototype for this version is

```
template <class InputIterator1, class InputIterator2,
   class OutputIterator>
OutputIterator set_union (InputIterator1 first1, InputIterator1 last1,
                          InputIterator2 first2, InputIterator2 last2,
                          OutputIterator result);
```

Here `[first1,last1)` and `[first2,last2)` define the respective ranges involved in constructing the union, and `result` refers to the beginning of the range holding the union. Note that the two ranges need not be restricted to ranges for `set` objects; they may represent ranges of values for any finite sequences, regardless of the type of container involved. In addition, `set_union` is stable in the sense that if a value should appear in both ranges (assuming that the ranges are for `set` objects), only the value appearing in the first range is copied into the range of the union. Finally, we should also note that `set_union` is not defined if the result range overlaps with either of the ranges `[first1,last1)` or `[first2,last2)`.

The Standard Template Library provides an auxiliary "helper" function called `inserter`, which is used to construct the range of the union correctly and efficiently.[5] The syntax for `inserter` may be given as

```
inserter(container_name,iterator);
```

where *`container_name`* identifies the container where the union's range is stored, and *`iterator`* references the initial position in that container. For example, if `set1` and `set2` name two `set<int,less<int> >` objects whose union is to be computed and `set_result` names the `set<int,less<int> >` object storing their union, then

```
set_union(set1.begin(),set1.end(),set2.begin(),set2.end(),
          inserter(set_result,set_result.begin()));
```

implements the union. The values of the sequence representing the union may be output using

```
copy(set_result.begin(),set_result.end(),
     ostream_iterator<int>(cout," "));
```

`inserter` creates an `insert_iterator`[6] reference to the position given by the value of the second parameter and writes the range of the result beginning at that position. As described in Section 5.8, insert iterators support the insertion of new values into a collection rather than copy the new value over that of an already existing value.

When `set_union` is applied to `multiset` arguments, and if these arguments contain duplicate values, `set_union` will construct a `multiset` object in which each duplicate value is reproduced the maximum number of times it appears in either argument.

Set Intersection

`<algorithm>` also contains two versions of `set_intersection`, which compute the intersection of two sets of values from a common data type. `set_intersection` is stable in the same sense as `set_union`. The default version of `set_intersection` has the prototype

```
template <class InputIterator1, class InputIterator2, class
OutputIterator>
OutputIterator set_intersection (InputIterator1 first1,
                                 InputIterator1 last1,
                                 InputIterator2 first2,
                                 InputIterator2 last2,
                                 OutputIterator result);
```

[5]See Section 8.3 for a discussion of helper functions.

[6] See Section 5.8 for more on insert iterators.

Assuming the same definitions as presented earlier for set1, set2, and set_result, the result obtained by applying

```
set_intersection(set1.begin(),set1.end(),set2.begin(),set2.end(),
                 inserter(set_result,set_result.begin());
```

is the ordered sequence referenced by the range [set_result.begin(),set_result.end()), whose values are just an ordering of the values lying in the intersection of set1 and set2. Example 9.3 illustrates the functionality of set_union and set_intersection on int-valued set objects.

EXAMPLE 9.3

```
#include <iostream>
#include <set>
#include <algorithm>
using namespace std;
int main()
{
 // Use int-valued arrays to fill slots in corresponding
 // int-valued sets.
 int int_array1[] = {2,3,7,9,15};
 int int_array2[] = {-4,0,5,3,6,7,8,10,14,15,20};
 // Construct int-valued set objects using default constructor
 set<int,less<int> > set_value1, set_value2;
 // Then fill these initially empty sets with values from the
 // corresponding arrays.
 set_value1.insert(int_array1,int_array1 + 5);
 set_value2.insert(int_array2,int_array2 + 11);
 // Echo values of each set:
 cout << "set_value1 has members:" << endl;
 for(set<int,less<int> >::const_iterator ptr1 = set_value1.begin();
      ptr1 != set_value1.end(); ++ptr1)
  cout << *ptr1 << " ";
 cout << endl;
 cout << "set_value2 has members:" << endl;
 for(set<int,less<int> >::const_iterator ptr2 = set_value2.begin();
      ptr2 != set_value2.end(); ++ptr2)
  cout << *ptr2 << " ";
 cout << endl;
 // Now apply set_union to set_value1 and set_value2:
 set<int,less<int> > union_result;
 set_union(set_value1.begin(),set_value1.end(),set_value2.begin(),
         set_value2.end(),inserter(union_result,union_result.begin()));
 cout << "The union of set_value1 and set_value2 has members:"
```

```
       << endl;
 copy(union_result.begin(),union_result.end(),
         ostream_iterator<int>(cout," "));
 cout << endl;
 cout << "size of union = " << union_result.size() << endl;
 // Now apply set_intersection to set_value1 and set_value2:
 set<int,less<int> > int_result;
 set_intersection(set_value1.begin(),set_value1.end(),
       set_value2.begin(),set_value2.end(),
       inserter(int_result,int_result.begin()));
 cout << "The intersection of set_value1 and set_value2 has members:"
       << cndl;
 copy(int_result.begin(),int_result.end(),
         ostream_iterator<int>(cout," "));
 cout << endl;
 cout << "size of intersection = " << int_result.size() << endl;
 return 0;
}
```

The program outputs

```
set_value1 has members:
2 3 7 9 15
set_value2 has members:
-4 0 3 5 6 7 8 10 14 15 20
The union of set_value1 and set_value2 has members:
-4 0 2 3 5 6 7 8 9 10 14 15 20
size of union = 13
The intersection of set_value1 and set_value2 has members:
3 7 15
size of intersection = 3
```

Set Difference and Symmetric Difference

Suppose `set1` and `set2` are `set` objects holding values of the same data type and referenced by the respective ranges `[first1,last1)` and `[first2,last2)`. The `set_difference` algorithm computes the *difference* between `set1` and `set2`, defined as the collection of values in `set1` with all of its values also lying in `set2` removed. Then if `set1` and `set2` are the `int`-valued sets defined by `set1 = {1,2,4,5,7}` and `set2 = {3,4,5,9}`, the difference `set1 - set2 = {1,2,7}`. Note that set difference is not a symmetric operation because `set2 - set1`, defined as those values in `set2` not also appearing in `set1`, is `{3,9}`.

The default version of set_difference has the prototype

```
template <class InputIterator1, class InputIterator2,
          class OutputIterator>
OutputIterator set_difference (InputIterator1 first1,
                               InputIterator1 last1,
                               InputIterator2 first2,
                               InputIterator2 last2,
                               OutputIterator result);
```

To illustrate, suppose set1 and set2 are the int-valued sets just defined. Then the result of invoking

```
set_difference(set1.begin(),set1.end(),set2.begin(),set2.end(),
                   inserter(diff,diff.begin()));
```

where we assume the constructor

```
set<int,less<int> > diff;
```

is the sequence 1 2 7 represented by [diff.begin(),diff.end()). On the other hand, if we invoke

```
set_difference(set2.begin(),set2.end(),set1.begin(),set1.end(),
                   inserter(diff,diff.begin()));
```

the result is the sequence 3 9 represented by [diff.begin(),diff.end()).

<algorithm> also contains the function set_symmetric_difference, which constructs the *sorted symmetric difference* of two sets. More precisely, if [first1,last1) and [first2,last2) reference the sorted sequences set1 and set2, respectively, then set_symmetric_difference constructs the sorted sequence of values consisting of those members of the union of the following two sets: set1 - set2 and set2 - set1. Thus, if we apply set_symmetric_difference to the int-valued sets set1 and set2 as previously described, the result is the sequence 1 2 3 7 9.

The prototype for the default version of set_symmetric_difference is given by

```
template <class InputIterator1, class InputIterator2,
          class OutputIterator>
OutputIterator set_symmetric_difference (InputIterator1 first1,
                                         InputIterator1 last1,
                                         InputIterator2 first2,
                                         InputIterator2 last2,
                                         OutputIterator result);
```

Note that the result obtained by executing

```
set_symmetric_difference(set1.begin(),set1.end(),
                         set2.begin(),set2.end(),
                         inserter(diff,diff.begin()));
```

is the same as that obtained by executing

```
set_symmetric_difference(set2.begin(),set2.end(),
                         set1.begin(),set1.end(),
                         inserter(diff,diff.begin()));
```

At this point, we should observe that each of the set operations described in this section is of order `O(n)`; that is, they have linear complexity because executing each of these involves making `2((last1 - first1) + (last2 - first2)) - 1` comparisons for sequences defined by the respective ranges `[first1,last1)` and `[first2,last2)`.

9.4 Implementation Details: Binary Search Trees and Red-Black Trees

This section gives a brief overview of how sorted associative containers are implemented in software. Sorted associative container classes should be used whenever we wish to store and retrieve values in an efficient and speedy manner using some type of key. As we will see, the choice of the underlying data structure is also motivated by the attempt to minimize as many worst case situations as possible for the operations of searching for and retrieving a value, inserting a new value, and removing values in the resulting container. For readers who are familiar with the data structures described in this section or who do not require this information for their work, the topics presented here may be easily skipped without interrupting the presentation of the remaining topics treated in this chapter.

We begin by defining the concept of a *binary tree.* A binary tree is a nonlinear data structure that either is empty or consists of a finite sequence of *nodes,* each of which consists of three components called `left`, `info`, and `right`, described as follows:

- `left` and `right` store references to other nodes or are void
- `info` stores the data (of some given type) to be maintained at that node

If we view this superficially, there seems to be no distinction between the basic structure of nodes presented here and those defined for the STL `list` class template in Chapter Six. However, there are significant differences between the way binary tree nodes are linked to others and those for `list` nodes. In the case of binary tree nodes, there is a uniquely determined *root node,* representing the only entry point into the tree. Once access is established at the designated root, passing to other nodes in the tree (if these exist) is possible in one direction only: from the root node to no further than a leaf node. A *leaf* (or *leaf node*) in a tree is a node for which no further downward movement is possible. Nodes that are not leaf nodes are called *interior nodes.*

Binary trees are characterized by the property that, if not empty, there is a maximum of two nonempty nodes coming from the root node. If the `left` component of the root is not empty, the node referenced by `left` is the *left child* (or *left descendant*) of the root. Similarly, if the `right` component of the root is not empty, the node referenced by `right` is the *right child* (or *right descendant*) of the root. The left and right descendant may each be viewed as the root node of a binary tree called the *left subtree* and *right subtree,* respectively, of the original binary tree. Since the left and right subtrees are each a binary tree in their own right, the definitions of left and right descendants, left and right subtrees, root and leaf nodes, and others to follow are recursive in nature.

A *binary search tree* is a special form of a binary tree in which the `info` component of any node (assuming the less than comparison operator) is greater than the value of the `info` component of any node in the designated left subtree (referenced by the `left` component of the current node) and less than or possibly equal to the value of the `info` component of any node in its designated right subtree (referenced by the `right` component of the current node). We also define the *level* of any node recursively as follows: The level of the root node is `0`, and the level of either child of any node is `1 +` level of its uniquely determined "parent" node. As an illustration, consider the binary search tree of integer values in Figure 9.2. Here

FIGURE 9.2

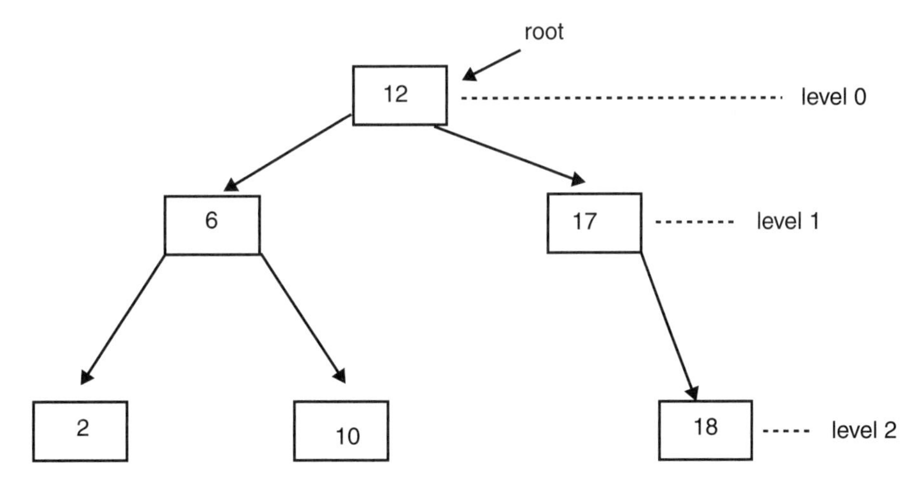

the root node and the nodes containing the values `6` and `17` are interior nodes, and the nodes containing the values `2`, `10`, and `18` are leaf nodes. The left child of the root is the node holding the value `6`, the right child of the node holding `17` is the node holding `18`, and so on. We can then characterize any leaf node as one whose left and right subtrees are empty; that is, a leaf node is one having no children. The implementation of the abstraction in Figure 9.2 displaying the complete layout of each node is presented in Figure 9.3.

FIGURE 9.3

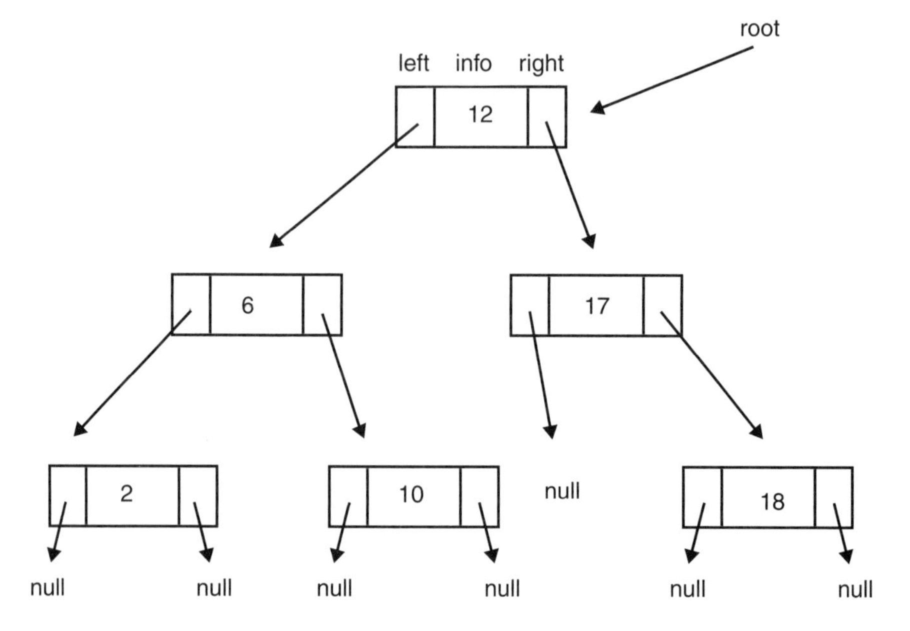

If the data type of the `info` components is more complicated, the basic structure of the binary search tree is maintained by defining a key from the values of the data type defined for the `info` components of the nodes and then comparing the values of the corresponding keys. The predefined C++ simple types all have a less than operator designated by `operator<`. But if we require an alternate comparison operator, the STL defines the `Compare` comparison type, allowing the programmer to define another comparison operator instead. In our presentation, unless we explicitly specify otherwise, we will assume the less than operator.

Not every binary search tree has the "symmetric" (perhaps better termed "short and thick") representation found in Figure 9.2. In fact, Figure 9.4 is also a binary search tree containing the same values as those in Figure 9.2.

What causes such differences? Using binary search trees as the implementation of sorted associative containers involves a heavy dependence on the order of insertion of values into the container. For example, the binary search tree depicted in Figure 9.2 implements the input sequence `12, 6, 17, 10, 18, 2`, and the binary search tree in Figure 9.4 uses the input sequence `18, 17, 12, 6, 10, 2`. So far as retrieval is concerned, since entry into the tree is possible only through the root, it would require, for example, only three comparisons to determine that ten appears in the tree in Figure 9.2, but `5` comparisons are required to reach the same conclusion

FIGURE 9.4

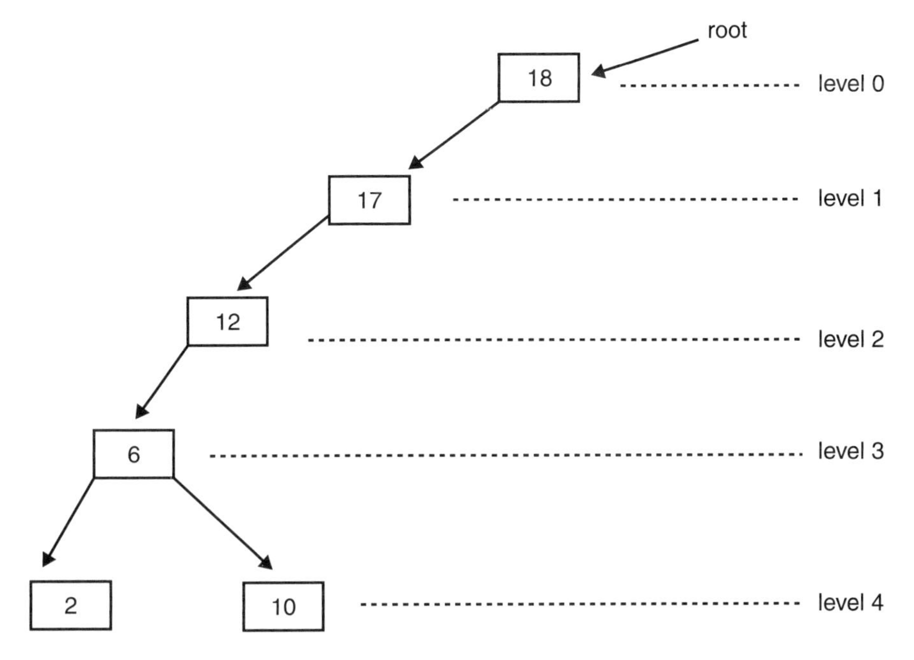

for the tree in Figure 9.4. Thus, we see in a very real and elementary sense that symmetric binary search trees are better suited for efficient retrieval of values and other related operations. This is primarily due to the fact that search and retrieval operations done in trees such as that depicted in Figure 9.4 are of nearly linear complexity, whereas those of trees such as Figure 9.2 are approximately of order `O(log n)`.

We define a *full* binary tree as one whose leaves are all at the same level `k` for some nonnegative integer `k` and for which each possible position at level `k` is occupied by a (leaf) node. Thus, the tree described in Figure 9.5 is an example of a full binary search tree, but those in Figures 9.2 and 9.4 are not. In addition, the definition of a full tree is extendable in a natural way to more general trees. We leave the formal details of this extended form of the definition to the reader.

How can we guarantee that the binary search tree is symmetric? The fact is that we cannot! This is quite obvious from the way the binary search trees in Figures 9.2 and 9.4 were constructed. We conclude that what is needed is a different form of a search tree where the order of complexity of the operations usually attributed to sorted associative containers is independent of the order of insertion of values into the associated container. A step in the direction of constructing a more suitable tree uses the definition of a *2-3-4 tree.* A 2-3-4 tree is a search tree that is no longer binary; rather, it extends the idea of search tree to those whose nodes may contain exactly one, two, or three values and have subtrees (if they exist) defined as follows:

1. If a node contains exactly one data value, it is called a *2-node* and has exactly two (possible empty) subtrees, defined exactly like the case of a binary search tree.
2. If a node contains exactly two values `val1` and `val2`, with `val1` less than `val2` (such a node is called a *3-node*), then three (possibly empty) subtrees exist: one whose nodes have values less than `val1` (designated as the *left subtree*), the next whose nodes have values between those of `val1` and `val2` (designated as the *middle subtree*), and the last, consisting of nodes all of whose values are no less than that of `val2` (designated as the *right subtree*).
3. If a node contains exactly three values `val1`, `val2`, and `val3`, where `val1` is less than `val2` and `val2` is less than `val3`, it is called a *4-node.* There are four (possibly empty) subtrees, representing the natural extension of the definition of subtrees for a 3-node as defined in 2.
4. The last row of the tree containing all of the leaves is completely filled.

We define a search tree to be *complete* if all of its leaves are at the same level and there are no gaps in the row of the tree in which all of its leaves appear or, at any earlier level, when such rows are scanned steadily from left to right. In other words, a binary search tree is complete if for every node having a nonvoid right child, that same node already has a nonvoid left child. Thus, we may conclude that the binary search trees in Figures 9.2 and 9.4. are not complete, whereas the binary search tree in Figure 9.5 is complete.

FIGURE 9.5

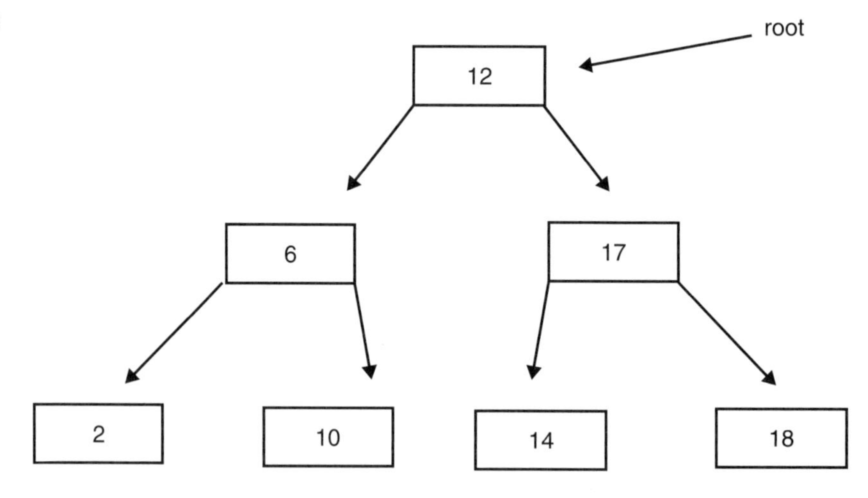

We define the *height* of the left (or right) subtree of any node in a binary search tree as the maximum length (number of distinct nodes) of any path in the left (right) subtree beginning with that node and ending at a leaf. Thus, the height of the node of the left subtree in Figure 9.2

containing the value 17 is zero, and the height of the left subtree of the same node in Figure 9.4 is 3. We define a binary tree as *balanced* if the height of any node's right subtree differs from the height of its corresponding left subtree by at most one. The binary trees in Figures 9.2 and 9.5 are balanced, but that in Figure 9.4 is not. The tree in Figure 9.6 is an example of a balanced binary search tree with leaves at different levels.

FIGURE 9.6

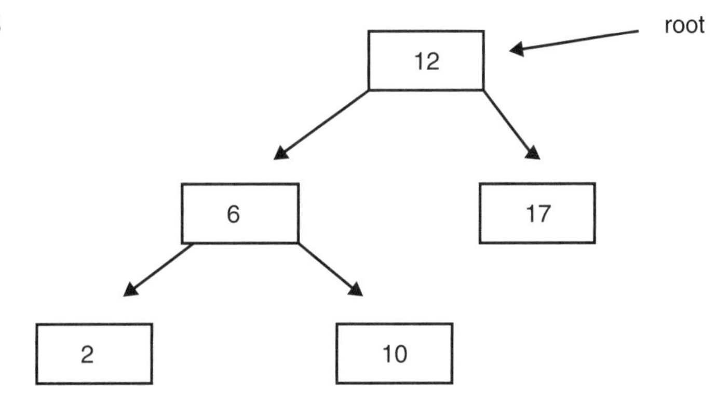

The motivation behind introducing 2-3-4 trees is to keep the level of the tree nodes as minimal as possible. In addition, the ideas of level, height, and completeness extend to 2-3-4 trees with little extra effort. In summary, the reason for becoming involved with 2-3-4 trees is to maintain the same level for a node as long as possible, until the insertion of new values into the tree "saturates" the current node to the extent that the only remaining alternative is to increase the height of the tree. As an example, consider the 2-3-4 tree in Figure 9.7 with no 4-nodes, constructed as the result of applying the insertion operation to the input sequence `18, 17, 12, 6, 10, 2`.

FIGURE 9.7

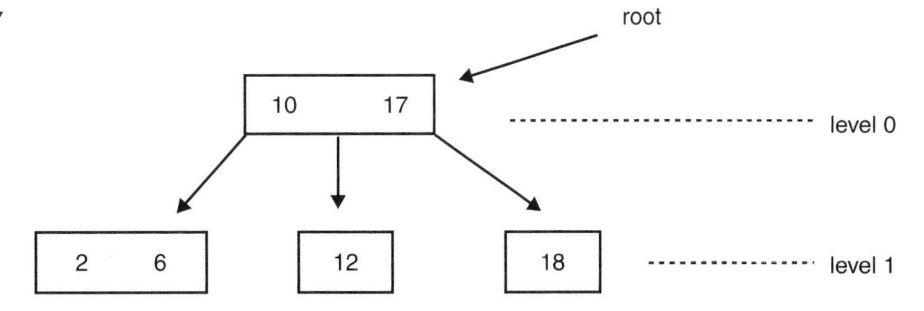

Thus, we go from a binary search tree of level 4 in Figure 9.4 to a 2-3-4 tree of level 1 in Figure 9.7. We can then conclude that the 2-3-4 tree is more efficient because the processing time required to compare several values at a single node is substantially less than progressing to a lower level of the tree, since following a pointer is slower than comparing values. Therefore, the efficiency of processing operations commonly attributed to sorted associative containers is generally enhanced when the 2-3-4 tree is used as an alternative to the corresponding binary search tree. To illustrate, look at the 2-3-4 tree of Figure 9.8. This tree is constructed from the same

FIGURE 9.8

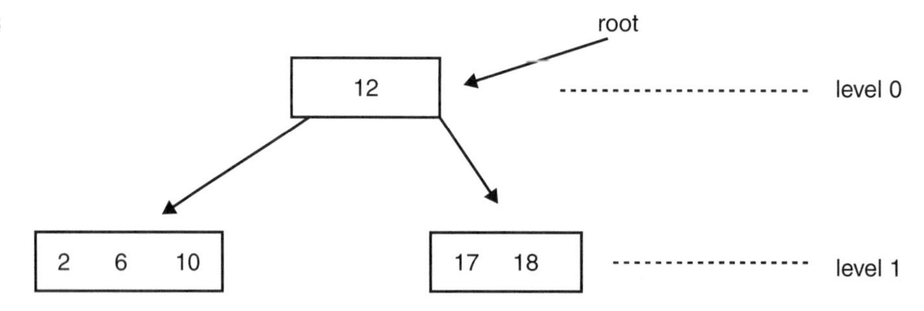

input sequence as that used to construct the tree in Figure 9.7. Although it is different from that of Figure 9.7, it is in no way less efficient.

There is, however, one major drawback in the use of 2-3-4 trees. Designing and coding efficient algorithms for searching and retrieving values, as well as inserting and deleting values, are substantially more complicated than the corresponding code for binary search trees. What we require, then, is some form of compromise between the ease of processing afforded by binary search trees and the efficiency of operations for 2-3-4 trees. This compromise is provided by the use of *red-black trees.*

A red-black tree is a binary search tree representing the following adaptation of 2-3-4 trees:

1. If we have a 2-node in the 2-3-4 tree, we make no changes in the corresponding red-black tree.
2. If we have a 3-node in the 2-3-4 tree, as in Figure 9.9a, we convert this to either Figure 9.9b or Figure 9.9c. The `(red)` designation of a node in the red-black tree is for a newly constructed node to complete the correspondence with the underlying 2-3-4 tree.

FIGURE 9.9a

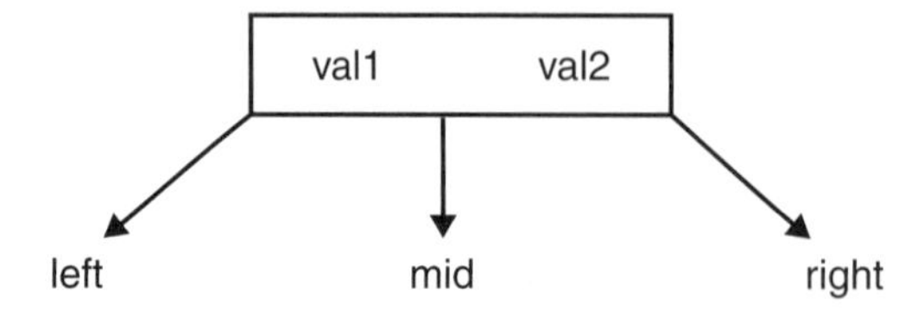

FIGURE 9.9b

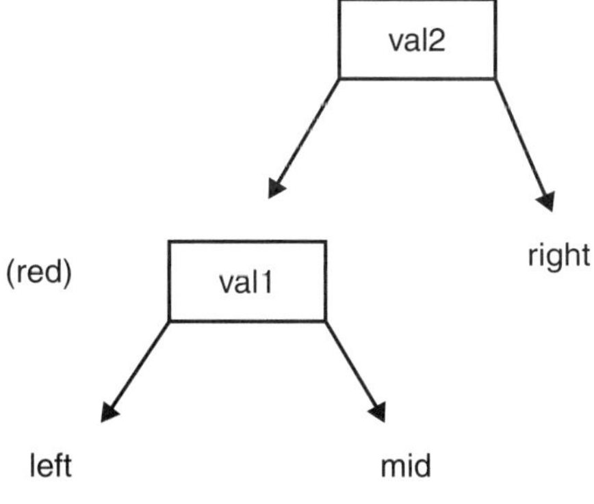

FIGURE 9.9c

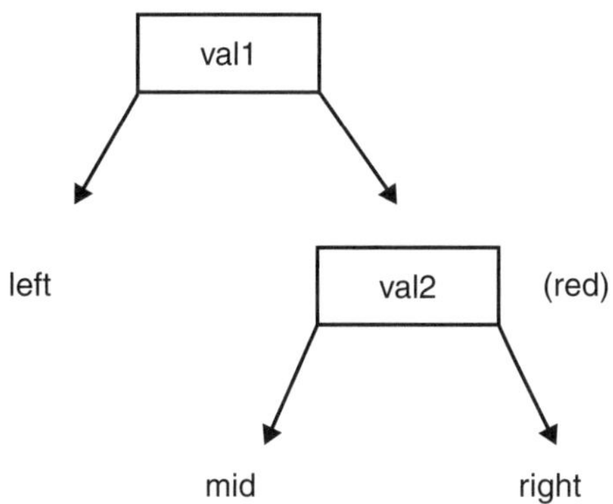

3. If we have a 4-node such as that described in Figure 9.10a, we convert this to the red-black tree structure given in Figure 9.10b.

FIGURE 9.10a

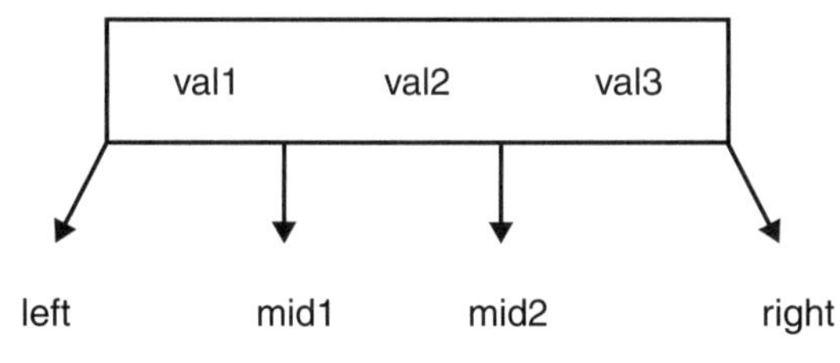

FIGURE 9.10b

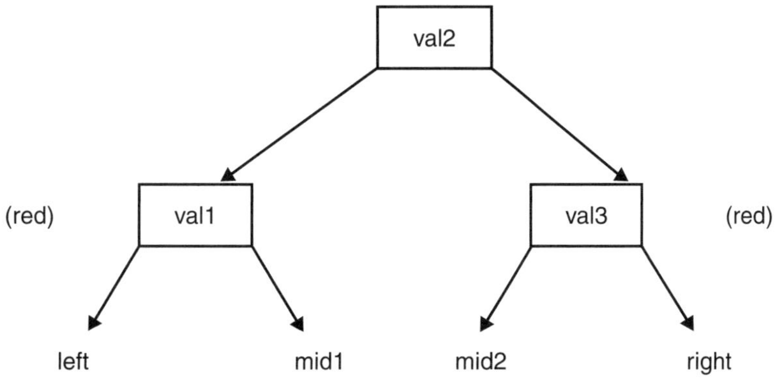

The idea is to reconstruct each 3-node or 4-node as a sequence of nodes and links in a binary tree in such a way that the ordering of the values of the nodes is preserved; that is, such that the corresponding binary tree is a binary search tree. As rule 2 shows, this representation is not necessarily unique. As an example, the 2-3-4 tree in Figure 9.7 may be converted to the red-black tree in Figure 9.11, and the 2-3-4 tree in Figure 9.8 may be converted into the red-black tree in Figure 9.12.

FIGURE 9.11

FIGURE 9.12

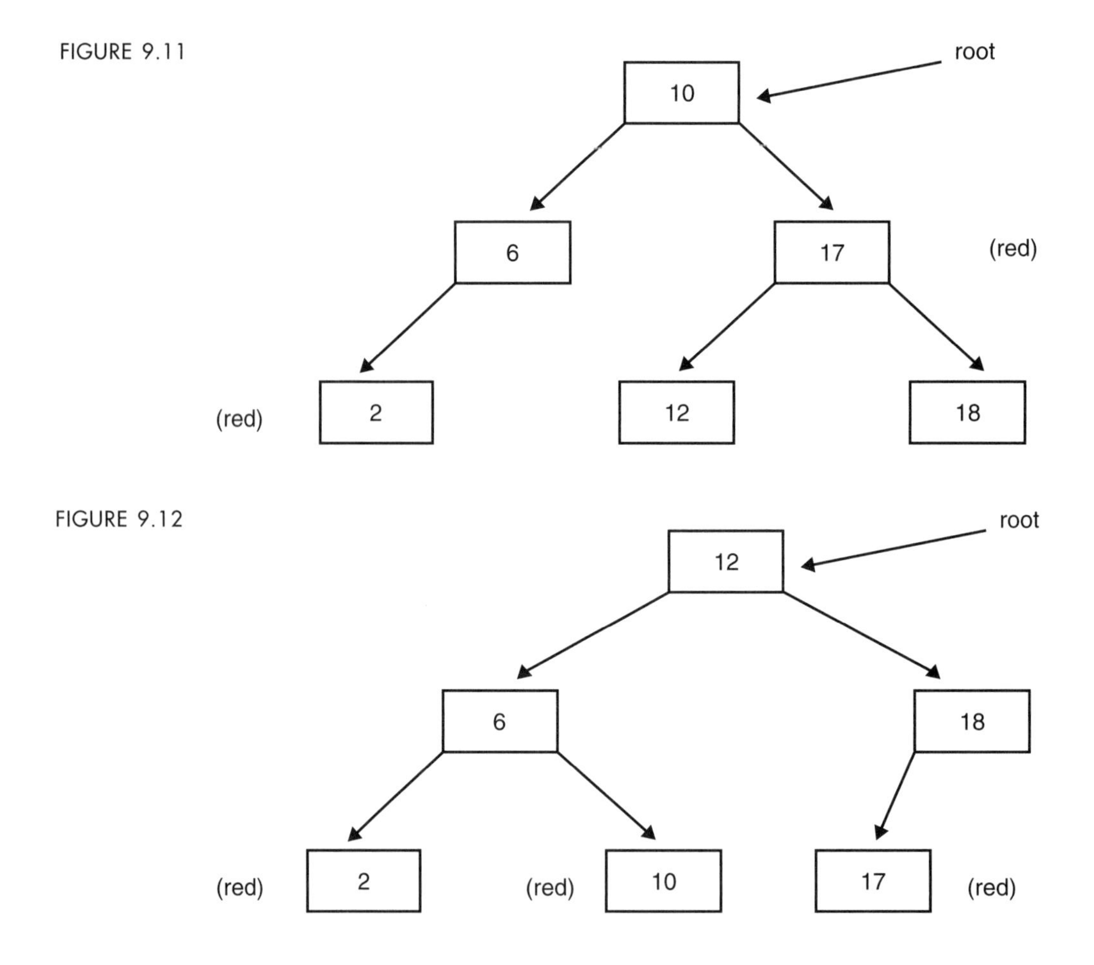

As Figure 9.11 shows, the corresponding red-black tree is not necessarily complete. In the conversion rules just stated, the original node in the 2-3-4 tree is designated a *black node,* as is the case of the root node. The only nodes that become red nodes are those in the corresponding red-black tree to which conversion rules 2 and 3 have been applied.

9.5 Maps and Multimaps

Maps and multimaps are forms of sorted associative containers that provide for speedy and efficient retrieval of data of some type `T` based on the existence of a collection of keys coming from some type `Key`. We assume that a comparison operator is defined for all members of `Key` (the default is `less`). It is quite common for `T` and `Key` to be distinct. Objects constructed from `map` and `multimap` are distinguished by the fact that `map` objects do not support duplicate keys, whereas `multimap` objects do support duplicate keys. In this sense, there is a similarity in the relationship between sets and multisets and maps and multimaps.

Although the syntax of the user interfaces for `map` and `set` is similar, there are several notable distinctions. For example, in `set`, `value_type` is defined as

```
typedef Key value_type;
```

while the definition of `value_type` in `map` is given by

```
typedef pair<const Key, T> value_type;
```

Thus, in the case of `map` objects, the keys are but one component of the information stored in the container, whereas the keys represent the entire information component of any `set` object. It follows that when we wish to construct a `map` or `multimap` object, we use the preprocessor directive

```
#include <map>
```

and then specify both a key type and a type for the information component for the object,
as in

```
map<char, int, less<char> > map_obj;
```

This constructs `map_obj` as a `map` object with key values of type `char` and component values of type `int`, where the comparison operator is the usual less than operator for `char` values.

Besides this, there are other more subtle and useful changes. One of these is the result of the following listing of operators in the `public` section of the `map` interface whose counterpart does not exist in `set`:

```
T& operator[](const key_type& x);
const T& operator[](const key_type& x) const;
```

Thus, we may apply the "bracket" operator to any of the key values of any `map` object. Consequently, any `map` object may be viewed as a one-dimensional array whose components are indexed by values of type `Key`, rather than exclusively by consecutive values in the integer sequence `0, 1, 2, 3, ...`. In other words, it is possible to create applications, with `map_obj` naming some `map` object, permitting values of the form map_obj['a'] (in case Key is instantiated by char) or of the form map_obj["March"] (in case Key is instantiated as char* or string). In light of this, we may adopt Stroustrup's terminology and name map objects as *associative arrays.*[7]

Because of this, map objects behave like arrays in other general-purpose programming languages, where the values stored in any such object may be referenced using subscripts coming from any well-defined discrete type admitting a comparison operator for any two or more of its values (we are using Key for this purpose here) and with values coming from any well-defined type T. The use of associative arrays gives C++ a level of flexibility common to many other general-purpose languages.

Another significant difference is the behavior of iterator types defined for set and multiset objects and those defined for map and multimap objects. For set and multiset objects, both iterator and const_iterator name nonmutable iterator types. In fact, these names are completely interchangeable. This is due to a design decision for the STL which demands that for sets and multisets, the only way to modify the value of a key currently stored in any such container is first to delete the current key value (using the erase member function) and then to insert the new value (using insert). If these iterators were mutable, the key value could be modified using operator=.

For example, suppose we inspect the code sequence

```
#include <set>
      .
      .
      .
set<int,less<int> > set_value;
set_value.insert(2);
set_value.insert(-5);
set<int,less<int> > :: iterator ptr = set_value.begin();
*ptr = 11;  // Compile error here.
```

The reason for the compile error at the last line is that ptr is viewed as a nonmutable iterator. If we wanted to accomplish the change, we would have to use the sequence

```
set_value.erase(ptr);
set_value.insert(11);
```

or

```
set_value.erase(*ptr);
set_value.insert(11);
```

[7]See Stroustrup in the References section at the end of this chapter.

Now consider the same situation for `map` and `multimap` objects. Look at the sequence

```
#include <map>
        .
        .
        .
map<char, int, less<char> > map_value;
```

Then `map_value` stores pairs of the form `pair<const char, int>`. This implies that the `char` values serving as keys in `map_value` cannot be modified, whereas the `int` values serving as the component of the associative array can be modified (perhaps using an `int`-valued version of `operator=`). To illustrate this, suppose we continue the last code sequence with

```
map_value.insert(pair<const char, int, less<char> >('i',2));
map<const char, int, less<char> >::iterator ptr = map_value.begin();
*ptr = pair<const char, int, less<char> >('i',3);// Compile error here.
```

This last line does not compile because the compiler sees it as attempting to modify not only the `int` value but the `char` value as well. This is not allowed because the `Key` type for `map` and `multimap` objects is `const`.

How, then, do we accomplish the change? There are in fact two ways to proceed. The first is to mimic what was done earlier for sets, namely, using the sequence

```
map_value.erase(ptr);
map_value.insert(pair<const char, int, less<char> >('i',3));
```

or the single assignment

```
(*ptr).second = 3;
```

There are further subtle changes between `set` and `map` objects, particularly with respect to the `insert` and `find` operators. We illustrate these in the following sequence of examples.

EXAMPLE 9.4 This example uses a `map` object to store pairs of values of the form `pair<const char,int>`, where the `char`-valued key is a lowercase vowel and the corresponding `int`-valued second component lists the sequential order of appearance of that vowel. We therefore represent the collection of vowels in the following sequential order of appearance:

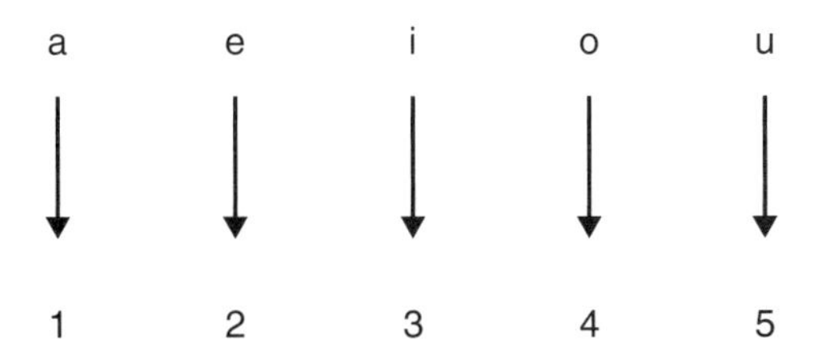

This version also expresses the values in the `map<char, int, less<char> >` object `map_value` using associative arrays with `char`-valued subscripts and with `int` values.

```
#include <iostream>
#include <map>
using namespace std;
int main()
{
 // Creating sequences of char and int values.
 // The first component will be a vowel, and the
 // second its corresponding number value.
 map<char,int,less<char> > map_value;
 map_value['a'] = 1;
 map_value['e'] = 2;
 map_value['i'] = 3;
 map_value['o'] = 4;
 map_value['u'] = 5;
 // Output the correspondence between the vowel subscripts and
 // their integer values.
 map<char,int,less<char> >::const_iterator ptr;
 for(ptr = map_value.begin(); ptr != map_value.end(); ++ptr)
  cout << (*ptr).first << "      " << (*ptr).second << endl;
 // Now find the number associated with the vowel 'i':
 map<char,int,less<char> > :: const_iterator qptr
   = map_value.find('i');
 // Output the integer associated with the vowel 'i':
 if(qptr != map_value.end())
   cout << (*qptr).second << endl;
 return 0;
}
```

Each of `map` and `multimap` support `find`, `lower_bound`, `upper_bound`, and `equal_range` . These appear as member functions for the same efficiency reasons as those described in Section 9.2 for sets and multisets. Specifically, `find` has two prototypes

```
iterator find(const key_value& x);
const_iterator find(const key_value& x) const;
```

because `map` and `multimap` support both mutable and constant iterators. In Example 9.4, the `find` member function appearing in `map` has been applied to `map_value` in the form

```
map<char,int,less<char> > :: const_iterator qptr
   = map_value.find('i');
```

The value of qptr returned is a reference to the pair stored in map_value whose first component is 'i'. When we then apply (*qptr).second, the int value returned is 3.

The complete output for this program is

```
a   1
e   2
i   3
o   4
u   5
3
```

Note that the sequence of associative array assignments

```
map_value['a'] = 1;
map_value['e'] = 2;
map_value['i'] = 3;
map_value['o'] = 4;
map_value['u'] = 5;
```

may be replaced by the sequence

```
map_value.insert(value_type('a',1));
map_value.insert(value_type('e',2));
map_value.insert(value_type('i',3));
map_value.insert(value_type('o',4));
map_value.insert(value_type('u',5));
```

with the same output.

EXAMPLE 9.5 This example illustrates the use of the predefined string type used to store the first components of multimap values of the form <string,int> where the first component represents the name of any month and the corresponding int value is the number of days in that month. The reason we have selected a multimap container is, of course, for the variation in the number of days for "February": either 28 or 29, depending on whether the current year is a leap year. We use string[8] for the designated key type because there is a natural lexicographic less than ordering for string constants. Also note that we cannot use associative arrays here because associative arrays apply exclusively to map objects (and not multimap objects). The formal code is

```
#include <iostream>
#include <map>
#include<string>
using namespace std;
```

[8]For a comprehensive treatment of the string type, see Stroustrup, pp. 579–602.

```
typedef multimap<string, int, less<string> > months_type;
// Main program follows
int main()
{
 // Create a multimap of months and the number of days
 // in the month.
 months_type months;
 typedef months_type::value_type value_type;
 // Put the entries in the multimap object.
 months.insert(value_type(string("January"),31));
 months.insert(value_type(string("February"),28));
 months.insert(value_type(string("February"),29));
 months.insert(value_type(string("March"),31));
 months.insert(value_type(string("April"),30));
 months.insert(value_type(string("May"),31));
 months.insert(value_type(string("June"),30));
 months.insert(value_type(string("July"),31));
 months.insert(value_type(string("August"),31));
 months.insert(value_type(string("September"),30));
 months.insert(value_type(string("October"),31));
 months.insert(value_type(string("November"),30));
 months.insert(value_type(string("December"),31));
 // Output the months and days for each month
 for(months_type::const_iterator ptr = months.begin();
      ptr != months.end(); ++ptr)
  cout << (*ptr).first << " has " << (*ptr).second << " days"
    << endl;
 // Apply find function to "February":
 months_type::const_iterator p = months.find(string("February"));
 // Output the number of days found for "February"
 while((*p).first == "February")
 {
  cout << (*p).second << endl;
  ++p;
 }
 return 0;
}
```

The program outputs

```
April has 30 days
August has 31 days
December has 31 days
```

```
February has 28 days
February has 29 days
January has 31 days
July has 31 days
June has 30 days
March has 31 days
May has 31 days
November has 30 days
October has 31 days
September has 30 days
28
29
```

The `string` values representing the months are stored in sorted lexicographic order because any `multimap` object is a sorted associative container.

9.6 Applications

We describe two specific application domains using the topics described in this chapter as well as topics described throughout the text.

Application 1: Separate Chaining Using Associative Arrays

In Section 4.5, we described the idea of a linked implementation of a hash table. This version of hashing was called *separate chaining,* and the Programming Project at the end of Chapter Four calls for the implementation of the `hash_table` class template using separate chaining. The solution of the problem as stated would involve constructing a `hash_table` object in the form of an ordinary one-dimensional array, using a key, of pointers to nodes in a linked list, each of whose `info` components contains the data to be stored at that position. As efficient as this may seem, the introduction of associative arrays allows for hash table entries to be constructed as `map` objects, using the key as the value of the hash function, and constructing an object in the form of an associative array component whose subscript is the key value and from which a node with the corresponding data value may be inserted as part of the hash table.

Admittedly, this is a complicated construction, but the payoff lies in the level of efficiency attained in the resulting structure. The important observation here is that there will be no components of the resulting hash table object referring to empty lists. This is because the associative array component will be constructed only for components whose data are known.

Application 2: Implementing Graph Types

Graphs are used to represent a sequence of data values described geometrically as points (or *vertices*), some of which are joined by line segments (or *edges*). The edges describe relations existing between pairs of these vertices. Indeed, suppose G defines a specific graph. Then G is defined by two sets: a nonempty set V of vertices and a set E (possibly empty) of edges whose members consist of certain pairs of vertices. The order of appearance of the vertices in an edge may be important, and if so, the graph is called a *directed graph,* or simply a *digraph.* In addition, edges with the same vertex at each end are permitted. Since any graph G is characterized by V and E, we use the notation G = (V,E). Figure 9.13 is a simple illustration of an (undirected) graph. Here $V = \{A_0, A_1, A_2, A_3, A_4\}$ and $E = \{\{A_0, A_1\}, \{A_0, A_2\}, \{A_0, A_4\}, \{A_1, A_2\}, \{A_2, A_4\}\}$, where, for example, the (undirected) edge with vertices A_0 and A_1 is denoted by $\{A_0, A_1\}$. Note also that G has no edge with vertex A_3.

FIGURE 9.13

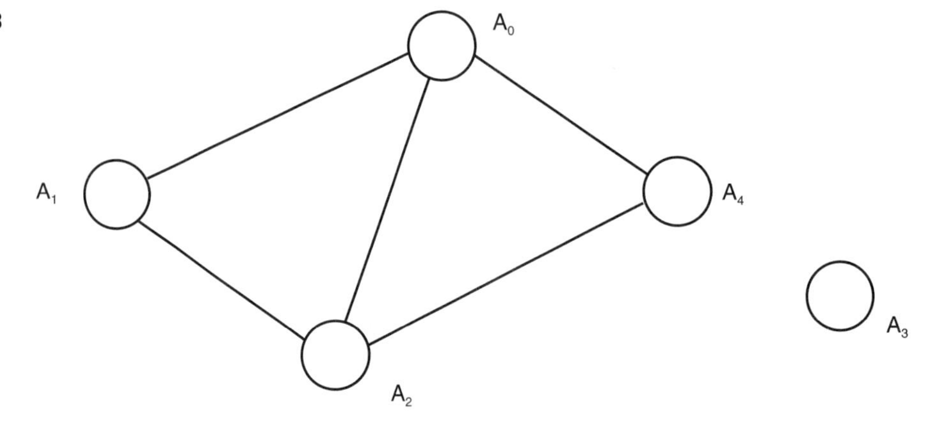

A *path* in any graph G between vertices X and Y is a finite collection of (undirected) edges of G: $\{X_1, X_2\}, \{X_2, X_3\}, \ldots, \{X_k-1, X_k\}$, where $X_1 = X$ and $X_k = Y$. For the graph described in Figure 9.13, there is a path between A_0 and A_4 given by $\{A_0, A_1\}, \{A_1, A_2\}, \{A_2, A_0\}, \{A_0, A_4\}$. We define a path to be *simple* if the path never passes through any vertex more than once. The example of a path just given is not simple, but the path $\{A_1, A_2\}, \{A_2, A_4\}, \{A_4, A_0\}$ is simple. Further, a *cycle* is a path that begins and ends at the same vertex and otherwise passes through no vertex more than once. The path $\{A_0, A_1\}, \{A_1, A_2\}, \{A_2, A_0\}$ in Figure 9.13 is an example of a cycle. A graph G is *connected* if a path exists for every pair of vertices. The graph in Figure 9.13 is not connected because, for example, there is no path joining A_3 to any other vertex. However, if A_3 were omitted, the resulting graph is connected.

A graph is *complete* if there is an edge between each pair of vertices. The graph described in Figure 9.14 is an example of a complete graph.

FIGURE 9.14

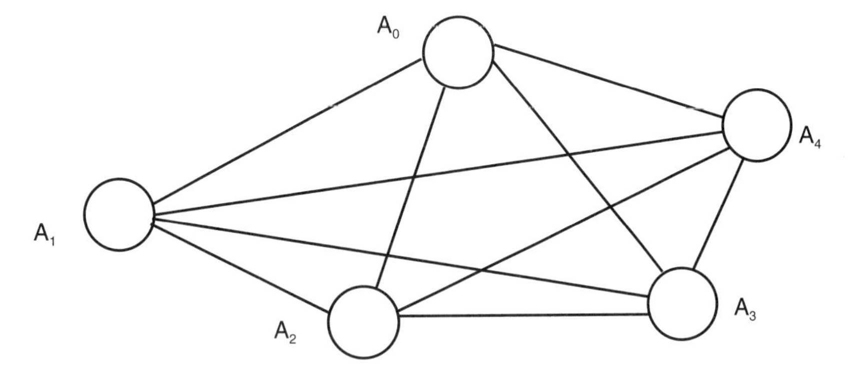

A graph is *directed* if each of its edges has a *direction;* that is, there is a well-defined initial vertex and terminal vertex. Thus, each edge in a directed graph determines a flow from its initial to its terminal vertex. We may represent a directed graph (or digraph) as `G = (V,E)`, where `V` is the set of vertices defined exactly as for (undirected) graphs and `E` is the set of *directed edges* represented as ordered pairs `(Ai,Aj)`, where A_i and A_j are in `V`. The ordering of the pair is used to indicate that the initial vertex is given by the left member A_i and the terminal vertex is given by the right member A_j. The graph in Figure 9.15 is an example of a digraph, where the arrows describe the direction of flow in each edge.

FIGURE 9.15

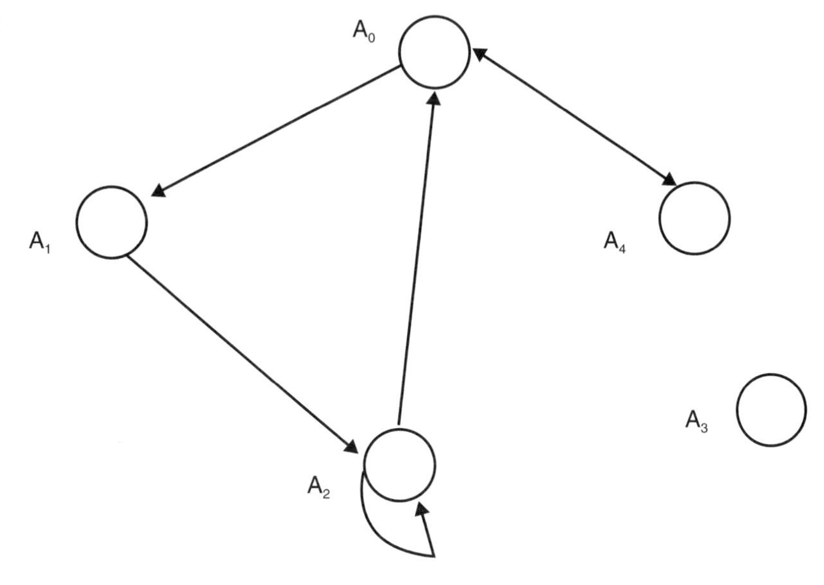

Here $V = \{A_0, A_1, A_2, A_3, A_4\}$ and $E = \{(A_0, A_1), (A_0, A_4), (A_1, A_2), (A_2, A_0), (A_2, A_2), (A_4, A_0)\}$. We define a cycle in a digraph as a path $(X_1, X_2), (X_2, X_3), \ldots, (X_{k-1}, X_k)$ in which $X_1 = X_k$. A cycle in a digraph is simple if X_1 and X_k represent the only pair of common vertices. A digraph is *acyclic* if it contains no cycles and is commonly referred to as a *DAG*. The graph in Figure 9.16 is an example of a DAG.

FIGURE 9.16

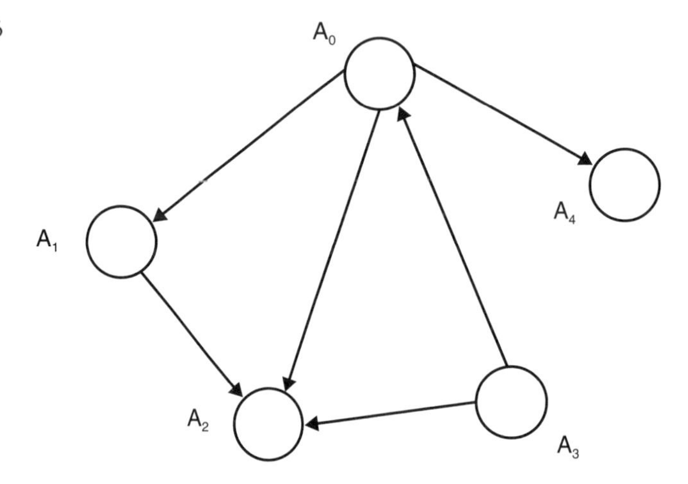

We are interested in answering several key questions regarding graphs:

- How do we define a graph ADT?
- How may we implement graphs using classes in the Standard Library?
- How are graphs *traversed*? That is, how do we move around from one vertex to another in a graph? How do we implement these traversals?
- Are there efficient algorithms for graph traversals?

In an object-oriented design, a graph ADT should address the construction and initialization of a graph object. We will define a constructor initializing graph objects with no vertices or edges and also supply a copy constructor. Besides this, we should consider the implementation of a destructor that returns as much reusable memory as possible to the free store. In addition, the user interface should contain member functions allowing for changes in the structure of the graph object by either inserting or removing vertices or edges or both. Further, the user should have the ability to issue messages to any graph (or digraph) object, testing whether certain vertices or edges appear in that object. Finally, the design should include the definition and implementation of functions for traversing the vertices of the graph in some particular order from some designated starting vertex.

In brief, our plan is to define class templates for (undirected) graphs and digraphs, each of whose objects is a graph (digraph) with vertices of type Key, where we assume Key supports a less than operator definable for any two of its values. These class templates should possess the following functionality:

1. constructors and destructors, allowing for the construction and deletion of all graph (digraph) objects with vertices represented by distinct values of type Key and where each such vertex stores a value of some type T
2. insertion operators for new vertices and edges in any graph (digraph) object
3. removal operators for vertices and edges in the current graph (digraph) object
4. a bool-valued function testing whether the current graph (digraph) object is empty—that is, whether the object has any vertices or edges
5. a bool-valued function with vertex parameters (of type Key) testing whether those vertices are joined by an edge in the current graph (digraph) object
6. a function with a single vertex parameter v (of type Key) returning the collection of all vertices in the current graph (digraph) object "adjacent" to v—that is, connected to v by an edge
7. functions implementing traversals of the current graph (digraph) object from a designated start vertex to a goal vertex, given as parameters

Our design will involve defining two user interfaces (and consequently, two implementation files), one for a Graph class template and one for a Digraph class template. We will relate these class templates by inheritance using Digraph as the base class and Graph as the derived class, using some basic observations about graphs and digraphs to exploit this inheritance relationship (Figure 9.17). In addition, we will use the map class template to implement these ideas in C++.[9]

FIGURE 9.17

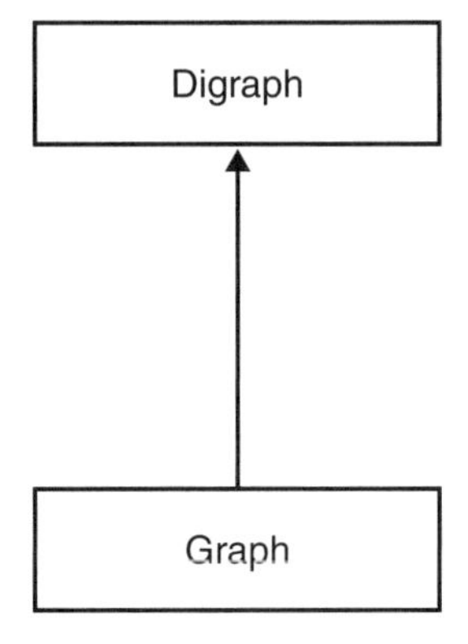

[9]A preliminary design using set was done by the author in collaboration with J. S. Mallozzi.

Digraph defines two constructors: One is the *default constructor*, constructing an empty Digraph object with no vertices or edges; the second is a *copy constructor*. In addition, we define a destructor for Digraph.

What about iterators for Digraph and Graph? Since neither of these class templates is predefined in the Standard Library, these iterators must be defined manually. We intend to define both mutable and constant iterators for either class. This simply means that iterators for any class of graphs or digraphs must be defined as special forms of iterators coming from predefined classes used in the definition of Graph or Digraph. As an example, let us preview part of the public portion of the interface for Digraph. It contains the sequence of typedef definitions given by

```
typedef Key vertex_type;
typedef T value_type;
typedef map<Key,T,less<Key> > vertex_map;
typedef vertex_map::iterator iterator;
typedef vertex_map::const_iterator const_iterator;
```

The list of member functions appearing in the public portion of the user interface of Digraph contains definitions for both mutable and constant iterator forms for begin() and end(). Our design also uses virtual member functions for inserting and removing edges in Digraph. This allows for the following application of polymorphism: If we have a Digraph object, then the operations of inserting and removing edges use insert and erase as defined in Digraph. On the other hand, if the object is constructed in Graph, determined as such at run time, the virtual nature of insert and erase causes execution to invoke the appropriate member function as redefined in Graph.

These preliminary observations lead to the description of the user interface of Digraph as

```
#include <map>
#include <functional>
using namespace std;
template<class Key, class T> class Digraph
{
 public:
 typedef Key vertex_type;
 typedef T value_type;
 typedef map<Key,T,less<Key> > vertex_map;
 typedef vertex_map::iterator iterator;
 typedef vertex_map::const_iterator const_iterator;
 typedef vertex_map::size_type size_type;
 typedef vertex_map::difference_type difference_type;
 // Constructor.  Constructs an empty digraph with
```

```
// no vertices or edges.
Digraph();
 // Copy constructor.  Makes digraph copy of source.
 Digraph(const Digraph<Key,T>& source);
 // Destructor.  Destroys current digraph.
 ~Digraph();
 // Assignment operator.  Assigns source to this digraph.
 Digraph<Key,T>& operator=(const Digraph<Key,T>& source);
 // Returns iterator indicating beginning of digraph.
 // That is, node corresponding to initial vertex in order
 // defined by vertex_type::operator<.
 iterator begin();
 // Returns const_iterator indicating beginning of digraph.
 // That is, node corresponding to initial vertex in order
 // defined by vertex_type::operator<.
 const_iterator begin() const;
 // Returns iterator indicating "past the end" of digraph.
 iterator end();
 // Returns const_iterator indication "past the end" of digraph.
 const_iterator end() const;
 // Returns whether current digraph is empty.
 bool empty() const;
 // Returns number of vertices in current digraph.
 size_type size() const;
 // Returns whether v is joined to w by an edge.
 // Precondition: v, w are vertices in current digraph.
 bool adjacent(const Key& v, const Key& w) const;
 // Returns set of vertices adjacent to v.
 // Precondition: v is a vertex in current digraph.
 vertex_map adjacency_set (constKey& v) const;
 // Inserts vertex v into digraph, with no incident edges.
 // Returns iterator referencing new vertex unless v is
 // already there, in which case returns "past the end".
 iterator insert(const Key& v);
 // Inserts edge from v to w.
 // v, w are vertices in current digraph.
 virtual void insert(const Key& v, const Key& w);
 // Removes vertex v from current digraph if present, along
 // with all incident edges.  Returns true if erased, false
 // if not.
 bool erase(const Key& v);
 // Erases vertex to which iterator refers.
 // Precondition: position references a vertex in current
```

```
  // digraph.
  void erase(iterator position);
  // Removes edge joining v and w, if present in current digraph.
  // Precondition: v, w are edges in current digraph.
  virtual void erase(const Key& v, const Key& w);
  // Returns iterator referencing vertex v or past the end
  // if v is not in current digraph.
  iterator find(const Key& v);
  // Returns const_iterator referencing vertex v or past the end
  // if v is not in current digraph.
  const_iterator find(const Key& v) const;
 private:
  // Details to be supplied later.
}; // terminates code for user interface for Digraph.
```

How do we reach the design decision that the `Graph` template is inherited from `Digraph`? The decision rests on an elementary observation: Each edge in an undirected graph may be viewed as a pair of edges in a digraph, where initial and terminating vertices exchange positions. That is to say, we may view the edge $\{A_i, A_j\}$ in an undirected graph as though it were a pair of edges (A_i, A_j) and (A_j, A_i) in a digraph. Thus, in particular, inserting and deleting edges in an undirected graph simply amount to inserting and deleting edges in a digraph. Applying this idea and inheritance, we may code the user interface for `Graph` as

```
template<class Key, class T>
  class Graph : public Digraph<Key,T>
{
 public:
  // Constructor.  Constructs an empty undirected graph with
  // no vertices or edges.
  Graph();
  // Copy constructor.  Makes undirected graph copy of source.
  Graph(const Graph<Key,T>& source);
  // Destructor
  ~Graph();
  // Assignment operator.  Assigns source to this graph.
  Graph<Key,T>& operator=(const Graph<Key,T>& source);
  // Permits continued use of iterator insert(const Key& v)
  using Digraph<Key,T>::insert;
  // Inserts edge from v to w.
  // Precondition: v, w are vertices in undirected graph.
  void insert(const Key& v, const Key& w);
  // Permits continued use of bool erase(const Key& v) and
  // void erase(iterator position);
  using Digraph<Key,T>::erase;
```

```
    // Removes edge joining v to w, if present.
    // Precondition: v, w are vertices in undirected graph.
    void erase(const Key& v,const Key& w);
}; // Terminates code for user interface for Graph.
```

How are `Digraph` and `Graph` objects represented internally? In other words, how do we describe the `private` section of the user interface for `Digraph`? To accomplish this, we begin by defining an *adjacency matrix* as a two-dimensional display of `bool` values whose rows and columns are indexed by the vertices of the underlying graph (or digraph). If the adjacency matrix is to represent a specific undirected graph with vertices $A_0, \ldots, A_{n-1}$, the adjacency matrix will be a symmetric matrix with `n` rows and `n` columns, where `true` appears in position `i,j` (row index `i` and column index `j`) if there is an edge from A_i to A_j in the graph. For undirected graphs, the `bool` value in each location `i,j` will be the same as that of location `j,i`. In the case of the undirected graph defined in Figure 9.13, the associated adjacency matrix is that described in Figure 9.18, and the adjacency matrix for the directed graph in Figure 9.16 is given by Figure 9.19. Note that this last matrix is not symmetric.

FIGURE 9.18

(column index)

(row index)		0	1	2	3	4
	0	false	true	true	false	true
	1	true	false	true	false	false
	2	true	true	false	false	true
	3	false	false	false	false	false
	4	true	false	true	false	false

FIGURE 9.19

(column index)

(row index)		0	1	2	3	4
	0	false	true	true	false	true
	1	true	false	true	false	false
	2	true	true	false	false	true
	3	false	false	false	false	false
	4	true	false	true	false	false

We may use these ideas to fill in the `private` section of the user interface for `Digraph` as

```
private:
 vertex_map vertices;
 typedef map<Key,bool,less<Key> > row;
 typedef map<Key,row,less<Key> > matrix;
 matrix adjacency_matrix;
```

This captures the idea of adjacency matrices in formal code.

Further sources of exploration involve traversals of directed and undirected graphs. Here the ideas of breadth-first and depth-first search are formalized for `Graph` and `Digraph` objects.

To traverse a graph (or digraph) is to systematically probe the structure by examining each vertex and edge. We seek efficient algorithms for graph traversals, where we judge such algorithms as efficient if all vertices and edges on the graph are examined (visited) in time proportional to the number of vertices and edges present. If a graph (digraph) has `n` vertices and `m` edges, we seek traversal algorithms of order `O(n+m)`.

We discuss traversals of undirected graphs here; the results for directed graphs are similar and left as an exercise. The objective in the depth-first traversal of a graph is to move as deeply as possible into the graph from a designated initial vertex to a goal vertex (presumed to exist in the graph) without having to backtrack to a set of previously visited vertices. Such a search strategy is important in a number of different applications, particularly in finding paths from one vertex to another or finding a *spanning tree* for a connected graph.

Suppose we consider depth-first traversals of the graph given in Figure 9.20, with initial vertex A_0 and goal vertex A_4. A depth-first search would

FIGURE 9.20

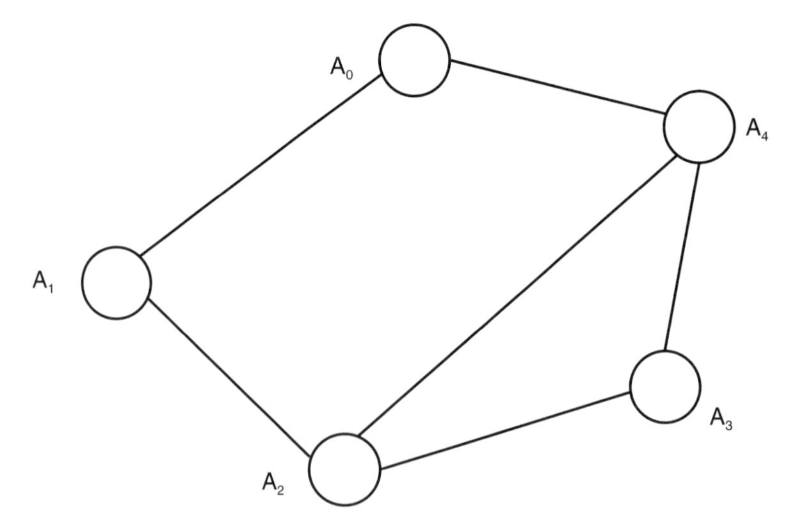

proceed to any vertex joined to A_0 by an edge—in this case, either to A_1 or A_4. Suppose the traversal proceeds to A_1. Then the next vertex to visit is A_2: We eliminate A_0 as a viable candidate because this would involve an early instance of backtracking. After A_2 is visited, the next vertex to visit may be either A_3 or A_4. If A_3 is visited first, the remaining vertex to visit without backtracking is A_4. Thus, a result of a depth-first traversal beginning with A_0 and ending with the goal vertex A_4 is expressed as the sequence A_0, A_1, A_2, A_3, A_4 (or more simply, as the sequence of integer subscripts `0,1,2,3,4`). Other depth-first traversals beginning with A_0 with goal vertex A_4 are A_0, A_4 (or `0,4`) and A_0, A_1, A_2, A_4 (or `0,1,2,4`).

In breadth-first search, the objective is to list all vertices adjacent to the current vertex before visiting some new vertex. This allows us to determine a path from the initial vertex to the goal vertex by performing a lateral sweep of all paths in the graph with the same number of vertices until a candidate is found with the desired goal vertex before considering candidates with additional vertices. If such a candidate is found, we have the desired result, but if no such candidate is found, we conclude that there is no path in the current graph beginning at the designated initial vertex and ending at the desired goal vertex. The proper data structure for holding the paths to be examined is a queue, each member of which is a path whose first node is the initial vertex.

The first value inserted into the queue is a path (in the form of a linked list) consisting of the initial vertex of the traversal. Then this vertex is removed and replaced by all paths (represented as linked lists of vertex subscripts) consisting of the initial vertex and whose remaining vertex subscript is that of any of the members of the adjacency set of the initial vertex. When a path is removed from the queue, it is replaced by a new path continuing the path just removed by inserting all paths with three vertices consisting of the initial vertex, followed by the vertex of the edge just removed, and then followed by any of the vertices in the adjacency set of the vertex in the path just removed. This process continues until either a path at the front of the queue ends with a terminating vertex equal to the desired goal or, if the queue becomes empty, an indication that no path is defined in the current graph from the designated initial vertex to the goal.

The underlying idea is that the queue maintains a repository of paths, all of which begin with the initial vertex, with the next candidate path at the front and which sweep through the graph breadth-first until the desired path is found or until no further candidate exists. To illustrate, we consider the graph in Figure 9.20 and a breadth-first traversal of the graph with initial vertex A_0 and goal vertex A_4. The algorithm first examines the possibility that the goal is the same as the initial vertex, but this is rejected immediately. The algorithm continues with a sweep of paths at the next level. In this case, there are two candidates: A_0, A_1 and A_0, A_4. The first candidate, presumed placed at the front of the queue, is rejected, and after this candidate is removed from the queue, the second candidate is tested and accepted. Thus, the result of the breadth-first search is the path A_0, A_4 (or equivalently, `0,4`).

9.7 Chapter Summary

Sorted associative containers are included in the design of the Standard Template Library to provide speedy and efficient access for the storage and retrieval of data. The four sorted associative container class templates are `set`, `multiset`, `map`, and `multimap`. In each such container, keys are used to provide storage of new values and the retrieval and removal of values already stored. The keys are maintained in sorted order, and traversing through the values of any such container amounts to visiting these values in sorted order. We assume that there is a binary relational operator defined for the keys, with less than as the default. This relational operator is the basis for the sorting of the values.

The `set` and `multiset` class templates provide member functions for manipulating objects in which the values coincide with the keys. That is to say, the values stored in such containers are the keys themselves. The main difference between a `set` object and a `multiset` object is that a `multiset` object allows for the storage of duplicate keys, whereas this is prohibited in a `set` object. The `map` and `multimap` class templates differ from those of `set` and `multiset` in that `map` and `multimap` objects distinguish between keys and values; that is, `map` and `multimap` objects involve both keys and a value associated with each key. The data type of the keys may be different from that for the values. The only condition is that the key type supports a well-defined binary relational operator (with less than as the default), providing the basis for the sorting of the values in the container. The main difference between a `map` and a `multimap` container object is that a `multimap` object allows for duplicate keys, whereas a `map` object allows only unique keys with associated values.

Another important difference between `map` and `set` is that the former supports a "bracket" operator `operator[]`, permitting access to the container in a manner similar to ordinary one-dimensional arrays. Stating this in other terms, `map` objects may be viewed as *associative arrays*, with many useful applications. The keys are the array subscripts, and the value associated with that key is viewed as the value stored at that array position. In addition, the iterators supported by `set` and `multiset` objects are constant iterators, whereas `map` and `multimap` objects support both constant and mutable iterators.

Besides constructors and destructors, each associative container class template supports other member functions, such as find, equal_range, lower_bound, upper_bound, and count. These are included as member functions based on their performance as speedier and more efficient than their generic counterpart because the implementation of each associative container is as a red-black binary search tree. In such an implementation, the tree is balanced, providing minimal time for retrieval of stored data. Thus, although these member functions also appear in generic form in <algorithm>, the more efficient alternative is in the form of the member functions previously listed.

There are generic functions defined in <algorithm> for such set-theoretic operations as set inclusion, set union and intersection, and set difference and symmetric difference. These are provided as generic functions because they are applicable to any STL container supporting random-access iterators, such as vectors and ordinary one-dimensional arrays.

There are a number of important applications of sorted associative containers. We have treated two important application areas: hashing using separate chaining and implementing various forms of graph ADTs. In the case of (undirected) graphs and digraphs, we saw a beautiful blend of many of the ideas of object-oriented design described in this text, particularly with the mingling of the ideas of the use of the Standard Library with virtual functions, polymorphism, class hierarchies, and inheritance. These ideas may be extended further to the implementation of *weighted* graph types, in which the vertices may be linked by edges carrying a numeric value (its *weight*). Such graphs are extremely useful in the application area of games and strategies as studied in artificial intelligence.

EXERCISES

1. Confirm the successful insertion of any int value into a previously empty int-valued set object using the first component of the pair value returned for the insert member function, with prototype

```
pair<iterator,bool> insert(const value_type& x);
```

2. Apply set_value1.swap(set_value2) for two int-valued sets set_value1, set_value2, whose before contents are 2 3 4 7 8 and -3 0 1, respectively.

3. Give alternative forms of red-black trees to those described in Figures 9.11 and 9.12 for the 2-3-4 trees given in Figures 9.7 and 9.8.

4. Write a program similar to that described in Example 9.1, but now the relational operator greater<int> replaces less<int>. Compare the result to that of Example 9.1.

5. a. Input the int values 7,30,9,1,20,30,120,20,12, 15 stored in a conformant array into a set<int> sorted associative container. Then output the contents of that container and the values of `size`, `equal_range`, `upper_bound`, and `lower_bound` for that container. Then insert the value `13` into the container. Finally, erase the value `12` from that container.

b. Apply `find` to the last form of the container from part a, first searching for `9` and then searching for `8`.

6. Redo Problem 5, but now for a `multiset<int>` container.

7. a. Write a program similar to that of Example 9.1, except that the input will now be the `char` values `'l','o','r','e','n','z','o'`, using `less<char>` as the (default) relational operator.

b. Redo part a of this exercise, except that now `greater<char>` replaces `less<char>`. Compare the result with that of part a.

8. Replace `set` by `multiset` in Problem 4 and compare the result with the output of Example 9.2.

9. Test set inclusion for the `char`-valued sets formed from the two conformant arrays defined as

```
char char_array1[] = {'e','l','e','p','h','a','n','t'};
char char_array2[] = {'a','a','r','d','v','a','r','k'};
```

10. Test `set_union` and `set_intersection` in a manner similar to that done for `int`-valued arrays, but now use the `char`-valued sets formed in Problem 9.

11. *de Morgan's laws* state that for any sets A, B, C,

```
A ∩ (B∪C) = (A∩B) ∩ (A∩C)
A ∪ (B∩C) = (A∪B) ∩ (A∪C)
```

Show that de Morgan's laws apply to the `set<int>` objects formed from the conformant array declarations given by

```
int int_array1[] = {2,3,7,9,15};
int int_array2[] = {-4,0,5,3,6,7,8,10,14,15,20};
int int_array3[] = {8,0,8,2,4,9,-7,4};
```

12. Find each red-black tree corresponding to the 2-3-4 tree described as

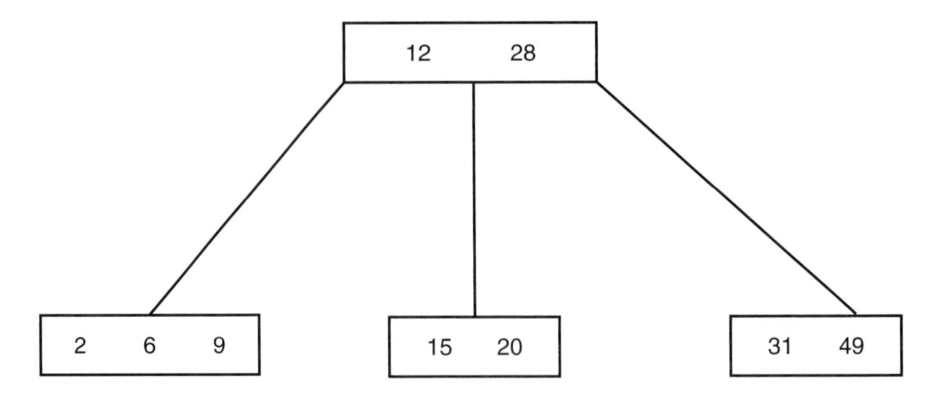

13. Write a program using a `map` object to store pairs of values of the form `pair<string,double>`, where the `string` values are the surnames of the eight position players for the New York Mets who started the baseball game against the Montreal Expos on September 17, 2000, and for which the corresponding `double` value is that player's batting average:

```
"Agbayani",0.294
"Payton",0.290
"Hamilton",0.284
"Piazza",0.327
"Ventura",0.231
"Zeile",0.274
"Abbott",0.274
"Bordick",0.267
```

a. Is it necessary to replace `map` with `multimap`?
b. Apply `find` to this container for `"Ventura"`.
c. Output the eight pairs in matching columns.
d. Erase `"Abbott",0.274` and replace it with `"Alfonso",0.325`.

14. Perform depth-first and breadth-first searches for the graph described by Figure 9.20 from A_0 to A_3 and then from A_1 to A_4.

15. Perform depth-first and breadth-first searches for the undirected graphs described in Figures 9.14 and 9.15 from A_0 to A_2.

16. Include an additional `public` member function in `Digraph` to retrieve the value (of type `T`) stored at any vertex in any `Digraph` object currently referenced by an `iterator` parameter.

PROGRAMMING PROJECTS

1. Supply the necessary implementation details for the `Digraph` and `Graph` class templates described in Section 9.6.

2. Use associative arrays with hash function

```
H(key) = key % 11
```

to hash the sequence of `int` values using separate chaining given by `23,36,89,12,134`. Also output the value of `size()` of the resulting associative array (viewed as a `map<int*>` object).

REFERENCE

Stroustrup, Bjarne, *The C++ Programming Language* (3rd ed.) (Reading, MA: Addison-Wesley, 1997).

APPENDIX

A Local Area Network Simulator

OBJECTIVES

- To introduce some of the basic concepts of local area networks and their design.
- To apply the concepts of object-oriented design and programming to produce an elementary version of a simulator of the activity associated with local area networks.
- To provide a concrete example of the use of C++ as a major tool for simulation commonly associated with industrial software design.

A.1 Introductory Concepts

A *network* is a finite set of communications links for connecting a number of terminals, printers, memory devices, and other hardware units used for processing and transmitting data. Every data communications network consists of units for sending and receiving data, computing units, and peripheral devices. Any point in the network where data are either received or transmitted is called a *node* or a *switch*. A *circuit* is a communications path between two nodes through which data may move in a single direction. The peripheral devices may include printers, disk and magnetic tape permanent storage devices, interactive or graphics terminals, or bar code scanners.

In this context, we define a *message* as a single item of communication. For example, if the network is an electronic mail system, a message is a document sent from one node in the network to another. Any message sent through the network consists of a *bitstring*—namely, a finite string of zeros and ones. We add other bits to the message to serve as a way of identifying the node for which the message is intended. This ensures reliable communication, correct routing, and avoidance of congestion and delay at some node in the network. Thus, it is generally the case that the messages sent through the network are very long bitstrings, which may not be capable of being transmitted all at once in their entirety due to hardware limitations. Hence, these messages are generally broken down into smaller bitstrings called *packets*. These packets are sent through the network to their intended destination and are reassembled at that destination to reproduce the original message. We will assume that each node is distinguished from any other by an *address*, represented by some positive integer and whose value is part of the bitstring sent along in the packet.

We define a *network topology* as the geometrical configuration of its nodes. One such topology is the *ring topology*, in which consecutive nodes are connected by links arranged to form a simple closed path as shown in Figure A.1. We also assume that the packets are transmitted from one node

FIGURE A.1

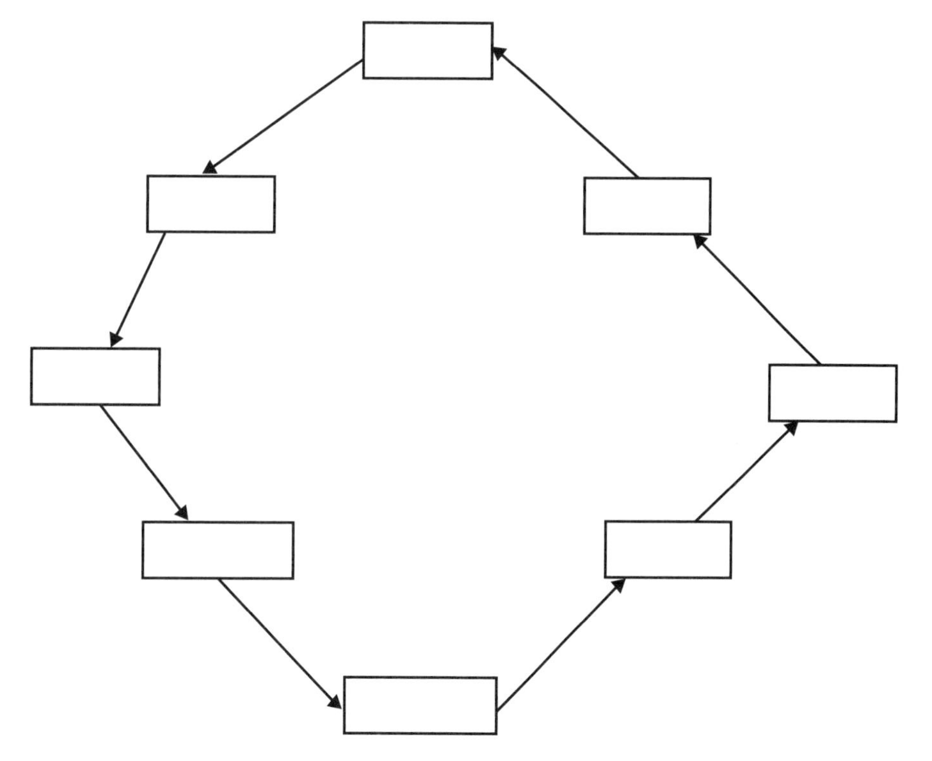

to another around the ring in a single direction, from the transmitting (or source) node to the receiving (or destination) node, and that the interface at each node has the ability to recognize its own address in a data packet in order to accept messages sent to it. The interface also has the ability to retransmit messages along the network intended for other nodes. At any time, a node can be in any one of three modes: `LISTEN`, `TRANSMIT`, and `BY-PASS`. When an interface is in the `LISTEN` mode, it scans the packet for the destination address and then copies the message into a *buffer* (a memory unit at that node) if the message was intended for that node. If not, the message is retransmitted to the next interface. When the interface is in the `TRANSMIT` mode, the node involved enters its own data into the ring. Finally, if a node is in the `BYPASS` mode, it is not fully operational or may be in the process of being removed from the network for maintenance or replacement. In this case, messages are sent through that node as though it were no longer part of the network.

We will assume that exactly one message is allowed to pass through the network at any given time. One possible way to ensure this is to use a *token,* which is a special bitstring that circulates in the network when no message is being sent. When a node is ready to transmit, it removes the token from circulation and stores it. This signifies that the node is now able to transmit its message through the network. It does so by changing its mode from `LISTEN` to `TRANSMIT`. In the meantime, the other nodes are continuously monitoring the messages passing through the network, remaining in the `LISTEN` mode. One key rule that we enforce is that each node must identify any messages passed to it and must transmit messages intended for other nodes. When a node finishes transmitting its message, it switches back to the `LISTEN` mode and passes the token back into the network. This enables another node to pick up the token and thus pass its message through the network. The type of network we have just described is commonly known as a *token ring network.*

Each node of the network is initialized in the `LISTEN` mode. If a message sent into the network is not accepted by any other nodes, it "laps" the network and is removed after completing one cycle. This implies that the node for which the message is intended either has not as yet been added to the network or is no longer part of the current network. We will also assume that any network may be in any one of two states: `ACTIVE` or `INACTIVE`. When `ACTIVE`, the network is performing its ordinary operations; it is `INACTIVE` when a node is being either removed from or inserted into the network.

A.2 Basic Design Components

How do we implement this in software? We use an object-oriented design in which these ideas are combined in a single abstraction, defining an ADT implemented in a class called `network`. For the member functions of `network` to operate properly, we will use the `list` class template and certain of its member functions.

Each node in any such network has the internal structure as given in Figure A.2. The `address` field contains the unique address of the network

FIGURE A.2

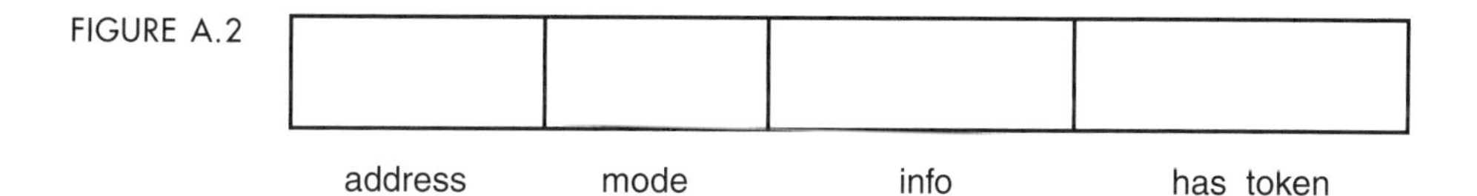

node. In addition, the `mode` field contains a value taken from the enumeration type

```
enum mode_type {LISTEN, TRANSMIT, BYPASS};
```

The `info` field is a string of a fixed size. This size is defined later as the value of `MESSAGE_LENGTH` because this simulates a typical hardware constraint. Thus, the value of the `info` field contains the message (in bitstring form) about to be sent by the node into the network once that node acquires the token or the message received by the node when its address is verified as the proper destination.

We define the value of `MESSAGE_LENGTH` as the maximum length of any packet capable of moving through the network, and the first six bits of any packet define the address of the destination node. Thus, the value of `MESSAGE_LENGTH` must be substantially higher than six. Finally, the `has_token` field contains a `bool` value that is `true` only when the current node has the token and is `false` otherwise. We capture this in formal code as

```
const int MESSAGE_LENGTH = some hardware-dependent positive integer;
```

The next definition represents an implementation of the data type (called `string_type`) characterizing the structure of a packet. We will single out the first six bits as `unsigned` values `0` or `1`, viewed as a bitstring yielding the address of the node for which the message is intended. The remaining `MESSAGE_LENGTH - 6` values, each of which is the *character* `'0'` or `'1'`, is a character string whose content is the message in the packet. Using this, we define

```
struct string_type {
 // First six bits are unsigned-valued of width one.
  unsigned bit0 : 1;
  unsigned bit1 : 1;
  unsigned bit2 : 1;
  unsigned bit3 : 1;
  unsigned bit4 : 1;
  unsigned bit5 : 1;
// Remaining bits are char-valued, either '0' or '1'.
  char msg[MESSAGE_LENGTH - 6];
}; // Terminates definition of string_type.
```

Thus, we view any value of `string_type` as in Figure A.3.

FIGURE A.3

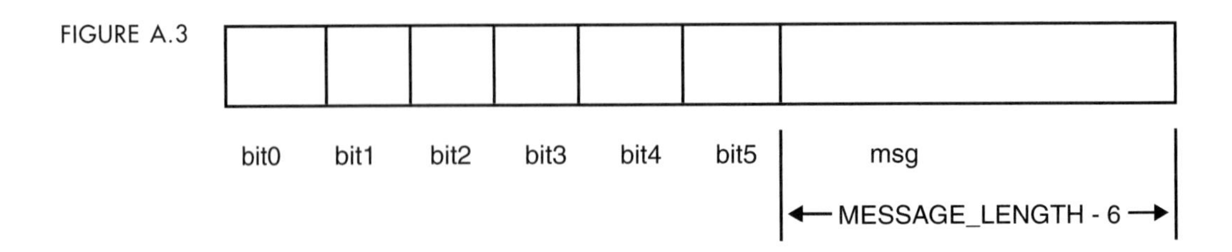

To illustrate these ideas, suppose the value of `MESSAGE_LENGTH` is `32` and suppose `message` is a `string_type` variable whose current value is `01100111010011001100111100101101`. Then the address of the destination node is the value of the bitstring `011001`, which is `25`.

A node of the network may then be defined as an object of the class `network_node`, whose formal definition is given as

```
class network_node
{
 public:
  int address;
  mode_type mode;
  string_type info;
  bool has_token;
  network_node : address(a) {}
 private:
  int address;
}; // Terminates definition of network_node
```

Since the implementation uses the `list` class template, we include the definitions

```
typedef list<network_node> network_list;
typedef list<network_node> :: iterator network_iterator;
typedef list<network_node> :: const_iterator const_network_iterator;
```

A.3 The User Interface

Using these preliminary design concepts, we may describe the user interface for `network` as

```
class network{
  public:
   //Constructor
   //Initializes network with zero size, initiates activity,
   //and with no current nodes.
   network();
```

```
  //Destructor
  ~network();
  //Inserts new node.
  //Postcondition: New node is inserted into the end of network
  void insert_node();
  // Removes node with address as parameter from the network.
  //Precondition: The current network contains at least one node.
  //Postcondition: Node referenced by parameter is removed from
  //current network.
  void remove_network_node(int);
  // Retrieves the current size of the network.
  int network_size();
  // Lists the addresses of the nodes currently active in network.
  //Precondition: the network contains at least one node.
  void list_network();
  // Sends the message from the source node to the
  // destination node if the source and destination addresses are
  // currently active in the network.
  void process_message();
private:
  int size; // Holds the current number of nodes
  bool is_active;  // true if currently active, false if otherwise
  network_list list_head; // Refers to the initial node of the current
                          // list.
  // Retrieves the address of the node appearing in binary
  // form as the first six bits of the parameter string sent
  // through the network
  int find_address(string_type&);
  // Retrieves a reference to the node whose address is the parameter.
  // If that node does not exist in the current network, NULL is
  // returned.
  //Precondition: The current network has at least one node.
  network_iterator find_node(int);
  // Simulates sending a message through the network from
  // a source node to a destination node.
  // Precondition: The current network has a least one node.
  // Postcondition: Message currently passing through
  // the network is received by intended destination node,
  // if such a node is presently in the network.
  void send_message(network_iterator&);
  // Precondition: parameter is non-negative integer
  // Postcondtion: two to the ith power is returned
  int powerof2(int);
```

```
    // Converts a decimal base node address to binary and appends
    // this new number to the bitstring fields of string type
    // Precondition: the address is a non-negative integer
    // no greater than 63.
    // Postcondition: The bitfields contain the binary number
    // valid addresses of nodes in the network
    void tobitstring(int, string_type&);
}; // Terminates user interface for network.
```

Each object of `network` is a specific network whose structure contains two data members: `size` and `is_active`. The `size` field is of type `int`, and `is_active` is `bool`-valued and `true` only when the network is currently active in the sense described earlier and `false` if otherwise. In addition, the `private` part defines a number of helpful operations used to simplify the coding of the member functions listed in the `public` part. These `public` member functions are listed as

1. `process_message`, used to simulate sending a message through the network
2. `remove_network_node`, used for removing any node currently in the network
3. `insert_node`, used for inserting a new node into the current network
4. `network_size`, used for retrieving the number of nodes currently in the network
5. `list_network`, used for retrieving the addresses of all nodes in the current network

A.4 Implementation Details

We include a constructor establishing initial conditions on the network, which places no node in the network. The coding of the constructor is given as

```
network :: network() : size(0),is_active(true) {}
```

The destructor is the default, given by

```
network :: ~network() {}
```

We now provide the formal encoding for the `private` auxiliary member functions `find_address`, `powerof2`, `find_node`, and `tobitstring`. Each of these plays a pivotal role in simulating the process of sending a message through the network to the appropriate destination node. The role of `find_address` is to convert the first six bits of any packet to the equivalent `int` value.

```
int network::find_address(string_type& message)
//Returns the address of the node stored in positions 0-5
//of message
{
 int value = 0;
 if (message.bit0)
  value +- powerof2(5);
 if (message.bit1)
  value += powerof2(4);
 if (message.bit2)
  value += powerof2(3);
 if (message.bit3)
  value += powerof2(2);
 if (message.bit4)
  value += powerof2(1);
 if (message.bit5)
  value += powerof2(0);
 return value;
}
```

The function `powerof2()` invoked in `find_address` is coded as

```
int network::powerof2(int i)
//Returns the integer value of 2 raised to ith power
//Precondition: i is a non-negative integer
{
 int base=1;
 while (i– > 0)
  base*=2;
 return base;
}
```

The auxiliary function `find_node` returns a reference to the node in the network whose address is the value of the parameter, if such a node exists in the current network.

```
network_iterator network::find_node(int address_value)
//Returns a reference to the node whose address is the value
//of the parameter, if such a node exists; otherwise nothing
//is returned.
{
 //Begin the search, moving through network
 network_iterator qptr;
 for(qptr = list_head.begin(); qptr != list_head.end();
       ++qptr)
  if ((*qptr).address == address_value)
```

```
            return qptr;
    return qptr;
}
```

The purpose of `tobitstring` is to produce the bitstring equivalent of the destination address.

```
void network::tobitstring(int destination, string_type& message)
{
 message.bit0 = 0;
 message.bit1 = 0;
 message.bit2 = 0;
 message.bit3 = 0;
 message.bit4 = 0;
 message.bit5 = 0;
 if (destination >= powerof2(5)){
  message.bit0 = 1;
  destination -=powerof2(5);
 }
 if (destination >= powerof2(4)){
  message.bit1 = 1;
  destination -=powerof2(4);
 }
 if (destination >= powerof2(3)){
  message.bit2 = 1;
  destination -=powerof2(3);
 }
 if (destination >= powerof2(2)){
  message.bit3 = 1;
  destination -=powerof2(2);
 }
 if (destination >= powerof2(1)){
  message.bit4 = 1;
  destination -=powerof2(1);
 }
 if (destination >= powerof2(0)){
  message.bit5 = 1;
  destination -=powerof2(0);
 }
}
```

The `private` member function `send_message` contains all of the formal coding details of the process of sending a message from the source node to the intended destination node. Since such detail is intended primarily for the successful completion of the sending process and is not of any importance to the user, its code is hidden in the `private` section. With this in mind, its source code is given as

```
void network::send_message(network_iterator& source)
//Simulates sending a message through the network from
//a source node to a destination node.
//Source node must have the token from network before
//sending the message, and cannot listen to any other message.
//Precondition: Current network contains at least two nodes, and
//the source and destination nodes are distinct.
//Postcondition: Message currently passing through the
//network is received by intended destination node, if such
//a node is presently in the network.
{
 //Prepare source node for transmitting the message
 (*source).has_token = true;
 (*source).mode = TRANSMIT;
 //Use auxiliary iterator to conduct a search through the
 //network, looking for destination node.
 //Initialize position of auxiliary iterator at the initial node.
  network_iterator qptr = list_head.begin();
  while(qptr != list_head.end())
  {
   cout << "Destination node " << find_address((*source).info) << endl;
   cout << "Searching node   " << (*qptr).address << endl;
   if(find_address((*source).info) == (*qptr).address)
   {
    cout << "Destination node " << (*qptr).address << " found."
          << endl;
    //The message is being sent to the proper destination.
    //Set the mode of the destination to TRANSMIT, since it
    //cannot receive any new message until the current
    //message is received.
     (*qptr).mode = TRANSMIT;
    //Copy message into the destination's info field.
     (*qptr).info = (*source).info;
    //Reset the mode of the destination node to LISTEN.
     (*qptr).mode = LISTEN;
  }//ends if-clause
  ++qptr;
  }//ends while-loop
  //Reset mode and has_token fields of source.
  (*source).mode = LISTEN;
  (*source).has_token = false;
  // Place empty message in the source node.
  (*source).info.msg[0]='\0';
```

```
  qptr = list_head.begin();
} // Terminates code for send_message.
```

The coding for the `public` member function `insert_node` follows. Its purpose is to insert a new node at the end of the current network.

```
void network::insert_node()
//Inserts node at the end of the network
//Postcondition: New node is inserted into network,
{
 static int address_counter = 0;
 //First shut down all network operations.
 is_active = false;
 //Create new node
 network_node new_node;
 new_node.mode = LISTEN;
 new_node.has_token = false;
 ++address_counter;
 new_node.address = address_counter;
 new_node.info.bit0 = 0;
 new_node.info.bit1 = 0;
 new_node.info.bit2 = 0;
 new_node.info.bit3 = 0;
 new_node.info.bit4 = 0;
 new_node.info.bit5 = 0;
 list_head.push_back(new_node);
 //Increase size of network.
 ++size;
 //Resume normal network activity.
 is_active = true;
}
```

We use the `static` variable `address_counter` to maintain an accurate count of the newly created nodes installed into the network, beginning with the initial node whose address is `1`. The current value of `address_counter` does not necessarily coincide with the number of nodes currently in the network. In fact, the address of each newly created node is given by the updated value of `address_counter`, and the value of `size` gives the number of nodes currently in the network. Note that if any node is removed from the network, its address is not recyclable. Finally, we initialize the values of `new_node.info.bit0` through `new_node.info.bit5` to zero because these bit values give the address of the destination node for a message. These values will change when a message is to be sent from this node to a destination node.

The code for the next `public` member function `remove_network_node` demonstrates how a node with the given addrress as the value of the parameter is removed from the current network, if that network currently contains a node with that address.

```
void network::remove_network_node(int address_value)
//Remove node with given address, if it exists in network.
//Precondition: Current network contains at least one node.
//Postcondition: Node referenced by parameter is removed from
//network, decreasing network size by 1.
{
 //Create iterator reference to find node with
 //given address and initialize.
 network_iterator qptr = list_head.begin();
 //Advance forward, looking for node with given address.
 while((qptr -> address != address_value) && (qptr != list_head.end()))
      ++qptr;
 if((qptr != list_head.end()) && (qptr -> address == address_value))
 //Node with given address is located.
 //Suspend all network activity at node to be removed.
 {
  qptr -> mode = BYPASS;
  //Suspend all other normal network activity.
  is_active = false;
  //Decrease network size.
  --size;
  //Remove node
  list_head.remove(*qptr);
  //If node removed is the entry into the network,
  //new entry is its successor.
  is_active = true;
 }
}
```

The next `public` member function returns the number of nodes currently in the network.

```
int network::network_size()
//Returns the size of the network
{
 return size;
}
```

The `public` member function `list_network` returns a list of the current network nodes and their `info` components.

```
void network::list_network()
//Outputs a list of the network nodes and their info components
```

```
{
 if (list_head.empty() == true)
  cout << "list_network: list is empty" << endl;
 else
 {
  cout << "node address       message" << endl;
  for (network_iterator qptr = list_head.begin();
              qptr != list_head.end(); ++qptr)
   cout << (*qptr).address << "      " << (*qptr).info.msg) << endl;
 }
}
```

The last `public` member function is `process_message`, simulating the process of sending a message to the destination node in the network. Its code is given by

```
void network::process_message()
//Simulates the sending of a message from sender.
// Precondition: The first 6 bits of message contains the address
// of the destination node.
//Postcondition: The destination node receives the message if
//the sender and the message contain valid node addresses.
{
  int source, destination;
  string_type message;
  cout << "Please enter the address of the source node:" << endl;
  cin >> source;
  cout << "Please enter the address of the destination node:" << endl;
  cin >> destination;
  cout << "Please enter the message to be sent:" << endl;
  cin >> message.msg;
  //Locate the sending node
  network_iterator qptr = find_node(source);
  //Send message if the sending node address is a valid network node.
  if (qptr -> address == source)
  {
   tobitstring(destination, message);
   qptr -> info = message;
   send_message (qptr);
   (*qptr).info.msg[0] = '\0';
  }
  else
   cout << "Error: message not sent" << endl;
 }
```

A driver for this implementation is

```
int main()
{
 network lan; //Constructs an empty network with no nodes.
 char ch_val = display_menu();
 while(ch_val != 'e' && ch_val != 'E')
 {
  process_choice(ch_val);
  ch_val = display_menu();
 } // ends while-loop.
 return 0;
} // Terminates driver.
```

The function `display_menu()` was not defined as a member function of `network` in our design. When invoked, it prompts the user for a choice of a network operation to be applied to the current network or to exit from the simulator. Its code may be described as

```
char display_menu()
{
 cout << "Welcome to the LAN system administration" << endl;
 cout << endl;
 cout << "Please choose from the following options:" << endl;
 cout << "A - add a new node to network" << endl;
 cout << "R - remove a node from the network" << endl;
 cout << "S - send a message" << endl;
 cout << "L - list addresses of nodes in network" << endl;
 cout << "E - exit" << endl;
 char choice;
 cin >> choice;
 return choice;
}
```

The final auxiliary function is `process_choice`. Its purpose is to select the proper `public` member function from `network` based on the user's choice after the menu is displayed.

```
char process_choice(char ch)
//Function used to perform selection made by user from display menu
{
 switch (ch)
 {
  case 'a': //add node
  case 'A':
   lan.insert_node();
   break;
```

```
  case 'r':
  case 'R': //remove node
   if (lan.network_size() == 0)
    cout << "Error: Remove node - network is empty" << endl;
   else
   {
    int r_address;
    cout << "Please enter the address of the node to remove"
         << endl;
    cin >> r_address;
    lan.remove_network_node(r_address);
   }
   break;
  case 's':
  case 'S': //send message
   lan.process_message();
   break;
  case 'l':
  case 'L': //list nodes
   if(lan.network_size() == 0)
    cout << "The network is empty" << endl;
   else
    lan.list_network();
   break;
  case 'e':   //exit program
  case 'E':
           //exit
   return (ch);
  default:        //error
   cout << "Error: incorrect choice entered" << endl;
   return 'x';
 }
 return 'x';
} // Terminates process_choice.
```

A.5 Description of a Typical Execution

A typical execution of this code begins with a call to `display_menu`, which displays

```
Welcome to the LAN system administration
Please choose from the following options:
```

```
A - add a new node to network
R - remove a node from the network
S - send a message
L   list addresses of nodes in network
E - exit
```

Initially, the user will respond with several successive choices to add new nodes to the network by pressing `'A'` or `'a'`. In each such case, `process_choice` calls `insert_node`. Each call to `insert_node` increments the `static` variable `address_counter`: The first node has address `1`, the next has address `2`, and so on. In addition, each such call increments the value of `size`, which keeps track of the number of nodes currently active in the network.

If a subsequent prompt results in the user's choice to remove a node, and if the current network is not empty, the user will be prompted to supply the address of the node to remove:

```
Please enter the address of the node to remove
```

The user responds to this prompt by supplying that address, and `remove_network_node` is called. Assuming that the address supplied is that of a currently active node, that node is removed, and the value of `size` decrements by `1`. On the other hand, if the network is currently empty, the response is

```
Error: Remove node - network is empty
```

Now suppose the user wishes to send a message from one node to another by responding to the choice generated from `display_menu` with `'S'` or `'s'`. Then `process_choice` responds by calling `process_message`, and the user must then respond to each of the following prompts:

```
Please enter the address of the source node:
Please enter the address of the destination node:
Please enter the message to be sent:
```

If we assume that the two nodes are currently in the network, the message is sent using the code segment from `process_message` given by

```
if (qptr -> address == source)
 {
 tobitstring(destination, message);
 qptr -> info = message;
 send_message (qptr);
 (*qptr).info.msg[0] = '\0'
}
```

Under other conditions, the error message

```
Error: message not sent
```

is returned.

If the user responds to the prompt in `display_menu` to list the addresses of the nodes in the network by pressing `'L'` or `'l'`, the size of the current network is examined. If `network_size` is currently zero, the response is

```
The network is empty
```

But if `network_size` is greater than zero, `list_network` is called, and a list of addresses and messages stored at each active node is displayed.

Finally, if the user responds to the prompt in `display_menu` to exit by pressing `'E'` or `'e'`, the `while` loop in the main function causes execution to terminate.

GLOSSARY

abstract class—a base class containing at least one pure `virtual` function. See also *pure* `virtual` *function.*

abstract data type (ADT)—an aggregate consisting of two components: (a) an *application domain,* consisting of a collection of objects (instances) and (b) a finite and nonempty collection of *admissible operations* applicable to any member of the application domain.

abstraction—the ability of a language to implement a theoretical concept in simple and precise terms.

accessor—a member function of a container type returning information about the container without modifying any of the container's current values or attributes.

actual parameter—a variable or expression appearing in a call to a function and passes to that function for computation. See also *formal parameter.*

adaptor—an STL entity assuming any one of three possible forms: container adaptor, iterator adaptor, and function adaptor. See also *container adaptor; function adaptor; iterator adaptor.*

adjacency matrix of a graph (or digraph)—a two-dimensional representation of `bool` values whose rows and columns are indexed by the vertices of the underlying graph (or digraph). See also *directed graph; graph.*

algorithm—a finite sequence of instructions which, when executed in order of appearance, produces a solution to a specific programming problem.

<algorithm> (or <algorithm.h>)—the STL library providing numerous implementations of the more commonly used algorithms in general data processing.

array—a data structure whose components are accessed in a random manner through the use of subscripts (or indices).

assignment—an operator taking the form `operator=` which, when applied to `v2 = v1`, changes the state of `v2` to match that of `v1`. See also *state.*

associative container—an STL container that associates a key value with each value stored in the container, providing speedy retrieval of these values based on the value of the associated key (also known as *sorted associative container*).

autodecrement operator—the operator defined as `operator--`, applicable to integer variables and iterators.

autoincrement operator—the operator defined as `operator++`, applicable to integer variables and iterators.

balanced binary tree—a binary tree in which the left and right subtrees have heights that differ by no more than 1. See also *binary tree.*

base class—the superclass in an inheritance relation between two classes (also known as *parent class*). See also *superclass.*

bidirectional iterator—an iterator whose functionality is similar to forward iterators, with the additional functionality of permitting the traversal of a sequence in either the forward or backward direction. See also *forward iterator.*

bidirectional pointer—a pointer applicable to nodes in a doubly linked list, permitting movement from one node to the next in either of two opposite directions.

big-O analysis—an analysis of the efficiency of an algorithm by counting the number of processing steps required for the algorithm to complete execution.

binary function—a function involving two arguments.

binary function object—a function object involving two arguments.

binary predicate—a `bool`-valued function of two arguments. See also *predicate.*

binary search—the process of searching that begins by examining the middle value of a sorted array and then moves to the half that is likely to contain the value sought, and so on, until either the value sought is located in the array or the search ends unsuccessfully.

binary search tree—a binary tree in which the value stored at each node is greater than the value stored at its left child and less than the value stored at its right child.

binary tree—a tree in which each node has a maximum of two children.

binder—a special form of function adaptor transforming a binary function object into a unary function object. See also *binary function object; unary function object.*

bit—a single binary digit described either as `0` or `1`.

bitstring—a finite string of bits.

bracket (`[]`) operator—an operator that permits random access to any value stored in a container supporting the use of random-access iterators, such as ordinary one-dimensional arrays, vectors, or deques.

breadth-first search of a graph—a traversal of a graph that visits each node of the graph at a given level before visiting a node at the next highest level. See also *depth-first search of a graph; level (of a node in a graph).*

bucket—an array of records maintained at each position in the hash table.

bucket hashing—a technique of hashing using open addressing in which several positions are available for storing values at each location of the hash table.

buffer—a memory unit maintained at any network node. See also *network node.*

child—an immediate successor of a node in a tree.

circuit—a communications path between two network nodes through which data move. See also *network node.*

class—the central construct of an object-oriented design; it is a specific description of the characteristics and behavior of a set of objects.

class template—a generic form of a class definition using type parameters.

comparative operator—a `bool`-valued operator defined as `operator==` or `operator<`, which permits comparisons between objects of the same container class.

compile time—the time segment during which a compiler translates a program from high-level code (source code) into an executable form.

compiler—a program used to convert a program written in a high-level language, such as C++, into a language that is more closely related to the underlying machine hardware—namely, into a language whose instructions are immediately executable by the computer's hardware.

complete binary tree—a binary tree whose levels, beginning with that of the root node, are full at each level except the last, where the nodes are situated in succession from left to right.

complete graph—a graph with an edge connecting each pair of its distinct vertices.

complexity—the formula that expresses the number of processing steps required for the algorithm to complete its execution, given a specific sequence of input data.

conditional (predicate) generic algorithm—a generic algorithm that executes on just those members of a sequence satisfying some specific condition (predicate). See also *unconditional generic algorithm.*

constant iterator—an iterator referencing a member of some sequence stored in a container whose value is not permitted to change during the course of a computation where that iterator is defined. See also *iterator.*

constant-time operation—an operation whose complexity is the same, regardless of the size of the collection to which the operation is applied. See also *complexity.*

constructor—a member function of a class used to create new objects of that class.

container—the data structure used to store finite collections of values of some type, defined and supported by the STL.

container adaptor—an STL class that uses objects defined as fundamental containers (vectors, deques, lists) as a background and provides a new interface, causing that fundamental container to be interpreted differently (as a stack, queue, or priority queue).

copy constructor—a constructor whose resulting object is an exact copy of an already existing object of that class.

copying version of an algorithm—an algorithm that copies its result to a different container or to a nonoverlapping version of the current container on which it operates; the name of any such algorithm ends in `_copy`, as in `reverse_copy`. See also *in-place algorithm.*

correctness—a quality of software design guaranteeing the production of the expected solution to a software problem for all possible admissible inputs.

CPU—that segment of a computer's hardware in which the actual computations are performed (also known as *central processing unit*).

data member—a component of a class describing data carried by any object constructed from that class.

depth-first search of a graph—a traversal of a graph that visits the successors of each of its nodes before moving to other nodes at the same level. See also *breadth-first search of a graph; level (of a node in a graph).*

deque—a fundamental STL container of varying length, providing random access to any of its values, with constant-time insertions and deletions at each extremity of the container. See also *constant-time operation.*

derived class—the designated subclass in an inheritance relationship between two classes. See also *subclass.*

descendant of a node A—any node on a path rooted at A to a leaf of a given tree.

destructor—a member function of a class performing the inverse operation provided by the constructor (it frees storage allocated to objects created by any constructor).

deterministic—the property inherent in algorithms stating that each of its steps, with the exception of the first step, has exactly one predecessor.

directed edge of a graph—an edge in which the order of appearance of the vertices it connects is significant.

directed graph (or digraph)—a graph such that the order of appearance of the pair of vertices constituting an edge is significant. See also *graph; undirected graph.*

directed path (of a directed graph)—a finite sequence of directed edges beginning at an initial vertex of the graph and terminating at another vertex of that graph.

dispatcher—a program in an operating system devoted to changing the state of the process at the front of the ready queue from ready to running and removing that process from the front of the queue. See also *dispatching.*

dispatching—the act of placing the process at the front of the ready queue in the running state and removing it from the front of the queue.

divide and conquer—a problem-solving methodology that repeatedly subdivides the solution into smaller and simpler subproblems.

double hashing—a technique of hashing using open addressing in which two hash functions are used; the primary function provides the initial probe into the hash table, and the second yields the interval length in the probe sequence.

driver—a program used to test implementations of algorithms.

edge—the link between two consecutive nodes on a tree or graph.

efficiency—a principle of design in which the solution is executed in a relatively fast manner, using only the resources that are absolutely necessary for the completion of the solution.

encapsulation—the process of hiding and restricting access to the implementation details of a data structure.

equivalence relation—a binary relation existing among members of a collection of data values that satisfies three properties: (a) every value "is equivalent to" itself; (b) for any two values `value1` and `value2`, if `value1` "is equivalent to" `value2`, then `value2` "is equivalent to" `value1`; and (c) for any `value1`, `value2`, `value3`, if `value1` "is equivalent to" `value2`, and if `value2` "is equivalent to" `value3`, then `value1` "is equivalent to" `value3`.

Euclidean algorithm—an algorithm that uses recursive methods to find the greatest common divisor of any two positive integers.

exception—an abnormal state or event interrupting normal program execution.

exception handler—a code sequence whose execution deals with an exception when that exception is raised during the course of a computation.

`explicit` declaration—a declaration used in the definition of a constructor to avoid any unanticipated type conversions.

Fibonacci function—a function generating the values of the Fibonacci sequence recursively by finding the sum of the previous two members of the sequence beginning with `1, 1`.

final segment—in quicksort, those members of the array whose values are larger than the pivot.

finite induction—a technique of mathematical proof involving verifying some initial step and then verifying that each successive step follows from the truth of its immediate predecessor.

FIFO property—a property of a queue in which the removal and retrieval operations access the value inserted earliest (also known as *first-in, first-out property*).

folding—a technique of hashing in which the digits of the key are involved in some computation, with the result lying within the scope of the subscripts of the associated hash table. See also *middle square technique.*

formal parameter—an identifier appearing in a function declaration that is replaced by an actual parameter when that function is called. See also *actual parameter.*

forward iterator—any iterator possessing the functionality of both input and output iterators. See also *input iterator; output iterator.*

4-node—a node in a tree containing exactly three data values and four children.

`friend` function—a function listed in the user interface of a class but coded in the implementation part without the necessary syntax for scope resolution as that for pure member functions.

full binary tree—a binary tree whose leaves are all at the same level `k` and for which each possible position at level `k` is occupied by a node.

function adaptor—a facility that adapts function objects definable in the STL for the purpose of extending their functionality. See also *function object.*

function object—a facility that permits the passing of a function as a parameter to an algorithm to adapt that function to the particular processing described by the algorithm.

function template—a generic form of a function definition using type parameters.

`<function.h>` (or `<functional>`)—the name of an STL library containing a number of useful function objects for commercial data processing.

generalized numeric algorithm—an algorithm coded in the STL that is useful in a variety of numerical computations, such as computing subtotals, inner products, partial sums, and differences of adjacent values.

generic pointer type—a useful alternative to class templates that permits instantiation using type casting.

global identifier—a name that is visible to any member function of a class.

global variable—See *global identifier.*

graph—a collection of points or vertices and a collection of edges connecting some of these vertices.

hash collision—the situation in which several different keys hash to the same value. See also *hash function.*

hash function—a function whose single argument is a key returning a value in the hash table. See also *hash table.*

hash table—a data structure (usually in the form of an array) whose entries provide a very efficient form of searching for a value.

hashed associative container—an associative container whose implementation is a hash table. See also *associative container.*

hashing—a search strategy that allows the user to specify a key value and employs a very fast and efficient lookup.

heap—a complete binary tree in which every node satisfies the property that its value is greater than or equal to the value assigned to each of its children. See also *complete binary tree.*

helper function—a useful and relatively simple function supplied by the STL to aid in the efficient computation of a number of predefined functions appearing in `<functional>` and `<algorithm>`. See also *`<algorithm>`; `<function.h>`.*

hierarchical organization—the ability of newly created classes to be derived from existing classes by inheriting certain characteristics of these already existing classes.

infix—a notation for writing expressions in which the operator lies between the operands (arguments).

inheritance—the process by which a derived class (subclass) may reuse characteristics and behavior defined in a base class (superclass).

initial segment—in quicksort, the sequence of values in the array whose members are no greater than the pivot.

in-place algorithm—a version of an algorithm that places its result into the same container on which it operates. See also *copying version of an algorithm.*

input iterator—an iterator whose functionality consists of moving forward through successive values of a container, reading any value it references, and responding to a condition halting its movement.

insert iterator—a form of an iterator adaptor that adapts the iterator to a version which inserts a value at a fixed position in some container.

insertion sort—a sorting algorithm that inserts the `ith` item into its proper position among the first `i` members of an array on the `ith` cycle through the array.

instantiation—the process of constructing an object and initializing its data members.

interactive user—a user communicating directly with the computer via terminals.

interior node—any node on a tree containing at least one nontrivial child; any nonleaf node. See also *leaf.*

invariant—See *loop invariant.*

is-a—a relationship between classes stating that a derived class is a special form of a base class using inheritance.

`istream`—an identifier naming the interactive input stream in C++.

iterative programming—a methodology of problem solving using loops.

iterator—a software construct that allows the user to access values in a given container in a specific manner.

iterator adaptor—an STL component that changes the interface of an iterator defined on some fundamental STL container.

key—the value used to access a member of a container or a hash table.

leaf—a node on a tree containing no children.

left child (of a node in a binary tree)—the root node of that node's left subtree. See also *left subtree; right child; right subtree.*

left subtree (of a node in a binary tree)—the subtree whose root is the left child of the given node.

level (of a node in a graph)—the smallest path length from the designated initial node in a traversal to that node.

level (of a node in a tree)—the level of the root node is zero; the level of any other node is `1` higher than the level of its parent.

lexicographic ordering—an order relation that imitates the ordering of character strings in a dictionary or the ordering of terms in a glossary.

LIFO property—a property of a stack in which retrievals and removals access the most recently inserted value (also known as *last-in, first-out property*).

linear probing—an open addressing strategy for resolving hash collisions in which a linear search is conducted (modulo the size of the hash table) for an unoccupied location in the hash table.

linear search—See *sequential search.*

linear-time operation—an operation on a container whose complexity is directly proportional to the size of that container.

list—an STL fundamental container of varying length that provides linear-time access to any of its values and with constant-time insertions and removals. See also *constant-time operation; linear-time operation.*

local identifier—a name whose current value is visible within the current block in which it is defined.

local variable—See *local identifier.*

logarithmic-time operation—an operation on a container whose complexity is directly proportional to the number of times size of the container is divisible by 2.

loop invariant—an assertion that in some sense captures the essence of the computation performed in the loop, is true when control of execution enters the loop for the first time, and is true each time control of execution reenters the loop.

map—an STL associative container supporting unique keys and permitting speedy retrieval of values of some type based on the underlying key values.

member function—a component of a class defining an operation applicable to objects constructed from that class.

merge—a member function applicable to list containers permitting the merging of two sorted lists into a single sorted list.

mergesort—a relatively fast sorting technique that first subdivides a finite sequence and then merges the two subsequences that result in sorted order.

message—a single item of communication in a network.

middle square technique—a form of hashing that involves squaring the value of a numeric key and then extracting a number of consecutive digits (usually three) from that result.

modifier—a member function of some container class that changes the current state of the container.

modularity—a design property in which the problem decomposes into smaller and autonomous units, each of which contributes to the solution and cooperates in producing that solution.

module—an independent program unit that is part of a problem solution; it may assume the form of a class or function in C++.

multimap—an STL associative container supporting duplicate keys and permitting speedy retrieval of values of some type based on the values of the underlying keys.

multiple inheritance—a form of inheritance in which a single derived class is inherited from two or more base classes.

multiprogramming—a multiuser technique in which several processing jobs are kept in main memory at the same time. See also *timesharing.*

multiset—an STL associative container supporting multiple objects with a common key value. See also *key.*

mutable iterator—an iterator referencing a member of a sequence stored in a container and whose value may change during the course of a computation where the iterator is defined. See also *constant iterator; iterator.*

mutating sequence algorithm—an algorithm processing data in some container and modifying the contents of that container.

mutator—See *modifier.*

namespace—a mechanism used by C++ to group together a number of logically related programming entities under a single identifier.

negator—a special kind of function adaptor used to reverse the values returned by any predicate function object. See also *predicate function object.*

network—a finite collection of communication links represented by hardware units used for processing and transmitting data.

network node—any point in a network where data are either received or collected.

network topology—a specific geometrical configuration of network nodes. See also *network node.*

node—a member of a list, graph, or tree that contains data and references to the succeeding and/or preceding member of the same data structure.

nonmutating sequence algorithm—an algorithm processing data in some container without modifying the contents of the container.

object—an instance of a class used to model a specific ADT; an aggregate of data and operations applicable to those data as specified by the member functions defined for that class.

`O(f(n))`—order of magnitude of `f(n)`. See also *big-O analysis.*

open addressing—a technique of hashing in which the actual value(s) sought lie in the hash table.

`ostream`—an identifier naming the standard output stream in C++.

output iterator—a form of iterator whose functionality is the complete opposite of that for input iterators; an output iterator permits values to be written to members of a sequence to which it refers but does not necessarily permit such values to be read. See also *input iterator; iterator.*

overflow—a condition applicable to array implementations of stacks indicating that there is no longer any space available for a successful push operation.

overloading—the ability of a single operator symbol or identifier to assume a number of different forms.

override—to redefine a member of a base class in a derived class.

packet—a finite collection of bitstrings of some predetermined size. See also *bitstring.*

palindrome—a character string that reads the same from left to right as it does from right to left, as in *level.*

parent (of a node A in a tree)—assuming A is not the root node, the immediate predecessor of A in the tree.

path—a finite sequence of edges connecting nodes of a tree or graph.

pivot—a value in an array around which the remaining values of the array are subdivided during execution of quicksort.

pointer-to-function adaptor—a function adaptor defined in the STL to permit pointers to ordinary unary and binary functions to operate in conjunction with function objects.

polymorphism—the ability of an operator to assume a number of different forms.

pop—the act of removing a value from a stack or priority queue.

`pop_back`—a removal member function defined for vector, deque, and list fundamental sequence containers.

`pop_front`—a removal member function defined for vector and list fundamental sequence containers.

portability—the ability of software to be transferred from one computer configuration (platform) to another.

postcondition—a description of the status of data at the point of exiting a function and returning to their caller.

postfix—a notation for writing arithmetic expressions in which the binary operator follows both of its operands.

precondition—a description of the status of data upon entry into the text of a function.

predicate—a function returning a `bool` value.

predicate function object—a function object returning a `bool` value. See also *function object.*

prefix—a notation for writing arithmetical expressions in which the operator precedes its operands.

primary clustering—a by-product of linear probing that results in a large number of keys hashing to a relatively small group of locations close to one another in the hash table.

priority queue—a queue that is either empty or a finite sequence of values of a single type, in which there is a well-defined comparison operation (ordinarily less than); each new value is inserted into its "proper position" according to the comparison operation.

priority queue container adaptor—an STL container adaptor possessing the functionality of a priority queue. See also *priority queue.*

`private` member—a member that is accessible only to member functions defined in its own class and to `friend` functions of that class.

`protected` member—a member of a base class that may be accessed only by member and `friend` functions of the base class and member and `friend` functions of the derived class, assuming `public` inheritance.

pseudocode—a stylized, somewhat grammatical semicode language that imitates formal C++ code.

pseudorandom numbers—an apparently random sequence of numbers that follows a specific recurring pattern.

`public` inheritance—a form of inheritance between base and derived classes that permits `public` and `protected` members of the base class to be inherited as `public` and `protected` members, respectively, of the derived class.

`public` member—a member of a class that is accessible throughout its scope and to all user functions.

pure member function—a member function of a class applied to any object constructed from that class using a qualified reference.

pure `virtual` function—a `virtual` function defined in the base class whose body is empty in the base class but has a specific meaning in each of the derived classes in which it is a member function.

push—the act of inserting a value onto a stack or priority queue.

`push_back`—an insertion member function defined for vector, deque, and list fundamental sequence containers.

`push_front`—an insertion member function defined for deque and list fundamental sequence containers.

quadratic probing—an open addressing strategy for resolving hash collisions involving probing the hash table at locations k, $k + 1^2$, $k + 2^2$, $k + 3^2$, and so on, for an unoccupied location.

quantum—a preset time interval during which a process is permitted to execute in the CPU.

queue—a sequence container that is either empty or contains a finite sequence of values of a single type, permitting insertion of new values from one end (the *rear*) and removal of values from the other end (the *front*).

queue container adaptor—an STL container adaptor possessing the functionality of a queue. See also *queue.*

quicksort—a relatively efficient sorting algorithm that rearranges the values in an array around a pivot value and uses recursion to sort these values.

random-access data structure—a data structure in which the time required to access any value in the structure is independent of the location of that value in the structure.

random-access iterator—an iterator having the functionality of moving from one position in a container to any other position in constant time. See also *constant-time operation.*

random number generator—a possible choice of a hash function involving generating a sequence of random integers lying within the scope of the subscripts of the associated hash table.

range of two iterators—the number of positions in the underlying container between their current positions.

ready queue—the queue containing all processes currently in the ready state, waiting to execute. See also *ready state.*

ready state—a state of a process waiting to execute in the CPU and currently appearing in the ready queue.

recurrence relation—a relation that equates a value of a function to values of that same function for smaller arguments.

recursive programming—a problem-solving methodology using functions that invoke themselves from their own scope.

red-black tree—a special adaptation of a 2-3-4 tree into a binary tree with red nodes and black nodes.

rehashing—a method of resolving hash collisions that involves more than one hash function.

reusability—the principle stating that a module designed to solve a specific software problem may also apply to the solution of other software problems.

reverse iterator—a special form of STL iterator adaptor whose direction of movement is the reverse of that of the original iterator. See also *iterator adaptor.*

right child (of a node in a binary tree)—the root node of the node's right subtree. See also *left child; left subtree; right subtree.*

right subtree (of a node in a binary tree)—the subtree whose root is the right child of the given node.

ring topology—a network topology in which consecutive nodes are connected by links to form a ring-shaped configuration. See also *network node; network topology.*

root node—the only node in a tree not having a parent; also the only point of entry into the tree.

run time—the time segment during which the program's instructions (in successfully compiled form) execute. See also *compile time; compiler.*

running state—a state that describes the fact that the process is currently executing in the CPU.

secondary clustering—a by-product of open addressing using quadratic probing in which only a small number of locations appear in the hash sequence, consequently limiting the effectiveness of quadratic probing.

selection sort—a sorting algorithm that sorts the components of an array in either ascending or descending order; the algorithm places the smallest (or largest) value in the initial position and then continues the process on the remaining array components.

separate chaining—a technique of hashing in which hash collisions are resolved by maintaining linked lists at each location in the hash table.

sequence container—a container that stores a finite collection of values of a single type in a linear arrangement, in which each such value occupies a specific position. See also *container.*

sequential search—the process of searching a finite sequence that begins by examining the first member and then examining successive members in their order of appearance (also known as *linear search*).

set—an associative container that supports unique keys and permits speedy retrieval of any key.

set difference—a generic function, written as `set_difference`, returning the sorted difference of two sorted sets, in that order, and represented by the ranges constructed from their respective iterators `[first1,last1)` and `[first2,last2)`.

set inclusion—a predefined `bool`-valued function in `<algorithm>` returning `true` if the set (or multiset) given by its first two iterator arguments `first1`, `last1` represents a sequence `[first1,last1)` that includes the set (multiset) `[first2,last2)` given by its last two iterator arguments.

set intersection—a generic function, written as `set_intersection`, computing the intersection of two sets of values from a common data type; these two sets are represented by ranges constructed from iterators `[first1,last1)` and `[first2,last2)`.

set symmetric difference—a generic function, written as `set_symmetric_difference`, returning the symmetric difference of two sets of values of the same type, where these sets are represented by the respective ranges `[first1,last1)` and `[first2,last2)`.

set union—a generic function, written as `set_union`, constructing the sorted union of two sets represented by ranges constructed from iterators `[first1, last1)` and `[first2,last2)`; the return value is an iterator reference to the end of the range constructed from that union.

Shell sort—a sorting technique that produces a sort of increasingly larger array segments until the final sort produces a sorting of the entire array.

sifting—a process used to distinguish even and odd integers.

signature—the list of formal parameters defined for a function.

simple inheritance—a form of inheritance in which a derived class comes from a single base class. See also *multiple inheritance.*

simulator—a program that models the behavior of an actual physical system.

sorted associative container—See *associative container.*

sorted collection—a finite, nonempty linear collection whose values are arranged in some specific order.

sorting-related algorithm—an algorithm coded in the STL involving sorting, such as `sort`, `stable_sort`, `partial_sort`, `partial_sort_copy`, `sort_heap`.

space efficiency—a measure of an algorithm's efficiency based on the amount of storage required to implement the algorithm.

spanning tree—a subcollection of vertices and edges of a graph containing all of the vertices of the graph and a smallest number of its edges to form a tree.

splicing—a member function operation applicable to two lists permitting the insertion of one list inside the other.

stable sort—a sorting algorithm that guarantees that equal values in the original unsorted sequence retain their relative ordering in the final sorted result.

stack—either the empty set or a finite sequence of values of a single type into which values may be added (pushed) and from which values may be removed (popped); the values are pushed and popped from the same end (called the *top*).

`stack` container adaptor—an STL container adaptor possessing the functionality of a stack. See also *stack.*

Standard Template Library (STL)—a C++ library that provides basic components for I/O, string processing, containers (such as vectors, deques, lists, stacks, queues, and others), algorithms (such as sort, search, merge, and others), and support for a wide variety of numeric computations.

state—the collection of all of the data values of a container or the collection of all of the current variables at any point during the execution of a program where these containers or variables are defined.

`static` data member—a value shared by all objects constructed from that class.

`static` member function—a member function of a class whose reference appears outside of the storage of any specific object constructed from that class.

std—the predefined namespace whose scope contains all of the facilities of the STL.

storage allocator—a member function available to vector containers reserving additional storage for the purpose of inserting new values.

stream iterator—an STL iterator operating on values in some I/O stream.

subclass—a class that inherits characteristics and behavior from another class (also known as *derived class*).

subtree—the tree whose root is any node of the current tree, together with all of the descendants of that node.

superclass—the class from which a derived class inherits characteristics and behavior (also known as *base class*).

switch—See *network node.*

3-node—a tree node containing exactly two data values and three children.

time efficiency—efforts to find the fewest number of processing steps for an algorithm to solve an underlying software problem.

timesharing—the fact that several processes are permitted to share processing time in the CPU, with one process currently executing and the rest in a ready state waiting to execute. See also *multiprogramming.*

token—a fixed bitstring that circulates in a network when no message is being sent. See also *bitstring; network.*

token ring network—a network whose nodes are configured using a ring topology in which a token circulates among the links between consecutive nodes. See also *network; ring topology; token.*

top (of a stack)—the end of a stack at which values are inserted, removed, and retrieved.

`top` member function—member function of a stack retrieving the value currently at the top of the stack.

traversal of a tree or graph—the act of moving from one node (vertex) to another in any tree (graph).

trickle down—a downward movement of values of the nodes described in a heap.

trickle up—an upward movement of values of the nodes described in a heap.

2-node—a tree node containing exactly one data value and two children.

2-3 tree—a search tree such that each node is either a 2-node or a 3-node and all leaves are at the same level.

2-3-4 tree—a search tree having nodes that are either 2-nodes, 3-nodes, or 4-nodes.

unary function—a function defined for a single argument.

unary function object—a function object involving a single argument.

unconditional generic algorithm—a generic algorithm that executes on every member of a sequence of values. See also *conditional (predicate) generic algorithm.*

underflow—a condition applicable to containers in which the container is currently empty and a removal or retrieval operation is attempted.

undirected graph—a graph in which the appearance of the vertices of any of its edges is insignificant.

user interface—that part of a class definition displaying the facilities available in the class to the user.

vector—a fundamental STL container providing random access to its values, and whose size varies dynamically, and permitting constant-time insertions and deletions at one end (the *back*). See also *constant-time operations; random-access data structure.*

`virtual` function—a function defined in an inheritance hierarchy that supports a dynamic form of polymorphism by permitting run-time selection of a member function associated with the current object.

`void` function—a function that returns no value to the caller.

INDEX